WHOSE EDUCATION FOR ALL?

STUDIES IN EDUCATION/POLITICS
VOLUME 6
GARLAND REFERENCE LIBRARY OF SOCIAL SCIENCE
VOLUME 1445

STUDIES IN EDUCATIONAL POLITICS

MARK B. GINSBURG, *Series Editor*

WHOSE EDUCATION FOR ALL?
THE RECOLONIZATION OF THE AFRICAN MIND

BIRGIT BROCK-UTNE

FALMER PRESS
A MEMBER OF THE TAYLOR & FRANCIS GROUP
NEW YORK & LONDON
2000

Published in 2000 by
Falmer Press
A Member of the Taylor & Francis Group
29 West 35th Street
New York, NY 10001

10   9   8   7   6   5   4   3   2   1

Library of Congress Cataloging-in-Publication Data

Brock-Utne, Birgit, 1938–
    Whose education for all? : recolonization of the African mind /
Birgit Brock-Utne.
        p.   cm. — (Garland reference library of social science ; v.
1445. Studies in education/politics ; v. 6)
    Includes bibliographical references (p.).
    ISBN 0-8153-3478-8 (alk. paper)
        1. Education—Economic aspects—Africa, Sub-Saharan.
    2. Education—Aims and objectives—Africa. Sub-Saharan.
    3. Educational assistance—Africa, Sub-Saharan.   I. Title.
    II. Series: Garland reference library of social science : v. 1445.
    III. Series: Garland reference library of social science. Studies
    in education/politics ; vol. 6.
    LC67.A435.B76   1999
    379.1′296—dc21   99-35515
                                                              CIP

Printed on acid-free, 250-year-life paper.
Manufactured in the United States of America

*Dedicated to my dear colleagues on the Faculty of Education,
University of Dar es Salaam,* hasa kwa Mwajabu, shoga yangu.

A Beautiful Tyranny Misnamed Partnership

*The relationship
To which we are wedded
Is a beautiful tyranny
Misnamed partnership.*

*Our partnership
Is a partnership of unequal partners
Of unequal powers and unequal opportunites
A partnership honeycombed
With labyrinths of genteel deception, division and exclusion.*

*In our partnership
One party represents
An imperial order of unprecendented sway and intrigue
Into whose hegemonic bosom
The other is conveniently entombed.*

*In our partnership
One party is the source, centre and symbol
Of all knowledge, civilization and salvation
The other a mere consumer of high culture and quips.[1]*

*We are stakeholders in a bizarre covenant
That folds enslavement
In intoxicating benevolence and grace
Our partnership is afflicted with saintly inhumanity.*

*In the cold mathematics of our partnership
Our partnership is our destiny.
Amen.*

HASSAN KEYNAN, 1995

---

[1]QUIPs are quick impact projects.

Contents

vii

Preface

It is now twelve years since my professorship was transferred from the Institute for Eductional Research, University of Oslo, to the Department of Education at the University of Dar es Salaam in Tanzania, for a four-and-a-half-year period (1987–92). For this arrangement I am especially grateful to three people: Sissel Volan in NORAD (the Norwegian Agency for Development), Professor Abel Ishumi at the University of Dar es Salaam; and Olav Trovik, the late Vice Chancellor of the University of Oslo. Sissel, a completely overworked woman in a donor agency, is in a position of bureaucratic imagination and if there had been more resources at her disposal it would have been to the benefit of the education sector in Africa. Abel Ishumi, who spent a year at my institute in Norway when I was the administrative head of the social education department of our institute, and with whom I had some cooperation then, was my initial contact to the University of Dar and did a lot to smooth my entry.

The years at the University of Dar es Salaam have had a profound effect on my authorship and research interests. Without those four and a half years this book could not have been written. I dedicate the book to my colleagues in the Faculty of Education in respect for the great work they do under difficult circumstances. I especially want to thank Naomi Katunzi, Suleman Sumra, Mwajabu Possi, and George Malekela for stimulating talks. I do hope that in this book I have recaptured some of the intellectually stimulating and critical tone in the student–staff seminars which were going on weekly in my time on the faculty. I have also tried to recapture the anectodal tone from the tea-time (*wakati wa chai*) conversations. Those were important times for me, not only for practicing my Kiswahili but also for learning about academic life at a poor African university.

I first embarked on this project in the fall of 1991, when after having been the head of the Department of Educational Psychology at the University of Dar es Salaam for two years, I took a sabbatical. I spent three months at the UNESCO Institute of Education in Hamburg on a German scholarship, granted me by DAAD (Deutscher Akademischer Austauschdienst). I want to thank DAAD for making it possible for me to stay those three months in Hamburg. I made extensive use of the good library at the Institut für Afrikakunde, at the University of Hamburg, and at the UNESCO Institute of Education (UIE). I would like to thank the wonderful staff of the UIE for always taking good care of me. The dear director of the institute, Paul Belanger, saw to it that I always had an office at my disposal at the Institute, eventually even one with a computer with e-mail facilities. I received great help from the very clever documentalist and researcher Ursula Giere, from the librarian Imke Behr, and from the young computer wizard Peter Nelke. I am grateful to the staff for the seminar on my project they arranged in the fall of 1991. It was a great help to focusing my thoughts.

I wrote a first draft of the book that fall but was not satisfied with it. More reading was necessary and more experience of other African countries than Tanzania. Four more stays, each lasting one month, at the UNESCO Institute of Education in Hamburg in the fall of 1993, 1995, 1997, and the fall of 1998 have been necessary for this book to reach its final shape. These stays were all paid by the Institute for Educational Research at the University of Oslo, to whom I am very grateful.

I spent the first couple of months of 1992 interviewing Tanzanian educators (see chapter 3) and the rest of the spring term as a visiting professor at the University of Antioch in Yellow Springs, Ohio. I taught one course in peace studies and another in African studies. For the African studies class I was able to bring over my close colleague from the University of Dar es Salaam, Mwajabu Possi, who was at that time finishing her doctoral studies in the States. The students and my colleagues in Yellow Springs enjoyed her talk and our preparation of African food at my house. It was in Yellow Springs that I first started my weekly seminar in "Education in Africa." I am grateful to the late Professor Paul Smoker for inviting me to his university as a visiting professor.

After I returned to Norway in the fall of 1992 and until the fall of 1998, I taught a weekly seminar called "Education in Africa" every term (except the fall of 1995, when I spent a sabbatical term in Namibia, South Africa, and Hamburg). Many of the participants attended the seminar almost every Tuesday for ten terms. It was a wonderful seminar with a good mixture of African and Norwegian students and with students from sociology, political science, social geography, social anthropology, and education. Seminar participants have included people outside of the University of Oslo, some working as secondary school teachers, a dear Kiswahili-speaking colleague, one participant from the Foreign Ministry, and one from the Ministry of Education. Several non-governmental organizations were represented among the participants. The permanent group consisted of between twenty and thirty participants, but more than a hundred people have visited the seminar on some occasion. We have also arranged a number of weekend seminars within the "Education in Africa" seminar series. These were on various topics like: "Indigenous Education in Africa" (fall 1993), "States or Markets? Neoliberalism in the Educational Policies of Sub-Saharan Africa" (spring 1994), "Decolonizing the African Mind" (fall 1996), "Higher and Adult Education in South Africa after Apartheid" (fall 1997), and "Educational Development in Africa from African Viewpoints" (spring 1999). The weekend seminars are continuing through 1999.

The "Education in Africa" seminar has been a great inspiration for my research and writing. Eleven students (one in sociology, one in political science, one from the University of Sports, and the rest in education) wrote their theses within the auspices of the seminar, and seven others (one in sociology and the rest in education) are in the process of doing so. I have been the principal adviser of all of them.

The history of the first five years of the "Education in Africa" seminars has been documented through a publication incorporating all our seminar programs as well as summaries of theses and papers written within the seminar (Brock-Utne and Miettinen, 1998). As of the fall of 1998, the seminar no longer exists as it used to. That fall we instituted a masters of Comparative and International Education, where I am responsible for those students who have chosen to major in education and development. This group consists of eight African students from seven different African countries, three Norwegian students and one student from Iceland. In the spring of 1999 I taught this group along with three exchange students from Italy, Germany, and Finland a course called "Education in Africa." We also arranged two weekend seminars where our former participants had an opportunity to meet the African students and learn from them.

We have received support from NORAD for one of the weekend seminars, as well as a small contribution from the Norwegian UNESCO Commission. On all other occasions the Institute for Educational Research has sponsored the many guest lecturers, mostly from Africa, most of whom have stayed with me.

In the spring of 1994 I was asked by the Namibia Association of Norway to evaluate a secondary school in the north of Namibia, Mweshipandeka, which was supported by them. Half of the children came from the Loudima school in Congo, where they had been with SWAPO (South West African People's Organization) in exile. This was an interesting assignment. The two other people on the evaluation team were Cliff Oliver of Namibia, and Isobel Appiah-Endresen of Ghana but living in Namibia. I learned very much about Namibia in the month I stayed there (July 1994). I became especially interested in the language policy of Namibia and tried to find out as much as I could about it, even though it was not part of the assignment. Not during that assignment, but the year after, I was asked by the National Institute of Education (NIED) under the Ministry of Education in Namibia to make a study of the situation of the African languages after independence. This was a challenging task, which I used the larger part of my sabbatical in the fall of 1995 to do. I would like to thank Patti Swatz of NIED and Roger Avenstrup, who at that time was an education reform adviser to the Ministry, for offering me the challenging task.

When Professor Mark Ginsburg from the Institute for International Studies in Education at the University of Pittsburgh saw that I had signed up for the conference of the Comparative and International Education Society (CIES) to be held in Kingston, Jamaica, on March 16 to 19, 1993, he asked me first to write a paper for his session on educating all for positive peace and then to come to his university after the conference to lecture. The paper he asked me to write helped me bring my two fields, peace studies and African studies, nearer. For this I thank him. The paper was later published in the *International Journal of Educational Development* (Brock-Utne, 1995a). It was also a great pleasure to stay with him and give seminars to his students and faculty colleagues.

At the Jamaica conference I was fortunate to meet Zaline Makini Roy-Campbell and to have an interesting exchange of views with her about the language situation in Tanzania. After the conference she sent me her doctoral thesis on the topic.

Of the many professional conferences within the field of comparative and international education I have attended over the six last years, the biannual Oxford conferences on education and development have been especially useful. I have attended the 1993, 1995, and 1997 conferences, and have had useful encounters with people including Lene Buchert, Keith Watson, Ulla Kann, Christopher Colclough, Angela Little, and Jon Lauglo. Their work has been referred to in this book.

At the Oxford conference in 1993 I also met Jürgen Hess of the Max Planck Institut für Bildungsforschung in Berlin, and Wolfgang Gmelin of the donor organization DSE (Deutsche Stiftung für Entwicklung). They were engaged in a program in southern Africa for building up research skills in qualitative research methods for young academics and wanted me to join them. This was the start of an interesting assignment and some personal friendships. I was a facilitator in a couple of meetings in Berlin, in Zimbabwe, and in Malawi, but first felt that I really became useful to the program when I, together with Kilemi Mwiria of Kenya, became the DSE-sponsored resource person to the program taking place at the historically black universities in South Africa. Together with four resource people from South Africa we have built up a research capacity program through four consecutive workshops. My first trip to familiarize myself with the black universities of South Africa was in the fall of 1995. Since that time I have been to South Africa five times. The last chapter in this book contains some of my reflections on the situation of the historically black universities today. I would especially like to thank Professor Jola Sobahle of the University of Fort Hare, my co-facilitator and jogging partner, who has taught me such a lot about what it is to be black in South Africa. I also want to thank Cecilia Moyo, the former director of SAAAD (South African Agency for Academic Development), for all she has taught me.

From the summer of 1996 through the summer of 1998, Janne Lexow, a good friend, a lovely co-worker, and the social-anthropologist from DECO (Development Consulting), and I were hired as consultants by the Royal Ministry of Foreign Affairs in Norway to follow up on the use of the 250 million Norwegian kroner (about $35 million in US dollars) that the Norwegian Foreign Ministry has granted UNICEF to use for basic education in Africa. The grant covers work in eighteen African countries, eight in eastern Africa and ten in western Africa (only in so-called francophone countries). My contract was made between the Ministry of Foreign Affairs and my institute, and has included money set aside for some of the students from my "Education in Africa" seminar to visit the project countries and write their theses on topics suggested by the country offices. Two of the students have been working in Swaziland, two in Uganda, one in Botswana, and one in Namibia. I have, in connection with this programme, made field visits to Guinea, Swaziland, Niger, Uganda, and Botswana. Impressions from these field visits also color this book.

The donors to education in Africa, and especially the World Bank, which lends money and sets tough conditionalities for its lending, are heavily criticized in the book. I would like to stress here that I am criticizing systems rather than people. There are some dedicated and wonderful people in the donor organizations. I know such a committed man in the Swedish International Development Agency (SIDA) and another in the Danish International Development Agency (DANIDA). I have already mentioned Sissel Volan in NORAD, and I could mention Wolfgang Gmelin in DSE, Wim Hoppers in the Dutch development cooperation working in South Africa, and Roger Avenstrup working for the British Council in Tanzania. I also know a very good and dedicated World Bank person, Stephen Heyneman. So I am not criticizing these people but the systems in which we, including myself, who are in the development business as consultants, as advisers, and as "capacity-builders," play a part. This includes consultants in both the North and the South as well as recipients of donor aid who also collaborate, even if unwittingly, in constructing the oppressive systems.

Many development consultants avoid criticizing the powerful donors. Those who know them well enough to be able to criticize them are normally dependent on them for funding of sectors or programs or for consultancies. Academics in the South are dependent on the consultancies for their living, as are the people working in consultancy firms in the North. Although their task is to appraise, evaluate, and review, they well know that they have to stay within certain parameters and critique within narrow limits if they wish to retain their jobs. The criticism should be impersonal and strictly within the terms of reference given by the donors.

Those who can criticize without fearing that they will lose their jobs are those, like me, who are independent university researchers from the North with comfortable salaries and tenured jobs. But what we lose if we criticize is the opportunity to work in developing countries, to learn more about the relationships and the phenomena we criticize. Donor agencies, even tough ones like the World Bank, do not like criticism and have their ways of punishing those who speak too loudly or are too direct.

Also for the more independent researchers working for donor organizations, it is not so easy to criticize, to speak up for the poor in the recipient countries. If we keep nicely within the limits of what we are allowed to criticize, write only in evaluation and review reports and within the terms of reference, we may be included on project visits, to do reviews and evaluations. And in such a capacity it is amazing how much interesting material one gets about a country which university colleagues in the same country have no access to and which one would not get if one came to the country as an independent researcher with no connection to donors. Working for donors one gets the most recent information and statistics, and has access to the top-level government officials, to ministers, permanent secretaries, and donor agencies.

It should be mentioned that it was a donor agency, NORAD, that first kindled my interest in the policies of donors or especially lenders of funds to the education sector in Africa. In the fall of 1987 Sissel Volan in NORAD asked me to make an assessment of the draft World Bank document *Education Policies for Sub-Saharan Africa,* which is still of great importance for the education sector in Africa. Chapter 2 in this work refers to this document as well as the many others which have come since.

Some Nordic colleagues and people in donor agencies accuse me of being too pro-African and claim that I am not objective when I write about education in Africa—that I am taking sides. Yes, I am, but so are those who side with the World Bank policies. I have taken a side in the struggle: I side with the masses in Africa and with their struggle for self-reliance.

To write a book is a heavy piece of work. So is finding a publisher, especially if you write in a language that is not your mother tongue and try to find a publisher in a country that is not your own. I was lucky to meet with Mark Ginsburg at the CIES conference in Buffalo in March 1998. He took a keen interest in my manuscript and said he would like to review it for the series he is editing for Garland. Not only did he recommend that Garland accept the book for publication, but he also gave me lots of valuable advice on how to rearrange my manuscript, tighten my arguments, and add information readers might like to have. Even though his advice meant another trip to Hamburg and another four weeks of intensive work, I find this version a great improvement over the earlier one. Thank you so much, Mark, for your practical help on the rewriting of the manuscript and your belief in the importance of this work. Thanks also to Kjersti Franciska Okkelmo for some typesetting help with the references.

As always I want to thank my husband, Gunnar Garbo, for his belief in me; for his support of my work, including this project; and for never criticizing my having to leave him for a month every other year to devote my time to writing or my going on many trips to Africa over the last years (on some of which he has accompanied me). I further want to thank him for his patient reading of the penultimate draft of the manuscript and his valuable comments. He is not only my closest friend but also my most valuable critic. We share so many of the same ideas. We share so much love, including a love of Africa.

Questioning Assumptions and Implications of an Educational/Political Slogan

MARK B. GINSBURG
University of Pittsburgh

"Take education out of politics!" "Education should not be a political football!" "Keep politics out of the schools!" "Educators should not be political!" These and similar warnings have been sounded at various times in a variety of societies. Such warnings, however, miss (or misconstrue) the point that education *is* political. Not only is education constituted by and constitutive of struggles over the distribution of symbolic and material resources, but education implies and confers structural and ideological power used to control the means of producing, reproducing, consuming, and accumulating symbolic and material resources (see Ginsburg, 1995; Ginsburg and Lindsay, 1995).

Political struggles about and through education occur in classrooms and nonformal education settings; school and university campuses; education systems; and local, national, and global communities. Different groups of students, educators, parents, business owners, organized labor leaders, government and international organization officials, and other worker-consumer-citizens participate (actively or passively) in such political activity. These struggles not only shape educational policy and practice; they also are dialectically related to more general relations of power among social classes, racial/ethnic groups, gender groups, and nations. Thus, the politics of education and the political work accomplished through education are ways in which existing social relations are reproduced, legitimated, challenged, or transformed.

The "Studies in Education/Politics" series is designed to include books that examine how in different historical periods and in various local and national contexts education is political. The focus is on what groups are involved in political struggles in, through and about education; what material and symbolic resources are of concern; how ideological and structural power are implicated; and what consequences obtain for the people directly involved and for social relations more generally.

The purpose of this series, however, is not only to help educators and other people understand the nexus of education and politics. It is also concerned with facilitating their active involvement in the politics of and through education. Thus, the issue is not whether education should be taken out of politics, nor whether politics should be kept out of schools, nor whether educators should be apolitical. Rather the questions are toward what ends, by what means, and in whose interests should educators and other worker-consumer-citizens engage in political work in and about education.

This volume by Birgit Brock-Utne, the sixth book to appear in the "Studies in Education/Politics" series, offers a critical analysis of the slogan and/or goal of many international agencies, governments, nongovernmental organizations, and school and university educators throughout the world. Much of the rhetoric and action stemming from the "Education for All" conference convened by UNESCO, UNICEF, UNDP, and the World Bank in Jomtien, Thailand, in March 1990, has highlighted the technical dimension of the issues. The focus of such discourse has been on strategies for increasing the number of schools and improving the quality of schooling, without problematizing the issues of what kind of education for what kind of world.[1] In contrast, Brock-Utne directs our attention to how global power relations shape not only the extent of educational provision but also the language of instruction and curricular content of schooling and higher education.

That education and educational reform are global—as well as national and local—phenomena (see also Ginsburg, 1991) is quickly brought home to the reader in Part I of this book on "Establishing Educa-

---

[1]For a critical review of the "education for all" slogan see Ginsburg (1998). In this essay I argue that it is not enough to answering "all" to the question, education for whom? We need to pose another question—education for what? In addressing this latter question, I propose that the education should be oriented to develop capacities and commitments to peace, defined broadly as the absence of physical and structural violence at interpersonal, intergroup, and international levels (see also Brock-Utne, 1989 [and 1995]).

tion Policies in Sub-Saharan Africa." While some accounts might begin with a description of national policy initiatives, Brock-Utne initially examines World Bank educational policy documents, which seem to guide projects funded by the Bank as well as those developed with the support of bilateral donors (e.g., the development agencies of European and North American nations). Moreover, she documents how the "structural adjustment programs" required by the Bank and the International Monetary Fund (IMF) actually make it more difficult for African nation-states to provide education for all its citizens. Such programs, which are included as conditions for obtaining loans, limit the amount of government expenditure on human services, such as education. The regressive consequence is the introduction of user fees and other forms of privatizing (versus socializing) the costs of education, which means that the poor, if they can gain access to schooling at all, pay a disproportionate share of their material resources.[2]

This analysis of the role that multilateral (and bilateral) agencies play in reproducing inequalities of wealth within and among nations is important (see also Braun, 1997; Cavanagh, Anderson, and Pike, 1996).[3] Brock-Utne, however, supplements and complements this structural analysis with a cultural analysis, focusing on curriculum knowledge and language of instruction. Thus, she contributes to the global level discussion of education what the "new sociologists of education" (e.g., Apple, 1979; Bernstein, 1971; Bourdieu and Passeron, 1977; and Young, 1971) did for national or institutional discourses on education.

---

[2]Structural adjustment programs tend to negatively affect females even more than males among the poor—a point Ashworth (1992, p. 233) discusses in recounting her personal journey of making "the impact of structural adjustment on women . . . known, . . . postulating damage limitation and even preventative measures, as well as proposing alternatives to the current forms of adjustment."

[3]Research by Cavanagh, Anderson, and Pike (1996, p. 97) suggests that such "World Bank and IMF policies hurt workers at home and abroad." There is also some question as to whether the structural adjustment programs even accomplish what they are supposedly designed for: reducing the debt of Third World countries. As Braun (1997, p. 87) reports: "In total, more than seventy countries have been subjected to 566 IMF structural adjustment programs [SAPs] in the past fourteen years [1980–94]. Despite their proliferation, all the austerity programs have done is lock more poor countries into debtor's prison for longer periods." Moreover, contrary to the public arguments for SAPs by World Bank and IMF officials, Braun (1997, p. 98) summarizes research based on thirty-two countries showing that "government spending reduces income inequality" and "an increase in economic growth does not lessen the degree of income inequality in these countries."

The second part of the book explores how and why "local" African knowledge and languages do not occupy the core of curriculum and instruction in many schools in African countries. Contributing to this situation is the dependency of African countries on foreign donors for financing education, the role played by foreign intellectuals as consultants in technical assistance projects and visiting scholars in exchange programs, and the requirements that textbooks purchased through such projects be produced in the donor (versus donee) country. But just as was the case under most forms of colonialism (see Ginsburg and Clayton, 1999), elites within the African societies have also contributed during the postcolonial or neocolonial period. Many of them were educated in European and North American institutions of higher education; and they not only learned the non-African languages and knowledge but often came to value such more than the languages and knowledge of their own continent. Given European and North American hegemony within the world economic and cultural systems, elites' preference for other nations' languages and knowledge is has a political and economic as well as a psychological identity basis. It is not only their familiarity and comfort with non-African language and knowledge, but also their perception of its utility for their countries' "development" that leads African elites to prize that which is "foreign."[4]

Can globalization (of the economy and culture) occur without "excessive Eurocentrism or any monoculturalist form" coming to dominate? Can there be "a strong Africa that speaks with her own voice"? Brock-Utne answers in the affirmative, and suggests that an important place to counteract the recolonization of the African mind is in African universities. In the third part of her book, where she makes this argument, Brock-Utne reminds us that World Bank policies, which also shape the actions of bilateral agencies, have in recent years deemphasized higher education, generally, and African studies research and teaching programs, more specifically.[5] Nevertheless, she provides us with examples both of "success" in this regard as well as with illustrations of where such efforts

---

[4]Neither Brock-Utne nor I are arguing for Africans to ignore or reject knowledge and languages originating outside the continent. Rather the point is for Africans (and non-Africans) to draw on such knowledge and languages in conjunction with equally valued knowledge and languages that are rooted in the historical and contemporary African scene.

[5]If one only considers the individual level, "human capital" development function of higher education, and ignores the collective level function of the discovery, preservation, and dissemination of indigenous culture (knowledge and language), one is more likely (as are the authors of World Bank policy documents) to downplay the importance of social investment in higher education.

have not been sustained, but could have been with greater attention and commitment by those involved—not to mention more adequate funding.

The issues raised in this book, however, are not only for African consumption. Indeed, given that much of Brock-Utne's argument and illustrations are derived from published work by and personal communications with African scholars and policymakers, this book is as much about giving voice as it is about speaking to citizens of the various African societies involved. While it is hoped that *Whose Education for All?* will contribute to debate and struggle among African intellectuals (academic or otherwise), this volume raises many issues upon which scholars and other citizens in Europe and North America need to reflect. For example, those of us who are non-Africans must consider the implications for the global distribution of power and material/symbolic resources of the answers we give to the following questions: (a) whose knowledge do we learn about and include in the curriculum inside and outside of Africa; (b) what languages do we teach, read, speak, and write in; and (c) how do we try to shape or enact the policies and practices of bilateral and multilateral agencies' "development" projects?

Brock-Utne has helped us to focus on these and other questions that are at the core of education/politics globally. It is now up to us to turn our reflections into praxis—preferably in collaboration with African colleagues.

REFERENCES

Apple, M. (1979) *Ideology and Curriculum.* Boston: Routledge and Kegan Paul.

Ashworth, G. (1992) "Politicizing Gender and Structural Adjustment." Pages 233–52 in H. Afshar (ed.), *Women and Adjustment Policies in the Third World.* New York: St. Martin's Press.

Bernstein, B. (1971) "Social Class, Language and Socialization." Pages 170–89 in B. Bernstein, *Class, Codes and Control,* Vol. 1, London: Routledge and Kegan Paul.

Bourdieu, P. and Passeron, J. C. (1977) *Reproduction in Society, Education, and Culture.* Beverly Hills, CA: Sage Publications.

Braun, D. (1997) *The Rich Get Richer: The Rise of Income Inequality in the United States and the World,* second edition. Chicago: Nelson-Hall.

Brock-Utne, B. (1989) *Feminist Perspectives on Peace and Peace Education.* New York: Pergamon.

Brock-Utne, B. (1995) "Educating All for Positive Peace: Education for Positive Peace or Oppression?" *International Journal of Educational Development* 15 (3): 321–31.

Cavanagh, J., Anderson, S., and Pike, J. (1996) "Behind the Cloak of Benevolence: World Bank and IMF Policies Hurt Workers at Home and Abroad." Pages 97–104 in K. Danaher (ed.), *Corporations Are Gonna Get Your Mama: Globalization and the Downsizing of the American Dream.* Monroe, ME: Common Courage Press.

Ginsburg, M. (ed.) (1991) *Understanding Educational Reform in Global Context: Economy, Ideology, and the State.* New York: Garland.

Ginsburg, M. (ed.) (1995) *The Politics of Educators' Work and Lives.* New York: Garland.

Ginsburg, M. and Clayton, T. (1999) "Imperialism and Colonialism." In D. Levinson, A. Sadovnik, and P. Cookson (eds.), *Education and Sociology: An Encyclopedia.* New York: Taylor & Francis.

Ginsburg, M., Clayton, T., Rakotomanana, M., and Rodriguez Gabarron Holly, G. (1998) "Education for All or Educating All for Peace?" In Shen-Keng Yang (ed.), *Education for the New Century: Lifelong Learning for All.* Tapei, Taiwan: Chinese Comparative Education Society.

Ginsburg, M. and Lindsay, B. (eds.) (1995) *The Political Dimension in Teacher Education: Comparative Perspectives on Policy Formation, Socialization and Society.* New York: Falmer.

Young, M. (1971) *Knowledge and Control.* London: Macmillan.

Introduction

This book takes as its point of departure the "Education for All" conference at Jomtien, Thailand, in 1990. It argues that in the wake of this conference there is an intellectual recolonization going on in many countries
of Sub-Saharan Africa. Countries that after independence had great
hopes for an independent development of Africa are becoming more and
more dependent on the West[1] for aid in the education sector, for textbooks, and even recurrent expenditures. With the aid follows Western
curricula and languages, Western culture, and the idea of education as
schooling. This book shows how Western donors together with parts of
the African elites trained in the West are involved in this recolonization
to the benefit of themselves but to the detriment of the African masses. I
am not claiming that this recolonization is purposeful, that it is part of a
conspiracy between the Western donors and parts of the African elites,
but I am claiming that the effects of the policies and practices followed
now are an intellectual recolonization.

---

[1]The "West" and the "North" throughout this book are used to denote the capitalist and industrialized countries mostly of western–Europe and North America.
Industrialized countries like Japan, New Zealand, and Australia can also be included in the concept though they are geographically east and south of Europe
and Africa. The "North" is sometimes used to contrast it with the "South," which
here stands for developing countries. Though most of the developing countries
are in the South, there are other countries in the South that are not developing
(again, like Japan, Australia, and New Zealand). They are not included in this
concept.

This intellectual recolonization is not only to the detriment of the African masses but also to the rest of the world. If globalization is not going to solely mean Westernization—Euro-American capitalism, culture, and standards—we shall all need a strong Africa that speaks with her own voice. A world culture is evolving fast—the task is to save it from excessive Eurocentrism or any monoculturalist form.

We in the West have so much to learn. We want to teach developing countries sustainable development, but ourselves lead a lifestyle that is not sustainable.

This book is divided into three parts: Part I looks at the powerful donors involved in education in Africa, their policies and influence. Part II examines the content of schooling in parts of Africa after the African states reached independence; and Part III analyzes the situation of the African universities.

Chapter 1 looks at the current donor preference for what is termed "Education for All" or basic education, the sector which is now "in." The effects of the structural adjustment policies on the education sector, especially on the provision of basic education, are analyzed and summarized. I show how the education sector in the adjusting countries of Sub-Saharan Africa have suffered through the adjustment policies. I also describe what the reintroduction of school fees has done to a poor country like Tanzania. Apart from drawing on research by critical economists, this chapter also draws on observations I made on my field trips to Guinea (1996), Swaziland (1997), Botswana (1997), Uganda (1997), and Niger (1998), to familiarize myself with some basic education projects —especially of the non-formal type—going on in these countries.

Considerable space is devoted in Chapter 1 to the Jomtien conference and the more unofficial discourse going on. I have included texts which were put into the "Framework of Action" during the conference as well as texts which were not adopted. The concept of "Education for All" (EFA) is also discussed. What does it mean? Is "education for all" the same as primary schooling? The dangers involved in donors telling Africa that it should now target basic education and limit its growth in higher education are pointed out. I show how this policy resembles the one the colonialists had previously meted out for Africa: only a rudimentary education for a few years for the masses of Africans, the cheap labor force, and little concern for higher education. Evidence is presented showing that donors are now actually shifting their funding from higher education to primary education.

Chapter 2 looks specifically at some World Bank documents of special interest for the education sector in Africa. I made the very first analysis of one of these documents as early as the fall of 1987. It was an analysis of a 1987 draft of the World Bank document *Educational Policies for Sub-Saharan Africa* (later to become World Bank, 1988a). I could not have written the analysis without the help of my colleagues at the University of Dar es Salaam, who held an entire student–staff seminar on 28 January 1988 focusing on my first version of the analysis. Their input made me rewrite large parts of my original paper. As I also mention in Chapter 9, several of my Tanzanian colleagues said they were very happy with my revised version, but they would not have dared to write it, dependent as they were on World Bank consultancies to sustain a living. The ideas in this ten-year-old document are still governing World Bank educational policies toward Sub-Saharan Africa, though many more policy documents have come from the World Bank since then.

In the second chapter I also name the most important of the newer documents and devote some space to the document *Priorities and Strategies for Education: A Review* (World Bank, 1995a). Not many things have changed in the Bank's analysis since 1988. There is still hardly any reference to researchers in the South or even to critical researchers in the North. The controversial rate of return analysis is still being used, leading to the conclusion that governments and donors alike should strengthen basic education to the detriment of other educational sectors, such as vocational education, which is "out," or higher education. No change in the basic assumptions of the World Bank seems to have taken place between the 1988 and 1995 papers. However, there are some signs in the 1995 document that the Bank has learned from some of the failures. This is especially evident in the World Bank's advice in the 1995 paper that no fees should be charged for primary school attendance.

The 1995 document also places more emphasis on the education of girls than the 1988 document did. Targeting the girl-child is now "in" in the donor community, but the World Bank advocates it for purely economic reasons (e.g., lowering the birth rate). In the 1995 document lip service is also paid to indigenous populations and the use of local languages. The basis for my conclusion that this is merely window-dressing is discussed in Part II.

Chapter 3 analyzes donor coordination and the quest for "accountability." Who should be accountable to whom? And who should coordinate? While the World Bank has been the target of much criticism in the first two chapters, examples of donor interventions in Chapter 3 are taken from a couple of the Nordic aid agencies. The influence of the Swedish International Development Agency (SIDA) to liberalize and privatize the school-book sector in Tanzania is commented upon. I include quotes from interviews with officials in the Ministry of Education and the Institute for Curriculum Development concerning what the Swedes call "a 180 degree turn in emphasis away from a government-led system towards a market oriented system" (Wickmann, 1993).

Chapter 3 also examines the introduction of the National Education Trust Fund (NETF) in Tanzania, a donor intervention coined by the World Bank, which the Norwegian Agency for Development (NORAD) has bought rather uncritically. I show how the distrust of the Tanzanian government by the World Bank and also by Norwegian officials has led to the undermining of the role of the Minstry of Education and a creation of an NGO that never would have been there had it not been for donor money. The local politicians and educational experts have been bypassed, and their warning that this fund would lead to greater inequalitites within the education system in Tanzania has been ignored. As several studies show, the NETF has increased the regional and religious inequalities in access to secondary education in Tanzania. Almost 40% of the NETF funds go to schools run by Christian missionaries. Not a single Muslim school has received any funds. Three of the most wealthy regions of Tanzania — Kilimanjaro, Ruvuma, and Arusha — have received more than 50% of the funds, while Kigoma region, which is very poor and has few secondary schools, has received no funds.

Later in Chapter 3 I quote the aid coordinator of the education sector in Namibia. She tells how donors assume that they are the ones to do the coordination and insist that their specific "logical frameworks" be used for projects in "their" countries without paying any attention to the fact that the recipient country has its own "logical framework" it could have wanted to use.

Part II looks at the content of education in Africa: curriculum, textbooks, and language of instruction. The first chapter of this part (Chapter 4) discusses curriculum reconstruction and the renewed curriculum dependency of African education. I look first at the pre-colonial education with its linkages to production and social life, then at colonial education teaching African children that the whites were the discoverers of their waterfalls, mountains, and rivers. I look at some of the attempts at curriculum reconstruction at the time of independence in most countries in Sub-Saharan Africa, innovations like "education with production," "education for self-reliance," and the establishment of curriculum centers. I then analyze the recently renewed curriculum dependency whereby textbooks are again being produced in the West, and the curriculum experts are coming in from the West with their ideas of school effectiveness. Based on my visit to the nonformal schools of Guinea in 1997, I ask whether it is not high time to revisit some of the ideas from the liberation struggles, ideas like education with production. I suggest that there is also a need to study the indigenous learning systems of Africa, to revive them and make them part of the curriculum.

In the next two chapters (Chapters 5 and 6), I look into the educational language policies of several countries in Sub-Saharan Africa. I examine the role of the donors, Western scholars, and parts of the African elites. On several occasions I have noticed an alliance between donors, the economic elites, and part of the intellectual elites that makes it hard for governments to embark on the language policies of their choice. The first of the two language chapters, Chapter 5, starts by describing the language situation in Africa generally and then looks at the language situation in several countries in Africa: Madagascar, Guinea, Uganda, Swaziland, and Niger. I discuss the role of the anglophone and francophone consultants who often have a blind spot for languages (especially in the case of the anglophones, who themselves are often monolingual). Chapter 5 shows that while English is strengthening its position in the former British colonies, French is strengthening its position in the former French colonies.

Madagascar, like Tanzania, has a national and uniting offical African language, Malgash (Malagasy). Madagascar had for many years succeeded in having Malgash as the language of instruction, not only in the elementary school but also in the secondary school. During a visit to Madagascar in 1989, a headmaster of one of the larger secondary schools in Antananarivo explained, however, that the previous year Madagascar had reintroduced French as the language of instruction in secondary school. "There were simply no more books available in Malgash," the headmaster said with considerable regret. "But Alliance Française has supplied us with textbooks as a type of educational aid." A recolonization of the mind is going on.

In Chapter 5 I also point to the interests of the African Ministers of Education in a strengthening of the African languages, knowing that those languages are the mediums of communication for more than 90% of the African people. How can one develop democracy in a country where the masses do not understand and use the official language? I tell about a recent discussion with the Minister of Education in Guinea, who told me that he was bent on reintroducing African languages as mediums of instruction, as he viewed French as a barrier to knowledge for most of the schoolchildren. Some Western scholars are concerned about the costs involved in publishing textbooks in many languages. One also has to be concerned about the costs involved in children spending valuable years of their lives in an alienating environment where the language of instruction is a barrier to acquiring knowledge.

I have been able to follow the educational language policies of two countries especially well: Tanzania, where I lived for five years, and Namibia where the National Institute of Education under the Ministry of Education in the fall of 1995 asked me to make an assessment of their language policies, especially analyzing the state of the African languages after independence. Chapter 6 looks especially at the language policies in these two countries. Tanzania is one of the very few countries in Africa that uses an African language as the language of instruction all through primary school. At one point, Tanzania also had plans for using that language, Kiswahili, as the language of instruction in secondary schools and even the universities. In Chapter 6 I look at what has happened to the language policy after the introduction of uncontrolled market forces, capitalism, multi-party systems, and under pressure of a project like the English Language Teaching Support project sponsored by the British Council.

The last part of Chapter 6 focuses on Namibia, a country that recently obtained its independence. In this post-independence and post-apartheid period, Namibia could have adopted a language policy that would have strengthened the African languages but did not do so. The language policy of Namibia was formed in exile and since then an enormous effort has gone into making English the official language of Namibia. This effort has been strongly supported by overseas agencies, like the Overseas Development Administration (ODA) of the United Kingdom and US-AID. The intention from the Government's side was that English should replace Afrikaans, but I show that the strong emphasis on English has been to the detriment of the African languages. A new colonial master of thoughts and intellect has moved in.

After describing the various African languages of Namibia, I dwell somewhat on their history as written languages, showing the influence of missionaries and later the apartheid regime of South Africa. Toward the end of Chapter 6 I discuss publishing in the Namibian languages and show that such publishing is going on much less since the end of the apartheid regime.

Part III looks at the role of the universities in Africa. Is there a life after Jomtien for the African universities? How much are they a part of the intellectual recolonization? Could they be something else? Could they restore the dignity of Africa by building on African culture, on indigenous knowledge? In this part of the book the other two parts come together: the role of the donors, of the universities in the North, as well as the possibilities to build a curriculum on African culture. And what about the language issue at African universities?

In the first chapter of Part III (Chapter 7) I point to the problems and challenges facing the universities in Sub-Saharan Africa and also to some creative solutions. I give an example of a university department and a research institute using an African language for all their work and what that has meant to the coinage of new vocabulary. The donor policies pertaining to higher education in Africa are examined and the attitude of the World Bank to higher education in Africa is revisited. How is it at all possible to develop an "Education for All" without strengthening the African universities?

I describe the many links with universities in the North that the universities in Africa have had to build up, and the inherent inequality of many of these linkage arrangements. Several examples of dominance by the Northern universities, who insist that they are coming to Africa to transfer their knowledge, to teach rather than learn, are given in this chapter. An example of an empowering link arrangement is also described. The examples are taken from linkages involving Norwegian universities with funding from NORAD.

At the end of Chapter 7, I describe the link that is really missing in the African university system, namely, the link between the university and the people its graduates are meant to serve. The university graduates, whose training is usually paid for by the people, have also been trained away from them, trained in foreign theories and in a language most Africans do not speak. I also write about the necessity of doing research from an Africanist perspective, about the need to record the experiences of Africans and let the voices of Africans be heard. It is a type of research only Africans can do but we researchers from the North can help them in their endeavor and learn a lot ourselves in the process.

The situation in South Africa is very different from the situation in other countries in Sub-Saharan Africa and is therefore treated separately in Chapter 8. In that chapter I discuss the situation of the universities in South Africa generally, and the situation of the so-called historically black universities of South Africa especially. Will the latter institutions be third-rate places of learning, modeling themselves after the white universities in South Africa which again are judging themselves according to Euro-American standards? Or can they become places of learning and research into the culture and history of the majority population of South Africa, centers that would attract scholars from other parts of Africa as well as white South Africans and people from overseas? Could they become centers that would stop the recolonization of the African mind? I mention in Chapter 8 how much higher the tertiary enrollment rate is in South Africa compared to other countries in Sub-Saharan Africa. However, the high enrollment rate glosses over large inequities. The majority population of South Africa are not much better off than the inhabitants of other African countries, while the white minority population have built up universities that are replicas of the universities in Europe. Seven of the eight universities with the largest libraries in Sub-Saharan Africa are in South Africa—but they are all in historically white universities. The great disparities one finds within tertiary education in South Africa are a result of the inequitable distribution of financial and material resources.

In Chapter 7 I argue for a transformation of the universities of the South to include local knowledge. When it comes to the universities in South Africa, the historically black universities are in the best position to tap this local knowledge since the students there and many of the lecturers speak the languages of the majority and have grown up in the culture of the majority population.

The concluding chapter (Chapter 9) tries to bring the three parts of the book together. I discuss the "Education for All" drive as fundamentally misconstrued. Maybe the declining enrollment rates and increasing drop-out rates in the primary schools in Africa have to do with the fact that parents do not find that the education their children get in primary school is worth having. "Education for All" has become "Schooling for Some," having a content and taught in a language that alienate children instead of making them proud of their culture.

"Education for All" requires relevant curricula in the languages children speak. But the construction of culturally relevant curricula and the strengthening of the use of local languages require that emphasis is put on the building up of institutions of higher learning in Africa where independent, or at least not foreign colonized, minds are fostered. It also requires the existence and further development of independent curriculum centers as well as a strengthening of teacher training.

PART I

Establishing Education Policies for Sub-Saharan Africa: A Critique

> *The very use of the word "policy" in the title of the World Bank documents is rather presumptuous because policies are made by national governments. The documents are rather reflections of the principles which govern Bank lending to education.*
>
> (ERNESA, 1987: 32)

CHAPTER 1

Whose Education for All?

Every person—child, youth and adult—
shall be able to benefit from educational
opportunities designed to meet their basic
learning needs. . . . The scope of basic
learning needs and how they should be met
varies with individual countries and cultures.

(WDEFA, 1990: ARTICLE 1)

THE WORLD CONFERENCE ON EDUCATION
FOR ALL BY THE YEAR 2000: THE ISSUES RAISED

Over the two decades ending in 1980, primary enrollments doubled in Asia and Latin America, while in Africa they tripled. This pattern was reversed, however, after 1980, when growth rates of enrollment declined so much in Africa that they actually were lower than the rate of growth of the population.[1] Over the 1980s, in about two-thirds of the countries of Sub-Saharan Africa (SSA) educational expenditures per head were cut in real terms. In some cases the cuts were very large; for example, between 1981 and 1989, real expenditures per head on education fell by 67% in Nigeria and Zambia and 60% in Tanzania (Stewart, 1996). This decline in enrollments was an effect of the general economic recession that hit the African countries in the 1980s. The economic recession was mostly caused by worsening terms of trade which again gave rise to mounting

---

[1] Both the gross and the net enrollment ratios for Sub-Saharan Africa (SSA) taken as a whole fell through the 1980s. Most available data suggest that this decline continued at least through 1992, such that by that year, scarcely more than half of the primary school-age population of SSA were actually attending school (Colclough, 1997). The net enrollment ratio (NER) takes account of the age structure of those enrolled by excluding all those children who are older or younger than the officially eligible age group. The gross enrollment ratio (GER) expresses total enrollment at a given level of schooling—irrespective of the age of the students—as a percentage of the population which, according to national regulations, is of an age to attend that level.

3

debts. The introduction of economic structural adjustment programs (ESAPs) had a further negative impact on the social sector in most developing countries.

It was this steady deterioration of the education sector in the developing countries in the 1980s that led some of the multilateral organizations to organize the 1990 World Conference on Education for All (WCEFA). This conference, called by Simon McGrath (1997: 3) "the greatest education jamboree of all," took place in Jomtien, Thailand, on 5–9 March, 1990. What happened at this conference? What issues were raised? How much was the South[2] able to influence the declaration coming out of the conference? What critiques and alternative visions were formulated? What does education for all (EFA) or basic education mean? Does it equal primary education? These questions form the first part of this chapter. To place them in a historical context we shall briefly look at the colonial legacy of the African countries and what they have tried to achieve after independence. We shall discuss how the gains of the independence period were reversed under the structural adjustment policies of the 1980s.

The World[3] Conference on Education for All was sponsored by the World Bank, the United Nations Development Program (UNDP), the United Nations Children's Fund (UNICEF), and the United Nations Educational, Scientific and Cultural Organization (UNESCO). Some 1,500 participants met at the EFA conference in Jomtien. There were delegates from 155 governments, 20 intergovernmental bodies, and 150 nongovernmental organizations (NGOs). Forty-eight roundtables were arranged along with some seventy exhibits. There were cross-regional caucuses among NGOs, donor agencies, and national delegations. There were South–South caucuses, as well as North–South. The overall aim of the main organizers of the conference was to get developing countries and donors to turn around the downward trend of falling enrollments, falling completion rates, and poor learning outcomes within primary ed-

---

[2] When the expression "South" is used in this book, it is not being used as a strict geographical term since it does not include industrialized countries in the South like Australia and New Zealand. I use the expression to denote developing countries—most of which are located in the southern hemisphere.

[3] The Ugandan researcher Catherine Odora Hoppers (1998: 177) shows how the conference called a "World" conference, had as its target, not humankind, but the Third World, once more making educational discourse miss a crucial opportunity to develop among people as people and educators as educators irrespective of affluence levels.

ucation in developing countries. This aim was targeted to be reached by the beginning of the new millennium, by the year 2000.[4]

CHANGES MADE AT JOMTIEN
IN THE DRAFT DOCUMENTS

Delegations to the Jomtien conference were actually encouraged by the organizers to propose changes in Draft C of the *World Declaration on Education for All* (WDEFA) and the *Framework for Action,* which were circulated before the meeting. Before a further discussion of what has happened to the policies laid down at Jomtien in the years following the conference, it is important first to have a clear picture of what major changes were proposed and accommodated in the final version of WDEFA. What came out of this last round of consultation and lobbying? NORRAG News (June 1990) reports that significant changes were made in the document during the conference. For instance, the disabled were accepted as important beneficiaries of education for all, and stronger emphasis was put on education for girls and women. Here a whole new section was adopted to emphazise the need for the programming of aid to be much more gender conscious. This section now constitutes point 45e of the *Framework for Action* which now reads:

> *Education programmes for women and girls.* These programmes should be designed to eliminate the social and cultural barriers which have discouraged or even excluded women and girls from benefits of regular education programmes, as well as to promote equal opportunities in all aspects of their lives. (WCEFA,1990—also in Little et. al. (eds.), 199: 249)

The four international teachers' associations present at the Jomtien conference succeeded in getting into the *Framework for Action* a stronger emphasis on teachers' trade union rights and professional freedoms. But as we shall see in the following chapter, after five years the teacher unions were among those groups whose influence on the education sector the World Bank (1995a) claimed must be curbed.

Groups from the countries in the South, especially from Latin America and the Caribbean, and from Africa and Asia, together with signatories

---

[4]The notion of the approaching millennium is, by the way, as McGrath (1997) correctly observes, rooted in the Christian calendar and represents another example of globalization as Westernization.

from Europe and the IDRC (International Development Research Center based in Canada), were at Jomtien successfully lobbying for more explicit safeguards for higher education. IDRC was also instrumental in introducing into the final text an emphasis on traditional knowledge and indigenous cultural heritage.

*The Reluctance to Deal with the Effects of Debt Service
and Structural Adjustment Policies on the Education Sector—
An Unsuccessful Attempt at Change.*

By far the most contentious issue at the Jomtien conference was related to the trade-off between the debt burden and the search to extend education to all. No fewer than thirteen Latin American countries along with the Ivory Coast were signatories to a recommendation that targeted debt as the main problem preventing poor countries from meeting their citizens' basic needs (including education), and placed responsibility on the North to take the initiative. A different version of this dilemma about debt versus education for all was prepared by World University Service, the International Coalition for Development Action and twenty other NGOs. In a proposal for the preamble they argued the need for rethinking debt in the context of macro-economic relations, maintaining that:

> A resolution of the economic crisis associated with debt and North–South economic relations is a necessary precondition for the achievement of Education for All. Resources currently flowing from South to North in debt service, if reoriented to the service of education and development, could provide the debtor countries with an enhanced capacity to ensure the survival of children to school age, and release families, communities and nations from the poverty which prevents universal participation in pre-school, school and adult education. (NORRAG News, June 1990: 7)

Even stronger than this was the set of proposals from the African Association for Literacy and Adult Education (AALAE) and the Association for Participatory Research in Asia (PRIA), supported by several other NGOs. These, too, set the responsibility solidly in the North[5] for

---

[5] The expression "the North" denotes modern, industrialized countries mostly located in the northern hemisphere, though a couple of the countries, like Japan and Australia, are actually located in the southern hemisphere and are included in this concept.

the conditions that constrained the South. The following is an excerpt from the proposal by AALAE:

> We call on all governments of the North and all international financial institutions to cancel all existing debts as these are an intolerable burden on the people, make it impossible for them to mobilise the resources necessary for basic education, and ferment revolt and strife. It is necessary further to put an end to structural adjustment programmes[6] and attendant conditionalities which have caused so much suffering to the people and undermined their capacity to mobilise resources for their basic needs. (quoted in NORRAG News, June 1990: 7)

AALAE also suggested that a special development fund be set up into which all canceled debts would be deposited in local currencies and to which the countries in the South as well as Northern donors would make additional contributions to finance development activities in the South, including basic education.

When we now read what the final text says about the debt burden, we are safe in concluding that the African and Asian countries behind the AALAE proposal were not paid much attention to. The development fund is nowhere mentioned, nor is the heavy responsibility of the North for the sad state of the social sectors in the South acknowledged. In the final text the South as well as the North are compelled to act and there is no mention of a straightforward trade-off between debt service and educational development. This is how the debt problem is treated in the WDEFA:

> Creditors and debtors must seek innovative and equitable formulae to resolve these burdens (heavy debt burdens), since the capacity of many developing countries to respond effectively to education and other basic needs will be greatly helped by finding solutions to the debt problem. (WDEFA, 1990: Article 10, point 2)

AALAE held a workshop in Mauritius from the 28 October to 10 November 1990 to assess the outcomes of the EFA conference. After the workshop the Second General Assembly of AALAE adopted a declaration giving its views on EFA. The preamble states:

---

[6] I shall later discuss the effect of the structural adjustment programs on the education sector in Africa and also the conditionalities imposed by the World Bank.

> Though the Declaration on "Education for All" is positive in its aims, its broad and universal framework fails to take specific account of the prevailing socio-economic conditions in the different parts of the world, Africa in particular. (AALAE, 1990: 1)

A similar assessment was offered by one of Thailand's leading papers, *The Nation*, which ran a special supplement each day of the EFA conference called the "Jomtien Journal." The editorial of the "Jomtien Journal" of 10 March 1990 was titled: "After the World Conference on Education, What Next?" This editorial raised some very critical comments about the way the conference had been organized and the failure sufficiently to address the question of debt.[7] The editorial reports that all delegates agreed that the debt crisis has had a major impact on the quality and quantity of education in the South. But banks and aid agencies maintained that structural adjustment was for the large part not responsible for the general deterioration of the education sector in most of the South over the 1980s, arguing that Southern delegates were "confused" about the cause of their problem. Structural adjustment is the medicine, not the cause of the disease, and Africa's economy will improve during this decade as a result of it, they said. African and Latin American delegates, however, repeatedly expressed doubts about these sorts of predictions. They complained that charging school fees caused parents to pull their children out of school, bringing down the enrollment rate; that increasing class size and introducing double shifts in rural areas affected the quality of teaching, causing the literacy rate to drop.

It is easy to understand why the WDEFA could not contain an appeal to the North to cancel the debts in the South or to abandon the structural adjustment programs. The representatives from the North meeting at Jomtien had no mandate from their governments to alter the macroeconomic policies, even though those policies, and here I agree with my African colleagues, are of the highest importance for the education sector in developing countries. The policies have to do with the liberaliza-

---

[7] In particular, the editorial reported on the Jamaican Errol Miller's statement at the EFA conference on the tendency of the conference to lean too much toward Northern research findings. This is the same tendency found in the World Bank (1988a) document on the education policies of Sub-Saharan Africa (which will be discussed in the next chapter). Miller also held that the conference paid the most attention to Northern advice about the means of reaching Education for All in the South. Applications of many suggestions made by Northern experts made his country's situation worse, not better, he maintained.

tion of trade, opening up the economy to private, often foreign, investors, abolishing state regulations and protective measures, and "adjusting" the economy by downsizing public expenditures in sectors like education and health. In the next section we shall give an example of how the liberalization of the economy and the so-called structural adjustment policy meted out for a poor country like Tanzania means a threat to the gains that had been won in the education sector. We shall also show how the reintroduction of school-fees, so-called cost-sharing policies, along with privatization means building up structures to the benefit of children of the affluent and to the detriment of children of the poor.

DOES BASIC EDUCATION OR EDUCATION FOR ALL EQUAL PRIMARY EDUCATION?

As we shall see in the following chapter, the part of the education sector in Africa which the World Bank has singled out for support is *primary* education. At the World Conference on Education for All, representatives of the developing countries stressed that the concepts "basic education" or "education for all" had to include more than primary education. Those concepts had to include non-formal education and adult education, and sometimes even secondary education. As already mentioned, representatives from the South were also concerned that an emphasis on basic education should not mean a deemphasis on higher education (a point we shall return to in part III).

It is interesting to note that in the book *African Thoughts on the Prospects of Education for All* (UNESCO-UNICEF, 1990) the main concern is preserving African culture through education.[8] Primary school is hardly mentioned at all. The twelve authors of the book claim that making education available to all raises the question: "What education to what classes of the population at what specific periods in their lives, by what means and for what purposes?" (UNESCO-UNICEF, 1990: 6). Their concern is that the type of education needed should be culture-oriented and incorporate African norms and values, African traditional practices, and help shape the historical identity of Africans. We shall return to this point in our discussion of the content of schooling.

---

[8] The book was published as part of the African preparation for participation in the EFA conference. The volume was conceived by a joint working group of the UNESCO Regional Office for Education in Africa (BREDA) and the UNICEF Regional Office for Western and Central Africa (WACRO).

In publications written after the Jomtien conference, especially by authors from the North, we find that Education for All is frequently equated with primary education or Schooling for All (SFA).[9] The book: *Educating All the Children* by Christopher Colclough with Keith M. Lewin (1993) has as its subtitle *Strategies for Primary Schooling in the South.* It deals with primary schooling or Schooling for All, an expression used frequently in the book. A more honest title for the book would have been *Schooling for All.* The use of the title *Educating All the Children* leads our thoughts to Jomtien and the expanded vision of education expressed in Article 2 of the Declaration.[10]

When we look at the types of basic education attracting donor support, the two largest bilateral funders of basic education in Africa in 1990, USAID and SIDA (the Swedish International Development Agency), allocated 80–90% of their funds to primary schooling (Colclough, 1997).

Among multilateral funders of education, the World Bank is the largest, accounting for about 90 % of funding. It should be remembered, however, that the Bank is lending money, not donating it. A high priority is given to primary education within multilateral programs; it has accounted for all of UNICEF's educational support in recent years. According to Chrisopher Colclough (1997: 8): "Almost all of this multilateral finance was, in 1991, allocated to primary schooling, rather than to other basic education programmes."

As an observer representing the Norwegian Foreign Ministry I was present at two conferences in Africa leading up to the 1996 conference in Amman, Jordan, which was held to give a mid-term review of the

---

[9] For instance, Sarah Graham-Brown introduces her chapter on Basic Education for All by referring to the World Declaration on Education for All issued by the conference in Jomtien and then goes on to say:

> For the poorest and most conflict-ridden countries, the prospects of achieving *primary education* for all by the year 2000, as the declaration envisages, seem remote. (Graham-Brown, 1991: 269, emphasis added).

Also a book edited by Angela Little, Wim Hoppers and Roy Gardner (1994) following up projects in developing countries responding to the challenges of Jomtien bears the title "Beyond Jomtien: Implementing *Primary Education* for All" (emphasis added).

[10] Article 2 states:

> To serve the basic learning needs of all requires more than a recommitment to basic education as it now exists. What is needed is an 'expanded vision' that surpasses present resource levels, institutional structures, curricula, and conventional delivery systems while building on the best in current practices. (WDEFA, 1990: Article 2)

progress on "education for all." It was interesting to note that in the conferences, both the one held in Yaoundé, Cameroon for western Africa and the other held in Johannesburg for eastern and southern Africa, there were two themes which especially engaged many of the African ministers of education: the need to reinstate African languages as languages of instruction, and the need to define basic education in broader terms than primary education. For these two needs they have received no support from the World Bank. The one multilateral organization which has supported the African ministers of education was UNESCO (Brock-Utne and Lexow, 1996).

Catherine Odora Hoppers, who has followed the implementation of the EFA strategies rather closely, finds that the Jomtien conference represented a missed opportunity to reclaim an education for freedom and self-reliance. She finds that the Education for All conference gave disproportionate focus on formal primary schooling. "It was school education for all," she claims, "just being labeled 'Education for All' " (Odora Hoppers, 1998: 177). This school education, which the donors so wanted, was presented "complete with target dates accompanied with the imperative to make it 'universal' "[11] (Odora Hoppers, 1998: 177).

WHY DID THE CONFERENCE TARGET PRIMARY EDUCATION?

Why did the great educational jamboree target primary education, not vocational education which was in vogue with the World Bank some years ago and could have helped children earn a living, nor higher education, which could have made it possible for Africans to develop a counter-expertise, their own experts?

---

[11]Odora Hoppers sees education in Africa as an instrument of both foreign and ideological policy of countries external to the recipient countries of aid to the education sector. These donor countries have their own agendas that are often labeled "universal." As an example she cites the phenomenon of universal access which is taken as a neutral, ethically disinterested concern without any question being asked about universal access into what type of education (Odora Hoppers, 1998: 2). She quotes Huntington, who claims that at the end of the twentieth century, the concept of universal civilization helped to justify Western cultural dominance over other societies. The use of this concept made it necessary for other societies to ape Western practices and institutions. Like Huntington she also sees "Universalism as the ideology of the West in confrontation with non Western cultures" (Odora Hoppers, 1998: 18).

While many of my African friends have told me that the World Bank intends to recolonize Africa by giving Africans only a poor and rudimentary education and letting advanced knowledge belong to the West, I do not believe this is the intention of World Bank planners—but it might well be the effect.

Economists in the education sector try to argue that the education sector is not just any public sector, it is an investment sector, a sector dealing with human capital. When the right investments are made, the benefits both for the individual and the society will be great. Education is not looked at as a right, a joy, a tool for liberation and empowerment, but as an investment. In the words of the authors of the 1995 World Bank document *Priorities and Strategies for Education. A Review* (World Bank, 1995a—hereafter called *the Review*): "We believe that education is an investment and in every sense just as hard as building bridges and roads"[12] (Burnett and Patrinos, 1996: 273).

By means of rate of return analysis of education systems (ROREs), these economists have concluded that the rates of return are highest within primary education and therefore this level should receive the most public funding.[13] Paul Benell (1996) shows in his article that there are enormous national variables, that much of the data the World Bank economists base their ROREs on is now very dated, and that it is difficult to acquire accurate data for such analyses from many advanced countries, let alone the least developed countries. Keith Watson (1996) agrees with Benell that the research methodology of much of the Bank's approach is highly questionable. He also mentions that perhaps the biggest indictment of ROREs comes from Stephen Heyneman (1995), a comparative educator for many years on the staff of the World Bank. He says that

> the bulk of the economics research has been superfluous to making educational decisions. It has overemphasised rates of return to expansion by level, and under-emphasised the economics of educational quality, new subjects, target groups, teaching methods, and system reforms. It

---

[12] This type of argument might be necessary—especially for internal consumption—in the World Bank, which is not a donor but a bank. This means that any project proposed for approval must be presented as "bankable," that is, likely to yield returns that justify the loan investment. But unfortunately, this thinking has had contagious effects also on the donors to education in Africa. We shall return later to the human capital theory the Bank builds its policies on.

[13] RORE, according to Benell (1996), is used over thirty times in the *Review*.

has virtually ignored the dependency of one part of the education system on other parts, for example the essential contribution made by secondary and higher education to the quality of basic education. When dealing with vocational education, the economics literature has followed a traditional misspecification now three decades old. (Heyneman, 1995: 559–560)

But to challenge the World Bank economists is an uphill struggle, even if one is inside the World Bank, it seems.

TARGETING THE GIRL CHILD

The argument that basic education should target the girl child is also based on an economic analysis. Even some years of schooling of a girl child are said to be beneficial to curbing population growth.[14]

In a provoking paper Christine Heward (1997) maintains that in developing countries girls' schooling is being used as a contraceptive. She takes her point of departure in the UN Conference on Population and Development in Cairo in September 1994, which made girls' education the favored policy for delivering lower fertility and improved child health. Cairo was notable for the rather aggressive debates between groups representing a broad range of "feminist" interests and the patriarchal religious interests of countries like the Holy See and certain Islamic states. Abortion became a focus of bitter disputes about women's control of their fertility. Heward (1997) claims:

> Improving girls' access to education is a policy which neatly side-steps these difficult issues. Enlightening the potential ignorance of that appealing innocent, the girl child, is an indisputaby laudable goal upon which consensus is assured. (Heward, 1997: 2)

Six months after the Cairo conference, at the UN Conference on Poverty and Development in Copenhagen, Hillary Rodham Clinton pledged

---

[14] This argument, when coming from Western donors, to me always seems racist. Who are we, who are using so much of the world resources, to say that those who use much less should not have more children? In most of the countries in SSA I have visited, there is space enough for many more people. The most heavily populated area in the world is Central Europe. We also know now that it is not large population growth that leads to poverty, but the other way around: poverty leads to big families.

$100 million to girls' education, as a media-hyped U.S. gesture to the reduction of world poverty. In September 1995 the UN Women's Conference in Beijing made the strongest case for raising women's status by improving women's access to education. To Heward's arguments one can, however, add that already the Jomtien conference, four years before the Cairo conference, argued for strengthening education for girls.

Recent surveys of all the available studies show that the relationship of fertility to girls' education is complex. It is mediated by the social, cultural, and political contexts of girls' and women's lives within patriarchal gender relations.

Christine Heward draws on an analysis of the findings of studies of fertility and education in thirty-eight different countries derived from the World Fertility Survey and the Demographic and Health Survey of the United Nations Population Fund and the International Union for the Study of Population. This analysis shows that there are thresholds of development below which education has little effect on fertility.

Education appears to reduce fertility in countries with higher levels of development and more egalitarian gender regimes. Autonomy is crucial to women's control over their fertility. The relation between education and autonomy is mediated by the cultural relations of patriarchy. In many highly patriarchal settings a woman's autonomy increases only if she has a secondary or higher education.

There are good reasons to ensure that girls are educated, and it may be necessary to target them especially, but the arguments for doing so should have to do with fairness, equity, and securing the best talents in important jobs rather than with having women give birth to fewer babies.

THE SOCIAL DEMAND FOR EDUCATION

The assumption of the Jomtien *Declaration* and *Framework of Action* was that the low enrollment, completion, and attainment rates in primary education in developing countries had to do with the supply, location, and quality of educational provision rather than the demand for it. But a quite separate set of circumstances may lead to nonachievement of the objectives both of aid and of policy reforms. As pointed out by Colclough with Lewin (1993), there are factors inhibiting the demand for primary education irrespective of the relative supply of schools.

Drawing on the research of some countries in ex-French colonies in Africa, Jacques Hallak (1991) suggests that opportunities for education are underexploited and that the social demand for education is low. He cites four reasons for this low social demand. The first two are economic:

the continuing importance of child labor and the high costs incurred by poor families who have to contribute to construction and school facilities even before paying school fees for individual children. A third reason cited by Hallak is a perceived drop in quality. He maintains that for many parents the notion of quality encompasses more than simply a better school environment, more qualified teachers, and an adequate supply of textbooks. Quality also means relevance to local needs and adaptability to local cultural and economic conditions. We shall return to this point in Part II. Education, according to Hallak, must help children get on better in their daily lives. It must also help children adapt to other environments. If education is not perceived to be meeting such felt need, then parents, especially poor parents and those who need the labor of their children at home, may well withdraw their children from school.

A fourth reason is the lack of perceived prospects after the completion of primary education. If one of the main motivating factors for parents in rural areas for sending their children to school is to prepare them to also be able to live outside the rural environment, then one may suppose that they also expect post-primary education and training opportunities. If the supply of post-primary education is inadequate, it is likely to weaken the demand for primary education. Conversely, if the supply of post-primary education is strengthened, it is likely to strengthen the demand for primary education. Hallak raises the question whether EFA is a realistic social project if it does not account for, and build into its framework for action the implications, in terms of supply for the secondary and tertiary tiers of the education system.[15]

In an analysis of what has happened after Jomtien, Lene Buchert (1995b) shows that many donors have actually shifted their priorities within the education sector in Africa to supporting basic education more and higher education less. But as she also states:

> Since the maintenance or shift of resources for Basic Education by the donor agencies have to be understood within a framework of overall decline in education aid,[16] the impact is far from substantial. This leaves the national governments with the continuous, primary

---

[15] These were, as we shall remember from the earlier discussion in this chapter, also some of the concerns of the representatives from the developing countries at the Jomtien conference, who were afraid that the emphasis on basic education might mean a dismantling of higher education in their countries.

[16] Total official development assistance (ODA) from the OECD countries—which in 1990 provided approximately 90% of all ODA in SSA—decreased as an overall percentage of GNP, from 0.35% in 1990 to 0.25% in 1996 (OECD, 1997).

responsibility of the fulfillment of the goals of Education for All. (Buchert, 1995c: 540)

In her analysis of recent trends in aid to the education sector in Africa, Buchert (1995b) finds that agencies that have traditionally supported higher education and/or vocational education (for example the German development agency (GTZ), the Finnish International Development Aid (FINNIDA) and the British Overseas Development Administration (ODA) have begun to switch to basic education. Other agencies that have traditionally supported higher education have expressed an intention of supporting basic education. We shall return to these trends in Part III.

After analyzing the then current foreign aid patterns and policies on education in developing countries in three bilateral aid agencies: the Danish Internatonal Development Agency (DANIDA), the Swedish International Development Agency (SIDA) and the Dutch international development agency DGIS,[17] Lene Buchert (1993) concluded that the primary point of departure for the three aid agencies seems to be that the needs identified in the specific recipient countries are not followed up by careful curriculum design to match such identified needs.

Basic education, according to her analysis, seems to be equated with primary schooling. Apparently forgotten is the need expressed in the declaration from Jomtien to pay attention to the variations in basic learning needs and how they should be met in individual countries and cultures. The aid as well as the lending to education seem to be built on the definitions and philosophy of the World Bank expressed, for instance, in the 1988 document: *Education Policies for Sub-Saharan Africa: Adjustment, Revitalization and Expansion* (World Bank, 1988a). We will analyze this document in the next chapter.

THE COLONIAL LEGACY AND ITS EFFECT
ON EDUCATION IN AFRICA

David Scanlon (1964) starts his book, *Traditions of African Education*, with a chapter on indigenous education, then analyzes the educational policies followed by the Germans, the British, the French, and the Belgian colonialists in Africa. He also refers to the Phelps-Stokes Report of 1922, to which we shall return in Chapter 5, discussing the language of

---

[17] The Diretoraat-General Internationale Samenwerkung.

instruction in basic education in Africa. Scanlon relates how the education of the African before the arrival of the European was an education
that prepared the young African for responsibilities as an adult in the
home, the village, and the tribe. Learning took place through doing and
practicing, imitating the grown-ups. By this process, simple instruction
was given and know-how transmitted. There were also more formal
teachings by the fire-place at night, when the older members of the family taught the younger the history of the locality and developed abstract
reasoning through riddles. We shall return to this point in Part II. Scanlon
also mentions that there were complex educational systems in Africa before the coming of the European. He discusses the initiation rite of the
Poro society of western Africa. To go through that rite took several years.
The first formal attempts at European schooling in Africa were made by
Portuguese missionaries and date back to the middle of the sixteenth
century, but little is known about these missions and very little of their
work remains (White, 1996).

The vast European exploration of Africa in the early nineteenth century and the evangelistic and trading activities that followed led to the
"scramble for Africa" in the 1880s, and the eventual establishment of
colonial rule over large portions of the continent. The first general remark on the history of education in colonial Africa is that foreign missions (Christian or Islamic) with interests in Africa pioneered and
dominated the educational sector for many years. The foundations for
European education in Africa were laid principally by nineteenth-
century missionaries from Great Britain, France, and later, America. This
pioneering work in education should be judged in the context of the missions' early recognition of the supreme importance of education in the
successful execution of their evangelistic assignments. Therefore, as
Babs Fafunwa (1982: 21) argues, "education to win African souls for
Christ was made a central objective of mission education in colonial
Africa."

In the later years of colonization, when the colonial governments
began to show interest in education, the general goal of education did not
seem to change. What did seem to change was the shift in emphasis: a
shift from a purely religious education to what Fafunwa (1982: 21) calls
"a diluted semisecular education which emphasised the role of the
school in the continued furtherance of colonial interests in Africa."
Africa's colonial system of education was, according to Fafunwa, characterized by conscious and obvious attempts, first by the foreign missions and later by the colonial governments, to educate Africans away

from their cultures. This feature was most pronounced in the French colonies, where education meant "frenchifying" Africans.

There were clear differences in how much the French and British governments were involved in the education efforts in the colonies. *The French,* who colonized large parts of western and equatorial Africa, stressed a colonial policy of assimilation. Although here the missionaries again arrived first, the French government was not far behind. Legislation in France between 1903 and 1924 eventually gave complete control of the colonial schools to the French government. France had a very tight grip on the development of educational systems in its colonies. In 1922 France put forth a decree announcing that the establishment of a new school in the colonies required government permission, government-certified teachers, a government curriculum and the exclusive use of French as the language of instruction (White, 1996).

The British government was much less involved in educational policy in its African colonies than was the French government. Mumford's (1936) book *Africans Learn to be French* although presented as a review of French colonial policy and practice, lends great insight into the assumptions underlying British policy during the same period in other parts of Africa. Mumford writes about the prominent role of missionary education in the history of the British African colonies. In fact, the missions figured so prominently in the British conception of colonial education that they were often referred to as Britain's "unofficial partner." The collaboration between the government and the missions characterized British colonial education and distinguished it from the French system.

Throughout most of the British literature there is a sense of appreciation for local culture and tradition in the colonial setting. British colonial policy has often been referred to as "indirect rule" since it used chiefs and kings as allies in colonial administration. The sons of these chiefs and kings were trained in English to serve as middle-men between the Africans and the colonial administration. The other Africans in anglophone Africa just had a few years of schooling. Their education typically involved learning to read an indigenous language before they were introduced to English. When the mission schools were taken over by the British government, they also introduced English at an earlier stage and relegated the vernacular languages to an inferior position.

Fafunwa (1982) tells how the highly sophisticated Poro school system in Liberia and Sierra Leone was almost completely eradicated in the colonial period. In colonial Africa, schools were used basically for preparing the African for the semi-skilled job market. As Fafunwa (1982: 22) argues:

"In fact the volume and quantity of education the colonial administrators were willing to give to the Africans were the barest minimum necessary for such auxiliary positions as clerks, interpreters, preachers, elementary teachers and so on."

When we look at colonial education in Africa, we find an unwillingness to give Africans (called natives) higher education, to make them independent and critical. We find that education was used as an ideological tool to create feelings of inferiority in Africans, to create dependence on white people, and to spread the thinking, ideas, and concepts of the "master" race.[18]

The Tanzanian professor of the history of education, the late Z. E. Lawuo (1978), maintains that the European slave traders at one point found it more lucrative to retain the Africans in Africa and make them cultivate crops like cotton and oil seeds for overseas markets. In order to make Africans participate in this new economic structure, it was found necessary to change their culture, beliefs, and value system and to colonize them politically. Thus, European economic interests in Africa were largely responsible for the appearance of missionary activities in Africa accompanied by the introduction of Western education. Lawuo argues:

> Christian missionaries used education as their tool for gaining converts and making entry into new areas to pave the way for western socio-economic and political structures. According to David Livingstone, who first came to Africa as a missionary sent out by the London Missionary Society, the most important duty of the European Christian Missionary in Africa was to integrate the African into European economic structures. Africa, he declared, should not be allowed to industrialize but instead it should serve as a plantation for the metropole, growing the crops demanded by industrial Europe. (Lawuo, 1978: 43)[19]

When Abdou Moumouni (1968) writes about the colonial education system in his book *Education in Africa* he takes his examples from western Africa but what he says about colonial education in Africa seems to hold for all of the colonial countries:

---

[18]For an analysis of how education has been used as an ideological weapon against blacks in colonial times and how it has worked to oppress girls, see Brock-Utne (1989a).

[19]Having read such analyses of the colonial educational system, the attentive reader may have a feeling of deja-vu when reading in later chapters about donor policies to education.

The essential aim of education was to supply the subordinate personnel necessary to the effective functioning of the colonial administration, such as clerks and interpreters, employees in commerce, nurses and veterinary assistants, elementary and secondary school teachers, assistants to doctors and workers in various fields (Moumoni, 1968: 37).

Walter Rodney (1976) has termed the colonial school system: "Education for under-development." He has found that the main purpose of the colonial system was to train Africans to man the local adminstration at the lowest ranks and to staff the lowest jobs in the private capitalist firms owned by Europeans. It was not an educational system designed to give young people confidence and pride as members of African societies, but one which sought to instill a sense of deference toward all that was European and capitalist.

THE EFFORTS OF THE INDEPENDENCE PERIOD

Fafunwa (1982) tells how education became a top priority when the African states attained their political independence.[20] In a book edited by A. Babs Fafunwa and J. U. Aisiku (1982), the educational efforts in ten African countries are described. Irrespective of the philosophical position of each country covered in their survey, there is a very clear indication that each country has had phenomenal growth in educational development, and consequently in the financing of education as compared with their respective colonial eras. Increased primary school enrollment was one of the direct results of a significant development in post-independence Africa. Universal and free primary education was introduced in country after country.[21] As we shall discuss more thoroughly in Part II expansion of the already existing educational system in many places took priority over the creation of new systems in education, though there were exceptions to this rule. Mali, for instance, soon after independence in 1960, embarked on a thorough educational reform move-

[20]The pioneer African country to attain independence was Ghana, in 1957, while Namibia gained its independence in 1990.
[21]By the Education Act of 1961 in Ghana, primary education became free and compulsory. Kenya introduced partially free primary education in 1971 when a presidential decree abolished tuition fees in those parts of the country considered educationally backward, and in 1974 free primary education was extended to all parts of Kenya. Similarly, primary education became free in all parts of Nigeria in 1976.

ment to give it a truly Malian system of education. Tanzania's "education for self-reliance" policy was outlined by the first president of the country, Julius Nyerere.

Another mark of progress in African education after independence came in the area of increased facilities for higher education. Prior to independence most African countries had no universities of their own. Those were not needed for people who were meant to only occupy jobs of low status. After independence each African country erected a university; in most of the countries several were erected.[22] In 1982 Fafunwa and Aisiku concluded their edited book *Education in Africa,* by noting that Africa since independence had recorded phenomenal progress in the provision of more education for more people, but what seemed to be lacking in most African countries at the time was more concern for the relevance of the education provided.

Not long after their book came out, the effects of the economic structural adjustment policies started to be felt also in the education sector of those African countries that were forced to apply these measures to their economy. The whole educational system from primary through university was hit by these measures. The gains made after independence were eroded.

THE EFFECTS OF ESAP ON THE PROVISION OF BASIC EDUCATION

The economic structural adjustment programs (ESAPs[23]) of the World Bank starting in the mid-1980s were meant to be the medicine that would help African and other "developing" countries repay their debts by having their exports grow. The medicine consisted of measures like trade liberalization, privatization, forced devaluation of the local currency to "get the prices right," and reducing public expenditures by laying off people in public administration as well as cutting sectors like health and education. The medicine came from people who believed in the blessings of the free market and the downsizing of the national governments—the State—attributing to African states a lot of the blame for the economic recession.

They seemed to forget that African states may be weak and inefficient, but so are African markets. And as Simon McGrath (1997) rightly

---

[22] We shall return to the situation of the African universities today in Part III.
[23] Many of my African colleagues have told me that the abbreviation ESAP really stands for Extreme Suffering for the African People.

argues, much of the limitations of these markets arises because of the limited strength and reach of states rather than their excessive influence. What is required, he claims, is a viable approach to strengthening both states and markets to mutually reinforce each other's operations. In poor countries a strengthening of the role of the state is especially important to create national unity, indigenous development and greater equity among districts and among groups of people. As we shall see in Chapter 3 even the socalled "like-minded donors"[24] among them Norway and Sweden, have followed the policies of the World Bank by-passing of the national governments, privatization of the secondary schools, and liberalization of the textbook market.

The ESAP medicine led to a starvation of the social sectors, including the education sector, in most developing countries. At the end of the decade this was also known by the World Bank. For instance, in the World Bank publication *Improving Primary Education in Developing Countries* Marlaine Lockheed and Adriaan Verspoor (1991) attribute the declines in net enrollment ratio in primary schools in fifteen out of twenty-five "adjusting" countries during the 1980s to the reduction in public expenditure on education arising from structural adjustment. A number of other studies (e.g. Cornia, 1989; Tilak, 1992; Blundell, Heady, and Medhora, 1994; Jayarajah and Branson, 1995; Cornia, Jolly, and Stewart, 1987) have consistently reported that school enrollments declined in those countries embarking on ESAPs.

In 1993 Fernando Reimers and Luis Tiburcio published a study comparing countries in Africa that had undergone structural adjustment[25] with those that had not.[26] They found that betweeen 1980 and 1988,

---

[24] This expression was coined within the donor community denoting a group of donors who often vote the same way in the UN and who in their development policies adhere to principles like poverty alleviation and recipient responsibility. The group includes all the Nordic countries as well as Holland and Canada.

[25] In Africa the adjusting countries were Algeria, Angola, Benin, Burkina Faso, Burundi, Cameroon, Central African Republic, Chad, Congo, Cote d'Ivoire, Equatorial Guniea, Gabon, Gambia, Ghana, Guinea-Bissau, Kenya, Madagascar, Malawi, Mali, Mauritania, Mauritius, Morocco, Mozambique, Niger, Nigeria, Rwanda, Sao Tome and Principe, Senegal, Sierra Leone, Somalia, Sudan, Togo, Tunisia, Uganda, United Republic of Tanzania, Zaire, Zambia, and Zimbabwe.

[26] In Africa the non-adjusting countries at the time of the study were Botswana, Cape Verde, Comoro Islands, Djibouti, Ethiopia, Lesotho, Liberia, Libyan Arab Jamahiriya, Namibia, Seychelles, South Africa, and Swaziland.

while education expenditures declined in twelve of the twenty-eight "adjusting" countries, a similar decline took place in only two of the twelve "nonadjusting" countries. On average the share of recurrent expenditures going to education increased 8% in non-adjusting countries in Africa, while it increased only 2% in adjusting countries (p. 37).

Reimers and Tiburcio (1993: 54) conclude their analysis of the effects of the structural adjustment measures on the education sector in Africa this way:

> It is clear that the adjustment programmes supported and promoted by the World Bank and the IMF during the 1980s have not worked for many countries. Lip service to a new emphasis on social development and rhetoric about difficulties in establishing causality between adjustment and deterioration in living conditions have to give way to a new sense of accountability.
>
> International financial institutions are supposed to be part of the solution, not part of the problem, and their record has to be assessed by the number of success stories they can claim, not by whether they can or cannot be blamed for the failure.

The following two examples illustrate the trends described by Reimers and Tiburuco (1993) and Lockheed and Verspoor (1991). The first example is a study of the impact of adjustment on education in Nigeria that showed how enrollments in primary education declined from 14.7 million in 1983 to 12.5 million in 1986. Relations between the Ministry of Education and teachers soured; some teachers left their jobs while others were fired. The budget categories for educational materials, buildings, and furniture almost disappeared (Hinchliffe, 1989). The same report indicates that universities have suffered the financial squeeze as well, with impact on the supply of scientific equipment and materials, books and journals, staff development and research.

Another example illustrating the trend is a case-study of the situation in Zambia which concludes that public education finance suffered as a result of economic adjustment. Per pupil expenditures in 1985 in real terms were half those in 1970. The impact of this adjustment was greater in primary and secondary schools than for universities. The basic education budget became increasingly equivalent to a payroll. Capital expenditures also fell disproportionately and Zambia became increasingly dependent on donors for teaching materials (Hoppers, 1989).

Likewise the basic conclusion of the studies undertaken by UNICEF shows that the extent of the deterioration of the situation of children and other vulnerable groups in Africa in the 1980s was largely dependent upon the type of adjustment programs adopted (Cornia, Jolly, and Stewart, 1987).

Concerned with the disasters provoked by orthodox structural adjustment programs of the kind described in the Cornia, Jolly, and Stewart (1987) study removing food subsidies and reintroducing school fees, the Economic Commission for Africa (ECA) in 1989 drafted an *African Alternative Framework to SAP for Socio-Economic Recovery and Transformation (AAF-SAP).* AAF-SAP clearly condemns SAPs for their limited objectives and short-term perspectives.

THE REINTRODUCTION OF USER FEES

The market philosophy associated with adjustment, under the powerful auspices of the IMF (International Monetary Fund) and the World Bank, led to the introduction of user-fees for schools in most adjusting countries. An analysis of a sample of World Bank loans showed that introducing or raising various educational charges was a feature of about one-third of World Bank Education Sector loans (Stevenson, 1991). Primary school fees were introduced in Malawi, Zaire, Mali, and Nigeria, in each case followed by reduced school attendance (Stewart, 1996).

But as Christopher Colclough claimed, there is no guarantee that the imposition of user fees for attendance at primary and secondary schools will increase enrollments at those levels. That would happen if and only if the revenues so gained are spent on the provision of new school places, if there also is excess demand for schooling, and if the fees are not so high that the negative enrollment response among the poor exceed the positive response from those who are willing and able to pay (Colclough, 1995). Scholarships for the poor would be needed, which may substantially undermine the revenue raising objectives of user charges. On the other hand, if low enrollments are caused by demand deficiency, any increase in private costs will reduce enrollments even further. If the quality of schooling is low because of irrelevant curricula taught in a language children seldom hear outside of school and by untrained and poorly paid teachers, there may be little demand for schooling. Charging fees in such a situation would be another argument for parents not to send their children to school.

THE EFFECTS OF THE STRUCTURAL ADJUSTMENT POLICIES ON THE EDUCATION SECTOR IN A COUNTRY LIKE TANZANIA

Through the Arusha Declaration and the policy of Education for Self-Reliance (Nyerere, 1968) the whole country of Tanzania was mobilized to eradicate illiteracy, to provide universal primary education and to change the content of the inherited educational system. After twenty-six years of independence, Tanzania, with a population of 20 million, could boast of 3.5 million children in over 10,000 primary schools, with at least one primary school in every village (Roy-Campbell, 1992: 147). The achievement of universal primary education, where all Tanzanian children had access to a basic education, was commendable for one of the poorest countries in the world. As a result of its vibrant adult education program and because Tanzania had succeeded in having its own national language, Kiswahili, as the language of instruction both in primary school and in adult education, Tanzania increased its literacy rate from 33.3% in 1970 to 90% in 1984, the highest in Africa. However, with the structural adjustment of the Tanzanian economy in the 1980s, culminating in the signing of the IMF agreement in 1986, the very essence of Education for Self-Reliance has been threatened. Whereas in 1966, five years after independence Tanzania spent 14.2% of her national budget on education and 8% on debt servicing, in 1987–1988 she spent only 5.4% of her national budget on education while 33.2% was spent on debt servicing (URT, 1972; URT, 1988). In 1992 the percentage used for education had fallen further to 4% (BEST, 1994).

The situation in Tanzania comes easily to mind when we read the warning words from the Economic Commission for Africa (ECA):

> Reductions in budget deficits must not be accomplished at the expense of expenditures on the social sector, i.e. education, health, and other social infrastructure . . . Efforts must be made to ensure that the annual average of at least 30 percent of total government outlays is devoted to the social sector and that in any case, the annual rate of growth of social investment is significantly higher than the population growth rate. (ECA, 1989: 3)

When these words were written, Tanzania was already in a situation where less that 10% of the national budget was devoted to the social sector.

The illiteracy rate, which by 1984 was only 10% had gradually risen to the region of 20–30% in 1992 (URT, 1993: 6), and further to 32.2% (20.6% for men and 43.2% for women) in 1995 (UNESCO, 1997).

According to the 1993 report on Tanzania's education system universal primary education was supposedly attained in 1981 with a gross enrollment ratio of about 98%. However, the primary school gross enrollment ratio has gradually declined, to 70% in 1992 (URT, 1993: 6).[27]

The problem of non-enrollment in the primary school in Tanzania is a national problem and it is on the increase. Sumra (1994) holds that the population is about to relapse into levels of illiteracy that were present under the colonial period. While the enrollment rate in primary school reached around 90% in the early 80's in 1993 only 53.2% of the 7- to 13-year olds were in school (Sumra, 1994).

EFFECTS OF THE REINTRODUCTION
OF SCHOOL FEES IN TANZANIA

During the colonial period the issue of school fees was one of the issues in Tanzania around which mass discontent was mobilized against the colonial authorities. To provide equal access to secondary schooling in Tanzania, school fees were abolished in 1964. Primary school fees remained until 1973 as they were considered minimal compared to secondary school fees. They were, however, abolished in 1973 (Galabawa, 1990). The abolition of school fees was one of the measures to ensure the legitimacy of the post-colonial state.[28]

Universal access to education is being undermined by the reintroduction of school fees. On the advice of the World Bank and the IMF primary school fees were restored in Tanzania in 1984 as a development levy.[29] Tuition fees were introduced at the secondary level in 1985 (Samoff and Sumra, 1992). As we shall see in the following chapter, this policy of so-called cost-sharing, especially at secondary and tertiary levels, was advo-

---

[27]This is the same figure given for 1993 in the last statistical yearbook from UNESCO (1997) (71% for boys, 69% for girls). The net enrollment rate that year was 50 (50 for boys, 51 for girls).

[28]In Namibia, which only attained independence in 1990, free education for all is an important part of the post-apartheid policy.

[29]To be fair to the World Bank, we should remark that the World Bank seems able to learn from its mistakes (but only after much harm has been done in poor countries). The 1995 *Review* states that no fees should normally be charged at primary level (World Bank,1995a). This is reiterated by Burnett and Patrinos (1996).

Table 1.1 Percentage of Students Reporting Difficulties in Paying School Fees

Students from:	Girls	Boys
Middle class families	20.6%	12.1%
Lower class families	53%	30.3%

Source: Sumra and Katunzi (1991).

cated by the World Bank already in the 1988 document on the educational policies of Sub-Saharan Africa. It is further advocated by the IMF as part of the structural adjustment program.

The reintroduction of school fees in Tanzania has been received as an extremely unpopular measure by the Tanzanian population. The heated debates in Parliament and the discontent of parents and students at the recent raising of the secondary school fees is an indication of such discontent.

Difficulty in payment of school fees is a gender issue as well as a class issue. Suleman Sumra and Naomi Katunzi (1991) found that the reintroduction of school fees in secondary schools affected girls more than boys, and girls from the middle and lower classes much more than girls from the upper classes.[30] Table 1.1 shows the results for children from less well-to-do homes.[31]

If students come to school without fees, they are sent home. In Handeni Secondary School, of the students not reporting during the first week, 68% were girls, and of those who were sent away, 80% were girls (Sumra and Katunzi, 1991: 27).

As one girl stated:

I have been sent home three times, twice this year. Last year I was sent away once. This year when I went to collect money, my father informed me that the money was spent to pay my mother's hospital bill. My brother was given the fees first and I was asked to wait till my father could sell his coffee again. (quoted in Sumra and Katunzi, 1991: 27)

[30] The research was part of the ongoing work of WED (Women, Education, Development)—an African research group based at the faculty of education at the University of Dar es Salaam. For more information about the group, see Brock-Utne (1991).
[31] Their sample consisted of 235 secondary school girls and 84 secondary school boys drawn from three locations, one in Dar es Salaam, one in Kilimanjaro, and one in Handeni.

While students are looking for school fees, the lessons continue at school.

> I remain behind my colleagues because I waste lot of time going back home to collect school fees. Teachers are unwilling to offer compensatory classes. I copy notes from my friends without understanding what they mean. (another girl quoted in Sumra and Katunzi, 1991: 27)

The nice words in the *WDEFA* about "promoting equal opportunities in all aspects of the lives" of girls and women (here especially pertaining to education) are of little value if the reintroduction of school fees forces parents to choose whether the little money available will be used for educating a boy or a girl.

The hope expressed in the Jomtien conference on education for all by the year 2000, if taken to mean primary schooling for all, is unlikely to be achieved if schooling is to be combined with so-called cost-sharing measures and the use of school fees. Delegation of the responsibility for funding to the communities, so-called "decentralization" will often mean that poor communities won't be able to fund much education for their children. After having analyzed case-studies from several developing countries on the funding of basic education for all Sarah Graham-Brown concludes: "If equity of provision in basic education is to be an important consideration, community financing cannot be regarded as a simple panecea for the problems of funding education" (Graham-Brown, 1991: 271).

In an analysis of national and regional enrollment trends in primary education in Tanzania, Suleman Sumra (1994), the director of the Bureau of Educational Research and Evaluation (BERE) at the University of Dar es Salaam, likewise shows how the delegation of responsibilities for primary education to the Ministry of Local Government (MLG) has created serious problems. Most district councils simply do not have resources to adequately deal with the rapidly expanding demands for primary education in the country. On the basis of his research, he draws the conclusion that the responsibility for providing quality basic education should rest with the central government.

WHAT ABOUT BASIC EDUCATION AFTER JOMTIEN?

Halfway through the EFA decade, data showed that the decline in both gross and net enrollment ratios in primary school had continued through 1995 in more than half of Sub-Saharan African (SSA) countries, and in one-fifth the absolute number of children enrolled actually declined. A majority of countries in SSA had a smaller proportion of their children in school in 1995 than was the case in 1980 (UNESCO, 1996).

UNESCO claims that the number of school-aged children not enrolled in primary school is expected to increase globally by approximately 34 million between 1990 and 2000 (UNESCO, 1993). To counteract this expectation and cater for children who have dropped out of school African countries, often through donor support, have embarked on various types of non-formal school programs. One of these is the COPE schools in Uganda, another the NAFA centers in Guinea.

A VISIT TO THE COPE SCHOOLS OF UGANDA

The COPE (Complementary Opportunity for Primary Education) program in Uganda caters for children who have either dropped out of school very early or never went to school. The teaching goes on for only three hours a day in order for the children to be able to participate in other activities and chores after school. Some of the children at the COPE centers are bread-winners in their homes. In the area we visited there were many child-headed households (Brock-Utne, 1997c). Their parents and other grown-up relatives have died of AIDS.

The communities build the school buildings and pay the salaries of the teachers. The pupils are expected to pay 1,000 Ugandan shillings (U.S.$1) per term in school fees (there are three terms in a year). Even though this fee is very low, we were told at Kabaari COPE Center that the school fees constituted a reason for children dropping out. Seven pupils were not attending school the day we were there and we were told that the reason was that they had not paid school fees. The pupils are also expected to buy their own exercise books.

At the same time, the revenue generated for schooling is quite limited. For example, the salaries the COPE instructors get are so low (30,000 Ugandan shillings per month, or U.S. $30) that they cannot live on them. Quite often their salaries are not paid on time, and the instructors can go months without any salary at all.

Donors pay the COPE schools for the training of instructors and for the teaching materials including the instructors' manuals.[32] Donors also

---

[32]A policy of international competitive bidding has been undertaken for organizing instructor training and for developing textbooks and instructor manuals for COPE schools in Uganda. The winner of the tender is an American firm, Creative Associates International, Inc., based in Washington, D.C.

pay for the monitoring of the reform and for vehicles for the COPE supervisors to visit the centers.

The teachers at the COPE centers are called instructors and not teachers to differentiate them from the regular teachers in primary school. They do not have initial teacher training. They normally have secondary school O-levels[33] and then receive training through the program. The initial training is three weeks. After that there is in-service training twice a month, once through a week-end and once including some more days. This training is supposed to be a training in more learner-centered instruction than has been the normal case in the regular primary schools. The training is given by tutors from the Teacher Colleges who themselves have gone through this type of training. No provision has so far been made for instructors who will be going through the whole cycle of in-service training to have this recognized as part of their teacher training.

In Bushenyi district, which I had the opportunity to visit, there are ten COPE centers, scattered far apart—some take four hour travel time from Bushenyi center to reach. Since I had only one day in Bushenyi and the schools only run in the morning, we could only visit two centers, Kabaari and Itendero. I was told that at each center about eighty pupils, aged 8 to 14, who had never gone to school or had dropped out very early, were enrolled in the centers when they first opened in November 1995. The pupils are divided into two classes, one for ages 8 to 11 and one for ages 11 to 14. They spend three years in the COPE schools with three hours a day of teaching. After those three years they are supposed to have learned as much as primary school pupils do in five years and to be able to enter form 6 in primary school. Whether this is realistic remains to be seen, since pupils in the first centers are only in their second year now. The drop-out rate has been high, so that the average number of pupils in the centers now is about fifty.

Among reasons for the high drop-out rate from the COPE centers the following may be mentioned:

- The centers do not teach vocational skills even though this is a wish of the parents. This type of teaching is said to be costly, the

---

[33]O-level stands for *Ordinary level*, an exam taken after four years of secondary schooling. Two more years are required to take A-level exams qualifying for university entrance. The system of O-levels and A-levels is inherited directly from the British system of secondary education.

instructors do not have the skills involved, and there is no money for the training materials the pupils would need and no workshops in the vicinity. But some instructors manage to get around this. The instructor at Kabaari told us that he had attended a technical school after O-levels at secondary school and was a bricklayer and a baker. He was going to teach the pupils brick-laying and baking of bread in his own home.

- Teaching is in English, and the textbooks are all written in English, even for the first grade and even though it is official government policy that the language of instruction in the first grades should be the mother tongue.[34] I was informed by George Ouma-Mumbe, education officer at the National COPE Focal Point, Ministry of Education in Kampala, that at least the first year of COPE would use the mother tongue as the language of instuction. This, however, is not what I found in Bushenyi.

- Some COPE pupils after the introduction of UPE (universal primary education) left COPE to join the regular primary school. Here again the teaching was not in the mother tongue, but children were taught some practical and vocational skills which were highly appreciated both by them and their parents (Grov, 1999).

THE UPE REFORM BROUGHT INTO EFFECT SINCE FEBRUARY 1997

When Yoweri Kaguta Museveni won the presidential elections in Uganda in May 1996, he had to fulfill a promise he had made during his campaign, namely, the introduction of UPE-free universal primary education. School fees should be abolished for four children per family, two of whom should be girls. Family has been defined in a way where the father is counted as the head of the family and four of his children may now receive primary education. There are many polygamous families in Uganda, especially in the countryside. Sometimes also a man has one wife in Kampala, another in his village, and a third wife in another village, and has more than four children with each of them. Many of those I spoke to felt that it would be better if the government had taken as a point

---

[34] These are Luo for the northern region, Runyakitara for the western region, Luganda for the central region, Itesot for the eastern region, and Lugbar for the northwestern region.

of departure the number of children a woman had. People tried to get around the four-children-per-family rule by enrolling four of the children in one school and four in another. (This is not allowed, but sometimes the authorities cannot monitor family enrollment well enough, so people get away with it.)

Museveni also made it clear that no child should be sent back home because the parents could not pay school fees. This decree has made it difficult to enforce any payment at all.

We visited two COPE centers in Bushenyi, Kabaari COPE Center and Intendero COPE Center. Both of the centers had experienced drop-out of students at the introduction of UPE but the total drop-out rate of pupils at Intendero was much higher than at Kabaari. Even though the teachers claimed that "UPE took a lot," they did not know how many of their initial pupils now went to the nearest primary school and how many had dropped out for other reasons (e.g. they found the teaching uninteresting, found they could make money by selling stuff in the streets nearby, or had parents who wanted them at home).

When the Intendero COPE Center started its work in February 1996, 120 pupils had shown their interest in following the three-year school, though 93 (48 girls and 45 boys) actually registered. The two teachers we met said that they now had 19 pupils each in their class, but the day we attended the center both of the teachers were working in the same room and they had only 23 pupils all together. They maintained that a lot of pupils had left and enrolled in primary school instead when that school became free. However, when their parents realized that it was not completely free after all and they were expected to contribute to school funds, the pupils dropped out of primary school again and found it difficult to reapproach the COPE center.[35]

At Rukindo primary school in Bushenyi we were told that of the 445 pupils (201 girls, 241 boys) in the school, 364 were UPE pupils, 40 were orphans (mostly because their parents had died from AIDS), and 41 others should pay, but did not do so. They said that the president had said that school fees were now abolished, education was free, and no one should be discontinued or sent home because of inability to pay. Before the reform which was put into place in February 1997 pupils in grades 1

---

[35]The instructors were strongly encouraged by the COPE supervisor Kabazeyo, and Jolly Uzamukunda, MoE (Ministry of Education), to trace the pupils who had dropped out of the center and get them back. Such a tracer study should also come up with the reasons for the drop-out.

to 3 had to pay 5,000 Ugandan shillings per year (about U.S.$5), and pupils in grades 4 to 7 were asked to pay 8,000 shillings per year. In addition they had to pay for textbooks and exercise books, contribute to the school fund, and buy uniforms. Since the reform was introduced, pupils are provided with textbooks. They still have to buy exercise books and uniforms, and parents are supposed to contribute to the maintenance and development of the school through cash payments or labor.

THE NAFA CENTERS IN GUINEA

The learning of vocational skills seems to be the reason for the success of the so-called NAFA[36] centers in Guinea. Guinea has one of the lowest enrollment rates in primary school of any African country. In 1990 Guinea had a gross enrollment rate of 31.8% (19.4% for girls and 44.2% for boys). That year saw the start of PASE (Programme d'Adjustement du Secteur de l'Education). This program, which is both a formal and a non-formal basic education program, has succeeded in bringing the enrollment rate up to 44.5% (28.8% for girls and 60.51% for boys). The non formal NAFA centers are part of the PASE program. There is hardly any drop-out from the NAFA centers even though the instruction is in French, and I discovered on a field-trip that many of the pupils who were asked to read for me from the black-board had just learned by heart the sentences that were there.

On that field-trip to the centers at the end of November 1996 I asked the pupils in the centers why they came to school, and they all mentioned the vocational activities which were part of the set-up. They learned soap-making, tie and dye techniques, sewing, carpentry, brick-making and brick-laying.

But the teaching of vocational skills is not regarded as cost-effective by the World Bank, an institution to which we shall turn in Chapter 2. We may mention at the end of this chapter on the Education for All initiative that the African Association for Literacy and Adult Education (AALAE) was critical of the *WDEFA* partly on the grounds that the initiative to the EFA conference was spearheaded by the World Bank, which, according to them:

---

[36] The word "NAFA" is no acronym but an Arabic word which in Guinea also is used in the domestic languages Malinké (the same language as Bambara spoken in Mali), Soso, and Pulaar, and means a profitable and useful enterprise.

has repudiated education as a public responsibility through its "Structural Adjustment Programmes" forced upon most African countries. Indeed there is every reason to believe that this broad framework is intended to give the World Bank and its allies a free hand to determine the detailed, specific education agenda on a country-by-country basis, and in particular apply the Bank's "Structural Adjustment Programmes" on the education sector.... Even the participation of UNESCO and the African governments would seem to have been used merely to give legitimacy to positions already taken by the Bank. (AALAE, 1990, preamble, p. 1)

CHAPTER 2

Education Policies for Sub-Saharan Africa as Viewed by the World Bank

> *It is the World Bank-donor analyses and pre-*
> *scriptions that dominate the ideological realm.*
> *They have so much human and financial re-*
> *sources at their command that to challenge*
> *them is an uphill struggle.*
>
> (TANDON, 1996: 3)

This book is my contribution to that uphill struggle. But before we continue on the strenuous uphill climb, it would be good to be nourished by a cosmic humility.

A PLEA FOR COSMIC HUMILITY

Yash Tandon (1996) of the University of Zimbabwe reminds us that when Europeans came to Africa toward the turn of the fifteenth century, they found a prosperous civilization and enormous wealth. Agriculture and cattle rearing, iron-work, pottery, fishery, salt-mining, gold refining and ornament making, weaving, hunting, and long-distance trading were well advanced at a time when Europe was still relatively backward (Diop, 1974). From the fifteenth century on, however, the fate of the two continents reversed. Through the intermediation of the Muslims in northern Africa and Spain from the ancient civilizations, Europe learned among other things the use of the compass and of gunpowder (Davidson, 1992).

Africa stagnated for over three centuries as a direct result of slavery and colonial conquests. This part of global history, for the sake of maintaining a correct historical perspective on Africa and Europe, must always be kept in mind when looking at the contemporary African situation. Tandon reminds us that civilizations come and go; and finds that this knowledge, if anything, should encourage what he terms "cosmic humility" (Tandon, 1996: 1).

The historian Joseph Ki-Zerbo gives us another example that may teach us some cosmic humility. He reminds us about the fact that Africa was the first continent to know literacy and to institute a school system (Ki-Zerbo, 1990).

The bulk of the African people fought heroically against the imposition of slavery and colonialism, though there were some Africans who collaborated with the white slave-hunters and colonialists as well. The struggle for liberation continued throughout most of the twentieth century, but began in real earnest after the end of the Second World War. It was a democratic struggle for self-determination, backed by several resolutions of the United Nations and by progressive people all over the world, that finally led to the political liberation of Africa. As I show in this book, political liberation did not translate into economic and cultural liberation. Attempts by leaders like Kwame Nkrumah to take advantage of the political climate during the 1950s to form a United States of Africa failed and Africa came out of its colonial past fragmented into fifty odd states. Despite Africa's fragmentation and weakness, political independence was a milestone in the contemporary evolution of Africa's history. It was a victory of democratic forces and it opened up the political arena to carry on the struggle for economic liberation. Yash Tandon (1996: 2) asks us to remember this aspect of Africa's history since "yesterday's colonialists and racists, who used all the undemocratic means at their command to suppress democracy in Africa, are today feigning to be its champions."

What is the nature of the present struggle in Africa? Tandon offers this answer:

> Primarily, it is to consolidate the gains of democratic victory against the forces of national oppression and class exploitation, and to liberate Africa from the continuing exploitation of its vast resources for the benefit of international corporate capital and its local agents in Africa. (Tandon, 1996: 2)

We may likewise ask: What is the nature of the present struggle within the education sector in Africa? An attempt at an answer would be: It is to consolidate gains made at independence, including opening up educational opportunities for the majority populations of Africa, introducing African languages as languages of instruction, constructing indigenous curricula, and liberating Africa from the intellectual recolonization imposed through educational policies designed elsewhere, the forced adoption of Euro-American curricula, tests, and textbooks, and the erosion of the African languages as languages for intellectual pursuit.

Tandon claims that in the short to medium run, Africa is on the road to "recolonization" by the West. Africa's political gains are under threat. I claim that this recolonization is strongly felt within the education sector of most African countries. Africa's intellectual gains made during both the pre- and early post-colonial period are under threat.

The title of Part I of this book, "Establishing Education Policies *for* Sub-Saharan Africa," points to the fact that there are outside influences establishing education policies *for* Sub-Saharan Africa. Were there a chapter on the way education policies are formed in Norway (or in other European or North American societies), the heading would be "Establishing Education Policies *in* Norway" (or in another European or North American country). Though Norway, with four million people, is also influenced by trends within the education sector in other countries (see Brock-Utne, 1997a, 1998b, 1998c), no one would dream of another nation or group of nations establishing education policies *for* Norway, deciding whether we should strengthen basic education or vocational education and cut down on higher education, deciding what curricula, textbooks, language of instruction, and examination systems we use. But this is the situation most countries in Sub-Saharan Africa find themselves in; their education policies are in many cases determined by bilateral and multilateral donors or money-lenders. As one interviewee put it when Lene Buchert (1997a: 52) tried to find out how the "education and training policy (1995)" in Tanzania had been formulated: "it has been stuffed down the throat of the Government by the IMF and the World Bank."

In spite of the fact that the World Bank is a lending institution and not an aid agency, the Bank has come to play a decisive influence in deciding on the educational policy and practices to be followed by African countries (Jones, 1992). After the Jomtien conference, when "Education for All" became the new buzz word for donors to education in Africa, a dear colleague at the University of Dar es Salaam wrote to me: "My own view is that education for all is fine as a goal. Who is against education for all? All wish to achieve that. But the problem is how to achieve it? What is the opportunity cost of achieving it? Reduced expenditure on higher education?"

My colleague feared that the EFA drive would mean further starvation of the poor university at which he was working. He feared that the already meager aid being given to higher education in Africa would be reduced further. As we shall see later in this chapter and also in Part III, his fears are warranted. My colleague also feared that donors, led by the powerful economic analysts of the World Bank, would put pressure on the governments of Africa to reallocate money from higher and secondary education to primary education, reintroduce school fees, and privatize part of the education sector.

This pressure, if followed up by the African governments, would mean an even more serious change of education policy than the reallocation of aid. It is estimated that the amount of foreign aid to education between the 1960s and 1980s fluctuated between 10% and 15% of public expenditures on education in developing countries (Sikwibele, 1996). The rest of the public expenditures, about 90%, is paid by the governments themselves. As we shall discuss in the following chapter, bilateral and multilateral donors to the education sector also seem to follow the policies of the World Bank.

The World Bank has over the last ten years produced five policy documents which have had great effect on the education policies of Africa. These are:

- *Education Policies for Sub-Saharan Africa: Adjustment, Revitalization and Expansion* (World Bank, 1988a)
- *Primary Education: A World Bank Policy Paper* (World Bank, 1990)
- *Vocational and Technical Education and Training: A World Bank Policy Paper* (World Bank, 1991a)
- *Higher Education: The Lessons of Experience* (World Bank, 1994)
- *Priorities and Strategies for Education: A World Bank Review* (World Bank, 1995a)

The first and the last of these documents will be dealt with in this chapter, while the 1994 document on higher education will be discussed in Part III when we take up the subject of the universities in Africa. For a critique of *Vocational and Technical Education and Training,* see Lauglo (1992).

We have singled out the document *Education Policies for Sub-Saharan Africa: Adjustment, Revitalization, and Expansion* (hereafter *EPSSA*) for special treatment here because, even though the document is ten years old, there is no other document that gives as fully the education policy suggested by the World Bank for adoption by the countries of Sub-Saharan Africa. With the benefit of hindsight it is also possible to see what has happened to the policies advocated in 1988. To what extent are the same policies advocated in the more recent publication of the Bank, *Priorities and Strategies for Education: A World Bank Review?*

A BRIEF DESCRIPTION OF THE DOCUMENT

EPSSA gives flesh and blood to an earlier World Bank publication called *Financing Education in Developing Countries—An Exploration of Policy Options* (World Bank,1986). The 1986 document is 43 pages long, with appendixes it comprises 67 pages. The 1988 document, by contrast, is 160 pages long, with appendixes it comprises 277 pages. An additional six pages of maps cover various aspects of Sub-Saharan Africa: population density, language groups, income groupings, and enrollment in primary schools in 1960 and 1983. *EPSSA* consists of three parts and nine chapters. Part I, "The Policy Context," is comprised of three chapters. The first chapter tells about the remarkable progress of African education; the second is called "Education and the External Environment: A Cycle of Deteriorating Prospects"; and the third chapter in Part I describes what the authors see as the major problems in the educational sector in Africa at the present time: enrollment stagnation and quality decline.

Part II describes what the authors[37] of the report see as policy options for African governments. It contains four chapters: one dealing with primary education, one with secondary, one with higher education, and one with educational management.

The third part of *EPSSA* called "An Agenda for Action" contains the last two and concluding chapters. Chapter 8 is mostly a summary of descriptions and arguments found in the preceding six chapters. It is called "Policy Packages for Educational Development" and builds on a description of the situation in the education sector in Sub-Saharan Africa which can be found in chapters 2 and 3 together with what the authors of *EPSAA* see as causes for the situation. It further summarizes policy suggestions

---

[37] *EPSSA* was prepared by a group of World Bank personnel including Peter R. Moock, task leader, and Ralph W. Harbison as the pricipal writers under the general direction of Aklilu Habte, who was the head of the Education Department of the Bank at the time and under the immediate supervision of Dean T. Jamison. Birger Fredriksen and John Middleton wrote the initial drafts of chapters 4 (on secondary education) and 7 (on educational management), respectively. It should be noted that all of the writers were males and, with the exception of Aklilu Habte who comes from Ethiopia, from the North. It is claimed in the preface that "thanks to financial assistance from the Norwegian Ministry of Development Cooperation, the study benefited greatly from discussion of an early draft by African policymakers at two international meetings held in Ethiopia and Cote d'Ivoire in early 1987" (World Bank, 1988a: xii). Africans I have met who have attended these meetings say that they cannot see that their input has had much influence on the document. The bibliography (pp. 113–118) hardly includes any writings by African policymakers or researchers.

which have also been made in chapters 4, 5, 6 and 7. The last chapter, Chapter 9, is titled: "International Assistance for African Educational Development." This chapter is a summary of arguments made in earlier chapters of what type of aid the group would recommend be given to developing countries and the conditions under which such aid should be given.

THE CRISIS IN THE EDUCATION SECTOR IN AFRICA

The authors of *EPSSA* point to the deteriorating conditions of the education sector in Sub-Saharan Africa. Though there are great variations among the countries in Sub-Saharan Africa, the World Bank Group (WBG) is generally making a correct observation: The education sector has been hit hard by the economic decline in Sub-Saharan Africa. In fact, the situation is even worse than described in the document. The World Bank Group (WBG) of authors suggested, for instance, that teacher salaries needed to be reduced, a proposal which made my Tanzanian colleagues only laugh because salaries for teachers at any school level in Tanzania already were too low to exist on. A primary school teacher in Tanzania in 1988 earned around the equivalent of U.S.$20 a month and taught forty hours a week to classes of forty to fifty kids in classrooms where often there were no desks, no windows, no books or other instructional material, and sometimes not even chalk. Apart from this the teacher was also required to teach adult classes at night twice a week for no additional pay. Teachers could not survive on the salary. They had to try to find other means to survive (e.g., farming or driving people to work in a pickup). The WBG's descriptions of "teacher absenteeism" and "low morale among teachers" have to be understood within this context. What strikes me as surprising is the fact that enthusiastic and committed teachers are found in some of the poorest countries in Sub-Saharan Africa in spite of the extremely harsh conditions they are working under. This can only be understood in terms of the dedication of the teachers to their nation, and to the freedom and independence of their people. It impressed me that my colleagues at the University of Dar es Salaam, who also received salaries much too small to live on, still conducted a high quality staff seminar each week, with well-prepared papers and excellent and critical discussions.

It has to be mentioned, however, that in *some* Sub-Saharan countries, like Botswana, teachers live quite well on their salaries. In the New South Africa, black university lecturers and professors at the historically black universities have a standard of living that is quite comparable to that of their colleagues in western Europe or in the United States and is far above the living standards of their colleagues in an African country like Tanzania.

Though the situation was bad in the education sector in most of Sub-Saharan Africa (SSA) when *EPSSA* was written, it has deteriorated further since that time. Class size—already much too high in many places in 1988—increased in almost two-thirds of SSA countries over the period 1990–1995 (UNESCO, 1996).

The crisis in the education sector is due in part to the larger economic crisis in Africa. This is also admitted by the WBG. But their explanation for the crisis, which has been given earlier in the introduction, sets the tone for the document and, unfortunately, is rather symptomatic of the attitude toward the problems of African countries which permeates the whole document. They give the following explanation for the crisis: explosive population growth, mounting fiscal austerity and tenuous political and administrative institutions (World Bank, 1988a, pp.ix, x). This description may also be called blaming the victim. The description, however, is consistent with the 1981 World Bank report *Accelerated Development in Sub-Saharan Africa*, often called the *Berg Report* after its lead author (World Bank, 1981).

This 1981 report, serving as the World Bank's manifesto for Africa in the 1980s, received more attention, debate, and criticism than any other economic study on Sub-Saharan Africa. Derek Mulenga (1995) claims that by the early 1990s virtually all of the policy prescriptions contained in that document had been implemented in one form or another in almost every country in Africa. When explaining the root causes of the economic crisis in Africa, the *Berg Report* dismisses the external factors, such as negative terms of trade and protectionism of the European and North American countries which contributed to Africa's poor economic performance, as peripheral to the real problems besetting Africa. The *Berg Report* focuses on internal factors (policy bias against agriculture, rapid population growth, and "inflexibility" of African economies) as the key causes of the economic stagnation. It further points to cost reduction as being central to all educational strategies.

The *EPSSA* also does not mention the negative terms of trade which most African countries were forced to accept. No mention is made of the heavy debt burden along with the rise in interest rates, the wrong technological choices encouraged by donor agencies, or the lack of high level training and education for development and independence. In addition no attention is given to the fact that the many devaluations forced on the

African countries by the World Bank/IMF conditionalities, along with the forced policy of reducing public expenditure, have led to a situation where in education, as in other sectors, there are only bones left; there is nothing more which can be cut.

SUB-SAHARAN AFRICA

There seems to be hardly any recognition in *EPSSA* of the fact that the countries of Sub-Saharan Africa are very different from each other in the way they have organized their economic and political systems, in the ideas and ideologies they adhere to, and in their goals for regulating their economic institutions and social service sectors like education and health. The WBG, praising market economy as a recipe not only for the productive sector but also for the social service sector, naturally gave good grades to countries where the governments practiced the same principles and bad grades to countries that were committed to some ideals of equal sharing of resources and saw health and education as services that should be provided for all people no matter which region they lived in or economic resources they had.

The countries of Sub-Saharan Africa reached their independence in different ways and at different times. At the time *EPSSA* was written, a country like Namibia had not reached independence and was still occupied by South Africa. There was no democracy, let alone economic equity, for the blacks of South Africa, who were ruled by a small white minority. The countries in Sub-Saharan Africa adhere to different ideologies as well as different educational philosophies. Even the conditions for teachers and pupils in the countries vary so much that a policy-paper dealing with all these countries, lumping them together and treating them as if conditions and ideologies should be the same for all, will seem highly inappropriate to *some* countries.

When it comes to the conditions in the eighteen universities in the eastern and southern African countries, these have been described rather thoroughly in the many publications from the now twenty year old research program Eastern and Southern African Universities Research Project (ESAURP). This research program has been carried out in fourteen countries in the region and has produced a lot of statistics and information about the conditions in the institutions of higher learning in eastern and southern Africa (e.g., see Maliyamkono (ed), 1980; Maliyamkono, Ishumi, and Wells 1982, ESAURP, 1987). To show how conditions vary throughout SSA, we may mention that the 1987 book *University Capacity in Eastern and Southern African Countries* shows that in 1985 the salary for a university professor in Zimbabwe, for instance, was more than four times the salary of a university professor in Tanzania.

In a field trip to Botswana in 1997 to examine a UNICEF project supported by the Norwegian Foreign Ministry, I learned that Botswana is one of the most prosperous countries in Sub-Saharan Africa (Brock-Utne, 1997b). I learned that basic education in Botswana comprises ten years, that is, seven years of primary schooling and three years of junior secondary schooling. Schooling is free for all children and a nutritious meal is provided at school for every child each day. The latest published statistics (1994) show a net enrollment ratio (NER)[38] of 96.7%.[39] In Botswana I was taken to the Kalahari desert, to Kweneng district west, where we visited Motokwe primary school. I here observed two lessons being taught, one in Setswana in the first grade and one in English in the seventh grade. Both of the classrooms were well equipped; there were chairs for each child and triangular-shaped desks placed in groups. Both of the classrooms were nicely decorated with pictures, wall charts, and drawings. The teaching in both classrooms was of a high quality. I was especially impressed by the break-through approach used by the first grade teacher. Her classroom was a workshop where children engaged actively with the abundant teaching materials provided. Though there where only 30 pupils in her class (18 boys and 12 girls), among those 10 Basarwa[40] children, she had a co-teacher to help out with the group work.

There is a need to take the differing conditions of the various countries in the region into account. There is also a need for a donor agency to acknowledge the fact that some of the African countries do not adhere to

---

[38] See footnote 1 for an explanation of the net enrollment ratio (NER) and gross enrollment ratio (GER)—the latter expressing total enrollment at a given level of schooling.

[39] On my departure from Gabarone, Mr. Makgothi, head of Planning, Research and Statistics, told me that the newly calculated statistics for 1997 showed a net enrollment rate of 97.7 % for girls. The enrollment rate for boys was somewhat lower but had not yet been calculated.

[40] Basarwa is a Tswana term for the people who are internationally known as the San minority of Botswana. In donor jargon they are called RADs (Remote Area Dwellers). They are much discriminated against. UNICEF (and Norway) wants to help them and have put them into hostels so that they can attend a Western type primary school. This may not be the best choice for them. The Basarwa children speak a Sesarwa language while the other children in the school speak Bakgala-gadi, a language which is much closer to Setswana than Sesarwa. The Basarwa children have to struggle with three African languages; Sesarwa, Bakgalagadi (to communicate with the other kids), and Setswana as well as English.

a capitalist viewpoint. Among them are various forms of socialist ideology and the desire to create a welfare state. Yash Tandon reminds us that Africa is still searching for the forms of governance that are best suited to its own history, culture, and environment.

> Western forms of democracy is "propertied democracy" that necessarily creates wealth on one side and poverty on the other. It has made deep inroads in contemporary African political economy, and it is relentlessly pushed by means of stick and carrot by Western countries to which most of Africa is still beholden for aid, technology and markets. (Tandon, 1996: 4)

The World Bank and the IMF [41] in various documents, including *EPSSA,* seem to think that market economy or capitalism will solve the problems in Africa. For instance: "As structural adjustment of African

---

[41] Both the International Monetary Fund (IMF) and the International Bank for Reconstruction and Development (the World Bank) were established in 1944 at an international monetary and financial conference at Bretton Woods, [therefore often referred to as "the Bretton Woods institutions"] New Hampshire, with forty-four states taking part. The formal founding took place the next year. The two institutions are governed by boards of governors, where all member countries are represented, with voting rights weighted on the basis of their capital contributions. Formally both institutions are specialized agencies of the United Nations system, but this relationship is only symbolic: None of them has accepted the coordinating role which the UN plays in relation to the regular specialized agencies (Garbo, 1995).

The IMF was assigned the task of promoting international trade, exchange stability, and a multilateral system of payments, countering the international disequilibriums of the past. The role of the World Bank was to assist in the reconstruction and development of territories of members and to encourage the development of the productive facilities of less developed countries.

Over the years the countries of the North, which thanks to the weighted voting have a deciding position in the Bretton Woods institutions, have permitted these institutions to take over the leading role in international economic and financial matters that the UN should perform according to its Charter. The strictly limited allocation of resources to the UN and its specialized agencies, combined with generous contributions to the Fund and the Bank, has created a growing asymmetry. Today the Fund and the Bank have become principal instruments in securing debt repayment from developing countries to their Northern creditors and in enforcing discipline over the developing countries and, more recently, countries in transition, transforming their economies into open market systems (The South Center, 1996).

economies is achieved and liberalization is institutionalized, markets will work better, during a potentially lengthy and painful transition to a more market oriented system of higher education" (World Bank, 1988: 13). There may be a danger that, even when it comes to the productive sector, the suggested recipe of the World Bank/IMF will work to the detriment of the great masses of the African people, of the poor, the hungry, and the women and children. (For analyses of this more general policy, see George, 1989, 1994; Loxley, 1987; McFadden, 1987; Mudenda, 1987; Onimode, 1992; Payer, 1987; UNECA, 1989).

But even those who would defend the use of market-economic principles in the productive sector will often hold that such principles are not applicable to a "non-productive sector" such as education, health, and other social services. The WBG carries over an advocacy for the use of market-economic principles from the productive to the social service sector without arguing for their claim that such a transfer is justifiable. Since EPSSA seems to be based on this assumption, the lack of arguments for this basic claim seems striking.

The Bank's view of education draws its inspiration from the modernization paradigm and derives its principles from its neo-liberal approach to economics. In particular, its present approach to education is informed by human capital theory.[42] As Fernando Reimers and Luis Tiburcio (1993) argue:

---

[42] It was in the 1960s that Theodor Schultz (1961) and Gary Becker (1962) developed Adam Smith's original notion that investment in education and skill formation was as significant a factor in economic growth as investment in physical plant and equipment, and the human capital theory was born. James Coleman (1988: 100) observes:

> Probably the most important development in the economics of education in the past 30 years has been the idea that the concept of physical capital as embodied in tools, machines and other productive equipment can be extended to include human capital as well. Just as physical capital is created by changes in materials to form tools that facilitate production, human capital is created by changes in persons that bring about skills and capabilities that make them able to act in new ways.

Since Becker and Schultz, huge amounts of research and analysis have been built on the notion of human capital (see, e.g. Carnoy, 1995). For a general and recent critique of the human capital theory, see Schuller and Field (1998). For a more detailed discussion of human capital theory and a critique of the theory within the context of education in Africa, see Mulenga (1995) and Colclough (1995b).

The underlying theoretical assumptions of structural adjustment programs (SAPs) rest exclusively on classical economic theory; but in the context of developing economies, economic aggregates (output, employment, prices, exchange rates) are not best determined by the free play of market forces and prices are not the most effective instrument for the efficient allocation of resources. (Reimers and Tiburcio, 1993: 17)

Both the identified "educational issues in Africa" and the proposed policy framework essentially reflect human capital assumptions within the broader context of the structural adjustment development agenda. Indeed, the main goals of the World Bank's efforts in education in Africa, both in terms of sectoral lending and as components of structural adjustment programs, seem to be to prepare people for the jobs that a global division of labor offers, which means primarily producers of raw material. The type of growth that is linked with the adjustment policies of the World Bank is an unequal growth. Bade Onimode puts it this way:

Adjustment growth reproduces the polarized and unequal development of the world capitalist system which is detrimental to Africa. It is constrained by the unacceptable requirement that Africa must pursue its imposed role of specialization in primary production within the international capitalist division of labour. (Onimode, 1992: 126)

Onimode shows convincingly how the World Bank's concept of adjustment growth is a minority project. It is growth for the primary benefit of a minority of the population in a given nation. It reinforces the effects of unequal global development within each country and threatens the very foundation of the liberation struggles of the African states.

A DOCUMENT FROM THE WEST

The document *Education Policies for Sub-Saharan Africa* was written from a Western perspective. There is little or no participation of African policy-makers or academics, as evidenced by lack of references to research carried out in Africa. There are, for instance, no references to the many seminars, reports and studies by ESAURP. Nor are very knowledgeable African professional bodies like ERNESA (Educational Research Network of Southern and Eastern Africa), whose members had discussed an earlier draft of the document and the policies it suggests, referred to (see ERNESA, 1987). Neither are the relevant African political bodies. There was, for instance, a joint meeting of the United Nations Economic Council of Africa and the vice chancellors of the universities in the region of Harare in the beginning of 1987. At that meeting the World Bank document on educational policies was heavily criticized because it would perpetuate Africa's dependency by discouraging the training of their own high level work force. It has been maintained that Africa needs "experts" from the industrialized countries because Africa has not developed the necessary expertise. The meeting in Harare stressed that if African institutions of higher learning do not undertake this training, the dependence on expatriates will again grow.

The *EPSSA* is heavily biased when it comes to the sources consulted for information. Only studies which support the arguments made are referred to. Sometimes these studies are rather insignificant and exploratory and have severe limitations and methodological weaknesses. Other studies, sometimes of a much more thorough nature, and sometimes even commissioned by the World Bank itself, are not cited when they go against the arguments made in the 1988 document. The document is clearly biased in the direction of American sources as evidenced by the bibliography at the back of the document. As mentioned earlier the absence of references to African researchers in African-based research institutes is remarkable.[43]

Joel Samoff (1993) has also shown that when it comes to World Bank thinking on education in Africa, the research base is largely restricted to that produced by World Bank staff or commissioned by the Bank. The result is a self-fulfilling prophecy. Research data support the policy that the Bank wishes to pursue because that research has helped to shape that policy.

SOME SPECIFIC POINTS

I shall limit the discussion to treat only a few of the specific points and proposals made in the EPSSA. I have tried to choose the points that I find best show the thinking in the World Bank. These are also the points

---

[43]As we shall see when discussing the 1994 World Bank paper on higher education, the World Bank continues to refer mostly to its own documents. The authors seem not to have read any of the research or writings from people in the South and hardly refer to any critical research undertaken by researchers in development education in the North.

which have received special emphasis in the Jomtien deliberations, are reiterated in the paper on higher education, and have proved to be of special importance for the bilateral donor policies so heavily influenced by the World Bank. These points are:

- Claims about "the quality of education" and how to restore it
- Privatization of education and cost-sharing
- The proposed stagnation of higher education

QUALITY IN EDUCATION AS THE WORLD BANK GROUP SEES IT

EPSSA is filled with assertions about what is claimed to be a "decline in the quality of education." Here the WBG first decides on what to assess as "quality of education", then judges the African countries as to how they perform in this dimension as defined by the WBG, and then tells them not only how they are going to restore the "quality of education" but also what does not help. The WBG sees three kinds of measures as necessary for the restoration of quality:

- More textbooks and instructional materials
- A renewed commitment to academic standards, principally through strengthening examination systems
- Greater investment in the maintenance of physical facilities (World Bank, 1988a: 131)

This way of defining educational quality is repeated over and over in the *EPSSA* in slightly different wording, for example:

The safest investment in educational quality in most countries is to make sure that there are adequate books and supplies. These are effective in raising test scores, and almost, invariably, have been under-invested in relative to teachers (p. 57).

The correctness of this rather debatable assertion is taken for granted. So also is the WBG's claim that it knows what does *not* lead to an improved quality in education:

The following kinds of investment are unlikely to have any noticeable effect on primary school quality despite their potentially high cost: reducing class size, providing primary teachers with more than a general secondary education, providing teachers with more than minimal exposure to pedagogical theory (p. 57).[44]

Several passages in the *EPSSA* assert that certification requirements for the teaching profession should be relaxed (e.g., p. 135). It is argued that this would facilitate another policy advocated by the WBG, that of lowering teachers' wages. It is also suggested that teachers could teach more hours per day and that class sizes of forty-four pupils in primary school are quite acceptable.

INSTRUCTIONAL MATERIALS VERSUS THE TEACHER

Even in highly industrialized countries I can see no professional argument for maintaining that a good supply of instructional material is better than a good teacher. This is especially not true in the lower grades and for immature pupils. On the contrary, what we try to do in such cases is to bring in an extra teacher, to lower the number of pupils in class, to teach small groups. The assumption of the early 1960s that self-instructional material, programmed learning, and computers would replace the teacher never proved to be right. Even in cultures where information is abundant, where people are bombarded daily with programs through multiple TV and radio channels, newspapers, magazines, books, and computers (which tie them up to the World Wide Web), the teacher is still as important as ever.

Most of the African countries we are discussing here are still largely oral cultures. The normal way to learn is through the examples and oral information given by the family, the elders, and the teacher. Teachers in Kiswahili *mwalimu*[45] still enjoy a high respect in these countries, their words carry prestige, and they are listened to. But the harsh conditions they are now working under; with salaries too low to live on, too many pupils in class, too many hours to teach, and hardly any teaching materials threaten to undermine their[46] position. Probably the best way to restore quality in education in Africa would be to restore the dignity of teachers,

[44] The trend limiting prospective teachers to exposure to pedagogical theory can also be detected in the policies of Thatcher's Britain (Editorial, 1994; Edwards, 1994).

[45] *Mwalimu* is also the name denoting Julius Nyerere, the first president of an independent Tanzania. He was looked at, and saw himself as, a teacher of his people, a highly respected title for a highly respected man.

[46] In most countries in SSA the teaching profession, especially in secondary school, but also in primary school, especially in the rural areas, is predominantly a masculine profession.

increase their salaries, shorten the numbers of working hours, especially their teaching loads, and lower the number of pupils in class.

When teacher salaries take up most of the primary school budgets, it is not, as the WBG seems to think, because these salaries are too high, but because the financial resources of the country and those allocated to the education sector are too low. It is not correct to say that instructional materials have been underinvested in relative to teachers. It is correct to say that the conditions of the teachers in most Sub-Saharan African countries are now so harsh that they threaten to undermine the position of the teachers and the quality of the education they can give.

In many countries in Sub-Saharan Africa, the salaries of teachers fell by some 30% in real terms during the 1980s. This reduction was compounded in a number of cases by failure to ensure regular payment. In Tanzania, for instance, rural teachers are required to travel to distant headquarters to collect their salaries, taking as much as an entire day, and in some districts payment can be delayed for months (Reimers and Tiburcio, 1993: 18). The Tanzanian educational researcher Herme Joseph Mosha (1988: 35), in an extensive study of the prevailing conditions in Tanzanian primary schools, made the following observation: "It was found that in most rural schools, teachers spent about three days getting their monthly pay, half of their monthly salary was spent on travel and accommodation."

Without openly admitting it, the World Bank must in the years following the *EPSSA* have seen that it was wrong in asserting that teachers were not that important and that their salaries could be cut. In the recent years a number of donor agencies, including the aid ministries of the Netherlands, Sweden and Germany as well as the World Bank, have recognized the desirability of supporting recurrent costs within the primary sector, even topping up teacher salaries (Colclough, 1997).

Of course, instructional materials are also important. But an inventive teacher with proper and challenging teacher training may be able to bring about more learning with just the simplest, home made instructional tools, using mostly the immediate surroundings, than can a mediocre and poorly trained teacher using even the most advanced self-instructional materials. The following describes how an inventive teacher in Zimbabwe provides excellent education with the simplest tools:

> In a remote school in Matabeleland there was a young student teacher whose working conditions and social background were just as poor as that of any other student teacher and as that of the fifth grade children

he was teaching. The children in his class were busy doing different things. They seemed interested in what they were doing.

In one corner of the class-room there was a book-shelf made of old bricks and planks wrapped up in newspaper. There were a few booklets and some magazines which the teacher had collected together with the children. In the windows, some with broken panes, big seeds had been threaded on strings and were waving happily as decoration in the light breeze from the broken windows. In one corner the organization of SADCC was illustrated by means of empty coke-tins and stones. Newspaper pictures were glued to the boxes, symbolizing different SADCC departments.

On the floor maps of different countries were shaped with pebbles. There was hardly an empty space on the mud-floor. But children stepped carefully around the creations not to destroy them. In another corner was a "spelling tree", just a few branches with cards hanging on strings like a Christmas tree. Children worked in pairs, asking each other to spell the difficult words. In another group some children were playing with a set of home-made math cards.

To honour the guests, the children picked their self-made costumes from the hooks on the wall, one drummed and the others performed a joyful and very rhythmic dance.

To teach children about traditional handicraft techniques, like how to build a proper hut or how to make a hob-kerry, elderly people from the village were invited to the school to share their wisdom and knowledge with the children.

This wizard of a young teacher had also taught the children, boys and girls, how to knit and had just started to teach them sewing, but this was a problem since material was scarce. His wisdom lay in seeing the future for these children, how hard it would be for them to get a job, like any of the other 200,000 pupils in Zimbabwe leaving school every year. Therefore he wanted to teach them useful things which they could make and which they would need, for their own use, hopefully for sale as well as for consumption (Nagel, 1993: xviii).

In fact, the World Bank in 1978 (ten years prior to the publication of *EPSSA*) commissioned a very thorough study of the effect of teacher training on the school environment and pupil performance both in developed and developing countries. This study is not referenced by the WBG. The study made an extensive review of the relevant literature with respect to both developed and less developed countries as well as a reanalysis of earlier data collected in India and Chile. The conclusion of the study, discussed in the introduction by Professor Torsten Husen, is that "teacher education makes a difference both in developed and in developing countries, particularly in the latter" (World Bank, 1978, introduction).

Herme Mosha (1988) in his study of factors that promote good performance in Tanzanian primary schools observed:

> The findings showed that factors that accounted for good performance were to have adequate and well qualified teachers who are motivated to work hard. A school climate that supported co-operation among teachers was also a prerequisite of good performance (Mosha, 1988: 35).

Of instructional materials the most important are: blackboard and chalk for the teacher, and paper and pencils for the pupils. In some places even these basic necessities are lacking. It is important that pupils and teachers together make their own learning materials and that written and printed materials are clearly relevant to their own situation and their own curriculum. The learning materials should preferably be produced locally. I completely agree with the then Tanzanian Minister for Health, Chiduo, who claimed in a conference in March 1988: "Third World countries should endeavour to produce their own learning materials instead of depending on imported ones" (Chiduo, 1988: 1).

The Education Sector Policy Paper of 1986 from the African Development Bank also stresses that "there is an urgent need not just for any teaching materials and textbooks, but for materials that are more closely in tune with the realities and needs of African societies" (quoted in World Bank, 1988a: 137). This then is the challenge facing African scholars and writers of textbooks and learning materials. But to do this work, which is of the greatest importance to restore the best parts of African culture, history, and dignity after a long period of colonization, it is necessary to strengthen institutions of higher learning and to provide for research in fields like African history, African art, African languages, traditional medicine and meteorology, and so on. It is also important to promote publishing within the African countries themselves.[47] The World Bank (1988a:137) policy put forth in *EPSSA* is not reassuring. It says:

---

[47] This point will be dealt with more extensively in subsequent chapters on curriculum reconstruction and the language policy of Africa.

Difficult issues will have to be confronted: what pedagogical material to develop locally and what to purchase from abroad, the trade offs between higher cost local printing and least cost printing elsewhere . . . usually outside Africa.

What is needed most is pedagogical material developed and published locally in Africa for primary schools, and nationally or regionally within Africa for secondary schools and institutions of higher learning. For these institutions some books will also have to be imported, but it is important that the African countries themselves decide on which books to import and are not merely given books from donor countries which these countries, for ideological or other reasons, would like to give away.

ACADEMIC STANDARDS: RAISING TEST SCORES

The concept "academic standards" is a highly controversial concept.[48] Who has the power to define "academic standards"?[49] The whole controversy about the concept is not made an issue in the *EPSSA*. Whose academic standards are we talking about? What are test scores supposed to measure? Testing for what purpose?

Professional educators know that those who construct the tests and decide on the examinations to be used are really the ones who decide the curriculum. It does not matter that curriculum guidelines say that children should learn to cooperate, learn to till the land or to help in the neighborhood, if all that is measured through tests is individual behavior and narrow cognitive skills. This behavior and these skills then become the curriculum; they become what the children learn. Ideally, it ought to be the other way around: first a country decides on the education it wants its citizens to acquire, then it decides how to evaluate whether desired learning has taken place. The first president of Tanzania, Julius Nyerere, the *mwalimu*, expressed this professional understanding well in his policy directive published in March 1967 called *Education for Self-Reliance*:

[48] In Chapter 8 we shall return to a discussion of this concept in connection with the situation of the universities in post-apartheid South Africa.
[49] In his last book, *Whose Reality Counts?* Robert Chambers (1997) discusses the power to define concepts. He demonstrates how academics with a long university education, having lived up to high academic standards, frequently hold erroneous beliefs about development because they have been taught to communicate laterally and within academia. They have not been able to "learn from below," to learn from the people in the developing countries.

The examinations our children at present sit are themselves geared to
an international standard and practice which has developed regardless
of our particular problems and needs. What we need to do now is to
think first about the education we want to provide, and when thinking
is completed, think about whether some form of examination is an appropriate way of closing an education phase. Then such an examination should be designed to fit the education which has been provided
(Nyerere, 1968: 63).

In the same policy directive, Nyerere notes that for the education which
independent Tanzania wants to build, "the purpose is not to provide an
inferior education to that given at present. The purpose is to provide a
different education" (p. 63). He wanted the educational system of Tanzania to emphasize co-operative endeavor, not individual advancement,
and to stress concepts of equality and responsibility (p. 52).[50]

In one passage in the *EPSSA* the WBG also seems to pay attention to
the professional understanding of the relationship between curriculum
choices and examinations:

Most African examination systems need modification so that the broader
range of cognitive competencies sought by a nation from a given level
of the educational system is sampled on the tests, rather than their concentrating, as is now often the case, narrowly on those skills most
needed for success at the next level of the system. Only if examinations
are so structured will the curriculum be made pertinent for the majority
of students for whom any level of education is now terminal (World
Bank, 1988a: 138).

If one added to the expression "broader range of cognitive competencies" also practical and social skills, the statement could serve as a
good guideline for test construction. But unfortunately it seems the
WBG through this statement is mostly paying lip service to insight developed in the community of professional educators. The thoughts are
not developed any further; on the contrary, they are contradicted in several other passages in the *EPSSA* where "academic standards" are looked

---

[50] We shall see in subsequent chapters how imported assessment systems from
the West along with the destruction of indigenous publishing and curriculum development have strengthened the policies outlined in the *EPSSA* and have undermined the policies professed by a newly independent Tanzania.

at as a well-defined and fixed entity and where performance on tests developed in the West is taken as a measure of "academic standards."

When the WBG argues that academic standards in African countries are low, it does so by referring to low test-scores earned by African pupils and students on tests developed in the West, for instance, by the IEA (International Association for the Evaluation of Educational Achievement). It has to be remembered that these tests stem from a Western culture and entail Western concepts.[51] It also has to be remembered that the majority of African students who are required to take the tests often have to do this in their second, and frequently even in their third or fourth, language, while the majority of students in the West answer them in their mother-tongue. The WBG refers to an IEA mathematics test on which students in Nigeria and Swaziland answered just over half as many items correctly as students in Japan, the highest scoring country, and about 65% as many as students in the 17 better off countries (14 of these were industrial market-economies) (World Bank, 1988a: 39). Further results of IEA tests in reading comprehension, general science, and mathematics administered to some African countries led the WBG to draw the following conclusion: "The general conclusion to be drawn from these studies is that the quality of education in Sub-Saharan Africa is well below world standards" (p. 40).

Educational researchers in Africa are constantly debating what quality in education may mean in their own context and how it is going to be assessed. The issue of quality in the education and training system was a main issue in the seminar on educational research in Tanzania at the University of Dar es Salaam in 1984 (see Ishumi et al., 1985). The participants discussed what the concepts of quality "might mean in a country concerned with wider meaning of this concept than conventional measures of educational achievement" (p.12). The researchers were extremely skeptical of importing the whole apparatus of American research on classroom interactions and to "measure up Tanzanian students against batteries of tests that have been used transnationally by bodies such as the IEA. These approaches come out of very specific cultural milieux in northern industrialized countries" (p. 13).

In an article on the interaction between quantity and quality in Tanzanian primary education, Kenneth King and David Court (1986) write

---

[51] In Part II I shall show an example, taken from Namibia (MEC/NIED, 1994), of how examinations can be monitored in order to include African cultural expression.

about the "problems of assessing quality in a nation pledged to non-conventional measures of school success" (p. 22). They write about the vast difference between Kenya, where "quality is defined almost entirely in terms of intellectual skills that are examined in the Certificate of Primary Education" (p. 24), and Tanzania,

> where the ideal quality consists of knowledge and skills relevant to the immediate life of the terminating majority rather than the future requirements of those going to secondary school. More important, it also consists of sets of attitudes, values and commitments such as non-cognitive attributes which are felt to be relevant to socialist citizenship (p. 25).

Though Tanzania, under the pressures of the globalization of capital[52] and a neo liberal agenda[53] largely put on them by donors, has had to give up its policy of a tradition-rooted socialism called *ujamaa* and is moving in a capitalist direction, the country still tries in some instances to state its own eductional goals.

One cannot talk about "falling standards" without taking into account that the standards themselves have changed. Throughout the *EPSSA* (e.g. pp. 39, 40, 47, 105, 121, 125) with the one above-quoted exception, the WBG is an uncritical advocate of using standardized tests developed in countries with a different culture, and different political and

---

[52] In many ways globalization has become the buzzword of the day. In their book *Global Village or Global Pillage* Jeremy Brecher and Tim Costello (1994: 4) claim that the word is "on the lips of politicians, professors and pundits alike." Corporations, markets, finance, banking, transportation, communication, and production more and more cut across national boundaries. This globalization of capital is being deliberately accelerated by most national governments, by international institutions like the International Monetary Fund (IMF) and the World Bank, and by global corporations themselves. Bradshaw and Wallace (1996) find that the most striking feature of globalization may be summed up in one word: *disparity*. An effect of the globalization of capital is increased differences between the haves and the have-nots. The share of the poorest 20% of the world's people in global income was 2.3% in 1960, and sank to 1.4% in 1991, and sank further to 1.1% in 1997, according to the latest *Human Development Report* from UNDP (United Nations Development Program). It continues to shrink. And the ratio of the income of the top 20% to that of the poorest 20% rose from 30 to 1 in 1960, to 61 to 1 in 1991, and to 78 to 1 in 1994 (UNDP, 1997: 9).

[53] For a general assessment of the neo liberal contribution to development theory and policy, see Colclough (1991).

educational ideals and concepts of quality, when assessing students of a given African country. The following uncritical passage is illustrative:

> There is a long history of educational testing in Africa, beginning in the colonial era with extensive use of examinations administered from Europe. After independence such multinational groupings as the East and West African Examinations Councils played critical roles in helping develop a cadre of experienced African testing professionals and psychometricians. (p. 121)

African educational researchers have shown that the history of formal examinations in Africa is as old as colonialism itself since formal education and examinations were part and parcel of the colonial rule. They have also indicated that the East and West African Examinations Councils were completely foreign-dominated. Mukyanuzi (1978) argues that the examination system contributed to underdevelopment of Tanzania, testing the mastery of verbal skills and the cultural knowledge of colonizers. "The consequence of this was to have no regard whatsoever for non-academic activities" (Mukyanuzi, 1978: 100). He further relates that in 1971 "Tanzania disengaged herself from the foreign-dominated Examination Council of East-Africa because it did not consider performance in manual work" (p. 101).

MAINTENANCE OF PHYSICAL PLANT

The suggestions put forward under this point, and they are made several places in the *EPSSA* (e.g. pp. 53, 65, 66, 138), are among the few suggestions in the document it is easy to agree with. The use of local materials in the construction of school buildings and classroom furniture is stressed several places. The use of local building materials is said to be both cheaper and to give better results such as more comfortable classrooms. It is mentioned that in Niger, for instance, the cost of a classroom constructed in concrete is five times that of one constructed from "banco" (the most commonly used material in rural areas). Yet the latter is cooler in summer and warmer in winter than the former (World Bank, 1988: 65). An interesting example of low cost school construction on a large scale is from Senegal, where a new construction technology that is labor intensive and maximizes the use of local materials has been put into use. More than 80% of total construction materials are locally available. The foreign exchange components of this technology represent approximately 28%, compared with about 53% for imported construction methods. Examples like these are useful and may be of help for other African countries striving to build good, but inexpensive schools.

The *EPSSA* also stresses the importance of pupils, parents, teachers and students being engaged in both the construction of schools and in maintenance of school buildings. I find it easy to accept this suggestion and would also argue that it fits in well with the ideology in Tanzania of combining manual and intellectual work with self-help schemes and community spirit. The Educational Research Network of Eastern and Southern Africa in their discussion of the EPSSA, however, makes an important comment: "The paper ignores the fact that self-help is a form of indirect taxation and that peasants in most rural areas are already overburdened by their support to other service sectors (e.g. by building health clinics, roads, cattle dips, etc.)" (ERNESA, 1987: 32).

Since peasant-parents are already stretched to the limit of their ability to contribute, pupils and teachers might be able to carry out the maintenance, repair, and construction of school buildings and furniture as part of the curriculum.[54] Nyerere says in his *Education for Self-Reliance*:

> Many activities now undertaken for pupils, especially in secondary schools, should be undertaken by pupils themselves . . . In many of our schools we employ cleaners and gardeners, not just to supervise and teach but to do all the work . . . Is it impossible for these tasks to be incorporated into the total teaching task of the school? . . . The children should certainly do their own cleaning (boys as well as girls should be involved in this) and should learn the value of working together! (Nyerere, 1968: 68–71)

Thoughts like these have been put into practice in secondary schools in some African countries. The WBG could have cited a good example of a school-maintenance project in Zambia that is supported by the Norwegian Development Agency (NORAD) but has an explicit educational policy of training the school community, in particular, the secondary school pupils, to maintain the physical plant and to take pride in nice surroundings. Funds for the project have come through a World Bank credit, from the Zambian government, and from NORAD (see ZAM 021, 1986).

---

[54]Another suggestion would be that national government funds (or international organization financing) be used to buy materials from local families and to pay them for some of their work in building and maintaining schools.

In particular, one of the schools in the project, the Bwacha secondary school, may serve as an example of what is possible with a self-help spirit in the school, good and enthusiastic support from local educational authorities, and an educational rather than only a narrow technical approach from the country mission of the donor agency. In the Bwacha secondary school the pupils work in groups, who are responsible for taking care of particular parts of the school (e.g., the furniture, the plants and physical surroundings). Pupils learn the necessary skills to repair and maintain the buildings (replacing broken windows, for instance) and the school furniture, and to do the gardening, all as part of the school curriculum. With their acquired skills and their pride in nice surroundings, many of these pupils also are initiators of repair and maintenance work in their family houses and those of others in the community.

But work like this, in line with basic self-help thinking in many African countries, will be downgraded and difficult to undertake if examinations measuring narrow cognitive abilities are the sole assessors of pupils' achievements and are allowed to be all-important in deciding the future educational and vocational careers of pupils.

QUALITY IN EDUCATION—ALTERNATIVE VIEWS

Elsewhere (Brock-Utne, 1993) I have referred to a seminar we arranged on the *EPSSA* at the University of Dar es Salaam on the 28 January 1988. The views expressed in that seminar suggested that to improve the quality of education, especially primary education, in African countries, the most important thing to do is to restore the dignity and quality of the teacher. The measures to do this will have to be exactly the opposite of what the WBG suggested in *EPSSA*. The needed measures include: reduction of the number of pupils in class, increased salaries (which are paid locally to the teachers on a fixed day of the month), a reduction of the numbers of hours a day a teacher has to teach, and improvement of teacher training, both initial training and in-service training. In-service training should include seminars with other teachers to work out plans for educational innovation in school and to construct locally based instructional materials.[55] The relevance of the curriculum in relation to the African situation was

---

[55]Another suggestion on which there was full agreement at the seminar was the desirability of introducing free or at least subsidized school meals for both teachers and pupils.

mentioned as another extremely important aspect of a quality education in African countries. To what degree does the curriculum restore the dignity of the African people and build on the best elements of their culture? To what degree does the curriculum taught and the education organized reduce Africa's dependence on foreign aid, foreign "experts", and expatriates? To what degree does it aim at self-reliance and decreased dependence on the outside?

This way of looking at quality in education in an African context contrasts rather sharply with the way education in Africa is thought about in the *EPSSA*. But it fits quite well with the way quality education is described by the important group of ministers, policy-makers, high officials in education and researchers interested in education of women in Africa called Forum for African Women Educationalists (FAWE). FAWE defines quality education this way:

> Quality education is defined as going beyond quantitative inputs such as the number of qualified teachers, adequate and appropriate physical structures and facilities, and equipment, to include teacher competence and commitment, curricula relevance and gender sensitivity (FAWE, 1995: 14).

PRIVATIZATION OF EDUCATION AND COST-SHARING

In the *EPSSA* the World Bank voices the opinion that a revitalization of education in Africa and a selective expansion (which to them primarily means increased enrollment of primary school pupils and a restoration of "quality in education") cannot take place without major structural adjustments in the way education has been financed in most African countries. These adjustments represent major breaks with the policies of most African countries. These countries have wanted to look at education as social service and a right for all people and have wanted to use education to eliminate regional and class differences instead of creating such differences.

In line with this thinking the WBG advocates the establishment of more private schools at the primary and secondary levels, a policy which Norway for instance has not wanted to adopt precisely because of the undemocratic consequences such a policy easily leads to. It creates a dual school-system in which the elites have their children in private schools where teachers have good salaries and enough instructional materials while the government-financed schools continue to be poorly financed and offer inferior education for the masses.

The policy called "cost-sharing," under which parents/families are assessed fees when their children are in school, also will have many of the same undesirable effects. The WBG partly acknowledges this fact but still advocates the introduction of the policy: "It is probably inevitable that parents' contribution to the costs of primary education, and particularly secondary education, will increase, despite very real concerns about the impact of this on overall equity and efficiency" (World Bank, 1988a: 95).

The WBG might have tried to answer the question: Why is it "probably inevitable?" Is there anything the industrialized countries of the North, with all their wealth and international agencies like the World Bank and the IMF, could do to prevent the pessimistic trend away from a policy of equity to one of survival of the fittest? My answer is yes. The countries of the North could cancel all debts and create more equal and fair terms of trade.[56]

The cost-sharing policy entails the use of fees, having parents pay for instructional materials and students pay their own living expenses, and a shift from boarding schools to day-schools. Such measures are likely to increase social inequities, regional inequalities, and inequalities between sexes.[57] The WBG seems to be aware of this fact and offers the following suggestion:

> Governments can reduce the private costs of girls' education relative to boys' by, for example, providing girls with free books and other instructional materials, charging them with lower tuition fees, or recovering less of the cost of boarding and welfare services from girls' families than from boys' (World Bank, 1988a: 85).

It *can* be done, but will it be done, especially when governments are being urged/forced to cut back on public expenditures as part of structural adjustment programs?

---

[56]As we saw in the previous chapter, these were the wishes voiced by the South (the less industrialized, mostly formerly colonized countries) at the 1990 EFA conference in Thailand.

[57]In the previous chapter we gave an example of the consequences of the reintroduction of school fees in the secondary schools in Tanzania. We saw how this measure in particular affected the schooling of girls from the lower classes.

When the WBG advocates a shift from boarding schools to day-schools, it argues that living expenses should be carried by parents. It is said that these expenses do not belong to the education sector since they are expenses which would have had to be met by the students or their parents had they not gone to school. Yes, but in that case the students would have been working instead! This argument is not taken into account.

Schooling will have to be paid for and is never "free." The question is: Who should pay for the education? If schooling is "free," all taxpayers pay for schooling. Those who earn most and often have the fewest school children pay the most.[58] Free schooling becomes an equity measure and a way of redistributing a society's resources from the richer to the poorer. The reintroduction of school fees and so-called cost-sharing measures mean that the poor parents, who often have many children, have to bear a disproportionate share of the burden of their education. Often they will not be able to do so and greater inequities will occur both because some children will not be able to attend school and the resources available in school will vary greatly depending on local community wealth levels.

When discussing with my colleagues in Tanzania, Zambia, and Malawi the suggestion put forward in the *EPSSA* of having students pay part of the expenses for university studies, I found that opinions vary. Some say that sometime in the future students should have to pay their living expenses while studying, for instance, by getting student loans which they have to pay back. The WBG in *EPSSA* advocates the use of loan schemes. Such schemes, however, have been tried in many places in Sub-Saharan Africa but there have been enormous problems, including the high cost of getting former students to repay the loans (Maliyamkono, 1987: 7). Keith Watson (1996) points to the fact that student loans have been notoriously difficult to recoup because of administrative inefficiency and mentions that while Sweden has a loss rate of 30%, Kenya has a staggering 103% loss rate (he has taken figures from the World Bank, 1995a: 108).

New ways of creating loan schemes may be tried at a later stage if economic conditions among people are better, and also when there are enough educated/skilled workers for jobs in the government and the new industrial sector, which is not the case in some African countries. As it is

---

[58] How much more the well-to-do tax payers pay depends of course on how progressive the tax system of a country is.

now, highly qualified people are so badly needed that the government has to pay for them.[59] I fully agree with Keith Watson's analysis of cost-sharing schemes advocated by the World Bank. He concludes: "By encouraging fee paying as a contribution at least for secondary and tertiary levels the Bank is actually favoring the better off" (Watson, 1996: 55).

Even though opinions were divided when I discussed cost-sharing measures with colleagues at the Universities of Zambia, Malawi, and Dar es Salaam and discussions were heated both among students and university teachers and administrators, they all seem to agree on one point: their right to decide their educational policies themselves through their own internal debates. For instance they felt that it was very humiliating when the University of Malawi was forced by the World Bank in 1987 to reduce the book allowance given students—as a condition for receiving World Bank loans to the primary school sector.[60]

PROPOSED REDUCTION OF HIGHER EDUCATION IN SUB-SAHARAN AFRICA[61]

Even though African policy-makers at earlier meetings about World Bank policies for the education sector have strongly opposed the suggestion of a stagnation in enrollments in higher education, this suggestion is advanced over and over by the World Bank. In the EPSSA we find:

> To meet minimally acceptable targets for coverage and quality of lower levels of education in most countries, as a general rule the tertiary sub sector's share of stagnant real public education expenditures cannot expand further, and in some cases may have to contract. Some combination of efficiency improvements, increased private

---

[59] Others argue that those students whose parents are better off should have to pay their own cost of travel, books, and maybe even living expenses while studying. This presupposes a system where the earning power of the parents was assessed and one could argue that such a system could rather be used to tax such people more heavily than is now the case.

[60] Personal communication from the then vice chancellor of the University in Zomba in a discussion with me on the *EPSSA* in the fall of 1987.

[61] As mentioned in the previous chapter, African ministers of education at the Jomtien conference in 1990 as well as in the mid-term conferences in Yaounde and Johannesburg in 1995 voiced their concern that the Education for All drive might lead to a further starvation of the higher education sector in Africa. We shall return to this point in Part III.

contribution to costs, and constrained growth of—in some countries and fields, outright cutback in—production of graduates must be sought (World Bank 1988a: 95).

The fields singled out for cut-backs are the arts and humanities. But, as pointed out earlier in this chapter, in order for African scholars to teach and write teaching materials in tune with the realities and needs of African societies, it is important to expand and give priority to a vivid research environment for African arts and humanities.

THE POWER TO DEFINE CONCEPTS AND DICTATE POLICY

The Educational Research Network of Southern and Eastern Africa (ERNESA) in their criticism of an early draft of *EPSSA* pointed out that the very use of the word *policy* in the title of the document is rather "presumptuous because policies are made by national governments. The paper is rather a reflection of the principles which govern Bank lending to education" (ERNESA, 1987: 32). But, unfortunately, ERNESA is only describing the desired and not the actual state of affairs for the poorer countries of Africa today. As will be clear from the following chapters, the policies of the poorer countries in Africa are more often determined by terms set by the World Bank, the IMF, and bilateral donor agencies.[62] Those who lend or give the money also have the power to define concepts and to enforce their educational policies by rewarding those countries showing willingness to follow the "recommendations" and punishing—or at least not funding—the others.

The WBG demands substantial and rapid adjustment in the educational sector of the countries of Sub-Saharan Africa in order to give money to the revitalization and expansion program. The promises here are rather vague, however, and are made on the condition that the African governments follow up the recommendations made under adjustment policies. This is said explicitly several times in the EPSSA. For instance:

> In the context of ongoing austerity in Africa, resolute movement toward adjustment is a necessary condition for implementing forward looking policies on the other two dimensions (p. xi).

---

[62] Sometimes the terms set in loan or SAP programs actually undermine or contradict the "policies" set out in Word Bank documents on what should be done in the education sector.

Countries which have demonstrated their willingness to address policy issues should have access to increased, longer term and more flexibly offered international aid (p. xii and p. 153).

African countries unwilling to embark upon sectoral development programs are unlikely to be attractive candidates for conventional project assistance (p. 150).[63]

In the 1988 *EPSSA* document countries are urged to make the structural adjustments *rapidly*. This is stressed over and over again with expressions like "there is need for expeditious action" and "Any initiatives that would take more than a year to be adopted and implemented cannot be judged an adequate response to the needs of African governments" (p. 15). The fact that democratic processes normally take a long time is disregarded. It is a democratic principle that people who will be affected by initiatives adopted and implemented—in this case, pupils, parents, teachers, students and professors, should have a say about these initiatives, and preferably participate in deciding on them. This is a principle we try to practice, or at least subscribe to, in Western democracies. The WBG does not seem to think they apply to the countries in Sub-Saharan Africa, the same countries they want to teach democracy and "good governance." The aid policies of most OECD countries now include human rights and good governance as additional conditionalities over and above the economic ones (Tandon, 1996; Tomasevski, 1997).[64]

---

[63] In a 1993 article Adriaan Verspoor of the Education and Employment Division of the World Bank suggests that considerable pressure be put on countries in the developing world to follow what the World Bank sees as "sound policies." He claims that agencies giving or lending aid to the education sector must: "have the courage to target education aid to help those governments that adopt sound policies rather than to disburse aid to countries that are their foreign policy priorities" (Verspoor, 1993: 112).

[64] Yash Tandon (1996) mentions the conditionalities of good governance laid down in the Swedish aid policies passed as a white paper by the Government in early 1996. And Katarina Tomasevski (1997) has studied Report No. 19 to the Norwegian Storting (1995–96) from the Royal Norwegian Ministry of Foreign Affairs. The report is called: *A Changing World. Main Elements of Norwegian Policy Towards Developing Countries*. On page 17 she finds Norway's internal framework conditions: "Stable political conditions, efficient administration, sufficient legislation and regulations, general access to education, access to suitable technology and improved opportunities for export" (Tomasevski, 1997: 12). She asks the inevitable question which follows from the list of conditions mentioned: Why would a country where all those conditions are fullfilled need aid?

Consider the following advice offered in *EPSSA*:

> Political considerations will inevitably limit the feasibility of some desirable elements and sequences of measures, many of which will in the short term be perceived as threats to deeply ingrained interests of powerful groups in society (civil servants, professors and students) Determined and very high level leadership will be needed to overcome resistance. (World Bank, 1988a: 113)

Desirable for whom? And who is going to provide that leadership? In a democratic state, high level leadership must be elected and come from the government. The more autonomous the government, the more capable it will be to render "high level leadership." But such autonomous countries may not be demonstrating "their willingness to address policy issues" the way the World Bank wants them to. After all, policies are supposed to be made by governments in a democratic country, governments that are accountable to their people, representatives of their constituencies and influenced by a civil society, including NGOs such as teacher and student unions and other stakeholders. Even "high level leadership" in democratic countries will have to carry out policies determined in the context of all of these democratic influences. And wasn't it democracy that the Western donors wanted to teach Africa and not to promote a "high level leadership" that functions as a dictator or puppet in the hands of the World Bank?

PRIORITIES AND STRATEGIES FOR EDUCATION: A WORLD BANK REVIEW

The 1995 World Bank document called *Priorities and Strategies for Education: A World Bank Review*—(World Bank 1995a, hereafter the *Review*) appeared seven years after the *EPSSA* and five years after the EFA conference. We shall now compare certain aspects of the *Review* with *EPSSA*. What type of change has there been in the thinking of the World Bank during those seven years?

The criticism that *EPSSA* was selective in referencing also holds true for the *Review*. As argued by Keith Watson (1996) in his analysis of that document:

> The present Review does not even recognise that there is a genre of social and philosophical research literature in the field of education and

development which shows that the justification for education is often far more subtle and complex than merely using labour market and economic arguments (Watson, 1996: 48).

Watson also mentions that of the several hundred research papers cited in the *Review* only a handful are from the very rich research base of United Kingdom and Australia.

> Contrary views are therefore not considered or recognised. Indeed so influential is the Bank over other donor agencies that when the British Overseas Development Agency (ODA) produced its "Aid to Education" in the 1990s (ODA, 1995) almost all the references were from the World Bank. The excuse was that this was what would impress ministers! Ironically the protests over this issue from British academics led ODA to publish a series of research documents that it commissioned from British scholars (Watson, 1996: 49).

In an article critiquing the *Review*, Noel McGinn (1997) claims that this report is distinct from earlier documents in its more explicit attention to policies to achieve proposed reforms. On this point I do not agree. If one compares the *Review* with the *EPSSA* from seven years earlier, one sees that also in the *EPSSA* very explicit attention to policies was paid.

But the *Review* goes one step further than *EPSSA* in naming the social actors the authors consider as obstacles to positive change. Strategies are proposed to weaken those actors and strengthen others that, the authors[65] believe, are more likely to provide the kind of education that is sought. The actors the *Review* wants to weaken are national governments, teachers' unions, the elite[66] and university students (World Bank, 1995: 135). Central governments, for example, are said to protect their interests "at the expense of parents, communities and the poor" (p. 137). The *Review* offers several strategies intended to strengthen the relative

---

[65] The *Review* was prepared by a World Bank team led by Nicholas Burnett and consisting of Tom Eisemon, Kari Marble, and Harry Anthony Patrinos, under the general direction of K. Y. Amoako and the immediate supervision of Peter R. Moock in the Education and Social Policy Department.

[66] The elites the World Bank wants to weaken must be the third world elites who disagree with the Bank. There are certainly also third world elites who profit from and advocate the policies of the Bank to the detriment of their own people. There were also Africans in the time of slavery that made profits out of capturing and selling slaves.

power of parents and communities vis-á-vis the central government and other stakeholders. These strategies include autonomy of educational institutions from the central government, and active participation of households. But even in affluent and literate societies in the North, where parents speak the same language at home as the language of instruction in school, the parents from the poorer households, the parents whose children do not do well in school, normally stay away from school meetings and do not get involved in running the school. The strategies proposed in the *Review* seem to have as their aim to weaken the state and ease the work of World Bank consultants in offering "high level leadership," to borrow a term from the 1988 *EPSSA*.

The *Review* is full of the same weaknesses as the *EPSSA*: selective reporting, gross generalizations, lack of attention to the massive critiques of earlier World Bank reports within education. The suggestion made in the *EPSSA* of shifting resources from teacher salaries toward textbooks and in-service training is repeated in the *Review*. As Samoff (1996) argues, such a general recommendation makes no sense and there is no research supporting it. Likewise the attack on higher education continues.

The advocacy for basic education normally means primary education, or rather primary schooling of a Western type that was so prominent in *EPSSA* continues in the *Review*. The World Bank is now as sure that basic education is the solution for the educational problems of the developing world as it once was that vocational and technical education would be the solution. In the Review it is argued that such education should now be left to private providers and employers. Keith Watson laments: "There is no acknowledgement that in the past the Bank had got this particular policy wrong. If some of the new ideas are proved wrong in the future, will there be any ackowledgement either?" (Watson, 1996: 47). No, probably not.

But it is up to us who are participating in this up-hill struggle against the Bank to point to the weaknesses in the policies they propose and bilateral and multilateral donors follow.

CHAPTER 3

The Formulation of Educational Policies and the Coordination of Aid—Some Examples

> *The most conspicuous absence in all the scattered literature on aid to education is any coherent account from the recipient perspective of how educational aid is perceived, negotiated, managed and reviewed.*
>
> (KING, 1986: 113)

THE RECIPIENT PERSPECTIVE

In the above quote Kenneth King speaks of *the* recipient perspective. Through my four and a half years of discussions with colleagues at the University of Dar es Salaam and on the basis of all the interviews I made the last half year I lived in Tanzania,[67] I think it is correct to say that there

---

[67] I thought that with my good personal knowledge of many of the leading people in the education sector in Tanzania and my command of Kiswahili (I conducted the interviews in CCM and in the Institute of Curriculum Development in Kiswahili) I would be able to get a better account of recipients' views than most consultants. Also I was not a consultant, and I had not been asked by anyone to conduct the interviews. I am not giving a coherent account from the recipient side of aid to the education sector in Tanzania, but I am letting some recipients of aid speak through their own voices. It is an attempt on my part to fill in part of the gap in our knowledge of how educational aid is perceived, negotiated and managed. The Tanzanians I formally interviewed to get hold of recipient views were government officials in the Ministry of Education, in the Institute of Curriculum Development, as well as in the President's Office. I have also had long conversations with some regional education officers as well as leading people at the CCM Headquarters in Dar es Salaam. The interviews were conducted in the spring of 1992. The methodology used has been a snowball technique since what one respondent said led me to want to interview another government official. It became important to me during my data gathering also to interview officials dealing with educational matters within the only legal party at the time, Chama cha Mapinduzi (CCM), which means "the Party of the Revolution."

I saw this as important partly because of the negative attitude toward the party I found held by some government officials and because the party officials had closer contact with the grass-roots. They could also be expected to take care of the original policy wishes of the Tanzanian government. The formal interviews written down by me were sixteen, but the less formal conversations to get hold of the recipient views were many, many more.

is not *one* recipient view on aid, but several. There was disagreement in the Ministry of Education as well as among university faculty when it came to politically hot questions, such as:

—Should Tanzania resume its original policy of making Kiswahili the language of instruction also in secondary schools and the university or continue to use English?

—Should the quota system to help girls and youngsters from disadvantaged areas be maintained?

—How much of the cost for schooling should be borne by the parents and how much by the state?

—What about privatization of the secondary school and the textbook sector?

There were some people at the university and also in the Planning Commission of the President's Office whose views were not very different from those of the World Bank and thus in stark contrast to the original equity concerns of Tanzania. As one of my interviewees in the CCM Office in Dar es Salaam expressed it: *"Ni watu wetu, lakini mawazo ya Benki ya Dunia"* (It is our people, but the thoughts belong to the World Bank). Whether the people the CCM officers were referring to felt compelled to voice World Bank views because they were economically dependent on consultancies or really *had* those views and were helped to voice them through the assistance of external donors, I cannot tell. There were other people at the university, in the Ministry of Education, the Institute of Curriculum Studies, and the CCM headquarters who were much more concerned with equity questions and the original promises of Nyerere's Tanzania to the people. This unorganized opposition to what is happening is the one which seems to be on the losing side through the policies now followed by the donors.

WHO FORMULATES EDUCATIONAL POLICIES IN AFRICA?

As already mentioned in the two previous chapters, the World Bank is the most powerful institution deciding on and formulating educational policies for Sub-Saharan Africa (SSA). But there are also bilateral donor agencies involved in this work. How different are they from the World Bank? And what is the role of the SSA governments in the policy formulation and in the coordination of aid to the education sector?

Much of the material in this chapter will be taken from the formulation of policies in Tanzania both because an interesting study (Buchert, 1997a) throws some light on how educational policies have been formed in that country during recent years and because of the interviews I conducted with some educational policy makers in Tanzania. Likewise, when it comes to the co-ordination of aid, I am building on an inside account from Ulla Kann, who has gained experience regarding aid coordination over more than twenty-five years, mainly in Botswana and Namibia. Though the Swedish born Ulla Kann is herself an expatriate, she has never worked for a donor agency or a bank but for the African governments. These more personal accounts are meant to give some flesh and blood to the more general analysis of aid coordination and educational policy formulations which will also be undertaken.

It should be mentioned here that an analysis by Tuomas Takala (1998) of the current national education sector policy documents from four African countries (Ethiopia, 1994; Mozambique, 1995; Zambia, 1996; and Namibia, 1993) found a considerable degree of agreement between the national documents and the donor agenda as presented in World Bank publications and in the documents of the Jomtien EFA conference. This was especially the case for the three first mentioned countries, all under structural adjustment programs. As argued by Takala (1998: 331): "It is also obvious that in the non-SAP [structural adjustment policy] case (Namibia) the current national education policies correspond to the donor agenda to a lesser degree than in the three countries following SAPs."

In an analysis of the formulation of educational policies in Tanzania in the most recent years, Lene Buchert (1997a) finds that the formulation of the social sector strategy has been heavily influenced by the World Bank and builds on the Tanzania Social Sector Review by the Bank (World Bank, 1995b). The *Primary Education. Master Plan* (Government of Tanzania, 1996) has likewise been heavily influenced by DANIDA, while the *Education and Training Policy* (United Republic of Tanzania, 1995) "has a clear government imprint" (Buchert, 1997a: 2). Even when it comes to the "Education and Training Policy" paper, however, Buchert (1997:52) reports that many of the government officials as well as bilateral aid agencies and people from the academic environment saw "a determined World Bank hand behind it." It is about this policy paper that the interviewee quoted in the previous chapter said: "It has been stuffed down the throat of the Government by the IMF and the World Bank" (Buchert, 1997a: 52). Buchert mentions that during 1994 and 1995 the World Bank held a number of education seminars in Africa and in Washington D.C. for key Tanzanian educators which had a direct and indirect impact on government thinking on education.

This reminds me of a day in my years at the University of Dar es Salaam when a colleague came into my office with a fax in his hand. He had been invited as a resource person to a seminar in Washington D.C. by the World Bank. They even wrote what his daily honorarium would be and what his per diems would be. He would be traveling club class, staying over-night in London with hotel paid for and he would get per diems even when he was on the plane. He showed me this and said:

> How can I possibly refuse such an offer? Just the per diems for these
> five days are more than I earn in half a year as a professor at the Uni-
> versity of Dar es Salaam. And how can I behave in such a way that I am
> invited back and still come with some of my criticism?

This is a real dilemma to many Africans, including academics and those in policy-making positions. Government salaries are meager. It is easy to be bought.[68] And when one hears the same ideas and solutions over and over again, it is easy to be socialized to the jargon and the solutions identified.

Work on the *Education and Training Policy* started in February 1993. According to Lene Buchert (1997b) it was initiated due both to an internally felt need for an official policy that reflected the state of the art of education in the 1990s and to agency pressure for a policy framework to guide education assistance.

The point of departure for the policy paper was the task force report *The Tanzania Education System for the 21st Century*—completed in 1992 and published in 1993 (URT, 1993). This report had been sponsored by DANIDA (Danish International Development Agency) but was never acknowledged by the government as official Tanzanian government policy. The document was produced by a predominantly academic task force and headed by the then dean of the Faculty of Education, Professor Herme Mosha. The Report analyzes educational needs in light of a future Tanzanian society able to cope in an increasingly globalized world. The emphasis is not only on political liberalization and sustain-

---

[68] It is not easy for an African intellectual who is unable to live on his regular university wage to write from an African perspective if this perspective is not what the donors want. He will often perform a type of self-censorship to write what he guesses the donors want to hear. I know there are donors who sense this kind of role-playing and dislike it.

able social and economic development but on the need for a long-term energy policy (solar energy, bio-gas), a long-term industrial strategy, and expansion of trade, transport, and telecommunication. There is strong focus in this document on the need to support research and development and the higher education subsector as well as to conduct fundamental curricular changes in schools in support of the envisaged society of the twenty-first century.

These foci have disappeared in the now authorized *Education and Training Policy* (URT, 1995). The policy formulation process for this document was lengthy, originating, as Buchert (1997a: 36) argues, "from the fact that the 1993 Report was never acknowledged as official policy." The *Education and Training Policy* was formulated by Tanzanian officials in an inter-ministerial committee headed by a professor at the University of Dar es Salaam. A first draft was discussed at an internal seminar with the directors of education and representatives of different ministries and agency officials. A summary paper was discussed at the University of Dar es Salaam. A reworked draft was shared widely at meetings with headmasters, principals, and regional and district education officers. But, according to Buchert, representatives of teachers, students, pupils, parents, community, non-governmental organizations, and other civil society organizations were not invited and there was no widespread debate on the document in the media or in Parliament. It would have been interesting to know whether there was any debate on this important education policy document in Parliament at all and where the politicians—as opposed to the civil servants representing the ministries—came into the formulation process. Civil servants are not the same as politicians.

"EVEN THE LIKE-MINDED DONORS"

The original intention of my interviews in the spring of 1992 was to find out something about the recipient views of aid in the education sector. It was not to look at aid given by the "like-minded" countries Norway and Sweden. The results of my interviews were rather surprising to myself.

When, in the summer of 1994, I complained to a Swedish expert in Namibia that the Nordic countries had been shifting their aid policies and were more concerned now about strengthening their own industries and jumping on the band wagon of the World Bank, she replied that they were still much better than some other bilateral donor agencies like US-AID and Canadian CIDA (Canadian International Development Agency).

When I held that too high of a percentage (50%) of the aid money to a particular project in Namibia went back to Norwegian expatriates or companies, she said that I should rather take a look at where the money given by
US-AID and CIDA went. These two aid agencies had both adopted the
general rule that at least two thirds of what they "gave" in aid should benefit their own countries.

I am not going to make an analysis of US-AID or CIDA but will give
a couple of examples that show a shift even among the so-called "like-
minded donors," like Norway and Sweden, in part of their aid policy to
the education sector in a poor country like Tanzania.

As part of my teaching of social psychology I had asked my students
to describe different nations through an adjective check list. In that small
survey of stereotypes conducted among my students, the people from the
Nordic countries were portrayed as generous, informal, easy-going,
witty, social-democratic, and non-racist, while, the British for instance
were seen as conservative, formal, and racist. When we discussed how
they had acquired these stereotypes, the students focused on the British
as colonial masters and the Nordic countries as the great donors to Tanzania. Even though their answers might have been somewhat biased
since I was the one who conducted the survey, I think they portrayed
some of the feeling of gratitude for Nordic aid which had up till then
been felt in Tanzania. As an example of the closeness and appreciation of
the Nordic countries felt by the Tanzanian government I may mention
that when Nelson Mandela made his first official visit to Tanzania after
his release from jail in 1990, the only ambassadors invited to the State
House to meet him personally were African and Nordic (Garbo, 1993).

Two recent interventions by Nordic donors will be used as illuminat-
ing examples of processes going on within the aid-supported education
sector in Tanzania, namely *The National Education Trust Fund* and *The
Future School Book Provision* for Tanzania. The need to go deeper into
these two interventions rose during data gathering. My original questioning was very open, intended only to learn how officials responsible for
the education policy of Tanzania experienced the aid they were given.

CHANGE IN THE DONOR POLICIES OF THE
NORDIC COUNTRIES

When I began interviewing of high officials within the education sector
in Tanzania, I had expected to find some negative attitudes toward the
former colonial masters and the World Bank. This I found. I had also expected that some bilateral donors, especially the Nordic countries, would

be regarded with much higher esteem. This expectation was *not* full-filled. Over and over again officials told me that at earlier times the Nordic countries would come to their rescue when the World Bank and the IMF wanted them to accept tough conditionalities like reintroducing school fees or privatizing the secondary school sector. But since about 1984–1985 this had changed.

I later learned that in 1983 a conference had been held with participation from all the Nordic governments and the government of Tanzania about the relationship between Tanzania and the Nordic countries. The results from this conference were mentioned in a Government White Paper to the Norwegian government (St. meld. nr. 74, 1984–1985): *Om Norges samarbeid med utviklingslandene i 1984* [On Norway's cooperation with the developing countries in 1984]). In this paper we read:

> The Nordic countries insisted that an agreement with the IMF (International Monetary Fund) had to be reached if Tanzania should get any external resources whatsoever in order to be able to turn the negative trend of their economic development and that *any extra support from the Nordic countries without such an agreement would not be given.* (St. meld. nr. 74., 1984–85: 27) (emphasis added, my translation)

It is an astonishing fact that there was no debate about this paragraph of the White Paper when it was presented to the Norwegian Parliament. All the donors, including the Nordic countries, seemed to agree to have their policies coordinated and decided by the thinking of the World Bank.

"WATU WA SIDA NI WATU WA SHIDA"

The Swedish International Development Agency (SIDA) was, according to several interviewees, on the whole much worse than the World Bank. Said one interviewee:

> The World Bank people come with their consultants, write their reports, are behind the scene. They don't bother us that much. But the Swedes say that if we don't do what they say, if we don't privatize the schoolbook sector, for instance, we get no money: Here we have started saying: "*Watu wa SIDA, ni watu wa shida*" The people from SIDA make trouble for us (people that mean trouble).

We shall now take a look at what is happening in the school book sector in Tanzania and the role, according to my informants, of the

Swedish development agency. The events are in line with World Bank policies and the structural adjustment program but reduce the chances of self-reliance and self-fulfillment for the people in the South. They also go counter to the emphasis on traditional knowledge and indigenous cultural heritage which IDRC was instrumental in introducing into the final text of the *WDEFA*.

THE PRIVATIZATION OF THE SCHOOL BOOK SECTOR

The market economic principles adhered to by the World Bank call for privatization and commercialization of all sectors. Cost-effectiveness and competitive bidding as guiding principles may easily undermine poorly financed national industries highly in need of protection. Imported technologies which often come with aid packages may easily increase dependency on donors.

In their 1990 guidelines for an African alternative to the "Education for All" strategy of Jomtien, the African Association for Literacy and Adult Education (AALAE) warns against "the use of imported technologies which in the majority of cases are inappropriate and reinforce foreign domination" (AALAE, 1990, paragraph 31) and "aid packages which include foreign personnel" (paragraph 33). AALAE recommends: "Loans, grants and donations should be accepted only when it is clear that they have no disadvantageous strings attached and that they will be for the benefit to the receiving organization and country" (paragraph 42). We may keep AALAE's warnings and recommendations in mind when we now turn to what is happening in the textbook sector in Tanzania.

The writing, publishing, and distribution of textbooks is of vital importance for the educational and cultural survival of a nation. About 50% of the total turnover of the publishing industry in developed countries is derived from educational publishing. In poor countries the percentage of educational publishing is upwards of 90% of publisher's turnover (World Bank/ODA, 1988). It is from the profits made in educational publishing that investments can be made to publish other categories of books—fiction, biographies, poetry, plays, and so on. Therefore, when textbook publishing suffers, all publishing suffers.[69]

---

[69] During the paper crisis in Tanzania in the early 1980s, for example, printers in Tanzania were forbidden to print magazines and other light reading matter so as to conserve all paper for textbook printing (Bgoya, 1990: 6).

Books originating in the developing countries, especially in Africa, are highly underrepresented in the world today. According to UNESCO's 1996 *Statistical Yearbook* (UNESCO, 1997) Norway (with 4 million inhabitants) in 1992 published 4,881[70] new titles, which was greater than the number of book titles published in Nigeria with 120 million inhabitants (1,562), Zimbabwe (232), Madagascar (85), Benin (647), Ghana (289), Mauritius (80), Uganda (162), Zaire (64) and Malawi (189) combined.

There was no model of publishing left in Tanzania at the time of independence that could be perpetuated or improved upon. The one that a number of African countries adopted—the early joint ventures with Macmillan, in Tanzania, Ghana, and Zambia—was a "state" model, which ironically was proposed by a private transnational company. As long as the partnership venture benefited the foreign transnational publisher, there was no criticism of the state publishing model where books were written by a state institution (Institute of Curriculum Development), published by a state publishing house (Tanzania Publishing House), and distributed by a state owned company (Tanzania Elimu Supplies). Walter Bgoya (1990), the former director of Tanzania Publishing House, tells that this model has fallen out of favor, not because it could not have been made to work. In fact, it worked well for a number of years, and Bgoya holds that when it is questioned today, it is because it does not favor the multinationals.

But at the time it worked, the same donors that are now pushing the "privatization" experiment in publishing were, through their policy, discouraging the building up of a private local publishing industry in Tanzania. Swedish SIDA support to the formal education sector as well as to the literacy campaign that was launched in 1970 was given in the form of paper and other inputs to the printing industry, relieving the foreign exchange shortage that printers faced. Walter Bgoya claims:

> One of the unfortunate outcomes of that support, however, was that in time the Ministry of Education and other institutions involved in formal and informal education developed such dependence on SIDA that other efforts to find a solution seemed unnecessary and even undesirable. As it was, support was given to the Government through the

---

[70] In Norway this number increased to 6,846 in 1994, but since statistics for most of the African countries are given only for the year 1992, that year is the one used for all of the countries mentioned here.

Ministry of Education. In turn, the Ministry gave the paper and other inputs to the parastatal printing firms; and publishers, parastatal and private alike, were by-passed because, it was argued, they were unnecessary middle men (Bgoya, 1990: 9).

In the spring of 1992 the Ministry of Education had recently received a SIDA mission on school books that had been great advocates of privatization and liberalization. A high official[71] in the ministry told me:

> SIDA gave us a deadline: "This must be done before we meet in March. Liberalization is a precondition for any future discussion," they told us. They told us that we must liberalize the production as well as the distribution of school and college books. "If you don't, you won't get any money. You don't get any support before you liberalize, that means privatize, the book production," they told us. We have produced the policy document you see on the table. We have been more or less forced to. They want us to do this also on the adult sector. But when it comes to that sector, the Government goes against it and therefore we shall get no Swedish support to that sector.

I was shown the five year plan for Swedish support to basic education in Tanzania (1991/92-1995/96), prepared by Graphia Consult AB (1991) which works in close connection with the well-known Swedish publishing company and producer of teaching aids, "Esselte." They suggested in the publication that a "care-taker" firm be made responsible for the liberalization of the book sector. In this publication a new textbook policy is established:

---

[71] High officials from the Ministry of Education in Tanzania with whom I discussed the writing of this chapter after my return from Tanzania have advised me to drop the names of the people I have interviewed since there might be repercussions taken against them . I have appreciated their frankness and shall obey the wish not to attach names to the direct quotes I give and try to conceal somewhat the identity of the Tanzanians interviewed. In a consultancy report prepared for NORAD, Dar es Salaam, we may find some of the reason why the government officials I interviewed preferred anonymity. It is said here about the appointment of the first board of the Education Trust Fund: "The government also has already pointed out/appointed the first Board of the FUND, *whose composition had to be ironed out with the World Bank"*(Galabawa and Alphonse, 1993: 2)(emphasis added).

The new school-book policy establishes that the school-books shall in the future not be written by ICD and not be printed by the PMO (Prime Minister's Office) . . . The new school-book provision system in Tanzania will be a market oriented system. It follows from this system that there will be several titles per subject and competition between publishers will increase which will result in better and cheaper school books. In this context it is proposed that the school-book approval procedure should be abandoned or at least reformed (p. ii).

The text-book approval procedure has been an important instrument in the indigenization of the curriculum in Tanzania. In Norway there is a rigorous procedure for approving school texts, by which not only is the language used in the books scrutinized, but the gender role models portrayed are also examined.[72] In a poor country like Tanzania where there are few books for use in schools, it would seem to be even more important that those few books meet the approval of indigenous curriculum experts.

The "competition between publishers," referred to in the quote above, is unlikely to mean between Tanzanian publishers but rather among the big multinational publishing companies. They are the ones that will participate in the competitive bidding and will profit from a world with "free market" prices. When the IMF and the World Bank impose free market prices as the core of their adjustment programmes, it must be realized that these are essentially global prices determined by the multinational corporations for the achievement of values and capital accumulation. In the world capitalist economy, as Bade Onimode (1992: 126) points out, African countries are simply *price-takers*—as determined by the dominant capital of the industrialized countries. So the growth which these so-called competitive prices produce must necessarily preserve unequal growth, polarized development, and the continued marginalization of Africa.

In the spring of 1992 when I visited the Institute for Curriculum Development (ICD), I was quite surprised to learn that the officials there had never seen the consultancy report: *Proposed Future School-Book Provision System in Tanzania* (Graphium Consult AB, 1991) which suggested new guidelines for Swedish aid to the textbook sector. They were

---

[72] The books are not approved for use in schools if they can be said to be discriminatory against women, for instance, by showing them only in traditional female roles. Gender sterotyping in text-books is also prevalent in Africa, for example in Tanzania (Kalugula, 1991) and in Swaziland, (Okkelmo, 1999)

upset. One of the officials made a copy of page 53 about the role of ICD and said:

> Who are they to say that we should reduce the staff or stop publishing? We want the philosophy of Tanzania reflected in our curricula. When you liberalize the school book sector, you are not helping the Tanzanian publishing industry. Right now Longman and Macmillian are so eager to get into Tanzania, saying: "We are the best publishers. We publish cheaply in India and China." But they are coming only because of the money which has come with the eighth IDA[73] project. Where will they be when that money is gone? Tanzania needs to build up its own publishing industry.
>
> What they are doing is like saying: "From now on there shall be no more agriculture in Tanzania. You shall live from finished products brought in from abroad." This is what they want to do to our book industry. Saying: *Leo utapata ugali, hakuna maragwe, kesho utapata uji tu* (today you'll get maize porridge with no beans, to-morrow you shall only get a thin soup).

The people at ICD told me about the importance of Tanzania deciding on her own curricula and the textbooks to go with them. They told me about the first O-level examinations given in Tanzania in 1971. They had helped with the examinations and saw that they were based on a Cambridge curriculum. One ICD official said:

> We could not use the curriculum from the UK. That curriculum did not promote the socialist values we want to promote. The books came from Britain. Nyerere talked about us becoming self-reliant, using our own curricula, our own books. We got the ICD Act.13. 1975 where it said in point 4 what the functions of the Institute should be. Point 4a says that the Institute shall assume the responsibility for the development of educational programs within the United Republic having regard to objectives specified by the government and to undertake the evaluation of courses of study and practices on the basis of such objectives.

In the 1991 consultancy report, *Proposed Future School-Book Provision System in Tanzania*, it was proposed to privatize the whole book sec-

---

[73] IDA (International Development Assistance) is a part of the World Bank that gives loans with very low interest to developing countries.

tor, the writing, publishing and distribution. It was proposed that the new system should be introduced as soon as possible. But the report also states:

> As several key functions, especially competent publishers and a retailer network, do not exist at present, the transition period will however take many years.
>
> In order to make the transition period as brief as possible, it is proposed that the whole present book volume is used to build up a retailer network instead of waiting several years while publishers develop new titles and bring them to the market. It is therefore proposed that all existing titles should be handled by a "caretaker company" during a limited transition period (Graphium Consult AB, 1991:iii).

The caretaker company was meant to be privatized; the government, according to the consultancy report, should only be allowed to keep a minority shareholding of no more than 20%. (Graphium Consult AB, 1991: 58) It was further going to be a restructured and refinanced merger of TPH[74] and EAP.[75] The reason given for this was that these two publishing companies had the publishing rights for most of the existing titles. Both of these publishing houses are Tanzanian and have experienced staff. It was therefore surprising to read the following paragraph in the consultancy report:

> Management of the "new" TPH/EAPL should during the transition period be operated by a foreign "caretaking" company with publishing background, which should also be shareowner during the caretaking period, possibly together with Swedecorp (if the Caretaking company is Swedish) (p. 58).

The following expatriate specialists were foreseen:

Manager and chief editor

Administrative and finance manager

Publishing specialist

---

[74] TPH (Tanzania Publishing House) is the state publishing house in Tanzania which before the 1980s was publishing textbooks as well as a number of critical books. Walter Bgoya was its first director.
[75] EAP (East Africa Publishing) is also a state-owned Tanzanian publishing company.

Distribution specialist

Marketing specialist

Design specialist (p. 82)

It is difficult to see this suggestion as anything other than an insult to Tanzanian publishers and an attempt at an intellectual recolonization of Africa. There is no lack of expertise in the Tanzanian publishing sector. There is only a lack of funds. One expatriate costs at least U.S.$200,000 per year. The six ex-patriates above will cost no less than U.S.$1,200 000 per year. One could print a large number of textbooks for that sum.

The suggestion of this care-taker company was met with great resistance from the Tanzanian authorities both in government and in the publishing sector and was in the end not accepted by SIDA either.

My point is not that it is necessarily wrong to reorganize the textbook sector in Tanzania, to establish an amalgamated publishing company, to limit the monopoly on textbook writing now given to the Institute for Curriculum Development. This *may* be a better way to organize the book sector but my point is that such decisions and even suggestions should be left to the Tanzanians themselves.

Even though the Swedes gave up on the care-taker company, they still insisted that the textbook sector be liberalized and opened up for foreign companies. In 1992 a new textbook policy was introduced in Tanzania under strong pressure from the World Bank and SIDA to loosen up the state monpoly in textbook commissioning, printing, and distribution, by giving more opportunities to the private sector. As a result there have been a number of problems which Brian Cooksey (1996) attributes to the haste with which the reforms were made and the institutional resistance against them.

In 1993, after the new textbook policy was introduced, a promemoria was written in SIDA. In this promemoria the role of the Institute of Curriculum Development seems to be non-existent. In the same promemoria the Swedes also admit: "The proposed new policy represents a 180 degree turn in emphasis away from a government led system towards a market oriented approach" (Wickmann, 1993: 3).[76] In the above-mentioned promemoria from the Education Office of SIDA the following questions are raised:

---

[76] It would be interesting to know how many degrees of the turn have been made under the pressure of not getting support if the turn is not being made.

Is it desirable that school book publishers are indigenous local firms? What bearing could that possibly have on developing local authors of fiction? What bearing on the production of post literacy reading material? Or could all these aspects as well be taken care of by foreign publishing houses? (Wickmann, 1993: 3)

Indigenous publication of school-books is important not only because the content of the school-books should be locally conceptualized and developed but also because developing a local school-book industry will help the publication of other books, thus promoting the intellectual life of a country. Certainly the school book publishing should not be taken care of by foreign publishing companies. Even the posing of the question by the Swedes seems disconcerting.

Under World Bank and SIDA pressure the Institute of Curriculum Development was reorganized under the name Tanzania Institute of Education (TIE) and had to stop textbook publishing. The director of TIE laments:

TIE has now been relieved of the task of textbook production. This move has changed the work culture at the Institute. It has also proved to be a cut in one of the major means of getting money to run TIE activities. Curriculum development in Tanzania has been put to a very delicate and difficult test. Will the private publishers who have been given the mandate to publish textbooks produce them as the school requirements demand? Will the private publishers accept to publish teachers' guides which are so few because they are only used by the teacher? A lot is left to be desired in this area. What remains as a fact now is that TIE is no longer writing or developing textbooks (Mbunda, 1997: 183).

Tanzania is not the only African country that has been subject to this kind of policy reversal in curriculum development and textbook publishing. Adama Ouane from Mali, who used to work at the UNESCO Institute in Hamburg, Germany, told me that exactly the same process of undermining local curriculum development and the local textbook industry is at the moment going on in Mali. After independence Mali had for many years been engaged in indigenous publishing of textbooks. Through educational reforms in 1962 the content of the textbooks was completely revised. A National Pedagogical Institute (IPN) was established to develop curricula and teaching materials of relevance to Mali.

Before this period the books had been written in France and were highly irrelevant in the context of Mali. In the late 1980s, while implementing its fourth educational project, financed by the World Bank and conceived within the structural adjustment policy, it was decided that local development and production of school textbooks by the IPN was too expensive. The responsibility of IPN was restricted to small-scale experimental work, and the textbooks are now being developed by EDICEF in France and later sent to Mali. It seems that donors are also involved in the downsizing of the Institute of Curriculum Development in Mozambique. This policy of down-sizing curricula centers in Africa to me seems to be the opposite of capacity building—it is downgrading of capacity.

Following the World Bank report *Sub-Saharan Africa: From Crisis to Sustainable Growth* (World Bank, 1989) "capacity building" suddenly became *the* aid metaphor and became linked particularly to Africa through the development of the Bank-inspired multi-donor project, *The African Capacity Building Initiative (ACBI): Toward Improved Policy Analysis and Economic Management* (World Bank, 1991b). Because one of the indicators of capacity building is the existence of functioning local institutions, it may be useful to judge aid components by whether they build, sustain, or entirely neglect the appropriate local institutions. The demolishing of national curriculum centers can hardly be called capacity building. It means recolonization of the African mind. The starvation of indigenous publishing in Africa is another example of recolonization and a disregard for a concept of frequent use in donor parlance: institution building. The former director of Tanzania Publishing House, Walter Bgoya, puts it this way:

> One cannot emphasise enough that what is at stake is institution building and that African publishing will not develop unless publishing houses, both private or parastatal, are able to command adequate resources to finance, train staff and equip them so that they may be able, in the next ten to fifteen years, to produce books that meet their countries' needs.
>
> Unless this is done, what is likely to happen, given that book production is being managed from Ministries of Education, is that when loans such as the one Tanzania has just signed with the World Bank are finished, there will be no publishing industries left in place and countries will go back to importing books (Bgoya, 1990: 12).

Though he would open up for private publishing companies in Tanzania, Bgoya shared the same fears that the staff at ICD had. He worried that, unless special provisions were made to support publishing in Tanzania by Tanzanians, liberalization of the textbook industry would only mean that the profit would go to foreign multinationals. He reminded me of what happened to textbook publishing under the English Language Teaching Support Project introduced in 1987.

The objective of that particular project, which was introduced in Tanzania through British development aid (1.46 million pounds sterling), was to increase the competence of English-language teachers and to provide books for that purpose. Nine specialists from the United Kingdom were brought to Tanzania to implement the project. In the early days of the project it was realized that there was a great need for relevant books in English, preferably written by Tanzanians, in place of books written primarily for students in Britain. Such books had already been given for free by the British Council in large quantities to many secondary schools. In my trips to secondary schools around the country, where I did student teaching supervision, I sometimes came across stacks of relatively new English textbooks sitting around in the teachers' staff room. One teacher commented when she saw me looking at them: "They are highly irrelevant for our situation here. But what shall we do? We got these books for free and this is all we have."

Through the English Language Teaching Support Project it was proposed that Tanzanians be invited to write books, or where such books already existed with publishers in manuscript form, they should be submitted to the project for approval, editing, and eventual publication. Walter Bgoya explains that a number of Tanzanian publishers thought the Tanzanian publishing industry might benefit from the project, which would buy no less than 20,000 copies of the English supplementary readers if published under the project (Bgoya, 1992: 179). They had books in manuscript form in which they had already invested a lot of time and work but had not been able to publish them because of lack of funds. But the Tanzanian publishers were not helped to survive through the project. On the contrary:

> As it turned out, the agreement stipulated that the first edition of all books published under the project had to be published in the UK and by either Longman, Macmillan, Oxford University Press or Evans. Only a reprint could be published in Tanzania under a co-publication arrangement between the UK publisher and a local one. But even this was revised, and no book was published in Tanzania. British publishers, it is said, insisted that they should publish the books in the UK even if the manuscripts originated in Tanzania. English-language teaching is also good business for publishers in the UK. (Bgoya, 1992: 179)

In all fairness it has to be mentioned that while the World Bank is only concerned about African school-children getting textbooks, regardless of where they are developed and published, the Swedes have been concerned about helping Tanzania to develop their own publishing industry. If the aim of indigenization of the school book industry is to have any chance of being fulfilled, however, regulations have to be passed allowing the government to regulate the import of textbooks to Tanzania in order to protect a very fragile publishing industry, be it private or parastatal. Foreign interests in the private Tanzanian publishing industry should also be severely limited to, say, 20-30%. According to the liberalization policy, which forms part of the structural adjustment program of the World Bank and which also Sweden has bought into, such protective measures are not allowed.

My interviews in Tanzania in the spring of 1992 revealed that not only SIDA but also the Norwegian Development Agency (NORAD) was seen to be "ganging up behind"[77] the World Bank. This they did by lending their support to the privatization of the secondary school sector and the creation of a National Education Trust Fund on terms formulated by the World Bank.

THE NATIONAL EDUCATION TRUST FUND

The World Bank had for many years been planning to hold a major donor conference together with the Ministry of Education in Tanzania to coordinate loans and aid going to the education sector. The conference was expected to take place in the spring of 1990 but was repeatedly postponed, mostly because of the reluctancy of the Tanzanian Ministry of Education to accept the views of external consultants hired by the World Bank. The ministry wished, according to my informants, to decide on the educational policy of Tanzania by using a Tanzanian perspective.

---

[77] In earlier writing on these two Scandinavian interventions I also used the expression that the Nordic countries were "ganging up behind" the World Bank. This is an expression I have heard over and over again by the Tanzanians I interviewed and covers well the feelings they expressed to me. All Tanzanians who have read my first writings on this topic have said I should keep that expression since I am writing from a recipient and not from a donor perspective.

The reaction to the use of this expression has, however, been very strong from donors and consultants who have worked very closely with donors. They find the expression "emotive" and insist that they have not been "ganging up behind the World Bank," but merely participating in "co-ordinating efforts."

In anticipation of the up-coming donor conference, the Ministry of Education held a "mini-donor" conference, 23–25 November 1989, in which on the donor side only one representative from UNESCO and two representatives from the World Bank participated. I was there in the capacity of staff member of the Faculty of Education. Most of the papers presented were written in English by my colleagues at the University of Dar es Salaam. The Washington D.C. representative from the World Bank confessed to me: "We have to have these papers summarized and rewritten in a language which will be attractive to the donor community. I have a good consultant from Norway who can do this. Maybe you know him?"

I did, but I think I was too shocked at her confession to comment on her suggestion. She must have approached me because I was the only other white woman present and she might have felt some sister solidarity from this fact. I was, however, already looking at aid to the education sector more from the recipient's view and felt more solidarity with my colleagues who had written the papers. Why should the papers be rewritten? Their English was better than most highly educated Norwegians would write. My African colleagues had their Ph.D.s from the United States, Canada, and Britain. Their English was excellent. If the papers needed to be summarized in a smaller and special report, it could have been done by one of my colleagues.

The consultant the World Bank representative had mentioned was not present at the pre-conference, yet he was actually given the task of writing a confidential report which was later rejected by the Ministry of Education. The larger donor conference for the education sector which the World Bank wanted to coordinate was then postponed.

Instead the World Bank wrote a staff appraisal report building on a study commissioned by UNESCO (Syrimis, 1988), on earlier World Bank reports, and on the papers from the pre-conference (World Bank, 1990b). Here they launched the idea of a *National Education Trust Fund* (NETF) to rehabilitate private secondary schools. They decided that NETF should be organized as an NGO (non-governmental organization). One of my interviewees in the Ministry of Education told me:

> Donors seem to be very fond of establishing NGOs. They do not seem to trust us in the government and do not want the Ministry to be in charge of the money. But if we shall have no control, no say, why should we see the money at all? Now NORAD in Oslo pays the money to the World Bank in Washington, which pays the money to the Treasury

which pays it to the Ministry of Education, which then hands over the money to the Education Trust Fund. I don't like this system. We here in the ministry have absolutely no control over the money.

The ministry has a good and yearly auditing system for the money it deals with, but this money is just being passed on. We have told NORAD and the World Bank that we do not want to sit here shuffling money that we have no control over.

In an article discussing the role of the NGOs on the development scene, Stellan Bäcklund and Anders Närman (1993) warn against by-passing the state. They also warn against the support NGOs may give to the African elite against its own people. Likewise Kenneth King, discussing the important aid metaphor "capacity building," asks the timely question: "Does it build analytic capacity in the Ministry if for every major aid project a separate project implementation unit is set up that effectively by-passes regular Ministry channels?" (King, 1992: 259).

The NETF is a donor initiative, conceptualized by the World Bank. A frank consultancy report prepared for NORAD on the FUND states: "There is lack of local support for the FUND. The FUND is designed for dependency on donor support. Whatever local support that exists is loaned from the Government. Thus without donor support the FUND would be non-existent" (Galabawa and Alphonse, 1993: 3).

NORWEGIAN INVOLVEMENT

On 10–12 April 1989, policy planning consultancies were held in Dar es Salaam between a Norwegian delegation headed by the then Minister of Development Aid, the Social-Democrat Kirsti Kolle Grøndahl, and representatives from the Tanzanian government. The *Agreed Minutes* (NORAD/AFR, 1989) from that meeting contain the following paragraph: "It was agreed that support to the education and health sectors should be expanded and constitute an important part of the country program."

When Kirsti Kolle Grøndahl, who had earlier been the Minister for Education, in 1989 proposed that support to the education sector in Tanzania be expanded, she probably had not foreseen that the U.S.$8 million that was granted based on her initiative would be given to the World Bank to create a new non-governmental organization which would be disliked by many officials in the Tanzanian Ministry of Education. Nor would she likely have predicted that this organization would further the privatization of the secondary school sector with the likely outcome of creating larger disparities between regions and groups of people in Tanzania. In Norway there are hardly any private secondary schools and the Social-Democrats have, because of equity concerns, been against the establishment of such schools. Indeed, the move toward funding programs that were developed by foreigners and imposed on Tanzania violates the first principle of Norwegian aid to developing countries, the principle of recipient responsibility. In the English version of the *Strategies for Development Cooperation* by NORAD (1990) we read: "Our partners in development must themselves assume responsibility for political priorities and the distribution of financial and technical resources. The capacity of the recipient country to control and co-ordinate all external development assistance must be reinforced" (p. 12).

A second principle of Norwegian aid is that aid should be given to improve the conditions of the poorest segments of the population. A third principle is that aid should be given to improve the conditions of women.

In *Agreed Minutes from Policy Consultations on Development Cooperation between Tanzania and Norway*[78] (NORAD/AFR,1989) we find:

> She (Ms. K. Kolle Grøndahl) stated that one of the fundamental aims of the Norwegian development aid policy is to contribute to the improvement of the conditions of the poorest sections of the population and thus contribute to the fulfillment of basic human needs as well as safeguarding and strengthening social and economic human rights . . . Other basic concerns of Norwegian development policy are the conditions of women and their role in the development process.

A committee might have been set up right after the decision was taken that more aid would be given to the education sector in Tanzania. This suggestion was made repeatedly to the NORAD Office in Dar es Salaam by the Norwegian ambassador to Tanzania, by the Education Division of NORAD in Oslo and by me. The Dar office chose not to follow it up. Maybe the main reason for this was that it was administratively simpler to just give a big sum of money to the World Bank to administer than to deal with the question of Tanzanian priorities. Also, as we shall remember from the earlier discussion in this chapter, there was a shift in

---

[78] Following the meeting held in Dar es Salaam 10-12 April 1989 (from NORAD/AFR (1989)—Storløkken/Aarbakke, 21.04.1989).

Nordic policies in the mid 1980s toward exerting pressure on developing countries to follow the World Bank.

It may have been simpler for the Norwegian administration to allocate the money to the World Bank, but this certainly was not the case for the Tanzanian administration of the FUND. The procedure for transferring money from NORAD in Oslo via the World Bank to the National Education Trust Fund has been long and cumbersome. In February 1993, though the money had already been granted from NORAD several months earlier, no money had come to the NETF (Galabawa and Alphonse, 1993).

WHAT IS THE PURPOSE OF THE NATIONAL EDUCATION TRUST FUND?

The National Education Trust Fund is meant to encourage and support the development of private secondary schools in Tanzania. The FUND is not meant for building new schools in poor areas[79] where there are no schools, but is meant to give support to areas where schools already are built or the people are in the process of building schools. In this way the FUND is meant to stimulate private efforts. The NETF is meant for day-schools, not for boarding schools or even hostels in connection with day-schools. The FUND is meant to be used for infrastructure like building materials, desks, textbooks, and student scholarships, but not for teacher salaries or pre-service training of secondary school teachers.

Any community that is too poor to build a school cannot benefit from this fund. It is as Sumra (1996: 219) argues, "a prescription for increasing regional inequalities in secondary education." Data from NETF (1994) show that of the total money disbursed between 1992 when the fund was started and 1994, schools in Kilimanjaro received 25.54%. Three regions (Kilimanjaro, Ruvuma, and Arusha) received more than 50% of the funds disbursed by NETF. Kigoma region, which has very few secondary schools, received no NETF funds during the period. The largest recipient of NETF funds were schools run by Christian missionaries. They received almost 40% of funds disbursed by NETF (see Table 3.1). Not a single school managed by Muslims received any funds.

Sumra (1996: 222) is on safe grounds when, after an analysis of how NETF works he concludes: "NETF funds are therefore used to increase

---

[79] The attentive reader will already have noticed that the NETF contradicts the second principle of Norwegian aid: helping the poorest.

Table 3.1 Amount of Funds Disbursed by National Education Trust Fund by Ownership of School

Ownership	No. of Schools	Amount (TSh)	Percentage
Government assisted	13	55.156.835	32.80
Christian mission	13	64.472.623	38.36
Wazazi	7	35.251.797	20.98
Others	3	13.182.160	7.84
Total	36	168.063.415	100

Source: Sumra (1996: 222).

the regional and religious inequalities that exist in access to secondary education in the country."

Sumra's paper, which was given at the NASEDEC conference in Norway in June 1995, predates an evaluation of the National Education Trust Fund undertaken by Knut Samset and Naomi Katunzi in September 1995 (Samset and Katunzi, 1995).[80] In the summary of this report three very minor achievements and ten grave problems are listed. Samset and Katunzi (1995: 3) also note that about 70% of the beneficiary schools are in the three more advantaged zones in the country: "the project is therefore reinforcing regional imbalances regarding access to secondary level education."[81]

A closer examination of zone characteristics made by Galabawa and Alphonse (1993) indicated that even within the zones, areas of educational imbalance exist. For example, in the Northern zone, Kilimanjaro[82]

[80] This evaluation reaches the same conclusion as my initial interviewing in 1992. Without wanting to sound self-righteous, I would like to mention that much damage could have been avoided had NORAD in Dar chosen to listen to my critique at that time. Instead the education officer at Dar wrote home to NORAD that it was sad that I should be so critical of the intervention Norway was supporting at a time when they had originally thought of making use of my services! As we have seen, the Galabawa and Alphonse evaluation of 1993 and the Sumra study presented at the NASEDEC conference in June 1995 reached the same conclusion that I had.
[81] It is interesting to note that Samset and Katunzi, both coming from a Christian tradition, have not looked at how NETF is also reinforcing religious imbalances.
[82] The advantaged regions are regions where the colonialists, because of good climate and fertile soil, established their plantations and the missionaries started schools.

is by far more advantaged than Tanga and Arusha. A similar picture is portrayed in the lake zone where Kagera region had more than half of the total applications from the zone and therefore received a much higher allocation of grants awarded compared to Mwanza and Musoma. Even within the regions and districts the distribution of grants may not necessarily favour disadvantaged areas or schools. A further breakdown of Kilimanjaro region shows, for instance, that Moshi Rural and Mwanga District are disproportionately represented (Galabawa and Alphonse, 1993: 13).

Samset and Katunzi further conclude that some of the main problems in this project are associated with the way the National Education Trust Fund has been designed and operationalized: "Instead of cooperating with and drawing upon the resources of the parent organisations at national and district level, it approaches their schools directly without consulting with their organisations" (Samset and Katunzi, 1995: 2). They further concluded that: "during its four years of existence only 25 per cent of the funds committed for this period has been used by NETF. The disbursement of funds to community schools is 80-90 per cent behind schedule compared with the project budget" (Samset and Katunzi, 1995: 2).

When it comes to the impact of this Norwegian-funded project (U.S.$8 million, or 56 million Norwegian kroner) on the quality of instruction the evaluation mission states: "There is no evidence from the field that there has been improvement in learning or increased enrollment of girls" (Samset and Katunzi, 1995: 34).

The official terminology for these schools, which have not been centrally planned by the government but initiated by members of Parliament (MPs) or groups of educationally interested parents, is "private" schools. This is the terminology used, for instance, in the biannual *Basic Education Statistics for Tanzania* (BEST). The Tanzanian goverment has been very reluctant to build up private schools, especially in the primary sector, but also in the secondary. My interviewees in the Ministry of Education told me that they would very much have welcomed support for the public sector.

On Tuesday, 3 March 1992, the Tanzanian newspaper *Daily News* reported that in a recent meeting Prime Minister John Malecela[83] had told leaders of charitable organizations that the government of Tanzania does not allow charitable organizations to open primary schools in the country as this would interfere with its efforts to mold a Tanzanian na-

---

[83] He was also first vice-president.

tion. He feared that such private primary schools would negatively affect the goal in Tanzanian education of bringing up Tanzanian youngsters as a cohesive generation. He said that public primary schools had been able to bring together children of all ethnic backgrounds: "The Prime Minister said that the Government welcomed assistance geared at the improvement of the standard of education in *public* secondary schools" (Daily News, 3. March 1992: 3—emphasis added).

Donors prefer to call the private schools "community" schools and claim that they resemble the Harambee schools of Kenya. In a penetrating article analyzing the Harambee movement in Kenya, Anders Närman (1991) finds it misleading to consider Harambee schools to be local initiatives. These educational initiatives are more likely to be important as a "show-piece of a development-conscious elite." He found that many Harambee schools were initiated due to personal prestige of a local elite. He also found that the building of these schools could be regarded as an extra tax levied on the people for social services that cannot be provided from government sources. Närman (1991: 114) concludes:

> The Harambee secondary schools have been shown to be a fairly expensive way of offering education to primary school leavers not entering government-maintained schools. The provided education is normally of low quality and the academic results are not encouraging . . . As there are not enough wage employment opportunities for secondary school leavers from government institutions, it is highly unlikely that students with lesser academic credentials from less reputable schools stand much of a chance to be gainfully employed . . . Provision of secondary education without any clear policies on fair regional distribution or actual man-power requirements is not advisable.

When I asked the CCM people responsible for the education and health sector for their views on the National Education Trust Fund (NETF), they told me that they had never been invited to give their opinions on the way NETF is organized or the priorities made. CCM was afraid that the NETF would strengthen the inequality between regions. Had they been invited to participate in the planning of this fund, they would have shared this concern.

The distribution by zones of the first awarded grants by the NETF also shows that the education sector people in the CCM office in Dar es Salaam were right in their assumption that NETF would lead to greater disparities in the education system of Tanzania. The distribution of awards reflects the unevenness of location of private secondary schools in the different zones. For example, the Eastern zone, which is one of the most disadvantaged zones in Tanzania, had only three applications for funds, all of which were awarded. The Northern zone, on the other hand, considered one of the most advantaged zones, had seventy-seven applications, of which forty-six were awarded. The central zone, yet another disadvantaged zone, had only four applications, and again all of them were awarded. While the NETF's official policy is to give priority to educationally disadvantaged areas, these areas do not respond in a manner that would attract increased funding.

HOW THE LOCAL POLITICIANS ARE BYPASSED

In most western European countries the leading political parties have a clear say in deciding on the educational policy. The parties are represented in offical committees dealing with policy frameworks for various sectors of society. I wanted to find out how much involvement there was from CCM, the leading (and at that time the only legal) party in Tanzania, in defining the educational policy of Tanzania.

The involvement of the official party in Tanzania is not the same as the involvement of the parties in the multi-party democracies of western Europe. Since most intellectuals and all higher officials in the ministries were members of CCM, one might assume that CCM was always represented on a certain policy committee. The whole committee might have been members of CCM though there was no-one who had been officially appointed by CCM headquarters to represent CCM views. At CCM headquarters they were aware of the fact that there was no regulation saying that they should always be represented on a government policy committee. The ministers might call upon them when they wanted ideological support, often to counteract the donors. When I visited the headquarters, they told me that the Minister of Finance had recently said: "We should have someone from CCM to go on that committee," dealing with the privatization within industry. They had just appointed a representative from CCM to go on the seven-person committee which was to give their views on the consultancy report, *Developing a Privatization Program for Tanzania: A Proposal* (Haggerty-Coopers & Lybrand International, 1991). The Minister of Finance wanted a representative from CCM to look at the privatization efforts that the donor community wanted Tanzania to undertake.

I was well received in the CCM headquarters. They were not that used to having visits from consultants and researchers from donor countries. In fact, they were disappointed by the fact that they were not much listened to. They felt that the donor community had a negative attitude to CCM. I was surprised to find some of the same negative attitudes among some of my interviewees in the government offices, especially in the Planning Commission under the President's Office. When I asked if CCM was represented in the new educational task force writing about the Tanzania education system for the twenty-first century (URT, 1993), my interviewee not only answered in the negative, but also claimed that the CCM officials were not trained enough to participate in such academic work. "No use involving those people," was the answer I got. This interviewee was a person who shared the views of donors on many crucial questions. He was a person with considerable power and claimed that he found the donors more easy to deal with than the CCM officials.

Contrary to what he had led me to expect, I found highly trained and well-educated officials in CCM who would have had no trouble whatsoever participating in writing a report on the educational system of Tanzania. But they had not been asked to participate.

When I told the CCM officials about the task force, one said:

> What sort of committee is that? We have never been asked to participate. We are not involved. That is stupid because we know the people, work on the grass-roots. We have solidarity with people who have no electricity and must walk eight miles to get water. They might be afraid of us because we are also concerned about the people in Lindi, Mtwara, and so on. Because of them we have to retain the quota system. How else are they going to get to school? The quota system can be abolished when we have reached equality in the country. Until then disadvantaged districts, as well as women, have to be given preferential treatment. We must have a positive discrimination. We don't want an uneven development.

The CCM representatives I met were not a bunch of unschooled politicians. Many of them were people with university degrees. Some had Ph.D.s. The ones I met were idealists who still believed in a type of social-democratic development for Tanzania. As one CCM official told me:

> Donors, and also quite often bureaucrats in the ministries, don't want to include us because they claim that *we* deal with politics while *they* treat apolitical issues. That is not true. They, as well as we, are dealing with politics, but we have different aims. CCM still holds high the

Tanzanian aims of *ujamaa and kujitegemea* (socialism and self-reliance). They are still officially the ideology of the country and CCM wants to see to it that they are carried through. We in CCM see stumbling blocks in the way; we have to make detours around them to get to our aim. Our aim is still the same.

The donors want us to change the aims. They do not seem to care about unemployment. The World Bank has a capitalist ideology—survival of the fittest. They forced us into SAP (the structural adjustment program). They want to reduce the work force. They will create an army of unemployed. Where are the unemployed going to go? What are they going to eat? The SAP ought to have been planned by the country itself.[84]

Through an alliance between bureaucrats from the donor community and some bureaucrats in the recipient countries, initiatives in the education sector are quite often taken by by-passing the official political party. In this case the political party seemed to have an ideology close to the rhetoric of the original donor in question.

The representatives of the education sector in the CCM headquarters in Dar es Salaam told me with pride about the Nyerere Educational Trust Fund[85] which was initiated about the same time as NETF, but was already working. People themselves had through solidarity walks been able to raise 30 million TAS (at that time U.S.$150,000), put them in a fixed deposit account and got 17,000 TAS in interest. The Secretary for the Nyerere Educational Trust Fund had gone on the radio, mobilized the people, got all that money. They had given at least five places in secondary schools to each district (more to the poorest ones) to children who would otherwise not have been able to go to secondary school. School fees, uniforms, and soap were funded by 40,000 TAS for boarding school students and 20,000 TAS for day-school students.

THE SECONDARY SCHOOL SECTOR IN TANZANIA

From the time of independence in 1961 and the following two decades, it was an official policy of Tanzania to limit the expansion of secondary schools. One did not want to create an army of unemployed sec-

---

[84] My translation. The interview was conducted in Kiswahili.
[85] Note that also for this trust fund the acronym is NETF—probably no coincidence.

ondary school leavers. Also the aim of universal primary education was given the first priority. Upon achieving independence Tanzania did away with the private schools[86] and the user fees of colonial times.

In his comments on the 1986 World Bank document *Financing Education in Developing Countries*, Professor Luta Maliyamkono, the executive director of ESAURP,[87] highlighted the promises of pre-independent Africa: "The point is that publically subsidized education is not only an obligation but also a price the governments must pay for political independence" (Maliyamkono, 1987: 2).

It was also a policy to build boarding schools. This was done partly as a policy of nation building. Children from various parts of the country and tribes were brought together in the same school. Their common language would be Kiswahili even though their mother tongues might be quite different. The language of instruction was English. Another reason for developing boarding schools was that such facilities provided students with better conditions for studying outside of classes. The conditions which prevail in many of the homes from which secondary school pupils come are not conducive to more academic learning; no place where the pupil can sit and do their homework, often no light at night, overcrowding of people and scarcity of food. George Malekela (1983), for example, found that youngsters, especially girls, do better in boarding schools than in day-schools.[88] In another study Malekela (1984) mentions that he had asked four former students whether, given a free choice, they would prefer to attend boarding or day schools. Ninety-one percent of the boys and 96% of the girls attending boarding schools chose boarding schools, while 66% of the boys and 78% of the girls attending

[86] In 1985 there were still more students enrolled in public than in private secondary schools. From 1986 this has changed. The expansion of secondary school places has since 1986 been mostly in the private school sector. Many of these private schools cover only the first four years, forms 1–4. Students who want to get into the university or a technical college have to complete forms 5 and 6.

[87] ESAURP (Eastern and Southern African Universities Research Program)—an African research program building networks between universities in eastern and southern Africa. ESAURP, headquartered in Dar es Salaam, arranges conferences and seminars, publishes books (e.g., Maliyamkono, (ed.), 1980, Maliyamkono et. al., 1982, ESAURP, 1987) and reports, and takes on consultancies. As mentioned in the previous chapter, their valuable work has not been referred to at all in the World Bank report *Education Policies for Sub-Saharan Africa* (World Bank, 1988a).

[88] The main reason for this is that when girls attend day-schools they are so burdened by housework that they have very little time to study.

day-schools also chose boarding schools. Asked to explain their prefer-
ences, the majority said that "in boarding-school there is more time for
one's studies." Also mentioned were the advantages of having free electricity, accommodation and food. Girls especially mentioned that they did
not have to do so many household chores.[89]

A third explicit aim of the boarding school system was to overcome
regional inequalities in the country by giving children from the rural
population equal access to secondary schools.

Malekela (1983) made a ranking of secondary schools in Tanzania on
the basis of data from the National Examinations Council of Tanzania.
Out of the 164 schools which were ranked, *all* those in the first quartile
(41 schools) were boarding schools, 3 of which were for girls and 2 were
co-educational, while the remaining 36 schools were for boys only.[90]

Maybe building more boarding schools for girls and opening up
some of the boys' boarding schools to make them co-educational would
have been a better way of assuring that there would be enough girls who
would apply for higher education. A less costly measure would be to
build girls' hostels connected to the private schools. The provision of
hostel facilities could substantially improve not only the enrollment figures for girls but also their academic performance because girls who stay
in hostels are known to perform better than girls who are day scholars.
Yet the constitution of the National Education Trust Fund does not provide support for constructing girls' hostels. In a consultancy report on the
implementation of the NETF, Galabawa and Alphonse (1993: 9) criticize
that several community schools which had put up applications for grants
to build girls' hostels "were of course rejected."

Most of the boarding schools are government schools, but there are
also a few well-equipped private boarding schools in Tanzania which are
financed and frequently also run by Euoropean and American missionaries. Most of the private schools are, however, day-schools. Day-schools,
to be profitable, have to be built in larger cities. The initiative to build
these private schools has normally come from educationally oriented
parents who are upset that their children did not get into the government

---

[89] Sumra and Katunzi (1991), in their research on the effects of the reintroduction
of school fees in secondary schools, found that girls spent three or four times as
much time on house chores as their brothers did.

[90] The policy of building many more boarding schools for boys than for girls was
started in colonial times (Hongoke, 1991).

secondary schools. Most of these schools are therefore in the more well-to-do areas of the country. The parents pay high fees to send their children to these private or community based schools, yet the schools are very poor, very crowded, ill equipped, often with teachers who have little or no training.[91]

A few years ago I had frequent contact with a cook in Dar es Salaam who told me with the greatest pride that he had managed to get his eldest son into a private secondary school. The father worked as hard as he could to pay the ever increasing school fees. After four years he asked me first to translate the school grades his son had got and then to try to find a job for this secondary school leaver. His grades were the lowest in all subjects except Kiswahili and *siasa* (social science)—the only two subjects taught in Kiswahili. I could not find a job for him, nor could anyone else. His father had thought that toiling so hard for four years to keep the son in the private day-school would open the doors to success for his son and the family. Instead he had an unemployed 17-year-old to feed.

What are the likely short term consequences of a donor initiative like the National Education Trust Fund? Some have been outlined in this chapter: elite formation and a growing disparity between regions, between rich and poor, between men and women in the country; growing discontent among the secondary school leavers, having left the private day schools. The many pitfalls of the Kenyan Harambee schools have shown us that the provision of secondary education without any clear policies on fair regional distribution or actual workforce requirements is not advisable. The regional distribution and labor requirements seem to be of concern to the politicians in CCM. These politicians were not listened to. A dangerous alliance was built between donor bureaucrats, some intellectuals and some bureaucrats in the concerned ministries, an alliance which was political in nature yet purported to be purely administrative. And what are the likely long term consequences of programs such as NETF? Further dependence on donor support and, contrary to the purported intentions of donor organizations, further underdevelopment. This is especially the case if we adopt the definition of development presented by the TANU Party of Tanzania in 1971: "Any action which gives people more power of decision and domination over their own lives is an act of

---

[91] Longterm pedagogical and professional training for teachers is one of the most hard core problems the private or community based schools have to cope with. Support for such training is, however, outside the scope of the NETF funding areas.

development, even if it does not increase health or food" (TANU Guidelines, 1971).

And as Sumra (1996) explains, the restrictions in the power of the Tanzanian people vis à vis foreign powers has meant that social inequalities within the country have been strengthened:

> Tanzanian education has come full circle. Inequalities in education based on race, religion, and socio-economic status having been reduced through deliberate government policies, are re-emerging. These inequalities were reduced through nationalization of schools. It is through having total control over all issues pertaining to education that the state was able to reduce these inequalities. With the donor pressure to privatize education, these inequalities are re-emerging. Donor support like that provided through NETF is responsible, at least in part, for deepening these inequalities (Sumra, 1996: 224).

It is also difficult to see that SIDA's handling of the Future School Book Provision for Tanzania will give more power of decision to Tanzanian curriculum makers and publishers. The rhetoric within Swedish development assistance emphasizes democracy and the building of democratic institutions, self-reliance, and sustainability. There seems, in recent years, to be an ever growing discrepancy between this rhetoric and the pressure put on recipients of aid to embrace market economies with liberalization and privatization as main strategies. There is a contradiction between the rhetoric of supporting governments in institution building and a series of initiatives, like NETF and the Future School Book Provision, which reduce government control and area of action as well as preclude government's development of experiences in a learning process that might lead the government to greater efficiency.

The recipient perspectives become muffled in the complex set of activities involving negotiations, feasibility studies, and related reports by external consultants and various donor practices that exclude local politicians as well as lower level educators from dialogue and decision-making. When the coordination of aid mostly becomes a coordination between donors (or between a bank and a donor, as in the case of the NETF where the cooperation was between the World Bank and NORAD), it gives the people through their governments less power and thus does not contribute to development as defined in the TANU guidelines quoted above.

COORDINATION OF AID TO THE EDUCATION SECTOR

Ulla Kann, who just after independence in Namibia had the position of adviser concerning aid coordination in the then Ministry of Education and Culture in that country, comments:

> I thought I understood what I was expected to do when I signed the contract. It was clearly stated in my Terms of Reference that I was to assist the Ministry in coordinating the inputs of the various donors, assist in arranging meetings with donors, and so forth. It was also stated in my contract that I had to show loyalty to the Ministry and the Government of the Republic of Namibia (Kann, 1997: 1).

She conceived of aid coordination as the coordination by the recipient government of the support provided by various donor agencies in order to see to it that wasteful overlaps between donor agencies were avoided, that donor support followed the national policies and priorities, and that aid would not be too costly in the long run for the recipient country. But during her time in the position of aid coordinator, she was forced to realize "that aid coordination was considered by the donors to be an issue for donors. But I did not, and still do not, agree with that understanding" (Kann, 1997: 5).

Kann explains how she learned that donor agencies (and not recipient governments) are in charge of coordination of aid, referring to her encounter with the "Round Table":

> For somebody who is not aware of the international jargon, Round Table sounds like a nice concept to use when you want to arrange a meeting between a government line ministry and one or several donor agencies. That is, if you are not aware of that by inviting to a "Round Table" you are stepping on the toes of UNDP, the World Bank and others. Inviting to and arranging a Round Table is the prerogative of UNDP. A UNDP Round Table is a meeting of bilateral and multilateral agencies with representatives of one country, its government, and sometimes also representatives of its private sector. Similar meetings and consultative groups are arranged by the World Bank (Kann, 1997: 4).

Kann had hoped that some coordination of aid could have been carried out by the recipient country through the working out of planning and monitoring documents of foreign aid projects in the country. She explains how the inclusion of a so-called logical framework has become almost mandatory in project documents. Kann finds that such frameworks help in the development and monitoring of a project. She relates that in the case of Namibia, the National Planning Commission has issued a manual for planners which includes a Namibian version of a logical framework, but notes:

> [the manual] is not being used by the planners. Instead they use a Swedish version for Swedish-funded projects, a German version for German-funded projects, an EU version, a Luxembourg version, and so on. Several agencies have arranged training sessions on their special logical framework version. Why not agree upon using the Namibian version for projects to be carried out in Namibia? (Kann, 1997: 5).

The problem here seems to be that the various donors want the framework they have worked out to be used in all "their" countries. They will all have the same reporting system no matter how this system coincides with the reporting system and routines in the line ministries of the countries that get the funding.

On my many trips to the African countries that get UNICEF funding from the Foreign Ministry in Norway, I have noticed what an extra burden it is on the government officials (and often on the local UNICEF representatives, who are more aware of the routines of the ministries they work with than the regional offices are) not only to have to get hold of different information for different donors, and adhere to different deadlines, but also to receive the many delegations from the donors who come as money-lenders, consultants, and in review and appraisal missions, often asking the same questions to the over-burdened government officials. When I travel for the Norwegian government I am always surprised how many top officials, including ministers give me of their precious time, always smiling, and being accommodating. But I know that they had another delegation like ours the day before and are expecting another one when we leave. No wonder donors can talk about inefficiency in the ministries. When are they going to get their work done? And how are they going to get in a position where they coordinate the projects, decide on the frameworks, and seek the donor funding they need for their priorities?

Yet both bilateral and multilateral funding agencies stress the importance of local ownership in policy development and project formulation. The development policies must, according to the agencies, be "locally owned" for agency funded reforms to be effective and sustainable. This is easier said than done, given the external origin of the structural adjustment programs and sectoral policies currently being implemented throughout the South. Brian Cooksey (1996) reminds us that reforms in education policy are part of a much larger structural adjustment reform program. Bilateral aid is more or less dependent on the government having an on-going adjustment programme with the World Bank and the IMF. But what if local priorities are perceived by the money-lenders or donors to be wrong? As Brian Cooksey (1996: 12) rightly asks: "Would funding agencies be prepared to finance a locally owned strategy with which they disagree?"

As early as 1984 the World Bank itself showed its awareness of the problem faced by national ministries when a lot of donors bombard them with different projects which are not necessarily those wanted[92] by the countries in question:

> The public investment program has become little more than the aggregation of projects that donors wish to finance. These projects have not always been consistent with the priorities necessary for achieving national development objectives. Donors finance the projects that spending ministries and agencies want, but these wants are seldom coordinated by the core ministries. (World Bank, 1984: 41, quoted in Colclough, 1997: 10)

Although written more than a decade ago, the generalization remains true of much of Africa. Ironically, as Colclough argues, part of this problem is induced by the process of aid-giving.

> The demands imposed by a large number of agencies upon small recipient administrations can be considerable, and are capable of diverting scarce resources from more important applications. Moreover, not only is donor activity often not coordinated, but it is actually marked by competitive behavior (e.g., competitively bidding for a small pool of qualified counterpart staff, or for high profile projects in fashionable sectors) which set up new cycles of wasted resources and opportunity (Colclough, 1997: 10).

[92] It can be difficult to say no to a project that a donor wants to finance because with the project there will always come some material benefits. For example some computers will be left when expatriates leave, and some officials might get to travel overseas.

The system of competitive bidding for project organization, evaluations, and writing of text-books is a system favoured by the World Bank. Being alert to threats to an independent intellectual development for Africa, I wondered during a field-trip to Uganda in 1997 about the soundness of a policy of international competitive bidding for organizing training, textbooks, and instructor manuals for the non-formal COPE schools. Especially when the winner of the tender is a Washington D.C. based American firm, Creative Associates International, Inc., and not even a Ugandan or affiliated African firm. I was told that the Institute for Curriculum Development in Uganda had also put in a bid but had not been chosen. No wonder, when the bigger and better resourced firms in the West have much better facilities and can make so much better and nicer looking applications.

Not only does the coordination of aid seem to be completely donor dominated, but so also does the whole question of accountability of funds received or loaned.

ACCOUNTABLE TO WHOM?

The word *accountability* in donor parlance has come to mean that the bilateral donors must be accountable to their governments, the multilateral donors to their constituencies, for the money given or lent to a developing country. That there is a much more important accountability at stake, namely, that the recipient governments must be accountable to their people for the aid they receive, often with strings attached, or loans they take which their people shall have to pay, seems to be forgotten among the donors that want to teach "democracy" and "good governance." But the African states are themselves treated by the World Bank/IMF in a very undemocratic manner and are forced by them to be dictators to their own people.

A former Norwegian ambassador to Tanzania tells how in meetings called by the government of Tanzania to discuss its economic policy, he observed that the economic plan—the so-called *Policy Framework Paper*—arrived at the last minute from Washington D.C., printed on World Bank stationery. The document was written in a way that was meant to give the impression that the policy to be embarked on had been chosen by the government itself. There was an abundance of expressions like: "The government will work energetically toward" and "The government has declared its intention to" and "The government has made a firm decision to" (Garbo, 1993: 106).

There are not many people outside of the inner government circles and the donor community who have ever seen a *Policy Framework Paper*, even though it is in this paper the economic policy of a country is laid down. The negotiations are confidential. The problems are not discussed in the press. The politicians in Parliament only get to know about the decisions when they are being enforced through government proposals for cuts in public expenditures and the selling and privatization of government enterprises. When the budget is presented to Parliament, the government is already tied up through enforced agreements with the World Bank and the IMF. As the former Norwegian ambassador to Tanzania argues: "The donors are today talking a lot about furthering democracy in the recipient countries. What do they teach through their own practice?" (Garbo, 1983: 107, my translation).

Akilu Habte (1997) of Ethiopia, earlier the head of the Education Division of the World Bank, reported that UNICEF had prided itself for having prepared national plans of action following the World Summit on Children. However, over 75% of those reports were prepared by external consultants. Similarly, all of 329 UNESCO- or World Bank funded sector studies on Africa conducted between 1990 and 1994 had been undertaken by expatriate-led teams with only minimal representation or inclusion of local researchers who never served as senior consultants or document authors. Habte (1997:5) felt compelled to conclude: "Sector studies in Africa seem to have been written more to be accountable to parliaments and decision makers of Europe and North America rather than of Africa."

Habte asks why there was no Africanization of the sector studies and why the World Bank today uses expatriates to undertake sector studies in African countries. He is also critical of the technical assistance[93] given by the North to African countries.

TECHNICAL ASSISTANCE AND CAPACITY DEVELOPMENT

Although technical assistance has purportedly been used by donors as an instrument for capacity building, Habte (1997) notes that there is an overwhelming consensus that the technical assistance provided to Africa has been more failure than success.

---

[93]According to Habte (1997), technical assistance represents one third of all external assistance to African nations.

Anne L. Sikwibele (1996), who was the head of the Department of Educational Administration and Policy Studies at the University of Zambia, claims that the general impression in poor African countries is that paying for the services of technical assistance from expatriates is too expensive, and that this is done at the expense of other priority sectors. Additionally, poor countries in Africa are apprehensive to spend borrowed money on experimental projects when there is no evidence of prior success in Africa.

> Although policy-makers agree to certain foreign aid projects, sometimes, this is done under pressure to be in line with requirements to get aid for another project or another sector . . . Further, when donors do not allow local input in planning, the results are often misplaced priorities, policies and projects (Sikwibele, 1996: 25).

Even though my informants seemed to disagree quite a bit on the type of educational policy to follow for Tanzania, there seemed to be more agreement on their wish to sort out differences of opinion among Tanzanians free of external threats or pressures from bilateral or multilateral donors. There was a unanimous annoyance with the way Tanzania was invaded by all types of donors of aid to the education sector, all with their philosophies and undebated agendas. As Abel Ishumi (1985:10) laments:

> For instance, in Scotland it would be impossible to have Russia construct a large technical school outside Edinburgh, the Cubans half a dozen secondary schools, the Danes 3 or 4 girls' boarding schools, without the Scots doing a great review, critique and analysis of the purpose of these interventions.

In Tanzania the former USSR built a Soviet-Russian technical college in Mbeya, Cuba helped develop agricultural schools, the former East Germany built polytechnical schools, West-Germany aided the development of Arusha Technical College, Norway provided assistance to the Faculty of Forestry and the Department of Animal Science and Production at Sokoine University, and Sweden built a vocational centre in Moshi. All of these projects were undertaken without these institutions and the ideologies they transmit having been analyzed by independent researchers from an African perspective. How relevant to an independent development in Africa is the training these institutions give? What are the underlying ideologies of the institutions? How do they correspond to the ideologies the Tanzanian government would like to transmit?

It is to such questions that we shall now turn, to the content of the education and training given. How much is expatriate technical assistance also being used when it comes to curricula in African schools? What about the curriculum reconstruction one African nation after the other planned to pursue when they attained independence?

PART II

African Culture and the Content of Schooling

We have never really stopped to consider why we want education—what its purpose is . . . although over time there have been various criticisms about the details of curricula provided in schools, we have not until now questioned the basic system of education which we took over at the time of Independence.

(NYERERE, 1968)

CHAPTER 4

A Renewed Curriculum Dependency?

When lost, it's better to return to a familiar
point before rushing on.

(AFRICAN PROVERB)

When discussing contemporary education in Africa the historian Joseph Ki-Zerbo (1990) of Burkina Faso quotes the African proverb above. In his book *Educate or Perish* he voices an SOS call to educators in Africa to set immediately to the task of designing an education of Africa and *for* Africa. It is important for Africa to return to her roots, to restore the cultural traditions of various parts of Africa.

Likewise, Katherine Namuddu (1991: 41) sees that the real and most fundamental problem in education in Africa is the fact that "the formal philosophy and organization of the educational system have remained predominantly foreign."

PRE-COLONIAL EDUCATION

Ki-Zerbo tells how the breakup of the African educational system was completed by colonial domination. The colonialists replaced the African educational system with an absolutely different system designed to serve the overall aim of the subjugation of the continent to European needs. For African societies, education lost its functional role. Ki-Zerbo (1990: 12) claims that in Africa "the formal system of classroom education looks like a foreign cyst in the social body, a malignant tumor."

The pre-colonial educational system had many positive points. The system can be described as a system of linkages between:

- General knowledge and practical life
- Education and production

- Education and social life
- Education and culture (through the use of the mother tongue; the incorporation of cultural practices like games, dancing, music, and sports; and the teaching of ethical values)

    Ki-Zerbo quotes Amadou Hampate Ba, who rightly said: "When an elder dies in Africa, it is a library that burns." The truth is even more tragic, however. For in the event of a library burning, other copies of the lost books may be found, and another library set up. Given Africa's situation of poor geographical, historical, and linguistic intercommunication, and with oral traditions being the dominant mode of transmission to this day, it can be said that an elder's death is the equivalent of the burning of a unique and living manuscript. Day by day, such living manuscripts pass away, and Africa's school system and society thus lose more of their cultural roots. These roots constitute the familiar point to which it might be better for Africa to return.

    The Tanzanian curriculum developer Charles Kalugula (1991) tells about the informal education which today occurs alongside formal education and sometimes as the only type of education children get. During story telling, both girls and boys tend to sit together around a grown-up parent, grand-parent, or other elder who relates to them stories of educational significance to the family, the clan and the wider society in which the children live. This aspect of the informal education — the story-telling — is non-sex specific. This contrasts with the informal curriculum of the traditional skill training in Africa taking place at the family level which is normally both sex specific and sex segregated. The girls learn what their mothers do daily, while the boys learn what the fathers do in the family.

    Whereas in Part I we looked at the structures surrounding education in Africa, the pressure by donors and lenders to privatize and liberalize the school sector, in Part II we shall be more concerned with the content of education, the attempts at curriculum reconstruction, the question of language of instruction, and the question of relevance. How relevant is the Western type of schooling that pupils in Africa today receive in relation to what they need? Maybe the drop in enrollment rate is a sign that parents and children do not find the type of schooling relevant. Maybe it is a very rational choice they are making. Maybe they find that the education children get outside of school is more worthwhile.

    As Catherine Odora (1992: 85) argues: "Educators interested in the local dimension could also revisit the phenomenon of drop-out from the perspective of other learning systems." At the end of the chapter we shall look at attempts that are being made to root education in African culture and at the renewed interest in other learning systems.

COLONIAL CURRICULUM DEPENDENCY, OR WHO DISCOVERED MURCHINSON FALLS?

The former primary school-girl and now educational researcher Catherine Odora (1993: 2) recalls the rigorous choir practices of her primary school and how the teachers spent weeks getting the Ugandan kids to sing "Auld Lang Syne," "I Sowed Barley in the Meadow," "London's Burning," and "Land of the Silver Birch, Home of the Beavers." None of the teachers had ever seen barley, let alone meadows, birches, or even London, either the one that was burning or the parts that survived the fire. She recalls how she received an award from the headmaster on a parents day, for reciting by heart a whole chapter from *Rip van Winkle*. The parents had clapped and cheered, but none of them had ever heard of Rip van Winkle, and most of them could neither speak nor understand English, which was the language of the text.

She further tells about the primary leaving examination and one question in it that has never left her mind:

> It was in General Paper and the question asked about who discovered the Murchinson Falls (a waterfall situated not too far away from my father's ancestral home). The objective options **a, b, c,** and **d** had several European names and **"e"** had **"none of these."** I had chosen the last one (**e**), but the teacher had insisted that it was one of the Europeans who had discovered this waterfall.
>
> This waterfall, on the river Nile, is part of the boundary between two major ethnic groups in Uganda, with the Acholi—my tribe—to the north of it, and Bunyoro to the south. It was a respected site for ancestral worship by the people who lived close to it. My great grandfather, who had died while on the Bunyoro side of the river early in the nineteenth century, had been brought to and buried on the Acholi side as he wished. A memorial tree had been planted on the grave (way before any of those explorers saw that waterfall) which our family visited regularly. But in the school we were to say it was some European who had discovered it. (Odora 1993: 3)

Odora wonders why the teachers felt so comfortable[94] educating the children on what Rip van Winkle did in the Catskills Mountains while ignoring the fantastic narratives of the kind her father regularly told the children in the neighborhood about famous events that had occurred to the Acholi people on different "mountains" long ago.

Like Odora, we should question why the teachers ignored the cultural heritage of the Acholi people. There may have been several reasons for this:

1. The narratives might not have been written down. They might therefore have belonged more to the curriculum of the indigenous and pre-colonial education conveyed regularly to children by parents and elders by the fire-side at night than to the Western type of schooling built on written sources.
2. Even if the narratives were written down, they might have been written in the indigenous language while the language of the school to which Odora went was the colonial language, English.
3. The purpose of schooling in colonial times seems to have been to make children familar with the cultural heritage of the colonial powers as a way to convince them of Europe's superiority. The cultural heritage of the African child was made invisible within the formal schools.

CURRICULUM RECONSTRUCTION IN AFRICA

But what about the cultural heritage of the African child *after* independence? We shall look at some attempts at curriculum reconstruction in Africa.

In May 1961, at the dawn of political independence in most African countries delegates of thirty-seven African states[95] and four European states[96] met in Addis Ababa under the auspices of UNESCO and UNECA

---

[94] Maybe they did not, but like Odora they acted out the script set for them!

[95] These were Basutoland, Bechuanaland, Cameroon, Central African Republic, Chad, Congo (Brazzaville), Congo (Leopoldville), Dahomey, Ethiopia, Gabon, Gambia, Ghana, Guinea, Ivory Coast, Kenya, Liberia, Malagasy Republic, Mali, Mauritania, Mauritius, Morocco, Niger, Nigeria, Federation of Rhodesia and Nyasaland, Ruanda-Urundi, Senegal, Sierra Leone, Somalia, Sudan, Swaziland, Tanganyika, Togo, Tunisia, Uganda, United Arab Republic, Upper Volta, and Zanzibar.

[96] These were Belgium, France, Spain, and the United Kingdom (UNESCO/ UNECA, 1961: 2–3).

(United Nations Economic Commission for Africa) to discuss education in Africa. The type of education discussed at this conference was formal schooling, the type which the colonialists had introduced into Africa. This was the first time that such discussions, conducted predominantly by Africans, had taken place at the continental level. The report of that conference (UNESCO/UNECA, 1961) has become one of the most important educational documents in Africa. In the report quantitative targets for the school years up to 1965 (short-term plan) and 1980 (long-term plan) were set.

The concern of the conference was, however, not only with quantitative targets. The Addis Ababa conference also observed that the content of education in Africa was based on a non-African background and therefore recommended that:

> African educational authorities should revise and reform the content of education in the area of curricula, text-books and methods, so as to take account of the African environment, child development, cultural heritage, and the demands of technological progress and economic development. (UNESCO/UNECA, 1961: 23)

Ayotunde Yoloye finds that "it is clear that the recommendation is addressed to the issue of the *relevance* of the content of education in Africa" (Yoloye, 1986: 150).

There seems, however, to be an agreement in the literature on the educational achievements of the newly independent states in Africa that increasing the quantity of education has had a priority over the work with quality inputs and relevance of the reconstruction of the curriculum (see Beshir, 1974; Uchendu, 1979; Jansen, 1989).[97] Beshir put it this way: "As education expanded, the problems of content and the relevance of the curricula have been given less attention not because they were not important, but because there were more urgent problems" (Beshir, 1974: 30).

The more urgent problems had to do with the expansion of education, with the building of new schools, with government take-over of private schools and the doing away with racially segregated schools. Of the few concrete promises made by national independence movements about the future educational system, expanded access and equal educational opportunity for the masses of Africans ranked high on the agenda. The

---

[97] "Curriculum" is defined in this book, as it is in Jansen's (1989) article on curriculum reconstruction in post-colonial Africa, mainly as content such as that reflected in textbooks, syllabi, policy documents, and teacher resources.

legitimacy of the new states, therefore, depended heavily on their ability to provide access to schooling for large parts of the African population.

So while the African educationists were busy fulfilling the promise of schooling for the masses of Africans, the curricula and textbooks along with the methods of teaching were in the hands of the educational industry and publishers of the North. One reason for this state of affairs was, according to Lillis (1985: 82), that "the African independence movement lacked a clear curriculum-policy dimension." Another reason had to do with a lack of resources and the fact that funds as well as technical expertise were coming from outside Africa.

Three major regional curriculum projects funded by USAID, for instance, were launched in the 1960s by the Education Development Center (EDC), a private company based in Newton, Massachusetts, under the general title "The African Education Program."[98] Under this program, EDC initiated the following three curriculum development projects:

1. The African Mathematics Program (AMP)
2. The African Primary Science Program (APSP)
3. The African Social Studies Program (ASSP)

The African Mathematics Program eventually split into two subregional programs: the West African Regional Mathematics Program (WARMP), and the East African Regional Mathematics Program (EARMP). The African Primary Science Program created Science Curriculum Centers in Ghana, Kenya, Malawi, Nigeria, Sierra Leone, Tanzania, and Uganda. The science educators in these centers, who mostly were from the United States, worked with local counterparts to prepare and test out primary science units in the African classrooms continuously over five years.

Lillis (1985) uses the term "curriculum dependency" to describe the control exerted by expatriate teachers, foreign "experts,"[99] imported models of training, and adopted examination patterns in ensuring a West-

---

[98] Labeling the projects "The African Education Program" was in itself rather presumptuous, as they were geared only to anglophone Africa. It may be looked at as a cultural/colonial/territorial bias to refer to "Africa" when one only means "anglophone Africa."

[99] In Tanzania my colleagues told me how they define an expert, or *mtalaam*. *"Mtalaam ni mtu ambaye anakuja nyumbani kwako na kuazima saa yako na kukuambia ni saa ngapi"* (An expert is someone who comes to your house and borrows your watch and tells you what time it is).

ern curriculum in independent Africa. In capitalist states, such as Kenya, as well as declared socialist regimes at that time, such as Tanzania and Zimbabwe, the problematic role of expatriates or experts on curriculum practices has been recognized.

In his book, *Education in Kenya since Independence*, George S. Eshiwani (1993) tells how the curriculum experts at the Kenya Institute of Education had to resort to imported curriculum packages because resources both human and financial, were too limited to do anything else.[100] He tells about the widespread dissatisfaction among teachers and students with the existing curricula in Kenyan schools, of which great parts are irrelevant and constructed for the children in the industrialized West, not for a largely agrarian population in an African context.

Eshiwani also reports on the *New Primary Approach* (NPA) project started in Nairobi with both financial and personnel assistance from the Ford Foundation and with books published by Oxford University Press. The NPA was really intended for effective use of English as the language of instruction. NPA was conceived by non-Kenyans. It was managed and financed by a foreign agency. The linguistic policy laid down by UNESCO.[101] that children's education should begin in their native tongue was completely ignored. No attention was paid to the problem of first language interference and the effect of the new approach on the pupil's self-confidence. Eshiwani (1993: 162) concludes: "It is no wonder that in the mid 1970s the NPA started to decline tremendously." Yet the NPA had been enthusiastically embraced by the Ministry of Education in Kenya. In its Triennial Survey 1964–1965 the Ministry stated:

> The Government has been actively attacking the problem of standards of primary education from the angle of teaching methods and curriculum. One of the most promising ventures in the history of education in Kenya has been the development of the New Primary Approach in the primary schools. (quoted in Eshiwani, 1993: 161)

F. F. Indire (1972) blames the problems in curriculum development on the British educational model which Kenya and many developing

---

[100] This issue of how lack of resources and dependency on aid leads to recolonization was also brought up in Part I, especially in Chapter 3.
[101] As we shall discuss further in the following chapter, in 1970 UNESCO had already recommended the use of the mother tongue as the universal language of instruction everywhere (UNESCO, 1970).

countries in the Commonwealth inherited. But as shown by the quote above, the inheritance was quite often embraced. Indire especially singles out the secondary school curriculum in his criticism and says that it is elitist; that the instructional methods used are formal; that the content is irrelevant and inappropriate; and that it emphasizes passing of examinations at the expense of acquisition of knowledge, skills, and attitudes appropriate for effective living.

Eshiwani describes how curricula in eastern Africa after independence have either been adopted or slightly adapted from the North. He tells about the conference comprised of representatives from Tanzania, Uganda, and Kenya which gathered in Dar es Salaam in 1964 to prepare a new syllabus in mathematics for the "O" level based on the British School Mathematics Project (SMP). Following this conference, the Kenya Institute of Education was charged with the responsibility of writing the first draft text for a new program. A team of expatriate secondary school teachers from Uganda and Kenya was assembled for this exercise. Eshiwani observes: "In the real sense, this team did not write new textbooks. What they did was to adapt the British SMP and call it the School Mathematics of East Africa (SMEA)" (Eshiwani 1993: 169). Eshiwani claims that the "indigenization phase of curriculum" has not yet taken off.[102]

Indire suggested earlier in 1972, that one approach that could be employed in dealing with the indigenization or Africanization of the curriculum would be to inject "the traditional African society education" into the formal education. This idea presupposes that educationists work with "the traditional African society education," know it, study it, and teach it. This means including in the study of education also the indigenous forms of learning, not letting this type of learning belong to the field of social-anthropology or the arts, being looked at as folklore and ancient ritual and customs. It means broadening and reclaiming the concept of "education." But our faculties of education are faculties of schooling, not of education. The ministries of education around the world are ministries of schooling.

---

[102]Likewise, Krishna Kumar (1991:13), on another continent but with the same colonial history, deplores the lack of de-linking from Britain which has happened since India got her independence: "Not only does a link exist between the selection of school knowledge that was made under colonial rule and present-day pedagogy and curricula, but the very idea of 'what is worth teaching' remains to this day clouded by a colonial view of Indian society."

FURTHER ATTEMPTS AT INDIGENOUS
CURRICULUM CONSTRUCTION

Pai Obanya (1995a), the director of BREDA, the UNESCO office for western Africa which is located in Dakar, Senegal, has examined some of the curriculum innovations that have been attempted in West Africa since the early 1960s. These include the promotion of national languages in schools, the introduction of environmental studies into the curriculum and the use of educational television. He reports that in nearly every case the desired goals have not been attained. In most cases this was because of unfavorable social, political, and economic conditions. Other reasons had to do with the failure to include the local population in the planning of projects. The population did not participate actively in the identification of its needs and so the programs developed seemed to have addressed the wrong issues.

Another explanation had to do with borrowing educational innovations from the West. Obanya comments:

> Innovative ideas like educational television, for example, collapsed after years of trial, mainly because the inputs and processes seemed to have been conceived in and for other regions of the world. They were not well received by Africans and the attempts to get them accepted were inappropriate. (Obanya, 1995: 335)

Obanya found that "expensive piloting" was another plausible reason for innovative projects not achieving their objectives. He reports that "in most of the pilot activities, expensive machinery was used, high level foreign experts were involved, and the projects never became fully domesticated." (Obanya, 1995: 335).

He also reported that there has been little critical analysis of the curriculum projects, how they came about and how they function. Instead there has been "propagandist reporting intended for the consumption of foreign donors" (Obanya, 1995: 335). He recommends that future innovative curriculum efforts in Africa should start with a societal needs analysis and full societal involvement in the entire process of curriculum construction, implementation, and evaluation.

In his article Obanya mentions that in most so-called "anglophone" countries,[103] one of the most immediate results of post-independence

---

[103]Which means countries formerly under British domination—more than 90% of the population speak African languages and not English.

educational reform efforts was the creation of national curriculum centers. The centers organized conferences to develop national curriculum goals. Grouped under the aegis of the African Curriculum Organization (ACO), the curriculum centers were able to establish a mechanism for the exchange of knowledge and experience which flourished from 1976 to 1985.

Obanya tells how the economic recession and structural adjustment measures of the mid 1980s led to a starvation of the curriculum centers. For example, Ghana's economic crisis of the 1980s led to lack of continuity in the curriculum development programs of that country. Sierra Leone and the Gambia relied heavily on external assistance in the early days and, as soon as external sources dried up in the mid-1980s, activities within the curriculum centres came to a standstill. However, the curriculum center in Nigeria—originally the Nigerian Eductional Research Council (NERC) and later the Nigerian Educational Research and Development Council or (NERDC), has been able to continue to mobilize the human resources available within the country to develop curricula for primary, secondary, and teacher education. But NERDC has not been able to satisfy the thirst for educational material. The major reason is that books take too long to be published. Secondly, distribution has been a problem. Most of NERDC's publications tend to languish in warehouses and do not easily get to the teachers and learners for whom they are intended.[104]

Obanya stresses that in spite of the not-too-rosy achievement of the curriculum development centers in anglophone western Africa and their dilapidated state today, one should remember that their existence had, among others, these good results:

> Training as textbook writers and curriculum developers was given to a large number of nationals of the countries with curriculum centers.
>
> Educators were given the opportunity and encouragement to think carefully about overall national development goals and their curricular implications.
>
> The emergence of terminal school examinations based on the school curricula developed by the curriculum centers replaced the erstwhile practice of using examinations created overseas.

---

[104] Problems of textbook publishing in poor Sub-Saharan countries today are discussed in more detail in the previous chapter.

The so-called francophone countries in western Africa, according to Obanya (1995a), have not made such far-reaching attempts to institutionalize curriculum development in a systematic manner. Post-independence educational reforms led to the setting up of IPNs (Instituts Pedagogiques Nationaux) in most countries, the mandate of which included curriculum development within a general framework of "implementation of educational reforms." Even though regional seminars on systematic curriculum development were organized for these countries under the aegis of UNESCO in 1978 and 1982, no follow-up action in the form of institutionalization of curriculum development has taken off in francophone Africa. The only possible exception to this general pattern is Cote d'Ivoire, which established a Centre de Production de Materiels Didactiques in Bouake in the 1980s. Bouake is now well-known for the training it has provided over the years and has grown into a regional centre for the other francophone countries in western Africa. The books produced at the center, however, are published by an established French publishing house (Nouvelle Editions Africaine) and seem too costly for parents to buy.

Visiting some of the non-formal (*écoles non-formelles*) NAFA schools in Guinea in November 1996, I experienced that in the school in Yaraya only the teachers had any textbooks at all, and these were produced in France. In another NAFA school in Boffa, three of the pupils had some very worn-out French textbooks produced in and donated from France. Through a UNICEF project with Norwegian funding, teaching materials are now being produced for the NAFA schools in Guinea, written in Guinea and reflecting the culture of Guinea, but unfortunately, according to the field officer taking me around, they are written in French.[105]

I noticed in the regular primary schools I visited in Conakry, the capital of Guinea, that there were hardly any textbooks in those schools either. I was told that it was the duty of the parents to buy textbooks and they could not afford to do so. In Coleah primary school, there were six seventh-grade pupils who had textbooks, and groups were formed around these six pupils so that everybody could share the textbooks. I asked to have a look at the textbooks. They were all published by French

---

[105] I personally observed how much the French language as the language of instruction was a barrier to learning for the children of the NAFA schools. I shall return to this point in the following chapter.

publishing companies, mostly by EDICEF or *Les Classiques Africaine* in Versailles.

When reviewing the literature on curriculum reconstruction in post-colonial Africa which had been written in the English language between 1974 and 1989, Jonathan Jansen (1989: 221) concluded that "there appears to be a small, but increasingly significant deviation from the technological, Western-oriented trend in curriculum development" which seems to be based on "a widespread perception of the ir-relevance of Western models of curriculum development in an African setting."

Unfortunately, the perception does not now seem to be as wide-spread as he claimed in his article of 1989. As examples of alternative curriculum thinking, he mentioned the model referred to as *Education with Production* (EWP) of Botswana and Zimbabwe, and the ideology of *Education for Self-Reliance* (ESR) in Tanzania as outlined by Nyerere (1967).

EDUCATION WITH PRODUCTION REVISITED

In a later article, a more pessimistic Jansen (1993) documents and then tries to explain why Education with Production (EWP) became a margin-alized socialist curriculum reform within the national school system in Zimbabwe. As long as the state failed to transform the economy in line with socialist objectives, EWP could not work, he claims. Socialist cur-ricula have difficulties surviving in a capitalist economy. Jansen states: "EWP will thus remain marginal in the national school curriculum as long as the economic and social rewards for competitive, urban-based, high-tech jobs are significantly greater than for employment in the im-poverished rural areas" (Jansen, 1993: 64).

Jansen writes about the hesitancy of the Mugabe[106] government to make decisive political moves when faced with educational dilemmas. The policy of reconciliation with the powerful white "settlers" has

---

[106] In 1980 the white minority of Zimbabwe finally consented to hold multiracial elections supervised by the British, and Robert Mugabe of the Shona-based Zim-babwe African National Union (ZANU) won a landslide victory. Mugabe as-sumed the duties both of prime minister and defense minister.

clearly led to capitulation on several issues, particularly with regard to the role and funding of private schools and the degree to which social studies books are positive and explicit about socialism. He quotes the then Minister of Education and Culture, Fay Chung, who in an interview with him said: "We wanted to provide outlets for white parents" (Jansen, 1993: 64). He continues:

> While white parents remain such powerful economic stakeholders and actors in national politics, and with the increasing capitulation of the political authority to foreign capital in the form of the World Bank among others, the state in its present form has gradually and, I would argue, irreversibly reduced its options for any form of radical change in either education or other sectors of the society. (Jansen, 1993: 64)

Anders Närman (1992) also analyzes the EWP model in Zimbabwe, referred to by him as the ZIMFEP (Zimbabwe Foundation for Education with Production) schools. He found that "presently there seems to be a lack of understanding of the importance of informal schooling and the world of work" (Närman, 1992: 149). He tells how ZIMFEP built on the experiences from the long war of liberation, and quotes Fay Chung, who relates:

> Zimbabwean children studying in refugee camp schools in Mozambique and Zambia spent half the day on academic work and the other half on productive work. This system enabled the pupils to link learning directly to practice, and was particularly useful because pupils had to provide their own accommodation, furniture and fresh foods. (Chung, 1985: 106, quoted in Närman, 1992: 149)

In my trip to Guinea at the end of 1996, I saw, as mentioned in the previous chapter, how this idea of education with production was being used in the informal NAFA centers where children spent half their day in productive work learning vocational skills. The main reason why children attended these informal learning places was to learn some skills which could help them make a living. They worked together with skilled workers where the teaching method was learning by doing. They learned the tricks of the trade while they were working alongside experienced craftspeople.

EDUCATION FOR SELF-RELIANCE REVISITED

In March 1967,[107] President Nyerere[108] issued the first of his 'post-Arusha' policy directives, on education, called: *Education for Self-Reliance* (ESR) (Nyerere,1967). It analyzed the system and attitudes of education as they had evolved in Tanganyika,[109] and then went on to demand an educational revolution—a recasting of the educational system in the light of Tanzania's needs and social objectives.[110] After the policy directive *Education for Self-Reliance* was issued, a whole series of working parties—involving teachers and educational administrators—was set up to examine the means of implementing the new ideas. At the same time, many schools in the country, and particularly the secondary schools, began the work of opening farms, establishing workshops, and undertaking "nation-building tasks."

The educational system of an independent Tanzania should, according to Nyerere, be geared at building the new nation on *kujitegemea* (self-reliance) and *ujamaa*.[111] This included a primary school for all children in Tanzania, secondary and tertiary education for a few. Already in primary school, where the language of instruction would be Kiswahili, children should be taught useful activities that could help them make a living; they should also be responsible for cleaning the school and producing food. Since secondary and tertiary school would be free for the few students who would go on, but expensive for the state Nyerere urged these students to contribute toward their education by productive activi-

---

[107] Tanganyika attained political independence on 9. December 1961. Two months before this date, the newly elected National Assembly passed an *Ordinance to Make Provision for a Single System of Education in the Territory*. This ordinance ended the separate education system for different races (whites, Asians, Africans) that had been practised during colonial times (Sumra, 1996).
[108] After Tanganyika drafted a constitution that made it a republic, Julius Kambarade Nyerere, was elected its first president on 1. November 1962.
[109] Tanganyika is the name of the mainland—exclusive of the island of Zanzibar off the coast of Tanganyika. When Zanzibar and Tanganyika were united into one country in March 1964, the official name of the union became the "United Republic of Tanganyika and Zanzibar," abbreviated to Tanzania.
[110] Mention of this directive has already been made in Chapter 2 where the World Bank thinking on "academic standards" (meaning standards set in the West) is contrasted with Nyerere's writing about the necessity of African countries to design their own curricula and then design examinations—if they deem such to be appropriate at all—to fit these curricula. It is further referred to by the CCM—people I interviewed regarding the current educational situation of Tanzania.
[111] *Ujamaa* is a Kiswahili term meaning "togetherness" and denoting the type of socialism Nyerere wanted to promote, a socialism built on African roots.

ties, growing their own food in the vicinity of the school, helping in the construction of new school buildings.

He insisted that all secondary school leavers, who were so lucky as to be allowed to enter the university, have a two-year period of community service before they could enter. The students at the University of Dar es Salaam made a strike against this directive when it first came, which resulted in President Nyerere sending them all back home.

Throughout the 1980s Tanzania, very much under the pressure of the World Bank and the IMF, had to give up her original ideas of an African socialism and education for self-reliance. In August 1986 Tanzania signed an agreement with the IMF/World Bank which contained conditionalities pertaining to liberalization of the economy, decrease in public expenditures, and privatization. As Buchert (1997:35) notes:

> The major contrast in the context for education policy making in Tanzania during 1967–1990s is the move from emphasizing the formation of a socialist state and public responsibility in education to emphasizing the development of a market economy which blends public and private initiatives.

The acting director of Tanzania Institute of Education, Alois Mbunda (1997: 180), also tells how difficult it is to convince parents to send their children to school in a country "where the provision of education used to be free" and where cost-sharing schemes have now been introduced. About the "production activities which are popularly known in Tanzania as self-reliance activities," he claims that they still continue in Tanzania primary schools "though not at the pace which used to be" (p. 181). He mentions that the new subject in primary school, *stadi za kazi* (work skills), encompasses eighteen work skills, among them gardening, plumbing and weaving. But this subject is not one that donors support.

BUT WHAT IS HAPPENING TO THE EDUCATION SECTOR IN SUB-SAHARAN AFRICA IN THE WAKE OF JOMTIEN?

The concept of cultural conditionality seems useful in analyzing the renewed curriculum dependency which may be a likely outcome of the World Conference on Education for All in Jomtien (for further discussion, see Brock-Utne, 1995b). A cultural conditionality is a conditionality set up by the lender or donor which has direct implications for the content of schooling, for instance, insistence on the purchase of textbooks written and published abroad, use of examination systems devised in the West, adoption of "international" (read: Western) standards, and the neglect of African culture, including African languages. In the article I also raise the question whether there is such a thing as "educational aid for empowerment," mentioning a couple of examples of aid projects within the education sector in Africa which have been helpful, one assisting in creating mono-lingual dictionaries for some African languages. I ask whether the countries in Sub-Saharan Africa will experience a renewed curriculum dependency in the wake of Jomtien. Will cultural conditionality in the lending for education become more explicit in the next decade?

There are at least two trends: 1) a donor trend bringing with it cultural conditionality in connection with privatization, more donor influence and control, and 2) a trend denoting a return to the roots, a trend that is partly being put in place by the African people turning their backs to the Western schools,[112] a trend that is also being voiced by independent researchers from the South and the North. We shall now look at both of these trends.

DONOR INVOLVEMENT IN EDUCATION IN SUB-SAHARAN AFRICA FOLLOWING THE JOMTIEN CONFERENCE

As a result of her analysis of foreign aid patterns, Lene Buchert (1993) concluded that educational content is likely to be an area which will be strongly affected by increased donor coordination based on the goals and priorities of the "Education for All" strategy.[113] She sees a clear risk that

---

[112] The division is, however, not as simple as it may seem since there are also among the African elites those who favor privatization (especially for their own children) and the use of the former languages as languages of instruction, while among donors—especially the German DSE (Deutsche Stiftung für internationale Entwicklung/German Foundation for International Development) and GTZ there are those who are culturally sensitive and want to support governments that want to build on African roots and use African languages as languages of instruction (see e.g., the recently published *Cross-Border Languages* edited by Karsten Legere (1998).

[113] Her analysis further showed that educational projects in the South in most cases have been designed and are now increasingly coordinated by donor agencies in the North, not by national governments in developing countries and certainly not by their local populations. Projects are tied to deliveries of equipment and key personnel from the donor country and, generally, only to a minor extent to the full utilization of local expertise and supplies.

donor-coordinated educational programs will be designed and implemented across the differences in individual recipient countries and in disregard of the education sector's considerations within the individual country. She finds that the Jomtien emphasis on cost, efficiency, and effectiveness is likely to re-emphasize a Euro-American curriculum rather than a locally adapted curriculum based on indigenous knowledge systems, socialization methods, and locally identified needs for specific skills, thereby impeding locally designed innovative experiments in recipient countries. When studying the interesting proceedings of the first sub-regional conference on curriculum development in southern Africa (Avenstrup (ed), 1997a), I could not help notice that although most of the curriculum developers from the ten countries in southern Africa present at the conference stressed the need for curricula that were more African in style and content, in most of the countries the same curriculum innovations had been introduced by the same donors.[114] We may mention here the concern of the African Association for Literacy and Adult Education (AALAE) expressed at their follow-up meeting after the Jomtien conference:

> there is a need to articulate and elaborate practical alternative strategies to develop policies and carry out educational programmes based on the basic needs of the African peoples and to identify and propose the areas and strategies through which we can act at the regional, sub-regional, national, and local levels to achieve our ideal of basic education for empowerment and self-reliance. (AALAE, 1990: 4)

In a discussion of the likely outcomes of the donor policies building on the EFA conference, Angela Little asks:

> "Will he who lends or gives financial resources insist also on lending the educational ideas and practices? Will *cultural conditionality* which is already implicit in much lending for education become more explicit in the next decade in the same way as economic and political conditionality have become explicit in the eighties and early nineties? If so to what extent will this prejudice the development of the local cultures which learners bring to the classroom? (Little, 1992: 20—emphasis added)

[114] These included environmental education, AIDs control education, family life (population) education, education for democracy (or citizenship education), gender sensitization and women empowerment, and a strengthening of the colonial languages English and French.

I am afraid that the cultural conditionality Angela Little describes will work against the indigenization of the curricula in African schools. A good example of donor involvement is given by Mbunda (1997:183). He tells how:

> Nearly all curriculum integration projects based at the Ministry of Education and Culture headquarters or TIE (Tanzania Institute of Education) are run by donor funds, without which they will stop. At TIE, for example, there is the Family Life Education Project funded by UNFPA; the Environmental Education Project funded by GTZ; AIDS Control Education funded by WHO. The donor pressure on what should be included in the content is tremendous.

He tells how the donors through their aid have an enormous influence on the curriculum, especially in those subjects and themes which they are interested in. Donors have exerted great pressure to have the themes they are interested in become full-fledged subjects in primary school. Mbunda tells how the government has tried to counteract this pressure and instead agreed to have the themes the donors wanted included in the new integrated subjects both at primary and secondary levels. But the donor pressure continues:

> So far the most affected subjects include the English and French languages, Unified Science (certain themes), Social Studies (certain themes), and primary teacher education. The projects were introduced with conditions laid down by both the donor and the implementing agency. Threats of withdrawing funds or other action to be taken by the donor where the implementing agency fails to honour the laid-down conditions are common. (Mbunda, 1997: 184)

The donors support what they deem important. It may often not coincide with the wishes of the recipient. In Swaziland I saw how the government, which received funding for one education project from USAID, obsessed with learning assessment and using American consultants, quickly tried to redefine the same project to have to do with basic education targeting the girl child to secure funding from Norway.

THE TESTING BUSINESS

The greatest threat to the adoption of locally adapted curricula based on indigenous knowledge systems is the reintroduction of exams created in the

West, often by the Cambridge Examination Syndicate for anglophone Africa. As all educators know, exams decide the curricula. What is measured in the tests that count for further advancement in the system is what the pupils will try to learn no matter what the teacher tries to teach them. Imported textbooks could be used creatively by a teacher also to emphasize an indigenous curriculum were the examinations locally made. Imported examinations will make any indigenous curricular work impossible.

The Finnish researcher Tuomas Takala (1995), who has conducted a consultancy assignment on the texbook provision in Zambia, Mozambique, and Namibia, mentions that at secondary level importation of textbooks from abroad is significant in these countries. About their influence he remarks:

> In policy discussions, the external influence ensuing from the use of foreign books has sometimes been criticized, but it is largely a consequence of giving preference to metropolitan secondary level examinations, or adopted versions of them, over locally designed examinations. (Takala, 1995: 164)

I noted earlier that Obanya saw it as one of the great achievements of curricular work in the anglophone countries of western Africa in the years after independence that terminal school examinations were based on the school curricula worked out locally by the curriculum centers in Africa. The renewed donor stress on "academic standards,"[115] according

---

[115]As noted in Chapter 2 when the World Bank (1988a) argues that academic standards in African countries are low, it does so by referring to low test-scores earned by African pupils and students on tests developed in the West, for instance, by the IEA (International Association for the Evaluation of Educational Achievement). I noted that these tests stem from a Western culture and entail Western concepts and also that most African students, who are required to take them, often have to do this in their second, or even in their third, language, while most students in the industrialized countries answer them in their mother tongue. I noted also that results on IEA tests in reading comprehension, general science, and mathematics, administered to some African countries and referred to by the World Bank in its 1988 *EPSSA* paper, led the World Bank to draw the conclusion that "the quality of education in Sub-Saharan Africa is well below world standards." (World Bank, 1988a: 40). I further noted that African educational researchers are extremely skeptical of assessing African students against batteries of tests that have been used transnationally by bodies such as the IEA, which they see as coming "out of very specific cultural milieux in northern industrialized countries" (Ishumi, 1985: 13).

to Angela Little (1992), may well mean Western standards and Western tests.[116]

The Donors to African Education[117] in 1989 created a Working Group on School Examinations (WGSE) led by the Irish development agency HEDCO to "help coordinate and collaborate on the development of national examination systems as a mechanism for improving primary and secondary education in Sub-Saharan Africa" (Lynch, 1994: 10). The WGSE has built a program of country-specific, five-year, costed action plans for the improvement of examination systems in fourteen Sub-Saharan countries. Its intention has also been to "draw attention to the role examinations can play in improving primary and secondary educa-

---

[116]The Danish researcher Joan Conrad has studied the effects of a basic education program which was put in place in Nepal as a consequence of the donor commitment to basic education following the Jomtien conference. She admits that donor agencies from the North may have the best intentions when they embark on a project like the Basic and Primary Education Program (BPEP), which was initiated in Nepal in 1992. They feel committed "to improve the quality of teaching and to meet basic educational needs in Nepal" (Conrad, 1994: 1). But the expression "the quality of teaching" is loaded with ideological content. Main components of the project include curriculum development and textbook production as well as improvement of the general examination system. Specific efforts will be directed toward developing an effective grade 5 examination, based on predetermined criteria.

The BPEP represents a model program generally regarded as being universally valid in relation to improving educational quality in developing countries with no regard to the characteristic cultural conditions of any specific country. Conrad, who is highly critical to the functioning of the BPEP in Nepal, laments: "The very similarity of such programs is alarming" (Conrad, 1994: 20).

[117]An organized group of donors from bilateral and multilateral aid agencies that meets regulary. The Donors to African Education (DAE) has its secretariat in the World Bank in Washington D.C. The quarterly newsletter is now published at IIEP (International Institute for Educational Planning) in Paris. The group also invites the African ministers of education to their meetings and in 1997 changed its name to ADEA (Association for the Development of Education in Africa). Under the leadership of Ingemar Gustafsson from SIDA and now Sissel Volan from NORAD, the group has become gradually more dominated by the African ministers of education. Their representation has been strengthened and there is a debate going on about moving the Secretariat to Africa. Kenneth King (1997: 1), however, argues that the proliferation of ever more working groups linked to ADEA "underlines a continuing preoccupation of donors with the coordination of policies in each of now, no less than 13 different education subsectors or thematic areas." He relates that during 1997 two new working groups were developed within the framework of ADEA, one in the area of early childhood development (with UNICEF as lead donor) and the other in distance learning.

tion" (Lynch, 1994: 10). The WGSE finds that it has met its objectives but concludes: "there still is, and will continue to be, a need for assistance to the African examination systems through advice, technical assistance and training" (p.10).

The technical assistance sought will most likely come from the North, from one of the "donor" countries, even though, as Pai Obanya claims, there exists a corps of capable curriculum and testing workers in Africa. The person(s) from a donor country who could be able to assist an African country in making school-tests would have to know the culture of the country, preferably speak one or more of the African languages spoken in the region, know the educational ideology of the state in question, be familiar with the curriculum they have been (or are in the process of) creating, and be aware of the hopes of parents and children for the future.[118]

Angela Little (1992) has analyzed the tensions between external standards and internal cultures. Cultural definitions of necessary levels of learning achievement vary; so, too, do strategies for assessing them. She detects an increasing trend toward the internationalization of educational assessment targets and practices and asks:

> If "international standards" which in many instances [in the African context] means "external standards" produced in the West begin to take precedence over national and sub-national standards what are the implications for nationally and culturally prescribed curricula?
>
> Will an internationalised education assessment technology begin to drive an internationalised curriculum reform? How much wider will become the gap between the culture of those who control education and who design "international" tests and curricula (i.e., the "supranational educators") and the culture of the child whose learning is the goal? (Little, 1992: 20)

But the fact that exams have such a great influence on the curriculum also provides an opportunity for conscious educationists working in the Ministries of Education to monitor and analyze exams and use the analysis for construction of different exams that will pay more attention to an

---

[118]As the Danish educational researcher Spæt Henriksen also realizes when describing a curriculum project the Danes are involved in, in a different part of the world, in Lithuania: "It should not be possible to embark on a project which defines itself as 'help to self-helping' without trying to understand as much as possible of the culture of the country, its history, and the structure and content of its education" (Henriksen, 1993: 71, my translation).

indigenous curriculum. In this way an indigenization of the curriculum can take place. We shall look at a good example of monitoring exams, taken from Namibia.

MONITORING OF EXAMS: A POSITIVE EXAMPLE

Attempts are being made in a recently independent country like Namibia to monitor the countrywide examinations as to their cultural bias and gender bias (MEC/NIED, 1994). This monitoring of exams is quite impressive and can serve as an example to other African countries.

The monitoring of the junior secondary certificate examination in 1993 showed, for instance, that the examination in the home science subject had a clear cultural bias toward urban living and European food. All the illustrations were of Europeans or European home environments; all the recipes were of European food. There was nothing in the examination paper indicating that it was from Africa or Namibia. When it came to the examination paper in art, it was found that only 16% of the marks could be earned on anything to do with Namibia; 84% of the marks were devoted to European art history. The monitoring paper concludes:

> With only a token [attention] to Namibian or African art, this examination continues the cultural disinheritance of Namibia, strongly criticised in Ministry documents, and counter to Ministry policy. The examination paper as a whole is also devoid of gender awareness. (MEC/NIED, 1994: 9)

Likewise, the examination paper in music is said to have a dreadful cultural bias. Of 100 marks, 74 could be gained on specifically European music, 10 on specifically African music and 16 on more or less culturally neutral music theory. Only male composers were referred to.

The history paper was, however, praised for promoting awareness of Namibian and African history.[119] The monitoring of exams in Namibia

---

[119] However, the history examination paper was criticized for making women and their contribution to history invisible. When it came to the examination paper in accounting, it drew on a variety of cultural settings but nearly all persons mentioned were male.

goes on and a small improvement in the examination papers set in the year 1995 has been detected (Avenstrup, 1995).

AFRICAN LEARNING SYSTEMS REVISITED: A CHANCE FOR EMPOWERMENT?

In spite of the economic problems Africa is facing, interest in studying indigenous education in Africa is emerging (Lawuo, 1978; Muyanda-Mutebi and Matovu, 1993; Namuddu, 1991; Nglube, 1989; Ocitti, 1973; Ocitti, 1990; Ocitti, 1991; Odora, 1992, 1993, 1994; Ki-Zerbo, 1990). For instance, Catherine Odora (1994) discusses the need for creating a space in contemporary education discourse that is more tolerant, more sensitive to realities *other than* the overwhelming Western one. She finds that discussing indigenous education today compels us to come to terms with the situation in which even the social construction of a people's reality is and has been constantly defined elsewhere. Discussing indigenous education, according to Odora, "is about asking why the school building is always quadrangled even where the local setting around it has round huts" (Odora, 1994: 62).

In the beginning of this chapter we referred to Ki-Zerbo, who described the injustice done to Africa by not rooting its education in African culture. It is easy to agree with him when he describes this injustice and also the disintegrating effects on African societies of the imported school curricula and imported languages of instruction, the "foreign cyst in the social body" (Ki-Zerbo, 1990: 12). His explanation for this sad state of affairs is, however, too simplistic. The colonialists may have designed an education system for Africa "to serve the overall aim of the subjugation of the continent to European needs" (Ki-Zerbo, 1990: 12). But the questions must be asked: Why have the foreign designed curricula continued after independence? And why has this continuation partly been applauded by well-known Africans (Fafunwa, 1990)? The role of the African elite, the *wazungo waeusi* (black Europeans), the "coconuts" or "bounties"[120] (as they are called in South Africa) also has to be taken into account. They have gone through such a long period of

---

[120] This name refers to the chocolate bar called "Bounty," which has brown chocolate on the outside (brown skin) but white coconut (white thoughts) on the inside.

schooling, much of it in the West, that they not only have become foreign to their own culture but also look down upon it.[121]

Clifford Fyle, a linguist, former head of the Department of Education at the University of Sierra Leone and now working at the UNESCO office in Senegal, sums up his chapter in the publication *Educational Research for Development in Africa* in these words: "In general it is best for Africa to look to herself for the development of her own curricula and teaching methods" (Fyle, 1993: 31) He claims that the best way by which Africa may look to herself is by an examination of the methods and techniques of traditional African education, for example, an examination of traditional practices for bringing up the young, for learning through play, for initiation into manhood or womanhood, for skills teaching, or for lifelong education. He assumes that such an examination may reveal practices that can be adopted directly or with little adaptation for use as part of African teaching methodology. Fyle comments:

---

[121] In their book *Education in the Far North*, Frank Darnell and Anton Hoem (1996) show that Norway, a country which most people do not see as an imperialist power, has treated their indigenous population in the Far North, the Saami people, much in the same way as Native Americans have been treated by settlers in the United States and Africans by the colonial powers. They quote Asta Balto, the director of the Saami Education Council, who did not learn to read and write her native Saami until age 30. She tells that from the 1870s until the last World War, the authorities tried to "Norwegianize" the Saami people in a very harsh way, and the Saami language was absolutely forbidden at school. In her own words:

> "The hundred years of convincing the Saami people that their language and culture were worthless have been effective. Many of the Saami parents are still believing that being Saami and speaking the Saami language is identical with defeat, poverty and contempt" (Balto, 1990, quoted in Darnell and Hoëm, 1996: 188).

When I read this I was reminded of an incident which happened around 1970 in Kautokeino, where the Saami people live. There was a seminar on education in that area which I attended. About half of the participants were of Saami origin. In the Saami culture there is a beautiful way of chanting "*joik*" that is being used for all sorts of festivities. *Joiks* have been created to celebrate various people and events. When the missionaries came to this part of the country they taught the Saami people that *joiks* were made by the devil and had to be abolished. When one of us Norwegians suggested that the *joiks* should be revived and introduced into the curriculum of the school, we were told by some of the Saami people that that could never be done because those songs were the song of the devil! The colonization of the mind had really taken place.

One may perhaps mention the great emphasis on education through practice generally evident in traditional African societies, and which is in line with current demands for linking education with productive work. Other examples may be of intellectual development through tales, riddles, and proverbs as in Zaire, and even the string games and tricks of Sierra Leone children which could be of much value in mathematics, science, and craft teaching. The point of emphasis here is that traditional methods and techniques have not yet received the research attention they duly deserve. (Fyle, 1993: 31).

There is a need not only to record this education as part of research studies and historical records but also to consider how it can be used to reconstruct a curriculum of and for Africa.

In my teaching of social psychology at the University of Dar es Salaam I explained to my students that they were in a much better position than I to understand the social psychology of Africa. I could help them with organizing their material and discuss it with them, but they were the ones who could understand their people and tap their learnings. The students went into their villages and made studies. They claimed that their studies of indigenous education were empowering, showing them how much value there is in the teachings of the village people, who were stamped by many as "uneducated" because many were illiterate. The students studied informal learnings around the fireplace, storytelling, joking relationships, and riddling activity.

J.M.R. Ishengoma (1988), himself a Mhaya,[122] wrote an interesting term paper titled: *Riddles as an Agent of Socialization and Social Learning among the Haya Children*. Having collected a vast amount of riddles still in use in Bukoba, Ishengoma analyzed the riddles as to their educational value. He found that they could be meaningfully divided into the following categories:

- Riddles that instruct children to compare, contrast and distinguish objects
- Riddles that promote mastery of Luhaya and proper communication skills

[122] The Haya tribe, or the Wahaya (Mhaya in singular) in Kiswahili (Bahaya in their language), live in the Bukoba region of Tanzania. They speak Kihaya (called in their language Luhaya). The region was colonized early and had a lot of Christian missionary schools. Many of the highly schooled Tanzanians belong to the Wahaya people.

- Riddles that teach cultural norms
- Riddles that are instructive about work, agriculture, and animal husbandry
- New riddles

He also found a category of riddles referring to sex organs. These riddles are, according to Ishengoma (1988), only asked in the company of friends or same-sex peers. Through his many examples he demonstrates what a useful tool riddles must have been, and partly still are, in the education of the young. He argues against Western social anthropologists such as Finnegan (1970), who looked at riddles as a form of entertainment and amusement for children. Ishengoma tells that Bahaya children, both boys and girls, are normally told riddles by their mothers or grandmothers.[123]

Ishengoma (1988) found in his study that children coming from families where riddling was still a normal practice had a better developed vocabulary in Luhaya (Kihaya) and were more sensitized to the cultural norms of the Bahaya than children in families where the art of riddling had been ignored or abandoned, for example, in devout Christian families. He claims that in many Christian families the practice of riddling is looked at as heathen.

There is a great need for studies of this kind, both the recording of educational practice like riddling activity still going on and a reanalysis of the history of indigenous education in Africa. Works by Western missionaries, travelers, or social anthropologists can be used with caution; they are often biased and need to be reinterpreted. For instance, the European travelers whose reports are summarized by Theal (1910) have, according to Ocitti (1991), a tendency of viewing indigenous African

---

[123] Lugoe (1989), however, relates that among the Wajita in Mara region in Tanzania, the riddling activity ceases to be an activity where all children participate from the child's fifth year. After the child is five, boys and girls form different riddling groups. The Jita boy is taught his role at the evening assembly commonly called *echoto* (in Kijita). Each home prepares a cow dung fire whereby the males, both elders and youth, gather while the females are busy preparing the evening meal. At this gathering, stories, riddles and narrations of events of interest to the growth of the boys are related. Most of the teachings are done by the grandfathers, as it is assumed that they have an accumulation of knowledge about the tribe. Also the grandfathers can say anything without hesitation or shyness.

education, especially of the Xhosa, as a phenomenon which was confined to the puberty years and achieved mainly through the rites of circumcision. Ocitti mentions that one finds a lot of parochialism and prejudice toward Africans and their traditional systems of education in some of the writers from outside Africa. All this information seems to have been gathered more out of curiosity than out of any intention of using it as a point of departure for the construction of school curricula.

INTEGRATING EDUCATION INTO AFRICAN COMMUNITY LIFE

An interesting educational program, known as the Village School Program, has been put in place for the Bushmen children in the Nyae Nyae area in the northeastern part of Otjozondjupa region in Namibia. When parents in that area go hunting, the children have to go with them. The philosophy of the Village School Program is that the teachers should also go with the hunters. The school should not divide children from parents. The older people are integrated in these village schools, too. Religion is not taught in these schools since the learners receive their own religion instruction from home.

The educational program is geared to the culture of the learner. The Bushmen children are known not to attend school, but they attend the Village School Program of the Nyae Nyae Foundation. The reason for this may be the cultural sensitivity of the program. Part of the reason why the Bushmen have not wanted their children to attend school is that schools have practiced corporal punishment (such punishment has now been outlawed in Namibian schools). Corporal punishment is a practice which goes completely against the Bushman culture. In the Village School Programme such punishment has never been practiced. When the learners get fidgety or bored, the lessons are simply stopped. They then do something else or stop completely for the day.

According to personal communication from the Nyae Nyae Foundation, the 220 children in the Village School Program are far ahead of other learners because they learn in their mother tongue and are exposed to culturally sensitive teaching material and teachers whom everyone respects (Brock-Utne, 1995d). The production of teaching material is done within the program and great emphasis is placed on local curriculum development. The 220 school-children get food through the World Feeding

Programme and are supplied with donkeys and donkey-carts as means of transportation.[124]

In the fall of 1976 I made some visits to teacher training colleges in Kenya. I remember two of these colleges especially well because the difference between them was so striking. The first one was Kenya Science Teacher Training College in Nairobi. This college was housed in nice, modern buildings—a gift from Sweden and furnished with a lot of advanced equipment. The language of instruction was English. I followed some lessons in curriculum theory and in educational psychology. The text-books were the same ones I had used when I took my master's degree in education at the University of Illinois ten years earlier. I would have had no trouble giving the same type of lectures as I heard. And I was in fact asked to apply for a vacant lectureship at that College. I was wondering as I sat listening to the theories of Bloom, Taba, and Cronbach how relevant they were for Kenyan school teachers and their pupils. I remembered how we in Norway had revolted against the very same theories because we felt that they were irrelevant for Norwegian pupils and that we had to build our own curriculum theory based on Norwegian experiences and in the Norwegian language. The theories would seem to be even less relevant here, but nobody seemed to question them.

The other teacher's college was situated a couple of hours' drive from Nairobi. The lecture halls there had only straw roofs to protect against the sun. The teaching was in Kiswahili, a language I had not yet mastered. In the music lessons the students used traditional instruments which they had built themselves and were proud of the music they played, which was based on local music and also inspired by Western music. The head of the college, who was a woman, proudly showed me around. She showed me the garden where the students both grew food for their own consumption and were taught how to teach villagers about the drying of cow dung for fuel. She showed me lessons in curriculum work where students were taught how to make lesson plans according to the interest of their learners. They were taught how to plan for educa-

[124]On my trip to the Kalahari desert in Botswana in the beginning of September 1997 (Brock-Utne, 1997c) I met another group of children of the San people, the Basarwa, and thought how much better it would have been for them to have had the teaching the Nyae Nyae Foundation of Namibia provided. The Basarwa children were living in hostels near a school far away from their parents and were taught through languages they did not understand. The food they received was of very low quality nutritionally.

tional experiences for their pupils. She, of course, did not ask me to come and teach at the college. How could I? I did not know the language, nor the culture. But there was a lot for me to learn here.

She could have come to Norway to teach us about ways to integrate education with culture. She taught the student teachers how to make instructional tools from readily available material. She tried to promote a child-centred, discovery-based method of learning. But she was also aware of the fact that rote-learning, much down-graded by Western educationists, may play a greater role in a culture where there are few books and little reference material. She agreed with her countryman, Eshiwani, criticizing educational ideas promoted and exported whole-heartedly from the United States or Europe into Africa:

> What was not realized by the educators then was that rote learning may be ineffective in a society where information is freely available for reference and where good memory does not play an indispensable role in daily life; however in a society where memory is highly developed, where much history and tradition is transmitted orally, and where sources of reference are not immediately available, rote learning may well have a more important part to play in a child's school education (Eshiwani, 1993: 157).

The head of the locally oriented teacher's college was proud of her school. Her aim was to base the teaching and learning firmly in the local culture and economy.

CHAPTER 5

Education for All—
In Whose Language?

It has always been felt by African educationists
that the African child's major learning problem is
linguistic. Instruction is given in a language that
is not normally used in his immediate environ-
ment, a language which neither the learner nor
the teacher understands and uses well enough.

(OBANYA, 1980: 88)

If the African child's major learning problem is linguistic, and I tend to agree with Obanya that it is, then all the attention of African policy-makers and aid from Western donors should be devoted to strengthening the African languages as languages of instruction, especially in basic education. The concept "education for all" becomes a completely empty concept if the linguistic environment of the basic learners is not taken into account.

Yet there is hardly another socio-cultural topic you can discuss with Africans that leads to such heated debates and stirs up so many emotions as the language of instruction in African schools. It is difficult to discuss this topic as strictly educational questions such as: Through which medium of instruction would children learn subject matter best? If the aim is to master a "world" language, would it be better to have that language as a language of instruction at the earliest time possible or first to further develop the vernacular or a commonly spoken national language? or; What does it mean for the development of self-respect and identity that the language one normally communicates in does not seem to be deemed fit for a language of instruction in school?

When it comes to the choice of language of instruction in African schools, socio-cultural politics, sociolinguistics, and education are so closely interrelated that it is difficult to sort out the arguments. Yet that is what we shall attempt to do in this chapter and the next. Following an account of the language situation in Africa in colonial times and after independence, we shall look at the socio-cultural, educational, and political issues involved. We will examine the role of donors and the educational development researchers from the West who guide them, as well as the role of the African elites. These roles will be illustrated further in Chapter 6 which will look in some detail into the language policies of Tanzania and Namibia. Toward the end of this chapter we shall take a look at some recent trends in countries like Madagascar, Guinea, Niger, Uganda, and Swaziland.

THE LANGUAGE SITUATION IN AFRICA

There has been some dispute as to the number of languages spoken in Africa today.[125] While David Westley (1992) claims that at least 1,400 languages are spoken in fifty-one countries in Africa (Westley, 1992), Barbarba Grimes (1992) puts the number of languages in Africa at 1,995.[126] Even in the Gambia, Africa's smallest country, seven distinct languages are spoken. Aside from the diversity of languages on the whole, the colonial presence created havoc when it, at the Berlin Conference of 1884, carved up the African continent according to its own whims. Thus, Hausa, Africa's second most spoken language, was bifurcated when the English and the French set up a colonial border between Nigeria and Niger.

THE LANGUAGE SITUATION IN PRE-COLONIAL TIMES

Zaline Roy-Campbell (1998), drawing on the works of Cheik Anta Diop (1974, 1991), who has written extensively on the African past, points to the achievements of Africans during the age of antiquity in mathematics, architecture, chemistry, astronomy, and medicine, all areas which required technical vocabulary and conceptual frameworks. This intellectual work was done through the use of African languages. Walter Rodney

---

[125] Roy-Campbell (1998) describes how missionaries' faulty transcriptions, some arising from inaccurate associations, occurred across the African continent, resulting in the creation of a multitude of dialects of the same language and different languages from what was one language. The difficulty of putting a definite figure to the number of African languages on the continent can be attributed to this process, as contention has arisen over whether certain language forms are indeed languages or dialects.

[126] A number of bibliographies have been published on the topic of *education and language in Africa*. Stafford Kaye and Bradley Nystrom (1971) have covered the colonial period in their extensive bibliography , while *Sprachpolitik und Sprachplanung in Africa* by Metchild Reh and Bernd Heine (1982) contains a vast bibliography with especially good coverage of the period from independence to 1980. David Westley (1992) has prepared an updated bibliography on the period 1980–1990.

(1976) has described the process by which Europe underdeveloped Africa, technologically and scientifically deskilling Africans. The accounts both of Cheik Anta Diop and Walter Rodney are a testament to the vast capabilities of African peoples realized through the indigenous African languages.

One of the oldest forms of written language in the world—Ge'ez—was found in Africa, in the area currently known as Ethiopia. It is still used as a liturgical language in Ethiopia. But European mythology about Africa, which came to be accepted as the early history of Africa, did not recognize the achievements of African societies in pre-colonial times. From the perspective of these Europeans, the activities worth recording began with their contact with this "dark continent." Africa was presented as comprising peoples speaking a multitude of tongues which did not have written forms. Roy-Campbell (1998) points to written African languages dating to 3,000 B.C. that are still used today.

The absence of a written tradition for many African languages, at least one which the missionaries could access (they would, for instance, transliterate existing orthographies into the Latin script) provided the opportunities for European missionaries to construct African languages according to their own specifications. For example in the case of Shona in Zimbabwe, five dialects were created by different groups of missionaries working in isolation from each other to render the language they heard into a written form. As will be illustrated in the next chapter, missionaries actually created several different languages out of the same language.

THE COLONIAL LANGUAGE POLICY OF THE BRITISH AND THE FRENCH IN PREINDEPENDENCE AFRICA

In Berlin in 1884, the European powers divided the continent of Africa into regions/territories that each would control and in which a particular European language would be associated. African countries, as colonies and even today as so-called "independent" countries, came to be defined and to define themselves in terms of the languages of Europe: anglophone, francophone, or lusophone[127] Africa.

---

[127] Lusophone means Portuguese-speaking. As noted in Chapter 1 the first formal attempts at European schooling in Africa were made by Portugese missionaries. The Portuguese, it seems, went further than any other colonial power in Africa in causing educated Africans to give up their mother tongue and substitute it with Portuguese. I have met several black academics from, for example Mozambique, who claim that their first language is Portuguese, their second English, and who can barely understand an African language.

There was a clear difference in the language policies pursued by the British and the French in their African colonies. White (1996) claims that the main feature characterizing French colonial education was the widespread use of the French language. Though France would permit the short-term use of African languages in order to meet "immediate" pedagogical needs such as health education and morality, all instruction had the mastery of the French language as its ultimate goal. Bakar (1988), of the Comoro Islands says of his school-days: "Since we were considered as French 'a part-entière', nothing but French was taught. The whole curriculum was based on France and anything that was French, whereas Comorian, our mother tongue, was never considered to be a suitable medium of instruction" (Bakar, 1988: 184).

White (1996: 14) writes that the French view on African intelligence enabled them to justify this policy. He quotes Albert Charton, inspector general of French West Africa, who attributed "the technical inferiority" of Africans to "their ignorance of the language." He further quotes Brevie, governor general of French West Africa, who in 1930 wrote that "the native's mind can become disciplined by the mastering of spoken French," implying that learning the French language is itself *the* education.

As noted in Chapter 1, the British government was from the start much less involved than the French in the educational policy of its African colonies. Missionary education played a prominent role in the history of the British African colonies, and the missionaries saw the value of the use of vernacular languages. White (1996: 19) cities a statement of the colonial office of 1953: "To preserve the vernacular languages of Africa is to preserve the tribes that speak them." The sons of the chiefs and kings Britain used for its "indirect rule" were trained in English to serve as middle-men between the Africans and the colonial administration. Other Africans in anglophone Africa had some few years of schooling. This education typically involved teaching students to read an indigenous language before they were introduced to English. When the mission schools were taken over by the British government, however, they too introduced English at an earlier stage and relegated the vernacular languages to an inferior position.

The Kenyan author Ngugi wa Thiong'o (1986) writes that language supplemented the sword and the bullet of the colonizers as the means of European subjugation of Africa: "But the night of the sword and the bullet was followed by the morning of the chalk and the blackboard. . . . The bullet was the means of physical subjugation. Language was the means of spiritual subjugation" (Thiong'o, 1986: 9). He then goes on to tell movingly about his own school experience. His mother tongue, Gikuyu, was the language of all the evening teach-ins around the fireplace when he was young, and the language used with friends and in the fields where he worked. In his first school years he went to a school run by nationalists grouped around the Kikuyu[128] Independent and Karinga Schools Association. The language of instruction in this school was Gikuyu, so for the first four years of his schooling there was harmony between the language of his formal education and the language he spoke at home, in the fields, and with his friends. He tells that after the state of emergency in Kenya in 1952, all the schools run by patriotic nationalists were taken over by the colonial regime and placed under District Education Boards chaired by Englishmen, and English was made the language of instruction.

Thiong'o recalls that in Kenya English became more than a language, it was *the* language, and all the other languages had to bow to it in deference. He tells how one of the most humiliating experiences was to be caught speaking Gikuyu in the vicinity of the school. The culprit was given corporal punishment—three to five strokes of the cane on bare buttocks—or was made to carry a metal plate around the neck with inscriptions such as *I AM STUPID* or *I AM A DONKEY*. Sometimes the culprits were fined money they could hardly afford. And how did the teachers catch the culprits? Thiong'o tells how a button was initially given to one pupil who was supposed to hand it over to whomever was caught speaking his mother tongue. Whoever had the button at the end of the day had to come forward and tell whom he had got it from, and the ensuing process would bring out all the "culprits" of the day. Thus, children were turned into witch-hunters and traitors to their own linguistic community.

But just as there are now donors as well as African politicians and academics who support the use of indigenous African languages as languages of instruction and those who do not, there were also in colonial times colonialists who favored policies introducing indigenous languages as languages of instruction and Africans who opposed such policies.

AFRICAN RESISTANCE TOWARD USING AFRICAN LANGUAGES AS LANGUAGES OF INSTRUCTION

One group that during the colonial times had full appreciation for the value of using the indigenous languages as languages of instruction was the Education Commission for Africa, set up by the Phelps-Stokes Fund. The commission delivered its report in 1922 (Jones, 1924).

---

[128]*Kikuyu* is the name of one of the largest tribes in Kenya. *Gikuyu* is the vernacular of the *Kikuyu* and their God.

The fund was a philanthropic American organization which had helped establish a segregated educational system for black Americans and had subsequently been requested by the British to organize a similar system for their colonies. Its 1922 Report (published as Jones, 1924) makes a strong argument for the use of African languages as instructional languages in school. In fact Sanou claims that: "The Phelps-Stokes Fund Report of 1922 advocates the use of African languages in schools in terms whose fervour would put today's African nationalists to shame" (Sanou, 1990: 85).

Some passages from this more than seventy year-old report are worth reading:

> With full appreciation of the European language, the value of the Native tongue is immensely more vital, in that it is one of the chief means of preserving whatever is good in Native customs, ideas and ideals, and thereby preserving what is more important than all else, namely, Native self-respect. All peoples have an inherent right to their own language . . . No greater injustice can be committed against a people than to deprive them of their own language.
>
> The use of a European language has been advocated from mixed motives by both Europeans and Natives. In the past, practically all controlling nations forced their languages on the Native people and discouraged the use of their Native tongue . . . Fortunately at the present time the only Powers that still maintain this attitude in some of their possessions are the French and the Portuguese. Whatever the motives . . . , the policy is unwise and unjust. *The disregard of the Native language is a hindrance even to the acquisition of the European language* (Jones, 1924: 19), (emphasis added).

Why did these language policies fail? Sanou gives the answer that it was the African resistance against them. The Africans felt, and Sanou thinks rightly so, that most of the colonial language policies suggesting that Africans use their vernaculars in school were inspired by racial prejudices regarding the supposedly intellectual inferiority of Africans, a factor making them incapable of benefiting from a Western education. The Africans suspected that the language policies were designed to keep them in their social ghettos in the same way black Americans had been disadvantaged by their education in separate institutions which were inferior to the ones the white children attended. They therefore rejected systems supposedly tailored to their needs and demanded to be educated to exactly the same standards as whites were. In particular, they insisted on the use of European languages as instructional media.

Berman (1975) cites the fierce Kikuyu reactions to the educational policies of missionaries in colonial Kenya. These policies called for the teaching of various local languages in the early primary years, with English introduced later, in gradual stages. The Kikuyu boycotted the missonary schools, and in 1931 they founded the Kikuyu Independent School Association (KISA). One of KISA's rules was that "English should be the instructional language at all levels" (Berman, 1975: 39). The reason behind the insistence on English as the language of instruction seems to have been that in the struggle against the injustice of British colonial policy the Africans felt a necessity to compete with the colonialists on their own turf. They unrightly believed that they would have a more proficient command of English if they used that language as the language of instruction. These emotional learning experiences may explain the fact that today one may find African parents who want their children educated in one of the languages of the former colonial powers.

AFTER INDEPENDENCE

At the time of independence, around 1960, African countries were faced with the prospect of choosing a language. The debate about educational language centered around whether a foreign language (the former colonial language) or one or more indigenous languages should serve as the medium of instruction in schools (Coombs, 1985; Wardaugh, 1987; Roy-Campbell, 1992a). The reasons given for adopting the language of the former colonizer would often be that with the multiplicity of local languages, choosing one or two of them as national languages might create conflicts which could eventually lead to civil wars.[129] Many African

[129]At a one-day research seminar on the language situation in Africa held at the UNESCO Institute of Education in Hamburg, Germany, in October 1991, solutions were discussed of introducing African languages as national languages without destroying African nations and sparking off tribal wars. A participant from Zimbabwe held that it would probably be wise if Zimbabwe were to choose Kiswahili as the national language rather than Shona to avoid problems with those Zimbabweans for whom Ndebele (the second largest language group) or other Zimbabwean languages are the mother tongues. It was also suggested that in a situation where it might be difficult to choose one African language among a multiplicity spoken in a country, it might be wise to choose a language belonging to a minority group in the country rather than to a majority group.

countries opted to retain the colonial language as the official language and the medium for formal schooling. Zaline Makini Roy-Campbell (1992a: 56) attributes this to the identification of education with learning the language of the former colonizer, which she calls "a tacit admission that it is the only suitable medium for assimilating education."

Babs Fafunwa (1990),[130] minister of education of the Federal Republic of Nigeria, noted in his linguistic profile of Africa that twenty-two African countries use thirty-four different African languages as mediums of instruction at primary level. Four countries (out of the twenty-two) also used nine (of the thirty-four African languages) as mediums of education at secondary level.[131] No country in Africa, according to Fafunwa, used an African language as medium of education at the tertiary level.[132] Ten countries had pilot projects in thirty-six African languages, while six of the countries were just at the exploratory stage. Five countries had, according to Fafunwa, not taken any action on African languages so far.

According to Pai Obanya (1995a), director of the UNESCO regional office for West–Africa, instruction at the primary level is still almost exclusively in French in the former French colonies, and 100% of the time in the following countries: Benin, Burkina Faso, Niger, Senegal, and Togo. The only exception in *francophone* West-Africa that he names is Guinea, where instruction is 95% in French. But as we shall see, both

---

[130] Professor Babatunde Fafunwa was Minister of Education from 1990 to 1993. He succeeded Professor Jibril Aminu.

[131] Among the four countries using an African language in secondary education Fafunwa included Madagascar. He was correct that Madagascar used its own national language, Malgash, as language of instruction in secondary schools for many years, but in 1988, the year before Fafunwa's article was written, Madagascar felt compelled to revert to French as the language of instruction in secondary school. We shall return to this point later.

[132] The medium of instruction in the teachers' colleges (training primary school teachers) in Tanzania is Kiswahili. At the University of Dar es Salaam, Kiswahili is the medium of instruction in the Department of Kiswahili and at the Institute for Kiswahili Research. We shall later discuss these examples in more detail. Apart from these few exceptions, the statement concerning the non-use of African languages in the institutions of higher learning in Africa mostly seems to hold true, if by Africa is meant Sub-Saharan Africa. In northern Africa, Arabic has taken over from French as the language of instruction at universities both in Tunisia and Morocco. The Ministers of Education in Africa (ED–82) define Arabic as an African language, although a historically non-indigenous language. Also in Sub-Saharan Africa there are some few examples of Muslim universities using Arabic as the language of instruction.

Guinea and Niger are planning a strengthening of the African languages, and Mali has a post-1994 policy of African languages in the first two years of primary school. In the anglophone countries in Western Africa the picture is different (Nigeria 70%, Sierra Leone 45%, Liberia 25%, the Gambia 25%), mainly because the early years of primary education in these countries involve instruction in the various national languages. Obanya (1995a: 321) laments: "This situation has persisted, in spite of the existence of national education policies which speak of giving due recognition and pride of place to national languages in education." Of the twenty-three African languages spoken across national boundaries, the most populous are Creole, Fulfulde, Hausa, Kiswahili, Yoruba, and Arabic.

LANGUAGE: "CULTURE EXPRESSING ITSELF IN SOUND"

In the *World Declaration on Education for All* (WDEFA), education through the mother tongue is mentioned just once, in the following sentence: "Literacy in the mother tongue strengthens cultural identity and heritage" (WCEFA, 1990: Article 5).

In 1982 the Ministers of Education in Africa met in Harare in Zimbabwe to discuss the use of African languages as languages of education. They stressed that

> there is an urgent and pressing need for the use of African languages as languages of education. The urgency arises when one considers the total commitment of the states to development. Development in this respect consists of the development of national unity, cultural development, and economic and social development. Cultural development is basic to the other two. . . . Language is a living instrument of culture, so that, from this point of view, language development is paramount. But language is also an instrument of communication, in fact the only complete and the most important instrument as such. Language usage therefore is of paramount importance also for social and economic development (ED-82: 111).

From the socio-political aspect, the use of national languages in the educational process represents, for those African states making the option, a sign of political sovereignty with regard to the old colonial power, as well as an assertion of their cultural identity, denied in the past by the colonialists through the harsh relegation of African languages to the inferior status of "vernaculars."

Even though educational arguments may be even stronger for using the mother tongue as the language of instruction, socio-cultural arguments are also strong. Folklorist Crats Williams defines language as "culture expressing itself in sound" (quoted in Ovando, 1990: 341). It gives individuals and groups their identity. There is a powerful connection between language and sociocultural identity. The language you learned your first words in, the language your mother and father talked to you in, the language used in your nearest surroundings and with your closest family and friends will always be a part of your personal identity. When the language one uses in daily communication is denigrated, for instance, not deemed fit as a language of instruction at higher levels of schooling, children may feel that a part of themselves is also being denigrated.[133]

When you learn a new language, you frequently also learn a new culture. That can be an enriching experience provided that the experience does not teach you to look down on your own mother tongue and thus at part of your own identity (Gaarder, 1972). Ngugi wa Thiong'o claims that during colonial times African children learned to associate their own language with low status, humiliation, corporal punishment, slow-footed intelligence, or downright stupidity. Because any achievement in spoken or written English was highly rewarded through prizes,[134] and through the prospects of climbing up the educational ladder, knowledge of English came to be associated with intelligence and prospects for success.

WHEN LANGUAGE BECOMES A BARRIER TO KNOWLEDGE

By 1970 there had been sufficient research for UNESCO (1970) to assert that it ought to be the duty of all school authorities to inform parents about the research results on bilingualism. These research results indicated that bilingualism may result in psychological problems if children

---

[133] Concerning linguistic minority children in Norwegian schools, Astri Heen Wold (1992:247) notes: "You do not accept a child when you convey a message saying that one of the central characteristics of the child, her or his language, is of no worth. When the Norwegian school enables the existence and further development of the minority child's vernacular, it signals the following: Your language is important and precious and so are you" (my translation).

[134] In Tanzania the English language support project used many luring incentives, like flying not only the successful students but also their teachers and the head of the school to the prizing center and back home. There was no such incentive for being an outstanding student of Kiswahili.

are taught in a foreign language and have not acquired a full mastery of their own language. UNESCO recommended the use of the mother tongue as the universal language of instruction.[135]

Paulo Freire (1985) defined the practice of imposing a foreign language upon the learner for studying another subject as a violation of the structure of thinking. Yet this is the situation most African children find themselves in today. In an interview, Ngugi wa Thiong'o (1992: 27) holds that "ninety percent of the population in Africa today speak only African languages." In the next chapter I shall report from my own observations of lessons in Tanzania conducted either in English or Kiswahili.

In Nigeria in 1971 a six-year primary education project was started using Yoruba as an instructional language. Evaluation exercises conducted from 1976 to 1978 yielded the finding that

> groups in the experimental classes obtained better results across the board, in both the arts and the sciences, than the control groups; that the differential could not be traced to teachers or educational aids, and that the most plausible explanation was the use of Yoruba as the instructional language (Bamgbose, 1984: 95).

Further work in Nigerian schools with the use of Yoruba as the medium of instruction has been going on. Evaluation studies repeatedly show that pupils educated through the medium of Yoruba are more proficient in school subjects, including English, than pupils educated through the medium of English (ILEA, 1990).

In a talk given at the National Workshop on African Languages in Basic Education held at NIED in Okahandja, 18 September 1995, Ben Elugbe of the Department of Linguistics and African Languages at the University of Ibadan in Nigeria had this to say about the language of instruction in the primary grades in Nigerian schools:

---

[135] The advantages of being taught in one's vernacular have also been discussed in public debates in Norway in connection with the many children of migrant workers in Norwegian schools. A Norwegian psychologist, Astri Heen Wold (1992), has taken the effort of going through a vast amount of international research on bilingualism and sorting out valid and invalid arguments in the public debate on bilingualism. She finds that many of the arguments furthered in the public debate on bilingualism do not hold when compared to the most recent research in the field. She also finds arguments which do hold and these point in the direction of the value of teaching in the vernacular.

The provision of the National Policy on Education (NPE) for this level is the mother tongue (MT) or the language of the immediate community (LIC)—either way, a Nigerian language. This provision is so logical and commonsensical that it may be properly asked if anybody ever saw or did it otherwise. The answer is that it was usual to go straight to English (Elugbe, 1995: 15).

In his talk Ben Elugbe referred to the research of Bamgbose and the growing conviction in Nigerian schools that children learn best through the mother tongue, that they even become more proficient in a foreign tongue through first developing proficiency in their own. The counterintuitive conclusion that more use of the first language and less use of the second may give better results in the second language seems to be well substantiated.[136]

In an article on education for all: policy lessons from high-achieving countries Santosh Mehrotra (1998) concludes about those countries that have achieved a high percentage of the population having a basic education:

> The experience of the high-achievers has been unequivocal: the mother tongue was used as the medium of instruction at the primary level in all cases . . . Students who have learned to read in their mother tongue learn to read in a second language more quickly than do those who are first taught to read in the second language (Mehrotra, 1998: 479).

The claim that "we need English as the language of technological development" is often heard. The claim is repeated several times in the

---

[136]To gain access to a second language via the first language may appear highly inefficient at first glance. As Crawford puts it: "Trying to convince a critic that bilingual education is the best route to full English proficiency is like trying to persuade someone that the best way to go west is to go east first." (Crawford, 1989: 439) Many commonsense notions regarding language are incorrect, but they contribute to public doubts about the usefulness of mastering one's own tongue. As Crawford writes:

Bilingual education still runs into the following powerful myths:

- That young children pick up new languages quickly and effortlessly.
- That prolonged reliance on the native tongue reduces students' incentives to learn English.
- That bilingualism confuses the mind and retards school achievement (Crawford, 1989: 86–87).

report on the *Education System for the 21st Century in Tanzania* (URT, 1993). Yet the claim seems unfounded. As Rugemalira and colleagues (1990: 31) maintain: "It should be demonstrated that countries such as Finland, Norway, China or Japan, which do not teach their children through the medium of an "international language" are isolated and have lost track of technological developments beyond their borders."

A. Mahinda Ranaweera (1976), Sri Lankan researcher and former director of education at the Curriculum Development Center, Ministry of Education, Sri Lanka writes about the great advantages to the population of Sri Lanka of the introduction of Sinhala and Tamil as the languages of instruction to replace English—*especially* for the teaching of science and technology:

> The transition from English to the national languages as the medium of instruction in science helped to destroy the great barrier that existed between the privileged English educated classes; between the science educated elite and the non-science educated masses; between science itself and the people. It gave confidence to the common man that science is within his reach and to the teachers and pupils that a knowledge of English need not necessarily be a prerequisite for learning science (Ranaweera, 1976: 423).

Ranaweera relates that the change of medium of instruction in science and mathematics always lagged behind the other subjects because of special difficulties, like the absence of scientific and technical terms, textbooks, and proficient teachers. Yet he found the greatest need to switch over to the national languages in the science subjects. He gives two reasons for this claim. First, science education was considered the main instrument through which national development goals and improvements in the quality of life of the masses could be achieved. Thus, there was a need to expand science education. He tells that the English medium was a great constraint which hindered the expansion of science education. Secondly, he notes that in order to achieve the wider objectives of science education, such as inculcation of the methods and attitudes of science, the didactic teaching approach had to be replaced by an activity- and inquiry-based approach which requires greater dialogue, discussion, and interaction between the pupil and the teacher and among the pupils themselves. As Ranaweera (1976: 417) notes: "Such an approach makes a heavy demand on the language ability of the pupils and will be more successful if the medium of instruction is also the first language of the pupils" (Ranaweera, 1976: 417).

A POLITICAL CHOICE

The difficulty of treating socio-cultural, psychological, educational, and political arguments separately can be illustrated by noting educational and linguistic research which shows that a familiar language frequently is not advocated as a language of instruction for some of the following reasons:

1. Some people distrust the motives of those who advance the arguments in favor of the mother tongue, particularly when such advocacy comes from foreigners.
2. An emotional learning from the colonial times may breed contempt for one's own culture and admiration of the culture of the colonizers — equating knowledge of the colonizer as *the* education.
3. Many Africans belonging to the elites feel that the use of a foreign language as a language of instruction, even though their own children would also learn better in a more familiar language, still will strengthen their children in comparison to other children in the country. This will happen since their children are likely to get more exposure to the foreign language. In this way language becomes a powerful mechanism for social stratification.

The choice of a language of instruction in Africa is also a political choice, a choice that may redistribute power in a global context as well as within an African country, between the elites and the masses. African political writers concerned with reaching the masses and not only the elites will often write in African languages. The Kenyan author Ngugi wa Thiong'o (1986) found that when he started writing plays in Gikuyu, they really reached the masses. But then he also became a threat to the government and was imprisoned for a year. His radical writing in English did not lead to repercussions from the government.

Fafunwa (1990) holds that one of the most important factors militating against the dissemination of knowledge and skills, and therefore of rapid social and economic well-being of the majority of people in developing countries, is the imposed medium of communication. He claims that there seems to be a correlation between underdevelopment and the use of a foreign language as the official language of a given country in Africa (e.g. English, French or Portuguese):

We impart knowledge and skills almost exclusively in these foreign languages, while the majority of our people, farmers, and craftsmen perform their daily tasks in Yoruba, Hausa, Wolof, Ga, Igbo, Bambara, Kiswahili, etc . . . The question is: Why not help them to improve their social, economic, and political activities via their mother tongue? Why insist on their learning English or French first before modern technology could be introduced to them? (Fafunwa, 1990: 103)

Fafunwa's claim of a correlation between underdevelopment and the use of a foreign language as the official language of a given country seems likely and is highly interesting. It is, however, not substantiated nor repudiated by references to any studies to this effect.[137] Roy-Campbell (1998), with further reference to Kwasi Prah, points out that "no society in the world has developed in a sustained and democratic fashion on the basis of a borrowed or colonial language."

The British researcher Keith Watson (1997) notes that most developing countries are characterized by "a myriad of languages, and generally speaking the poorer the country, the greater the number of languages" (Watson, 1997: 4).[138] The industrialized countries normally have one language[139] which is used as the official language and the language of instruction in the institutions of higher learning as well as on public radio and television and in parliament. Whether there is any causal relationship between development and the number of languages spoken has to be established. It seems, however, likely that if instruction is given in a language with which the learner is not familiar, not as much will be learned as would occur if the teaching were in a more familiar language.

In a recent article the Namibian researcher Brian Harlech-Jones (1998) refers to a useful classification of six factors[140] that are commonly debated in relation to the use of language in education. The order in which these factors are presented shows the hierarchy of importance

---

[137] The claim can be tested empirically. A study confirming or disowning this claim should be undertaken.

[138] Watson does not, however, take into account that many of the languages really are just dialects of each other and were created as different languages by missionaries.

[139] However Switzerland, with its three official languages, is a good exception to this.

[140] Harlech-Jones (1998) has taken this useful hierarchy of factors from Larson (1981:15–23).

accorded to those who favor a strong role for vernacular languages as the
languages of instruction. These people rank the factors as follows:

1. Psychological factors
2. Educational factors
3. Linguistic factors
4. Socio-economic factors
5. Political factors
6. Financial factors

People who strongly favor the use of non-vernacular languages[141]
(such as English in Namibia) as languages of instruction rank these factors in reverse order, emphasizing the financial, political, and socio-
economic advantages of the European language and de-emphasizing the
remaining factors.

In his 1997 paper Keith Watson is concerned about the costs involved in developing learning material in so many African languages.
This is indeed a grave concern. And, as the Namibian example shows,
material will not be published if it is left up to commercial publishers and
no profit can be made from it. Commercial publishers are not charity institutions. They are in the business to make a profit.

As we shall see in the following chapter, it is the educational language policy of the government of Namibia that has made it impossible
for the publishers to earn money on publishing in the African languages.
A language policy that strengthens the African languages may be costly.
But when the costs are calculated, it should also be calculated what it
costs to continue with a language policy where the language of instruction becomes a barrier to knowledge for millions of African children.
Those concerned about democracy and good governance in Africa

---

[141] Both Brian Harlech-Jones (1998) and Thomas Clayton (1998) talk about "languages of wider communication" when they mean European or Euro-based languages. Thomas Clayton explains this expression in a footnote: "Language of
wider communication is an updated term for lingua franca, meaning a language
which is used habitually by people whose mother tongues are different . . . to facilitate communication between them" (Clayton, 1998: 155). But then Kiswahili
is the language of wider communication in Tanzania but even this language is
threatened by the growth of the European language, English, the language of the
former colonial masters.

should also be concerned about the fact that in many countries information from the government to the people is given in a language that 90% of the people do not speak and hardly understand.

AFRICAN LANGUAGES IN THE DEVELOPMENT DISCOURSE

One of the strategies in the globally unequal distribution of power and resources involves the invalidation of the nonmaterial resources of dominated groups, including their languages and cultures. Non-material resources can be invalidated by making them invisible, as, for instance, African languages are in much development discourse, or by stigmatizing them as handicaps or problems, rather than resources, as in minority discourses in Euro-American contexts.

The linguists Tove Skutnabb-Kangas and Robert Phillipson (1996) make a point of the striking fact that in much educational policy work, even in policies on education for all, the role of language is seldom considered. This shows myopia on the part of the donors and the researchers who guide them: they urge targets for universal literacy to be set, but little thought is given as to the language in which literacy should be achieved.

THE ROLE OF DONORS TO EDUCATION IN AFRICA

As noted in chapter 1 some of the African Ministers of Education together with UNESCO representatives were the ones who, in the African midterm conferences to evaluate the progress of the "Education for All" initiative, raised the concern about the use of African languages as languages of instruction. There has, however, been little understanding for this concern among most donors, parts of the African elites, and Western scholars who write on Africa. However, some donor agencies, especially the German DSE and GTZ, some NGOs, and some Western scholars (see especially Phillipson, 1992; Brock-Utne, 1993b, 1997d; Skutnabb-Kangas and Phillipson, 1996; Watson 1994, 1997), through funding and writing are trying to support the development of the African languages.

As for multilateral donors, there seems to be no doubt that UNESCO is the agency that has done most for the promotion of mother tongue instruction. UNICEF, in spite of its heavy involvement in primary education, does not seem to give priority to the question of the language in which literacy should be obtained.

THE POSITION OF THE WORLD BANK ON LANGUAGE OF INSTRUCTION

Over the last ten years there has been a shift in the World Bank rhetoric concerning the value of the use of the mother tongue as the language of instruction. But to analyze the rhetoric of the Bank is not enough. As Jones (1997: 367) rightly notes, a key policy question facing analysts of World Bank operations concerns the practices the Bank is prepared either to support or reject, and how it financially backs its views. For example in the World Bank policy paper on primary education (1990a) the advantages of learning in a language with which one is familiar are not discussed. On the contrary, the World Bank asserts: "In developing countries instructional time for language is often divided between a national or local language and a non-indigenous official language, which may lower levels of achievement in either language" (World Bank, 1990a: 16).

However, both in writings by Lockheed and Verspoor (1991) and in the World Bank's 1995 review, *Priorities and Strategies for Education,* one may be able to detect a new understanding on the part of the Bank of the advantages of studying in ones own language. Lockheed and Verspoor note:

> Children who speak a language other than the language of instruction (which here refers to the European languages) confront a substantial barrier to learning. In the crucial, early grades when children are trying to acquire basic literacy as well as adjust to the demands of the school setting, not speaking the language of instruction can make the difference between succeeding and failing in school, between remaining in school and dropping out (Lockheed and Verspoor, 1991: 153).

Responding to Joel Samoff's (1996) and Jon Lauglo's (1996) criticism of the World Bank's 1995 review, Nicholas Burnett and Harry Anthony Patrinos (1996) principal authors of the review, claim that they have listened to their critics by showing the importance they now place on indigenous and ethnic minority issues in education:

> For example, there is unqualified support for bilingual education programs. And contrary to Samoff's claim that we do not consider the ways that education systems push students out, we, in fact, mention indigenous people who cannot easily benefit from a school system in which classes are conducted in a language they do not understand.

Therefore, we do not ignore those who discuss alienation of youth
from their cultural origins, as Lauglo suggests. (Burnett and Patrinos,
1996: 274)

In his analysis of World Bank policies toward language of instruction in Africa, Alamin Mazrui (1997) shows that the World Bank is just
paying lip service to the claim that mother tongue instruction in Africa
would be the preferable choice. In contrast to UNESCO, which holds
that the use of the mother-tongue ought to be extended to as late a stage
in education as possible, the World Bank seems to see the use of African
languages in the early grades of primary school just as a strategy for a
smoother transition to the European languages as languages of instruction. The World Bank continues to place heavy emphasis on the reduction of government subsidies in education, though such subsidies are
indispensable to the promotion of instruction in local langues. It is easy
to agree with Alamin Mazrui (1997:40) when he exclaims: "In effect, the
vaunted freedom of choice over education allowed to African nations by
the democrats of the World Bank is no freedom at all!"

Mazrui (1997) mentions that a World Bank loan to the Central African
Republic, allegedly intended to improve the quality and accessibility of elementary education, came with a package of conditions that required the
nation to import its textbooks (and even French language charts) directly
from France and Canada. It has been estimated that due to similar World
Bank projects and linkages, over 80% of schoolbooks in *"francophone"*
Africa are now produced directly in France (Nnana, 1995: 17).

In the process, the World Bank has not only positioned the West to
further control the intellectual destiny of African children, but has also
continued to weaken and destroy infrastructural facilities, primarily publishing houses, for the technical production of knowledge locally. Textbooks are of crucial importance for the publishing and printing industry
in Africa, as they represent 90% or more of the total book market in
Africa (Takala, 1995).

Mazrui correctly observes that in terms of sheer cost effectiveness,
French and Canadian publishers would have found it far more difficult to
participate in this World Bank agenda in West Africa[142] had the languages of instruction in African countries been an African instead of a

---

[142]As we noted in the discussion in Chapter 3 regarding textbook provision in
Tanzania, the use of English in "anglophone" Africa allows UK and U.S. publishers to become heavily involved in the textbook industry in these countries.

European language. Mazrui claims that because of the Euro-lingustic policy of Western donors (and, I would like to add, much of the African elite) intellectual self-determiation in Africa has become more difficult. Mazrui states: "For the time being, the prospects of a genuine intellectual revolution in Africa may depend in no small measure on a genuine educational revolution that involves, at the same time, a widespread use of African languages as media of instruction" (Mazrui, 1997: 46).

In view of such serious consequences for the educational future of African children arising from instruction in "foreign" linguistic mediums, finding ways of introducing and strengthening African languages as languages of instruction "would be expected to be a high priority for any institution that claims to have the educational welfare of the continent at heart" (Mazrui, 1997: 38). In spite of its proclaimed conviction about the pedagogic value of "mother-tongue" instruction, however, the World Bank claims that it cannot impose an educational language policy on any African country. Each country must itself determine the language policy it deems best fitted to its pecularities. Mazrui (1997: 39) remarks: "This same institution that has been coercing African governments into over-hauling their educational structures virtually overnight, has suddenly become mindful of the national sovereignity of these countries and of their right to linguistic self-determination."[143]

On a field trip to Niger in April 1998, where among other issues I discussed the language of instruction with a group of officials in the Ministry of Education, including their visitor, Makha N'Dao of the World Bank, N'Dao first claimed that the World Bank never involved itself in decisions that had to do with the choice of language of instruction. He stressed that it was his firm opinion that that question was not a question for donors to have any opinion on, it was for the governments themselves to decide. I mentioned that Alliance Française is involving itself in the language policy of the former French colonies and so is the British Council in the former British colonies. There are also strong publishing

---

[143] I have come across the same attitude among Nordic donors when I have maintained that the most important educational aid we could give to Africa would be help to strengthen its own languages. I have been told that the educational language policy is an internal matter in which we should not intervene. This could be an appropriate attitude if there were not others like the British Council and Alliance Française as well as strong publishing interests in the North already intervening and if we had held the same attitude on other questions concerning the organization of the education system in Africa.

industries both in the English- and the French-speaking world fighting for markets and being backed up by World Bank loans. These industries are certainly getting involved in the language policy in Africa. Mr. Makha N'Dao did not deny this, but claimed that donors like GTZ and the Swiss were also getting involved, even to the point of saying that there would be no aid to the publication of schoolbooks if a certain national language policy was not adopted. He said that these donors, who often accuse the World Bank of being arrogant and setting tough conditionalities, were doing this themselves, forcing a certain national language policy on a country like Niger.

Even though N'Dao claimed that the World Bank did not involve itself in the language policy question, he was quick to mention that though the experimental classes so far had shown an advantage of using mother tongues as languages of instruction, the outcomes were not so sure when it came to "learning achievement." How else the advantage was measured, he did not say. It seemed clear that he was skeptical of the development of African languages as languages of instruction. He held the typical World Bank attitude toward African languages described so well by Mazrui (1997)—they are to be used in the first grades to ease the transition to the Euro-languages.

BILATERAL DONORS

Both the British and the French seem to use development aid to strengthen the use of their own languages as languages of instruction. As we shall see in the next chapter, British Council has played no unimportant role when it comes to deciding on the language policies in Tanzania and Namibia (see also Phillipson, 1992; Brock-Utne, 1993b, 1995b, and 1997d). Skutnabb-Kangas and Phillipson (1996) tell about a succession of British conferences held to "assist" colonies in organizing their education systems when they became independent states in the 1960s. In these conferences language was given very little attention, and if the issue was raised, the focus was only on the learning of English.

A British Council annual report admits that although the British government no longer has the economic and military power to impose its will in other parts of the world, British influence endures through "the insatiable demand for the English language." The report maintains that the English language is Britain's greatest asset, "greater than the North Sea Oil" and characterized English as an "invisible, God-given asset" (British Council Annual Report, 1983: 9).

Madagascar has, like Tanzania, a national and uniting offical African language, Malgash (Malagasy). Madagascar has for many years succeeded in having Malgash as the language of instruction not only in the elementary school but also in the secondary school. During a visit to Madagascar in 1989, a headmaster of one of the larger secondary schools in Antanarivo told me that the year before the secondary school system in Madagascar had felt compelled to reintroduce French as the language of instruction in secondary school. "There were simply no more books available in Malgash," the headmaster said with considerable regret. "But Alliance Française has supplied us with textbooks as a type of educational aid."

Among bilateral donors, however, there are also those that support the use of African languages as languages of instruction, first and foremost the German development agencies DSE and GTZ and the Swiss. There are also examples of financial and technical support given by Nordic NGOs and Nordic donors to publishing of learning materials in local languages.

THE ROLE OF EDUCATIONAL DEVELOPMENT SCHOLARS IN THE WEST

Even among educational development scholars in the West, who see themselves as critics of the donor policies in the education sector in Africa and who believe themselves to be siding with the African people, there has been a conspicuous absence of analysis of the language question. Thus, in Kenneth King's (1991) major study of aid to the developing world, and in particular the role of donor agencies in the education sector, "language" does not even figure in the index.[144] Neither does the word *language* figure in the index in the large study *Educating All the Children. Strategies for Primary Schooling in the South* by Christopher Colclough with Keith M. Lewin (1993). The same blindness to the language issue, according to Tove Skutnabb-Kangas and Robert Phillipson (1996: 163) characterizes a major British study edited by Hugh Hawes and Trevor Coombe (1986) of education priorities and aid responses in Sub-Saharan Africa.

---

[144] In this study King (1991: 51) refers to a study of education in Tanzania which indicated that learners had too little English to enable them to benefit from the instruction, but this does not lead him to investigate language in education policy. Robert Phillipson (1992: 240) has elsewhere analyzed Kenneth King's "monolingual vision" which can be clearly detected also in an earlier study of African education.

Keith Watson (1997: 1) criticizes the "scant regard given to the complex language issues facing many national governments" in the South. He tries to explain this "scant regard" by pointing to the fact that the educational development discourse has been dominated by economists, planners, political scientists, or policy analysts, whereas language issues, whether in the form of language policy and planning or in the analysis of literacy and approaches to literacy, have been left to linguists or experts in literacy. There is certainly a need for a dialogue between these groups. The economists especially and policy analysts would benefit from the knowledge of the linguists.

THE ROLE OF THE AFRICAN ELITES

As among the donor community and Western scholars, there are also among the African academic elites opposing views on the role of the mother tongue as the language of instruction. Among African linguists the advantages of using the mother tongue as the language of instruction seem clear (see, for instance, Roy-Campbell and Qorro, 1997; Fafunwa, 1990; Tadajeu, 1989; Tadajeu, 1997; Ouane, 1995; Rubagumya, 1991). For example, Maurice Tadadjeu (1989, 1997) of Cameroon is arguing for a trilingual model in Africa whereby children learn first their immediate mother tongue, then an African language with a larger reach, preferably a national or regional African language, and then a European language. Such a policy would strengthen the African continent and bring it closer to a "communautarisme Africain" (Tadadjeu, 1989).

As noted earlier among other African academics the opinions are more divided. Sanou (1990) argues against the use of African languages as languages of instruction. Rubagumya (1991) argues for the use of Kiswahili, maintaining that the enormous increase in the literacy rate in Tanzania after independence would not have been possible had Tanzania not had a common national language which everybody could understand. While Rubagumya (1991: 70) defines literacy as the ability to read and write in *any* language, Kingsley Banya of Sierra Leone seems to have another definition of literacy. In an article on illiteracy in Sierra Leone, Kingsley Banya (1993) writes:

> Only about 25% of the country's population were (in 1961) literate in English, which is the official language. However, most people are literate in Krio, which is the lingua franca of the country. . . . in absolute numbers there has been a tremendous expansion in the number of

illiterates. As the population has increased, the number of literate people has not kept pace; 85 out of every 100 Sierra Leones are now illiterate. (Banya, 1993: 163)

Banya classifies as illiterate those Sierra Leones who cannot write and read English even though they may read and write Krio, the lingua franca of their country! If a native Englishman who reads and writes English but not any other language were likewise classified as illiterate there would be many illiterates in the English-speaking world.

We shall see in the following chapter that the role of the African academic elites concerning the language policy of Tanzania and Namibia has mostly been one of not supporting the use of local languages. Before we turn to this more detailed discussion of these two countries, we shall take a quick look at language policies in some other African countries.[145]

LUKEWARM LANGUAGE POLICIES THAT ARE NOT IMPLEMENTED

The Language Situation in Swaziland

The linguistic situation in Swaziland is quite different from most other African countries in so far as there is only one dominant language which is the mother tongue of 95% of the population, namely, siSwati (Mordaunt, 1990). This makes Swaziland a virtually monolingual society where one would think that it should be easy to make siSwati the language of instruction in all schools. Through frequent visits to schools in Swaziland over a two month period, Ragnhild Tungesvik (1998a) was struck by the fact that she found English to be the dominant language in every school setting, including the primary schools that she visited. Having analyzed policy documents describing the language policy in Swazi schools, Tungesvik (1998b: 2) concludes: "The language policy for Swazi schools is to some extent confusing. Some policy documents state that siSwati is the language of instruction in the first three or four years, while English is introduced later." She also notes that many policy documents on education in Swaziland hardly discuss the language issue at all.

On Monday, 3 February 1997, the Norwegian delegation of which I was a part had a discussion in the Ministry of Education in Swaziland

[145] I visited most of these countries in the years 1996–1998 as a consultant for the Foreign Ministry of Norway on a Norwegian-funded UNICEF project on basic education targeting the girl child.

with the permanent secretary, Mr. M. V. Vilakati, on the educational situation in the country. There was some discussion of the reasons for the high drop-out rates in primary school. Most of the educationists from Swaziland present admitted that the language of instruction might be one of the reasons behind the many failures. They claimed that the official policy required teachers to use siSwati as the language of instruction during the first four years and in those same years teach English as a subject. English should then be used as the language of instruction for the rest of primary and secondary school as well as at the university level. Vilakati stated, however, that he was aware of the fact that a good number of schools, especially in the towns and cities, now started with English as the language of instruction in the first grade. On the question of why the government did not attempt to enforce their language policy, he answered that they did not want to enforce anything and were more in favor of letting parents decide. Many parents decided that their children should start using English as the language of instruction as early as possible because they thought that would boost their learning of this very important language (Brock-Utne and Lexow, 1997).

In one sense the permanent secretary was arguing along the same lines as Mordaunt (1990), who writes:

> In the present situation, it does not seem that siSwati will become the medium of instuction, at least not in the foreseeable future . . . English is the major vehicle for the dissemination of the present century's knowledge. Furthermore, it is difficult to conduct business with powerful countries in the vernacular. In a sense, currently English is the language through which "modernization" for many developing countries takes place. (Mordaunt, 1990: 138)

Mordaunt is confusing several issues. The fact that it is difficult to conduct business with powerful countries in the vernacular is not a reason why the language of instruction in schools should be a foreign language. On the contrary, as we have just discussed, most linguists agree that the best way to learn a foreign language is through the best possible command of your own language, achieved by using your own language as language of instruction up to a high level of schooling.

As noted by Tungesvik (1998b), a lot of policy documents on education in Swaziland hardly mention the language issue at all. In that respect they resemble the policy documents in Zimbabwe. Herbert Chimundu (1997) holds that Zimbabwe has no explicit or written language policy.

He also states that: "the official neglect of language issues in post-independence Zimbabwe is deliberate and can be explained in terms of elitist rulership and fear of the unknown" (Chimundu, 1997: 129).

Chimundu (1997: 132) describes Zimbabwe as a country where English is the dominant language of business, politics, administration, and media, and "African languages continue to be down-graded in the schools and vernacularized outside in the wider community."

A Glimpse at the Language Situation in Uganda

A government White Paper (Government of Uganda, 1992: 16) states that: "The mother tongue should be used as a medium of instruction in all educational programs up to P.4. From P.5 onward, English should become the medium of instruction." Another official government policy is to strengthen the use of Kiswahili in school and in the population as a whole. The White Paper states:

> Unlike English, Kiswahili is an indigenous East African language. It has a strong local and regional cultural base cutting across the whole region. Therefore, the strengthening of Kiswahili, as Uganda's main language for official use and for national unity, will promote rapid and solid regional co-operation between Uganda and the neigbouring countries such as Kenya, Tanzania, Zaire, Rwanda, Burundi, etc. (Government of Uganda, 1992: 19).

But what are the realities? Annette Nyquist, who in the spring of 1998 spent a couple of months observing teaching both in the formal primary schools of Uganda and in the non-formal COPE schools, notes:

> Observations in primary schools showed that most of the teaching was done in English. The learning materials for the teachers and the students were all in English, including teacher guides for mother tongue teaching. The teachers I spoke to said that they were told that English should be the medium of instruction from P.1 . . . A teacher said: "In this sub-county only few know English. This makes teaching in English hard, but because of the final exams we have to use English a lot" (Nyquist, 1999: 20).

Prior to my visiting the centers of non-formal schooling in the western region of Uganda (the so-called COPE centers), I was informed by

George Ouma-Mumbe, National COPE Focal Point, Ministry of Education in Kampala, that the first year of COPE at least would use the mother tongue as language of instruction. This is, however, not what I found on my field-trip to Bushenyi (Brock-Utne, 1997b). Back in Kampala educational officers cited one of the reasons for the high drop out rate from the centers being the fact that the teaching is in English and the text-books are all written in English even for the first grade. This happens even though it is official government policy that the language of instruction in the first grades should be the mother tongue. The textbooks, as mentioned in the previous chapter, had been prepared by an American firm.

PRESERVATION AND REVIVAL OF AFRICAN LANGUAGES AS LANGUAGES OF INSTRUCTION IN AT LEAST THE PRIMARY SCHOOLS IN AFRICA

New Political Signals in Guinea

The courtesy call to Mr. Kozo Zoumanigui, the Minister for Education and Research of Guinea, that was scheduled as part of my field-trip to Guinea in November/December 1996, after some initial discussion on gender in education, quickly turned into a long conversation about the language policy of Guinea. He told me how Guinea, which had been a pacesetter on the francophone West African scene, using the mother tongue as the medium of instruction both at elementary and secondary levels of education, relapsed into French at the secondary level with the end of Sekou Toure's revolution in 1984. The minister informed me that the government of Guinea had recently decided to strengthen the national African languages as languages of instruction for primary as well as adult education. He told me about the period between 1968 and 1984 when education through the medium of African languages was the official policy of Guinea. This was suddenly changed in 1984 without any evaluation or research having taken place in connection with the language policy. This time the government of Guinea had decided to follow up on the reintroduction of the use of African languages as languages of instruction through an on-going evaluation process (Brock-Utne, 1996e).

It would be interesting to return to Guinea now to see whether the new language policy has taken root. On my field trip in November 1996, French was used as the language of instruction in all the primary schools I visited, even in the non-formal NAFA centers. I discovered that many of the children here had learned the sentences on the blackboard by heart. They could not actually read them. As noted in the previous chapter, all the text-books were published by French publishing companies, mostly by EDICEF or *Les Classiques Africaine* in Versailles, and were highly irrelevant for children in Guinea (Brock-Utne, 1996e).

New Political Signals in Botswana

Botswana has twenty languages; Setswana is the largest and the best understood by most people. African languages, especially Setswana, were for many years languages of instruction up to grade 5 but slowly a change occurred by which more and more schools began using Setswana only the first year and then switched to English. During 1977, however, there was wide debate in Parliament concerning the reintroduction of the mother tongue as language of instruction also in higher grades. Through the Revised National Policy on Education (RNPE 94), a Botswana Language Council has been set up, with the intent to strengthen the African languages (Brock-Utne, 1997c).

New Political Signals in Niger

Niger has eight national languages, including Arabic, apart from the offical language which is French, inherited through the French colonization of Niger. The language question was discussed in all of my meetings with education authorities in Niger during my field-trip to that country in April 1998.

The secretary general of the ministry of education, Hima Adiza, said that I had come at an exciting time for Niger because the Government had recently decided to promote all the eight national languages as languages of instruction during the first years. The government is going to start with a new policy, she declared. The first reports had come out from a few of the experimental schools where the national languages had been introduced, and the results seemed promising. Of course, the implementation of the new language policy of Niger would be costly and she praised donors like the German GTZ and the Swiss who helped Niger in their work with the promotion of the national languages. GTZ had promised help over a nine-year period. There was a great need for publications in the various languages, for teacher guides, and for translations.

In a later meeting Mai Manga Therese Keita, the national coordinator of the education of girls, said that she was so happy for the interventions I had made during several of the meetings on the language question. She thought that question was the most important concerning schooling of girls and she got upset when some people did not see this. Keeping French as the language of instruction was okay for the children of the intellectuals who heard a lot of French anyway, but she was thinking of the poor people, of the rural population, of those who did not use French outside of the formal school setting. She said she was happy for the help they received from GTZ in putting their new language policy in place. In answer to my question on the donor enforcement of this policy, she said that this was not true. The development of the African languages was certainly a priority of the government, but there was a lack of funds for implementation of the policy (Brock-Utne, 1998d).

On my visit to Niger, I also met with the regional education authorities, who showed me some of the textbooks which had recently been developed under a World Bank loan. The textbooks, developed by INDRAP (Institut National de la Recherche et Animation Pedagogic), were written by researchers and teachers from Niger and published in Niger. They were only published in French, however, in spite of the official policy of supporting the eight national African languages as languages of instruction in the first grades. But the content of a social sciences book that I studied more thoroughly seemed to be very relevant to the situation in Niger; almost all the examples were taken from their own country. The education authorities were quite proud of the books and told me that the earlier books, which had been written in France, were highly irrelevant. This was a big step forward. However, I did not see any of the children working with or carrying any of the books.

From my impressions from field-trips to Africa the last couple of years, it seems like a couple of "francophone" countries (I have mentioned Guinea and Niger), are especially committed to reintroducing African languages as languages of instruction. But a lot of support, both morally and financially, might be needed because the forces working for the strengthening of the colonial languages are strong. These forces are linked to policies favoring a free market economy and a reduced state. The success-story of Somali in Somalia may teach us something.

Somalia has the most propitious language situation for administrative efficiency in all of Africa, as at least 97% of its citizens have some understanding of the same indigenous language, Somali, yet the society has failed to take advantage of it. At independence, English, Italian, and Arabic became the official languages. It was only after twelve years of political independence that Somali was accepted as the language of the state. In 1972 the decision was taken by the military government, the Supreme Revolutionary Council, that Somali was to be the only official language of the country. To facilitate the use of Somali as the medium of instruction, the government had appointed a linguistic commission of twenty-one members to write textbooks for elementary schools, write the Somali grammar, and work out the compilation of a 10,000-word Somali dictionary (Roy-Campbell, 1992, with further references to Laitin, 1977). This resulted in the production of 135 textbooks in Somali by 1980. Somali is now the main medium of instruction in all schools and training centers at pre-university level. Somalia is an example of a poor country that formulated a policy of language planning, and allocated the requisite resources and personnel to implement it. Somalia showed that an African language could be modernized in a much shorter time than previously imagined.

Strong governments[146] may be necessary for the further development of African languages. With the building down of the state and the liberalization of the economy in many of the African nations over the last years, the former colonial languages have been strenghtened within African intellectual circles. There are certainly economic interests in France, Britain and the United States, such as the publishing industry, which benefit from the continued use and partial reinstatement of the colonial languages in Africa. But as we have seen, some African countries are trying to revive African languages as languages of instruction.

MULTI-PARTY SYSTEMS AND LANGUAGE

Many African countries are now in the process of establishing multi-party systems (Brock-Utne, 1992). This has come about partly through a domino-effect originating in the eastern European countries and the former Soviet-Union and partly through pressure on the African countries by the so-called donor community. There are also democratic forces within the African countries, especially among intellectuals working for a change in the direction of multi-party democracy. An important question for further study is whether the rapid and partly externally forced introduction of multi-party systems in poor African countries may lead to a

---

[146] The government of Somalia was a military government and in many ways was oppressive. But a participant from Somalia in my "Education in Africa" class, who was highly critical of the government, said that if there was one good thing they did it was to make Somali the language of instruction. But in Somalia today, in spite of all Somalis belonging to one tribe and having one language, there is no state and there is fierce fighting among clans.

strengthening of the old colonial languages to the detriment of the African languages.

There is a need for a study of the language policies of the new parties being born in Africa today. In Tanzania the ruling party, and until recently the only party, Chama cha Mapinduzi (CCM), conducts all its meetings, writes its party program, and distributes leaflets in the national language, Kiswahili. However, there is a tendency among the newer parties, which are currently coming into existence, to use English in order to attract sponsorship from foreign donors. Most of the new parties have also been started by "schooled" people, who have been trained abroad and many of whom have little respect for Kiswahili.

In the Seychelles, which I visited in February 1992, the language of instruction in elementary school is Creole. In secondary school it is English. French is taught as a foreign language. The ruling party has been a promoter of Creole. Officials in the ministry of education, with whom I had several conversations about the language policy of the Seychelles, claimed that all their studies showed that the switch to Creole had been of benefit to the great masses of children. Members of the elite with whom I also talked preferred English and French as official languages, and regarded the introduction of Creole, a language they looked down upon, as an imposition by the leftist government with which they were in disagreement. They wanted their children to be educated in English or French. Some of the new upcoming parties write their party programs in English.

Mr. Ferrari, the leader of the new Institute for Democracy in the Seychelles which was formed to distribute information on democratic methods of governance, told me that he had asked for some financial help from a development agency in France to further the work of the institute. He was promised aid on the condition that the institute would use French as the medium of communication and would work for the strengthening of the French language in the Seychelles and distribute their brochures written in French! He declined the offer.

One of the new parties in the Seychelles, led by Jacques Houdoul, states explicitly in their party program that they want to minimize the use of Creole, especially as a language of instruction. They argue that the use of Creole prevents the Seychellois from participating in world culture.

The donors to Africa are currently very concerned about democracy and "good governance" in Africa. It seems paradoxial in such a situation that most of them are not more concerned about the fact that some 90% of the people of Africa have no knowledge of the official language of their country, even though it is presumed to be the vehicle of communication between the government and its citizens.

IN WHOSE INTEREST ARE THE COLONIAL LANGUAGES STRENGTHENED AS LANGUAGES OF INSTRUCTION IN AFRICAN EDUCATION?

From the above discussion it seems obvious that there are Western interests like the publishing industry which profit directly from the continued use or reintroduction of the colonial languages in the schools in Africa. At the same time it seems like the masses of African school-children are losing intellectually through the language policy, and that the continued use of the colonial languages is an effective barrier, not only to their learning of modern science and technology but to the restoration of their own culture.

There is probably no strategy that could better decolonize the mind than restoring the African languages to their dignity, having them used as languages of instruction in school. This would make for better learning as well as strengthen the self-concept of the African learner. Alamin Mazrui asserts that: ". . . the prospects of a genuine intellectual revolution in Africa may depend in no small measure on a genuine educational revolution that involves, at the same time, a widespread use of African languages as languages of instruction" (Mazrui, 1997: 46). Yet in many African countries the majority language is now treated as minority languages are treated in the North.

The interests of the elites in Africa seem to coincide with the economic interests of the former colonial powers. The right to learn through an indigenous language seems to be undermined both by the elites in African countries and by economic interest groups within the Western powers. It is also given too little attention in the writings of Western scholars otherwise critical of donor influences on education in Africa. We shall now look into language policies of two African countries in more detail: Tanzania and Namibia.[147]

---

[147] I have been able to follow the educational language policies of these two countries especially well. I lived in Tanzania for five years, and the Namibian National Institute of Education under the Ministry of Education in the fall of 1995 asked me to make an assessment of its language policies.

CHAPTER 6

Language of Instruction in Tanzania and Namibia

As long as African countries continue to educate the continent's future leaders primarily through foreign languages, they will remain dependent. Education for liberation and self-reliance must begin with the use of languages that do not impede the acquisition of knowledge. This is a challenge for the 21st century.

(ROY-CAMPBELL, 1998: 16)

Tanzania is one of the very few countries in Africa that is using an African language, Kiswahili, as the language of instruction throughout primary school and, at one point also had plans for using that language in secondary schools and even at the universities. Namibia is also of interest as a country that has recently become independent, and at that time especially, was confronted with the question of what language policy to follow in post independence and post-apartheid Namibia.[148]

FOCUS ON TANZANIA

The uniting national language of Tanzania, Kiswahili, is really the mother tongue only of the population living along the east coast and in Zanzibar but is learned at an early age in most of Tanzania.[149] There are about 120 vernacular languages in Tanzania, yet Kiswahili is now spoken by more than 90% of the population (Rubagumya, 1991: 68; World

---

[148]As stated in the preface much of the information in this chapter stems from a consultancy I undertook in November and December 1995. The consultancy, commissioned by the National Institute for Educational Development in Namibia, dealt with the situation of the African languages in Namibian schools, especially after independence in 1990 (Brock-Utne, 1995c).

[149]The oldest preserved manuscript in Kiswahili dates back to 1723 (Knapert, 1969). The writing at that time was in Arabic script. The German missionaries transliterated Kiswahili from Arabic script to Latin script in the late nineteenth century (Kalid, 1977).

Bank, 1988b: 154).[150] Even those children who speak another vernacular at home with their parents often speak Kiswahili with their friends. This is the case in most if not all urban centers, and especially so in Dar es Salaam, to where people have moved from all over the country and where there are many marriages across vernacular language boundaries. Kiswahili is the medium of instruction in primary schools, in adult education, and in teachers' colleges. It is estimated that only 5% of the population has some knowledge of English, in addition to Kiswahili and a vernacular (Schmied, 1989).

A PERSONAL OBSERVATION

At the University of Dar es Salaam, though one can occasionally run across some few students from the same district addressing each other in their vernacular, for instance, students from Bukoba talking Kihaya, what one normally hears daily in the corridors and in the classrooms before classes is Kiswahili. Among the academic staff one finds the same phenomenon. Kiswahili is the common language of all in tea-breaks, at lunch, and at informal chats in the corridor. It is the language in which one is greeted in the morning, the language in which jokes are told, and confessions as well as pleas are made.

If you want to take part in informal chats, you have to learn the language. But an English-speaking person can manage a normal job at the university without knowing any Kiswahili at all, even when this job comprises supervision of education students in teaching practice in secondary schools. The language of instruction is English both in secondary schools in Tanzania and at the university. That is also the official language used in all departmental meetings as well as meetings of the faculty and senate at the university. But when tea and *mandazi* are brought in for tea breaks, people immediately switch to Kiswahili.

Because I was the head of department I found that the only time I needed Kiswahili for my official work was in writing the annual budget proposals and participating in budgetary meetings, which were the only

---

[150] Most words in Kiswahili are of Bantu origin, which makes the language relatively easy to pick up if one speaks one of the other vernaculars in Tanzania, most of which are also of Bantu origin. Kiswahili has proved to be a very flexible language, prepared to absorb words from the various vernaculars of Tanzania as well as from Arabic and English. The language is learned naturally within and outside the family and picked up through radio and television programs.

meetings conducted in Kiswahili. The reason for this is that the minutes of the meetings were sent directly to the Ministry of Education, where the working language is Kiswahili, as it is in parliament, in the government, in the radio broadcasts, in the banks, and the post offices. Since the first day I started teaching at the University of Dar es Salaam and through all the four and a half years I worked there, the artificiality of the use of the English language in these African settings struck me daily. Sometimes when I was lecturing to big classes of a couple of hundred students, I wanted to make them more active by giving them some questions to discuss in small groups for just five minutes. I gave them the questions in English but very soon heard that most of the groups had started discussing the issues in Kiswahili. Naturally, so would I.[151]

I do not doubt that the students at the University of Dar es Salaam feel more comfortable speaking Kiswahili than English; they express themselves better and their understanding is far better if the teaching is in Kiswahili. This holds even more true in the secondary schools. I have sat in the back of secondary school classrooms in Tanzania for more than a hundred lessons watching student teachers teach. What struck me in the first week I was supervising student teachers was the passivity of the secondary school students, how they were just sitting there, passively copying notes, not saying a word, not posing a question. Even when the student teachers tried their best to activate the class, they seldom got any response. The first two days I was sitting through lessons in history, chemistry, physics, mathematics, and English. I saw the same passivity everywhere. Then on the third day I was supervising the class in *siasa*[152] —political education, a subject which at that time was taught in Kiswahili. It was a different class! At once the secondary school students were participating, asking questions, and eagerly waving their hands. I made the same observation in a Kiswahili class, which was taught in Kiswahili. Again the class turned into an active group of secondary school students. In the school-yard everyone spoke Kiswahili, though there were big signs in English saying that only English should be spoken in the school-yard.

I started to wonder, Why does Tanzania continue thirty years after independence, to use the colonial language as the language of instruction?

[151] I have often had the experience of speaking English to Norwegians when there was another person in the group who did not understand Norwegian. At once when that person left the group, we would switch to Norwegian.
[152] *Siasa* is a type of social studies closely linked to learning and discussing the consequences of Tanzania's political ideology as outlined by the political party CCM, for many years the only legal party in Tanzania.

I started to ask my colleagues and other Tanzanian friends about this. I asked members of Parliament and former Ministers of Education about this. I also did some library research to trace the historical background for the use of Kiswahili as a language of instruction in Tanzanian schools.

A HISTORICAL GLIMPSE AT THE LANGUAGE POLICY OF TANZANIAN EDUCATION

The language of instruction in primary schools in Tanzania during the colonial period varied. During the German period (1886–1920) Kiswahili was made the language of colonial administration and was also promoted as the language of instruction for the four years of primary schooling for the few Africans who received any schooling at all. Zaline Makini Roy-Campbell maintains that there was concern within the German government that providing the Africans with access to the German language could be a potential disadvantage to German colonialism (Roy-Campbell, 1992b). Whatever the motivations behind the emphasis the German colonial government placed on the Kiswahili language, the use of Kiswahili in colonial administration and education provided the cornerstone for Kiswahili to become the lingua franca of Tanganyika.

When the British colonial government assumed control of the administration of Tanganyika in 1920, they chose to use English as the language of colonial administration but retained Kiswahili as the medium for primary education for African children. The British colonial administration developed separate school systems along racial lines. There were different school systems for the Africans, the Asians,[153] and the Europeans. In most Asian primary schools the language of instruction was Gujarati in the early years of schooling and English at a later stage.[154]

---

[153] During the colonial period people in Tanzania were categorized according to their race. There was very little social interaction between the races. In most cases they lived in separate areas. There were three main races. Europeans were the ruling class. The number of Europeans in Tanzania was never big, as there was no large white settler community as in Kenya and Zimbabwe. The trade in the country was dominated by people from India, called Asians. Government policies effectively barred the African population from taking part in commercial activities (Sumra, 1996: 206). The Africans were peasants or manual laborers working on plantations or in the mines.

[154] African education was limited to standard 6 until 1937, with limited expansion beyond standard seven after that, whereas Asians and Europeans had access to education beyond standard 8. As late as 1956 there were more Asian students in secondary schools in Tanzania than Africans, although Asians accounted for less than 1% of the population (Sumra, 1996: 206).

However, things changed slightly in the early 1950s, when it was decided that in the new middle schools English should be taught as a subject from standard 5 onwards and used as a medium of instruction in standards 7 and 8 as a preparation for education at the secondary stage. In 1953 the Binns Mission recommended phasing Kiswahili out of primary school and replacing it with the vernacular languages and English.[155] The recommendation of eliminating Kiswahili from the schools where it was taught was not accepted by the government, and Kiswahili retained its place in primary education.

In 1963, two years after Tanzania achieved independence, the Ministry of Education removed Asian vernaculars from the primary school curricula and made Kiswahili and English the only mediums of instruction at this level. In 1964 Kiswahili was made the medium of instruction from standards 1 to 4 in the former African schools, and English, which was studied as a subject from Standard 2, was introduced as the medium of instruction in Standards 7 and 8. Schools previously reserved for Europeans taught in English throughout the eight years. There was a difference in the quantity and quality of secondary school materials in the English language and Kiswahili language schools. This reinforced in the minds of Africans the "inferior status of Kiswahili" (Whiteley, 1969).

The Ministry of Education appointed a committee to seek ways of making Kiswahili intellectually respectable. The committee recommended converting most English-language schools to Kiswahili medium, beginning with standard 1 in 1968 and phasing to standard 5 in 1972, and adopting English as the language of instruction for some subjects in standard 5 and all subjects in standards 6 and 7. This policy, though approved in April 1966, did not take effect, for it was superseded by another policy emanating from the Arusha Declaration and the policy of Education for Self-Reliance. As a result of this latter policy, Kiswahili was, in March 1967, declared the medium of instruction throughout primary school, not just standards 1–5. In the teacher training institutions, the Colleges of National Education, the medium of instruction was switched from English to Kiswahili in 1973. In the second Five-Year Plan (1969–1974) the continued use of English as a medium at secondary and tertiary levels of education was deemed unsatisfactory. The move to Kiswahili as the medium of instruction in primary schools was thought to be only part of a larger plan to implement the use of Kiswahili as the medium of instruc-

---

[155] The Binns Mission report did not question the effect of the use of English as a language of instruction on the mentality of the African children. It also did not suggest how education could be made available in 120 Tanganyikan vernaculars.

tion throughout the educational system. In 1969 the Ministry of National Education sent a circular to all headmasters and headmistresses of all secondary schools outlining the plan for the gradual introduction of Kiswahili as the medium of instruction. According to Bhaiji (1976), secondary school teachers also favored a shift to Kiswahili as a medium of instruction.

The Ministry's circular suggested that Kiswahili and *siasa* should be taught in Kiswahili from the school-year 1969/70, domestic science from 1970/71; and history, geography, biology, agriculture, and mathematics from 1971/72 (Bhaiji, 1976: 112).[156] The initial plan was for Kiswahili to become the medium of instruction in all subjects in forms 1 and 2 by 1973 (Polome, 1979). The teaching of political education— *siasa*—and "Kiswahili" language through the medium of Kiswahili was introduced. But then the reform stopped.

Subsequently a study commissioned by the National Kiswahili Council showed that secondary school students had great difficulties learning the subjects taught in school because the medium of instruction —English—represented a great barrier (Mlama and Matteru, 1978). The study argued for the shift to Kiswahili both at secondary and tertiary levels of education.

At the end of 1980 the then president of Tanzania, Mwalimu Julius Kambarage Nyerere, appointed a Presidential Commission on Education to review the entire education system. He made J. Makweta the chair of the commission. The Makweta Commission presented its report to the president in February 1982. Its recommendations on the medium of instruction more than refueled the expectations by actually setting a date for a change from English to Kiswahili: in January 1985 the first year of secondary school (i.e., form 1) was to start using Kiswahili and in 1991 the university was going to start teaching through the medium of Kiswahili. However, this recommendation was deleted from the official report published in 1984 (Rubagumya, 1991).

In the years from 1969 to 1983 Tanzanian educators were waiting and preparing for the shift to Kiswahili as the medium of instruction in secondary and later also university education. But in 1983 "the government quite unexpectedly sought to turn the tide" (Lwaitama and Rugemalira, 1988: 2). In August 1983 the then Minister for Education, J.

---

[156]Bhaiji (1976) relates that by this time curriculum developers had already started to translate and compile all the technical and scientific terms of school subjects. Some schools had already received a booklet on mathematical terms in Kiswahili.

Makweta, was quoted in the press (UHURU, 8 August 1983) as saying that the expected change of medium was not going to take place. This statement must have been difficult for Education Minister Makweta to make. He himself had chaired the commission that had suggested the change from English to Kiswahili as the medium of instruction in secondary and tertiary education. When I discussed the issue with him, he told me that he personally favored a switch to Kiswahili but it was a government decision to stop the further development of Kiswahili at higher levels in the educational system. The decision seems to have been taken by President Nyerere himself, partly with the support of the British Council, the cultural arm of the British government. When discussing the same issue with Makweta at the end of April 1992, he partly put the blame for a reversion of the decision to switch to Kiswahili on the university people, especially on the then Department of Education. "You intellectuals betrayed us," Makweta said to the dean of the Faculty of Education. "We did not get the support from you we needed. How could we carry the decision through with so little support from the intellectual community?"[157]

During July/August 1984 Clive Criper, a linguist from Edinburgh University, and Bill Dodd, an administrator with long experience from Tanzania, were carrying out a British government funded study on levels of English presently existing across the educational system. Their study confirmed earlier research showing that the levels of English were too low in most schools for effective learning to take place. The following are three of the conclusions they reached:

- Only about 10% of Form IVs are at a level which one might expect English medium education to begin (Criper and Dodd, 1984: 14).
- We estimate that perhaps up to 75% of the teaching, at any rate in Form I, is being done through Kiswahili (p. 34).
- Less than 20% of the University sample tested are at a level where they would find it easy to read even the simpler books required for their academic studies . . . (p. 43)

In 1987 the Department of Foreign Languages and Linguistics published a *survey of the reading competence in English of secondary school*

---

[157] This is my translation of a conversation in Kiswahili between Makweta, now Minister of Communication; the dean of the Faculty of Education, Professor Mosha; and myself on 22 April, 1992 at a dinner party in the Swedish ambassador's residence.

students in Tanzania, conducted by Zaline Makini Roy-Campbell and M. P. Qorro. The study confirmed the findings by Criper and Dodd (1984) of the low level of competence in and understanding of English among secondary school students in Tanzania. They found that the overwhelming majority of students entering form 1 in secondary school could not comprehend sufficient English to follow what was being taught in class unless much of the lesson was conducted in Kiswahili. They conclude:

> When considering the appalling performance of secondary school students in English, one begins to question the wisdom of forcing students to learn through a medium in which they are inadequately competent . . . Language should not be a barrier to knowledge . . . If students are allowed to continue their education in a medium with which they are familiar, the language in which they have begun to conceptualise basic concepts relating to science and mathematics, as well as other areas, their cognitive processes will be provided the opportunity to blossom, as they will be further developed in a language with which they are comfortable. This study adds additional support to the call for changing the medium of instruction at secondary school level from English to Swahili. (Roy-Campbell and Qorro, 1987: 95)

But Criper and Dodd (1984: 73) unlike Roy-Campbell and Qorro[158] do not argue for a switch to a medium of instruction with which the students are familiar, namely Kiswahili. Criper and Dodd state: "The Ministry of Education should issue an unambiguous circular setting out the policy on English medium education." Lwaitama and Rugemalira (1988) claim that this statement was no coincidence. Rubagumya (1991: 76) explains that Criper and Dodd's recommendation has to be seen in the light of the English Language Support Project,[159] which the British government was prepared to fund but only on the condition that English continue to be the medium of instruction!

---

[158] In their book on the language crisis in Tanzania, Zaline M.Roy-Campbell and Martha A.S. Qorro (1997) argue convincingly for the need to switch from English to Kiswahili as the medium of instruction in secondary schools as well as in the universities in Tanzania. They hold that the English language should no longer be allowed to act as a barrier to the attainment of knowledge.

[159] The objective of that particular project, which was introduced in Tanzania in 1987 through British development aid (1.46 million pounds sterling), was to increase the competence of English-language teachers and to provide books for that purpose. Nine specialists from the United Kingdom were brought to Tanzania to implement the project.

The decision by the government that English will continue to be the medium of instruction in secondary schools was not taken because Kiswahili was not ready to be used as a medium. Rubagumya (1991: 77) asserts: "In fact this has never been given as a reason by the Government to justify its decision. The reason given is that we need English as the language of technological development" (Rubagumya, 1991:77). But in the 1992 report *Tanzania Education System for the 21st Century* (URT, 1993) it is argued that Kiswahili is *not* ready to be used as a medium of instruction:[160]

> As a matter of policy, Kiswahili should be a medium of instruction at the pre-primary and primary school levels. However, English should continue to be strengthened at primary level and used as a medium of instruction in post primary institutions *until such a time when Kiswahili is ready to be the dominant medium of instruction* (URT, 1993: 23, emphasis added).

There already exists a large technical vocabulary in Kiswahili.[161] But for Kiswahili technical terminology to develop there must be a firm

[160] We shall return later to this argument about the "readiness" of a language.
[161] Roy-Campbell (1992: 243) mentions that the *Primary Technical Dictionary of English-Kiswahili* (Ohly, 1987a) has 10,000 existing terms compiled from a larger work with more than 30,000 words. The core of the dictionary comprises technical terminology from agriculture, architecture, the motor and construction industries, electricity, fishing, handicrafts, mechanics, photography, mining, printing, railways, textile industries, etc. It is supported by theoretical terms from mathematics, chemistry, and physics, and by environmental terms concerning geography, geology, and meteorology.
There is also a dictionary of technical terms produced by the Institute for Kiswahili Research. This dictionary is titled: *Kamusi Sanifu Ya Biolojia, Fizika na Kemia, Taasisi Ya Uchunguzi wa Kiswahili* (Taasisi Ya Uchunguzi wa Kiswahili, 1990). Scientists collected the vocabulary for this dictionary, then sat together to accept words and agree on definitions. The dictionary provides terminology for the words used in biology, physics, and chemistry in the first four years of secondary school.
Roy-Campbell gives a good practical example of the coinage of technical words which was undertaken in the process of changing from English to Kiswahili as the medium of instruction in the Department of Kiswahili and the Institute of Kiswahili Research at the University of Dar es Salaam. Prior to 1970 the courses in this department were taught through the medium of English. There were no terms for linguistics and literature in Kiswahili. However, once the decision was made to teach this course using Kiswahili, words were developed in the process of teaching, and later standardized.

decision to use it. Nevertheless the task force behind the report *Tanzania Education System for the 21st Century* argues for strengthening English as the medium of instruction, apparently even in the primary schools,[162] and in teachers' colleges.[163]

LINGUISTIC OPPRESSION: IN WHOSE INTEREST?

The economic crisis in Africa has made it easy for the old colonial powers to move in all over Africa. In Tanzania the aid given by Britain has been in the form of an English Language Teaching Support Project, financed by the Ministry of Overseas Development as a "top priority of British aid to education in Tanzania" (Bgoya, 1992 : 179).

Rubagumya (1991) claims that the agreements Tanzania has been forced to make with the International Monetary Fund (IMF)—getting loans with the usual conditionalities: liberalization of the economy, devaluation of the currency, and cuts in public spending—led the second republic under President Mwinyi to shift emphasis from socialist rhetoric to pragmatic management of the economy. He finds that it is this political and economic change of focus which partly accounts for the increase of the symbolic value of English in the 1980s and today. It is considered imperative that economic recovery should go hand in hand with the raising of the standards of English.

Zaline Makini Roy-Campbell (1992a) maintains that some of the elements calling for liberalization are at the same time those calling for assistance in the improvement of English.

> It may seem ironic that at a time when British aid is being cut in other sectors, the British government would offer to invest in improving English in the schools, particularly when popular sentiment in Tanza-

---

[162]The report states: "Content is delivered in Kiswahili in all schools, except those earmarked for expatriates. *This negatively affects efficient learning of those joining Secondary Schools where English is the medium of instruction*" (URT, 1993: 17) (emphasis added).

[163]In secondary schools and teachers' colleges conducting A level courses, English is used as the medium of instruction. Otherwise, teaching is conducted in Kiswahili with respect to other teacher education courses. In describing the situation in the teacher colleges the 1992 task force on education in Tanzania states: *"The predominant use of Kiswahili in Teachers Colleges has tended to produce teachers who cannot read and understand the largely English written materials"* (URT, 1993: 17–18) (emphasis added).

nia is toward switching from English to Kiswahili as the medium of instruction at the secondary school level (Roy-Campbell, 1992: 164).

Roy-Campbell seems to think that it is the aim of the British government to stop the decolonization which for some time had been going on in Tanzania and strengthen the old colonial domination.

It is clear, even to the British government, that adopting an indigenous language as the instructional medium throughout the educational system in Tanzania is an important long-term step toward decolonizing knowledge. For this reason Britain seeks to reverse advances made in Tanzania in the context of the English-language syllabus (Roy-Campbell, 1992: 164).

ENGLISH-LANGUAGE TEACHING AS GOOD BUSINESS FOR PUBLISHERS IN THE UNITED KINGDOM

An example showing that English-language teaching is good business for publishers in the United Kingdom has been provided through the English Language Teaching Support Project. In Chapter 3 of this book, when discussing the textbook sector in Tanzania, I referred to Walter Bgoya (1992), the former Director of Tanzania Publishing House, who noted that no book was published in Tanzania under this project. He told how British publishers insisted that books be published in the United Kingdom even if the manuscripts originated in Tanzania. English-language teaching is good business for publishers in the United Kingdom. The English language support project deprived Tanzanians of employment and income as well as the possibility of developing advanced skills and expertise in publishing.

At a conference on *Decolonizing the Mind* held at UNISA (the University of South Africa) in Pretoria in South Africa in October 1995 I gave a paper which dwells on the language policy of Tanzania (Brock-Utne, 1995d, 1996f). In the question period after my talk a white South African woman in the audience said that strengthening Kiswahili in Tanzania should not be such a problem (yet it is a problem, as we have seen above). "But here the question of finding an indigenous African language to strengthen is hopeless because of the multitude of languages. We have eleven indigenous languages. Should we choose one of them, there would be domestic war." A black South African man in the audience answered her:

That is exactly what the apartheid regime has wanted you to believe. They have used our languages to divide us. If you really study them closely, they can all be grouped around two language families: Sotho and Nguni. It should be possible to develop Sotho and Nguni as two written languages all South Africans should learn apart from English.[164]

The language situation in South Africa is not very different from the one in Namibia, to which we shall now turn.

FOCUS ON NAMIBIA

I shall discuss the language policy in Namibia, how it was formed in exile, and how it has been formulated since. Namibia, situated in south-western Africa, has only 1.5 million inhabitants, yet the country officially has thirteen languages as languages of instruction in the first grades of schooling. Among these are three European and ten African languages. Of the three European languages two, German and Afrikaans, are connected to the colonial history of Namibia. Namibia was colonized by the Germans from 1884 to 1914. German is still an important business language in Namibia and the language one hears most frequently by shopkeepers in the capital, Windhoek. The South African colonization, which was supposed to be a trusteeship, lasted until 1990. In this period Afrikaans (a variety of Dutch) became the main official language and the language of instruction from grade 4 upward. After independence, English became the official language and the language used in commerce and government institutions (Davids, 1997). Since 1990 there has been a general strengthening of English and an eagerness, especially among the young and especially in towns, to learn the language (Brock-Utne,

---

[164]A similar thought has been expressed well in an essay by Neville Alexander (1989) titled: *Language Policy and National Unity in South Africa/Azania*. He argues for a "standardized Nguni" and a "standardized Sotho," envisioning a South Africa where the official languages will be standardized Nguni, standardized Sotho, and English, while other languages spoken by few, like Venda and Afrikaans, enjoy regional status. He is, in fact arguing for a trilingual model, not far from the one mentioned in the previous chapter and advocated strongly by Maurice Tadadjeu (1989, 1997) of Cameroon. For South Africa such a model would mean that everybody would first learn her or his mother tongue, then the standardized Sotho or Nguni, and then English. For the whites of South Africa this would mean that *they* would also have to learn standardized Sotho or Nguni. Today only 7.5% of white South-Africans can speak an African language (Watson, 1997).

1995c). The enormous work that has gone into making English the official language of Namibia, a work that has been strongly supported by over-seas agencies like ODA and US-AID, has born fruit.[165] There is, however, a real concern among language- and culture-conscious people that the growth of English has happened not only to the detriment of Afrikaans (an intended consequence) but also to the detriment of the Namibian languages (an unintended consequence). The following are some of the comments I have heard around the country:

> Instead of the donors giving us aid in English, they should give us aid to develop our own languages. The national education policy ought to be looked into again. Our children are fighting two enemies at the same time: the subject matter and the language. We must give more attention to African languages. After twenty years we shall all be speaking English.

> The Namibian languages are being marginalized. There should be more people fighting for the Namibian languages from official positions. All languages in Namibia should be treated equally. The emphasis has been too much on English to the detriment of the other languages. People are developing a negative attitude toward their languages. The Ministry [of Education and Culture] is doing nothing about this.

> If you know English well, you are considered educated. If you just know Namibian languages, even though you may know several of them and speak them well, you are considered dumb and uneducated.

> I think the indigenous Namibian languages should have been used for the whole of primary school. Now our own languages are left behind at a childish stage. We should strive for a situation like that in Botswana, where English is taught as a subject. If the languages were made languages of instruction right through primary school, they would become languages of learning. More books would be published in the languages. More publishing of schoolbooks would also make for more general titles in the languages.

---

[165] Teachers have attended upgrading courses, and most of those I have met had a good command of English. This impression also corresponds to some research carried out by Harlech-Jones (1995) at the University of Namibia, who found that among the 161 teachers in his original sample from 1986, only 43.4% would agree with the proposition that their own command of English is good. Among a comparable group of teachers (157) questioned in August 1995, 82.8% would agree that their command of English is good.

TOWARD A LANGUAGE POLICY FOR NAMIBIA: UNIN 1981

After independence in 1990 the language policy pursued by the SWAPO (South West Africa People's Organization) government reflects the decision to have English as the official language as stipulated in Article 3 of the Constitution of Namibia. Accordingly, English is to be the sole medium of communication in all executive, legislative, and judicary bodies from the central government level down to the grassroots. This decision was made even though the 1991 census figures on main languages spoken in Namibia showed that only 0.8% of the total population speak English as a mother tongue. And why was English made the official language? We shall look at what went on in the years preceding independence, during which SWAPO was in exile.

The principal aspects of the Namibian language policy were formulated and adopted before independence in the years of the liberation struggle. These aspects can be found in the key UN document *Toward a Language Policy for Namibia. English as the Official Language: Perspectives and Strategies* (UNIN, 1981). This document contains an extremely thorough survey of the language and educational scene in Namibia, a distillation of relevant experience in adjacent countries, a description of the options open to Namibia, and strategies for achieving language-planning goals. The text is based on the work of three named scholars attached to the United Nations Institute for Namibia (UNIN), one an American, one a British Council employee, and the third an Indian. The document was written after an international conference, with strong British and American representation, which was held to consider the implications of the choice of English as an official language for Namibia. The Ford Foundation financed the publication (Phillipson, 1992: 288). SWAPO decided that English should be *an* official language in independent Namibia—though it became *the* official language in the title of the report (Phillipson, 1992: 288; see also SWAPO, 1982: 40, Commonwealth Secretariat and SWAPO, 1983).

In order to judge the suitability of a language as the official language, certain criteria were employed. The choice of the following criteria was highly political: (1) unity, (2) acceptability, (3) familiarity, (4) feasibility, (5) science and technology, (6) Pan-Africanism, (7) wider communication, and (8) the United Nations. Criteria that are of extreme relevance but were *not* chosen were: (1) ease of learning, (2) Nambian cultural authenticity, and (3) empowerment of the underprivileged (which

could include democratization and self-reliance). The British socio-
linguist Robert Phillipson concludes: "It is difficult to avoid the conclusion that the criteria seem to have been selected so as to make English
emerge as the absolute winner" (Phillipson 1992: 293). The languages
judged according to these criteria were indigenous languages, Afrikaans,
German, French, and English. All of Namibia's own languages were
lumped together and none given a separate treatment, while the three European languages and the one European-based language (Afrikaans)
were all given separate treatments!

English was said to be the language that would best promote Pan-
Africanism. It is tempting to ask, among whom, the minute elite in so-
called anglophone African countries? Most of the people in these countries
never use English. The choice of a Bantu language like Kiswahili, spoken
by more than 40 million Africans, as the official language of Namibia
would have been more likely to have supported Pan-Africanism. Such a
view has been well argued by Phillipson, Skutnabb-Kangas, and Africa
(1985) in a publication of the Bureau of Languages in OAU (Organization of African Unity), but was not considered in the UNIN report. If
Kiswahili had been chosen, it would have been a language easy for all
the Bantu-speaking people in Namibia to learn. It would therefore have
promoted unity. Its spread to southern Africa would also have increased
its chances of becoming an official UN language—another criterion in
the UNIN report.

According to the report, choosing an official language had two related purposes: (1) the need to combat South African-engineered divisiveness, and (2) the unity of Namibians. Although these factors are
national rather than international, international factors get more prominence than national ones when the criteria are operationalized. For most
Namibians, international contacts will not be a pressing concern. Furthermore, it seems unlikely that a language spoken by less than 1% of the
Namibian population would create unity in the nation. Though many regard English as "the language of liberation," it is still a language built on
European and Western culture.

Among Namibians in exile, a merged Namibian language had developed based on Oshikwanyama but with ingredients from other languages
from the north. The possibility of developing this merged language further and giving it official status was not looked into. Neither was the option discussed of trying to merge some of the different orthographies of
languages which actually are simply dialects. This might have been a
better way to combat South African-engineered divisiveness.

The UNIN document first and foremost announces the replacement of Afrikaans with English for official communication and the medium of education from upper primary level. It does recognize the rights of the indigenous languages—the "Namibian languages" spoken by the overwhelming majority of the African population, but it does nothing to discuss how these languages can now be used to unite the people instead of dividing them. What about the many language committees that had been created by the South-African regime? One would think that an independent Namibia would do away with these committees and start thinking anew, maybe by creating two or three language committees (one for the Bantu languages, one for Khoekhoegowab, and one for the Bushman languages). One of the recommendations that emerged from the National Workshop on African Languages in Basic Education held at the premises of NIED (National Institute for Educational Development) in Okahandja, 18–22 September 1995, was the creation of a National Language Board which, among other duties, should pursue the standardization of languages. This National Language Board may at long last begin the unifying work that could have started at independence (NIED, 1995).

SWAPO'S POSITION ON THE EDUCATIONAL ROLE OF THE NAMIBIAN LANGUAGES

Partly as a result of their resistance against South African oppression and their link with the donors who had supported it, SWAPO seems to have been more interested in a rapid replacement of Afrikaans by English than in the role of the Namibian languages. Yet the organization also gave political backing for the support of the Namibian languages:

> A SWAPO government will pursue a language policy that accords equal status and respect to all locally spoken languages. The new policy will redress the present injustice whereby the German and South African colonial states have placed emphasis on the teaching, development, and use of German and Afrikaans at the expense of all other local languages. . . .
>
> . . . Mother language will be used as the medium of instruction at the lower primary school level. The concern here is not with so-called group identity or ethnic consciousness and exclusivity, as has been the case with the apartheid colonial regime, but with the fulfillment of cognitive and communicative functions. Since it is through the mother languages that infants first acquire social habits, manners, feelings, tastes,

skills, and other cultural norms, it is important that their formal schooling starts with those languages of everyday life at home. (SWAPO, 1989: 6)

SWAPO's position is not so different from the most recent one of the World Bank that we cited in the preceding chapter. The use of the mother language[166] is here looked at mostly as an educational device to ease the transition to teaching in English. The mother language does not in this statement seem fit to be used at higher levels of education. As we shall see, the mother tongue is not even used as the language of instruction at the lower primary school level.

Since independence, the basic documents dealing with languages in education have been the proceedings and reports of working groups of the Ongwediva Conference in 1992 (MEC, 1993a). The Minister for Education and Culture at the time, Nahas Angula (1993), sketched important features of language planning for schools. For example:

Education should promote language and cultural identity of the children through the use of the home language as medium of instruction, at least at the Lower Primary, and the teaching of the home languages throughout general education. (point 5.2, p. 19)

For the purpose of timetabling, learning and instructional process in schools, all National Languages (home languages and mother tongues) are regarded as equal and at par with each other. Thus all National Languages will receive equal treatment in the official school programme in State or State-subsidised schools. Language hegemony is in conflict with the equality principle enshrined in our Constitution. (point 6.2, p.20)

The development of the National Languages should receive due attention. Such development will include:

— codification

---

[166] Mother languages which here means a Namibian language, that is, those languages which are of African linguistic origin. The few children in Namibia who speak English as their mother tongue, can go on learning in their mother tongue. For children with German as their mother tongue there are schools where the language of instruction is German, bringing the children to a German *Abitur* (high school certificate). Those who have Afrikaans as their mother tongue in Namibia are two groups: the white Afrikaners and the coloured population. This last group especially had problems with the shift to English and felt that the low value given their mother tongue was a threat to their self-esteem.

—development of lexicographical reference materials
—development of literature in National Languages
—continuous research into National Languages
—elevating the hitherto neglected National Languages to equal status and value with other National Languages. (point 6.4, p. 21)

Namibia's response to the Jomtien conference was the 1993 policy document issued by the Ministry of Education and Culture titled *Toward Education for All: A Development Brief for Education, Culture, and Training (MEC, 1993b)*. This policy document aims at translating the Namibian philosophy on education into concrete and implementable government policies. In a foreword to the publication, President Sam Nujoma states:

> Access to education should not be limited to a select elite, but should be open to all those who need it—especially children and those adults who previously had no opportunity to gain education. The largest share of our budget goes to education. Will we as a nation be able to fund the envisaged educational programme? It may look costly but we should realize that educating the nation is perhaps the most important investment we can ever make. The only way we can redress the apartheid legacy is by a massive education and training programme for our people (MEC, 1993b: i–ii).

Regarding language policy, this document (MEC, 1993b: 65) states:

- All national languages are equal regardless of the number of speakers or the level of development of a particular language. All language policies must be sensitive to this principle.
- All language policies must consider the cost of implementation.
- All language policies must regard language as a medium of cultural transmission.
- For pedagogical reasons it is ideal for children to study through their own language during the early years of schooling when basic skills of reading, writing, and concept formation are developed.
- Proficiency in the official language at the end of the 7-year primary cycle should be sufficient to enable all children to be effective participants in society or to continue their education.
- Language policy should promote national unity.

In June 1993 the Ministry of Education and Culture issued a pamphlet titled *The Language Policy for Schools 1992–1996 and Beyond.* The above-mentioned principles were repeated in a slightly different wording in this document and called "criteria and key factors for policy development" (MEC, 1993c: 3). This policy document also notes the following:

- The 7-year primary education cycle should enable learners to acquire reasonable competence in English, the official language, and be prepared for English medium instruction throughout the secondary cycle.
- Education should promote the language and cultural identity of learners through the use of Home Language medium at least in grades 1–3, and the teaching of Home Language throughout formal education, provided the necessary resources are available.
- Ideally, schools should offer at least two languages as subjects.
- Beyond the primary cycle (grades 1–7), the medium of instruction for all schools shall be English, the official language.

A likely interpretation of these goals seems to be that they stress the importance of the home language as the language of instruction, at least in the first three grades, and even open the way for its being the language of instruction all through primary school. It is therefore strange to read this official interpretation of the goals presented in the same policy document under the title, "What the Policy Means": Grades 1–3 will be taught either through the home language, a local language, or English (MEC, 1993c: 9). This opens the way for English to be used as the medium of instruction right from grade 1. With the negative attitude toward their own mother tongue which has developed in several areas since English became the language of administration, government, and higher education, opening the way for English as the medium of instruction as early as grade 1 is likely to further undermine the status of the Namibian languages. Laurentius Davids, an education officer in Namibia, very much deplores the opening up of grades 1–3 to be taught in English:

> The choice of medium of instruction is now decentralized, and many schools are now opting for English-medium instruction from grade 1. I am very concerned about this as many principals and teachers lay the blame of failure in classroom efficiency on mother-tongue instruction,

but at the same time the very same teachers are not competent to teach the learners through the medium of English. This is the point where it becomes necessary that the language policy and its implementation should be revisited. The state, through its educational institutions, has a moral obligation to positively intervene where such decisions are taken to safeguard the future of the children. In my opinion the state still has a centralized responsibility. (Davids, 1997: 102)

NAMIBIAN LANGUAGES

As noted ealier, independent Namibia has granted ten Namibian languages of African linguistic origin the status of mediums of instruction in functional literacy and in the three lower primary grades.[167] Nine of the ten languages are also taught as subjects higher up in the education system. It is easy to agree with the linguist Karsten Legere (1995: 6) of the department of African languages at the University of Namibia (UNAM), who holds that the attempt to retain so many African languages as languages of instruction "deserves international appreciation, in particular in view of the fact that with dropping standards of education similar cases in Africa are rare."

The Namibian languages accepted for educational purposes in the Namibian formal education system belong to two main language groups, namely the Bantu group and the Khoe group. In Table 6.1 the first eight languages are Bantu languages[168] while the last two belong to the Khoe group.

SIMILARITIES BETWEEN THE NAMIBIAN LANGUAGES OF BANTU ORIGIN: QUESTIONS OF ORTHOGRAPHY AND STANDARDIZATION

Visitors to Namibia are first struck by the multitude of languages. How difficult and costly it must be for such a small country to publish reading material in all these languages! It is surprising that so many languages exist

---

[167]All of the ten Namibian languages are used as mediums of instruction in grades 1–3 and used for functional literacy, but the Bushman language, Ju'hoan, is not being used in the government schools but only in the private schools built by the Nyae Nyae Foundation.

[168]There are other dialects of the Bantu group spoken in Namibia, but these are currently not approved for use in the formal educational system.

Table 6.1 The Distribution of Namibian Languages in the Education System

Language	Subject up to Grade	Subject at the University[169]	Subject at College of Education
Oshikwanyama	12	Yes, from 1996	Yes, at Ongwediva
Oshindonga	12	Yes	Yes, at Ongwediva
Rukwangali	12	No	Yes, at Rundu
Otjiherero	12	Yes	Yes, at Windhoek
Rugciriku	0	No	No
Silozi	12	Some modules from 1996	Yes, at Caprivi
Setswana	7	No	No
Thimbukushu	8	No	No
Khoekhoegowab	10	Yes	Yes, at Windhoek
Ju'hoan	3	No	No

Source: Brock-Utne, 1995c

side by side. It is even more surprising that not only can Oshikwanyama speakers and Oshindonga speakers understand each other very well, they can also understand Rukwangali and Rugciriku speakers as well as Otjiherero speakers. Even Silozi speakers can be understood by the other groups, especially those who speak Sisubia, Sifwe, and Setswana.

Table 6.2 Number of Students of Namibian Languages at UNAM (1995)

	Oshindonga	Otjiherero	Khoekhoegowab
First Year	52	1	3
Second Year	35	5	2
Third Year	13	0	2

Source: Brock-Utne, 1995c

[169] Table 6.2 shows the number of students who were studying Namibian languages at the University of Namibia (UNAM) in 1995.

On my first visit to Namibia one of my Namibian students took me to his home in Katutura, the black township outside of Windhoek to where the black Namibians were forcefully moved by the whites. On the way he stopped at a gas station and spoke Otjiherero to the man who pumped the gas. I asked in surprise: "Is he an Otjiherero speaking person, too?" The man had responded to him in Oshikwanyama. "No," my student told me, "but if we speak a little slowly and distinctly, we can understand each other quite well."[170]

Oshikwanyama and Oshindonga (both belonging to the so-called Oshiwambo dialects or languages) are both spoken in Owamboland in the northwest of Namibia, where most of the indigenous population live.[171] More than 55% of learners in Namibia speak an Oshiwambo language at home. According to information conveyed to me during my many talks with speakers of Namibian languages, it is hardly correct to call these two dialects of Oshiwambo two separate languages. There are

---

[170] Some of the written languages are, however, very different. Often the same sound is written completely differently in the various languages. The th sound (as in English *th*at) is, for instance written dh in Thimbukushu and in Otjiherero z. Much money would be saved on tight education budgets if one orthography could be worked out, first for Oshikwanyama and Oshindonga, and later for some of the other languages. This would not mean that the spoken languages would give up their identity. With one written language for these languages, however, they would be strengthened. More books could be published in the languages, magazines and newspapers could be published, and the languages would have greater chances of survival in the long run.

[171] Oshikwanyama is also used in Angola but hardly anything is being published in Oshikwanyama in Angola. Gamsberg Macmillan Publishers have suggested sending books published in Oshikwanyama to Angola but the orthography they are using differs from the one used in Namibia. Portuguese missionaries in Angola wrote down the orthography differently from the German missionaries in Namibia. There is a need to harmonize the orthography of the same language in the two countries. Work to do this is in progress. According to the Education Officer for Oshikwanyama at the National Institute for Educational Development (NIED) at Okahandja (a couple of hours drive from the capital Windhoek) Mr. Paavo Hasheela this work is running very smoothly. It would, however, have been an advantage if also Oshindonga speakers were involved in this exercise. The problems of orthography of the same language spoken in neighboring countries were discussed in a regional workshop on cross-border languages (Legere, (ed.), 1998). Karsten Legere (1998) discussed the situation of Oshikwanyma in Namibia, while Zavoni Ntondo (1998) discussed the situation of Oshikwanyma in Angola. The workshop participants recommended that a working group on Oshikwanyama orthography consisting of language experts from Angola and Namibia be established.

other Oshiwambo dialects that are more dissimilar than Oshindonga and Oshikwanyama. As noted in the preceding chapter, historically this difference in writing can be explained through the work of missionaries coming from different nations and trying to transcribe the local languages through the way similar sounds were written in their own languages. While Oshindonga, which was the first of the two dialects to be written down, was transcribed by Finnish missionaries, Oshikwanyama was put into writing by German missionaries.

It must have suited the divide and rule of the apartheid policy to keep the two dialects as separate written languages. The more separate they were, the easier a policy of divide and rule would work. After independence the pre-independence type of divisive language committees from the Bantu regime were retained in a structure parallel to the colonial/apartheid system, despite the cultural policy of the Ministry of Education and Culture (MEC) of creating "unity in diversity." To outsiders it would appear that merging these two written languages into one while retaining the oral differences, should be possible (see Brock-Utne, 1995c). Work to this effect is also in progress by Oshiwambo speakers. The question is, however, politically sensitive, and there is also vocal opposition against a merger of the two written languages, especially from some of the Oshindonga speakers. The Curriculum Committee for Oshiwambo has split into one for Oshindonga and one for Oshikwanyama. There are also two education officers for the two dialects at NIED. According to Martha Namuandi of *Out of Africa Publishers*, who herself speaks five of the Namibian languages, Oshimbalantu could be used as a written language for both Oshindonga and Oshikwanyama. She also claims that Otjiherero and Oshikwanyama are more or less the same. There are, however, Otjiherero-speakers who do not agree with this statement. *Out of Africa Publishers* has published a grammar book for grade 9 titled *Ondungila* (Mixed Up), one chapter of which is written in Oshindonga, the next one in Oshikwanyama throughout the book. It seems that teachers like this book very much.

THE LANGUAGES OF THE KHOE GROUP

The Khoesan languages are often considered autochthonous[172] in this part of Africa (Elderkin, 1995). In the southern part of Africa, about 150

---

[172]Autochthonous means the original language spoken in the area.

Khoesan languages were still spoken by small communities roughly 140 years ago. Less than a third have survived till today and most of the remaining languages, according to Vossen (1990), will die out in the near future. The speech communities of most of the Khoesan languages today constitute hardly more than a few hundred people, and in most cases the number of speakers is diminishing rapidly.[173]

As noted earlier the languages of the Khoe group which are currently approved for use in the formal educational system of Namibia are Khoekhoegowab (formerly known as Nama/Damara) and San (also known as Bushman; approved dialect Ju'hoan). Khoekhoegowab is the language spoken by the second largest group of the Namibian society (after the Oshiwambo speakers). *Khoe* means a person, *gowab* to speak. Khoekhoegowab thus means person and person speak. It was earlier termed *Khoe se khoen di gowab*—"the language of the people." It can easily be identified by its clicks and sound rhythm.

Khoekhoegowab is the language of instruction in grades 1–3 and is also used for functional literacy programs. Khoekhoegowab is taught as a subject up to grade 7 in the Keetmanshoop region (now being extended to grades 8 and 9) and to 10 in the Khorixas region. Khoekhoegowab speakers are mostly found in these two regions and in Windhoek region. Khoekhoegowab can be taken as a subject at the University of Namibia, but, as shown, the enrollment is low. The fact that Khoekhoegowab cannot be taken as a subject in grades 11 and 12 is one of the likely explanations for the low enrollment figures.

There was a feeling among Khoekhoegowab speakers that their language is consistently being marginalised. "Our language is an endangered language" was an expression I heard several times from Khoekhoegowab speakers. There was a feeling that only Bantu languages were catered for. Khoekhoegowab was not being catered for in the IGCSE (International General Certificate of Secondary Education) syllabus and was not represented in the 1995 revision of the BETD (Basic Education Teaching Diploma) syllabus for teacher training. However, as part of the revision of the BETD in January 1996, it was included.

So far Khoekhoegowab has not been included in the Basic Education Support (BES) project which has identified five Namibian languages for materials production. These five are Oshindonga, Oshikwanyama, Rukwangali, Silozi, and Otjiherero—all Bantu languages. While two di-

---

[173]An exception to this is that the Khoesan languages spoken in Ngamiland in Botswana do not appear to be dying out (Vossen, 1990).

alects of one language (Oshiwambo) were included, Khoekhoegowab was not. When I made further inquiries about this fact in the Ministry, I was told that the project was concentrating on the most disadvantaged areas in the North. In the meetings arranged for me in Keetmanshoop I was informed about the problems faced by those responsible for the teaching and administration of teaching of Khoekhoegowab. I heard the following comments at the meetings:

> The young ones don't want to speak their own language,[174] they all want to be Americans. They watch TV and get all this American stuff. They want to be like Michael Jackson and look down on their own culture.
>
> The teachers have lost interest in the language. We must develop interest in reading in the language, but there are no newspapers in Khoekhoegowab.
>
> At one place children go to a primary school where the language of instruction the first three years is Khoekhoe, next three English, and then from seventh grade Afrikaans.
>
> We have a grave problem in our region—schools apply to switch over to English from first grade. The problem is that the language policy gives the parents the right to choose the medium of instruction. Parents think that if their children start with the mother tongue, they will not be so good in English.
>
> Parents seem to think, and are probably sometimes also being informed by principals, that by using Khoekhoegowab as the language of instruction the child will become stupid.

According to research carried out in twenty-four schools in Khorixas, Windhoek, and Keetmanshoop regions in August 1995, Afrikaans was still the medium of instruction in most of the schools in all three regions where Khoekhoegowab was supposed to have been the medium of instruction since most of the learners were Khoekhoe speakers (Boois,

---

[174] The decision to abandon one's own language normally derives from a change in the self-esteem of the speech community. In cases of language shift one can observe that members, very often the younger generation of minorities, regard their own community as inferior (Brenzinger, Heine and Sommer, 1991). They have adopted the value system of the dominant group. Language shift can thus be understood as one possible strategy for members of minority groups who have developed a "negative" social identity to change an inferior position.

Skrywer, and Namaseb, 1995). English is rapidly taking over from other remaining Khoekhoe schools as a medium of instruction. This may be looked at "as a threat to the existence of Khoekhoe language" (Boois et. al., 1995: 2). Moreover, Boois and colleagues found that:

> In the schools where Khoekhoe is implemented the headmaster assigned the most incompetent and/or under-qualified teachers for teaching in grades 1–3 where Khoekhoe is used as a medium of instruction and the qualified teachers are used for other subjects and in higher grades (Boois et.al, 1995: 2).

THE SAN OR BUSHMAN LANGUAGE GROUPS

In his statement at the opening of the workshop on African languages in basic education held in Okahandja, September 1995, the Minister of Basic Education and Culture, John Mutorwa, mentioned the Bushmen especially:

> In our country before independence was achieved African languages were developed on a piecemeal basis. The result was that some languages received more attention than others and some were hardly developed at all. For example one marginalized group of Namibian citizens, namely the Bushmen or San people, received so little attention that no education was available for them in any language except Afrikaans. (Mutorwa, 1995)

There are four main San or Bushman language groups, not mutually intelligible. Not even all dialects within the largest group (Khoe) are mutually intelligible. These groups are linguistically very rich (Mendelsohn, Swarts, and Avenstrup, 1995). Of the dozens of Bushman languages only Ju'hoan has an orthography recognized by the Ministry of Basic Education and Culture (MBEC). Ju'hoan is not even the most used language. Ju'hoan belongs to the Zhu dialects which constitute Northern Khoesan (Elderkin, 1995).

Namibian as well as other linguists have a great challenge in assisting the various Bushman groups to develop the other languages into written languages. This seems to be the main reason that Ju'hoan is not used as a language of instruction in any of the government schools. This situation has unfortunate implications, as the former Norwegian ambassador to

Namibia, Bernt Lund (1995: 11) observes: "As long as San children are not offered instruction in their mother tongue in lower primary, the school is actually excluding a part of the Namibian citizens from learning."

In Rundu I was told that the only primary schools in the region that used Afrikaans as the medium of instruction were Martin Ndumba and Omega primary schools because of the many Bushman children[175] in these schools. But these children and their parents would rather have the teaching in Thimbukushu, which they all speak, or preferably in their own San language.

Only the Village School Program in the Nyae Nyae area in the northeastern part of Otjozondjupa region lives up to the rules of children being taught in their mother tongue and provides instruction in Ju'hoan. There are five schools under the auspices of the Nyae Nyae Development Foundation, one of them having two teachers and the other four having one teacher each. The teaching is of a multi-grade type. The teachers have been trained under a program of the foundation. They are selected by the community to serve as teachers but sometimes have only three to six years of formal education themselves. The World Wildlife Fund gives some support to the foundation, while SIDA supports the five village schools.

AFRICAN LANGUAGES ACROSS NATIONAL BOUNDARIES

When in 1984 the European colonial powers carved up Africa among themselves, the existing boundaries of African languages were of no concern to them. One therefore finds that many of the African languages are spoken across the artificial national boundaries. For instance, Silozi, which is spoken in the Caprivi near the border of Zambia and in Botswana, is also spoken in Zambia. It is a written language both in Zambia and in Namibia, but here also the orthography differs. There are some minor differences in orthography between the Silozi written in Namibia and that written in Zambia (see also Kashoki, Katengo, and Mundia, 1998; Elderkin, 1998). Yet in the Caprivi, books from Zambia are used as supplementary reading. Zambians buy grammar books in

---

[175] I was told that before independence the Bushman children were not allowed by the South African authorities to continue schooling past grade 6.

Silozi developed in Namibia. From 1968 Namibia was cut off from Zambia for political reasons. In this period the orthography developed differently. There is a need for joint work with Zambian counterparts to sort out matters of orthography.[176]

Silozi speakers can also understand Sesotho spoken in the Transkei (South Africa) and Setswana spoken in Botswana. For Setswana it should be possible to make use of books published in Botswana. The syllabi are, however, different. This problem should be possible to overcome with the use of teachers' guides prepared especially for Namibian children and some supplementary reading. According to the senior education officer for Namibian languages at NIED, there are only three primary schools in Namibia using Setswana as the language of instruction for the three first grades and as a subject up to grade 7. There is a wish to have Setswana also offered as a subject at a secondary school, but that wish has not materialized yet.

In the homes in the Caprivi, learners use different languages such as Sisubia, Sifwe, Thimbukushu, Siyeyi, and Sitotela—dialects of Silozi. Thimbukushu and Siyeyi differ most from the others. A large number of people in this area speak Thimbukushu. At school all must adapt to Silozi, which is the only one of the said languages written down. Silozi is actually the home language of less than 18% of the learners in grades 1 to 3 (EMIS, 1994). Yet it seems to function as a lingua franca in the region.

In Bukalo in the Caprivi, where Sisubia is spoken, I met on 30 November 1995 with the traditional leaders, the Indunas. They held that Sisubia should be the language of instruction and that funds should be made available so that Sisubia can be written down. They claimed that Silozi is a foreign language to the children of Bukalo, now being promoted at the expense of Sisubia. Their teachers would try to explain in Sisubia, but Silozi was supposed to be the language of instruction. Exam papers were set in Silozi. The spokesman of the Indunas said:

> Sisubia should be taught to the Subia people. First we had Setswana, the language of the Botswana people, then Silozi, the language of the people of Zambia, then Afrikaans and English, the languages of the

---

[176] Fortunately, a meeting on linguistic cooperation between Namibia and neighboring countries took place 23–27 September 1996. The meeting was sponsored by Deutsche Stiftung für Entwicklung (DSE, German Foundation for Development)(Legere (ed.), 1998).

whites. When do we get our own indigenous Namibian language Sisubia? We have achieved independence, so our language should be written now.[177]

THE FUTURE OF NAMIBIAN LANGUAGES

As noted earlier, there is an increasing shift from Khoekhoegowab to English as the language of instruction in grades 1–3 and a downgrading of the mother tongue. Third-year UNAM students in teaching practice also find much of the same attitude in the Oshiwambo-speaking area:

> All my respondents told me that both children, teachers, and parents prefer English to be the medium of instruction from grade one onward, because of political reasons. In this regard they told me that there is a general understanding in society that a person who does not know English is useless and unimportant in society ... The principal of Omuhonde Combined School has strongly emphasized that most parents are still demanding the immediate abolition of Oshindongo at that school in order to be replaced with English. Four respondents at Uukwango Combined School told me that there were eight pupils at their school who were transferred by their respective parents this year to English medium schools in the South which do not offer any African languages. They told me that these parents had expressed the opinion that schools whose medium of instruction is Oshindonga are useless for the future of their children.
>
> One teacher at Onantanga Junior Primary School told me that there is a general understanding in their community that Oshindonga teachers are less educated and therefore sometimes regarded as incompetent teachers while those who know English are regarded as the highest qualified ones (Assignment by Max Uutoni, May 1995, quoted in Legere, 1995: 10).

---

[177]A study carried out in the Caprivi region by Mbala, Maayumbelo, and Matongo (1995) found that about 47% of the parents preferred Silozi to continue to be the medium of instruction in the lower grades, 20% preferred English while 33% preferred their own local languages. Like the Indunas in Bukalo, these parents regarded Silozi as a foreign language being imposed on them. There is a problem of identifying the generic or "core" languages for dialects in the Caprivi. More linguistic research needs to be carried out.

Other student teachers of African languages at the University of Namibia learned that the *children* preferred the language of instruction to be Oshiwambo because that was the sole medium they understood. Many of the parents, especially the educated ones, preferred their children to be taught in English. The parents seem to feel that if children are taught in a vernacular language during the first years they would stay behind and not be as skilled in English as they would if they had been taught in that language from the start.[178]

In many ways the preindependence Bantu education scheme,[179] with its stress on the mother tongues in the first years of schooling, was a sound educational policy but for the wrong reasons. It is difficult to make Namibian parents understand that when the same policy is advocated over again but now in an independent Namibia, it is for quite other reasons. It has nothing to do with divide and rule but with furthering the intellectual learning in the best way.

The regional director in Windhoek told me he had trouble with a school in Epukiro that had recently applied to have Otjiherero as the language of instruction and wanted all the books to be in this language. This caused problems since the books had already been ordered in English, the print run had been calculated and so on. This attitude seemed not to indicate an adherence to the spirit of the curriculum guide, in which the use of the mother tongue as language of instruction should be the normal policy and not need any permission while the use of English should need extra permission. Point 9.1 of the curriculum guide for formal basic education (MBEC, 1995) concerning the language of instruction in grades 1–3, reads:

---

[178] However, as argued in the previous chapter, this belief is erroneous, but difficult to do away with when even educated Namibians hold it.

[179] The white South African government had devised a scheme for a separate education for the blacks both in South Africa and in Namibia, known as the Bantu education scheme. The education was designed to keep the blacks in their areas, both physically (in the creation of separate schools and, in the case of South Africa, universities) and mentally (in allowing the various mother tongues to be the languages of instruction for the first years of schooling along with an early introduction of Afrikaans). The policy was one of divide and rule and was strongly resented by the blacks both in Namibia and South Africa, even though lots of money was spent by the white rulers in building and maintaining the black universities in South Africa and subsidizing the cost of textbooks in mother tongues in both locales.

All learning at the early stages is done best in the mother tongue, and this also provides the best foundation for later learning in another language medium.

Therefore, wherever possible, the medium of instruction should be the mother tongue/familiar local language. In schools with learners with different mother tongues, every effort must be made to give teaching in mother tongue medium. Where there are enough learners, classes with each their own mother tongue medium can be organised. *Where it is not possible to offer teaching through the medium of the mother tongue or familiar local language, schools must apply to the Regional Director for permission to use English as a medium* (MBEC, 1995: 21, emphasis added)

PERCENTAGE OF GRADE 1–3 LEARNERS TAUGHT IN THEIR MOTHER TONGUE

Almost all of the Namibian languages have become less popular as languages of instruction in grades 1–3 than they were at the time of independence. According to the *EMIS Statistical Yearbook, 1994,* in 1994 only 7.1% of Otjiherero speakers in grades 1–3 received instruction in their home language. This, however, represents a small increase from the previous years. Only 35.7% of Khoekhoegowab speakers were taught in their home tongue; the majority were taught either in English (47%) or Afrikaans (16%) while 92% of the Oshindonga speakers and 84.2% of the Oshikwanyama speakers were taught in their home language. In both cases there has been a slight decrease (EMIS, 1994). In Windhoek in 1995, only a couple of primary schools had a Namibian language as the language of instruction in the first grades. Even in Katutura, the black township outside of Windhoek, English is the language of instruction from the first grade in almost all of the primary schools. Two lower primary schools in Katutura offer Otjiherero as a subject only.

The school principals play a decisive role in the choice of medium of instruction. They inform the parents and explain the policy. They also chair the important school committees making the decision on language of instruction for each school. Often the principals do not have enough knowledge themselves on the importance of mother tongue instruction.

One of the recommendations from the NIED workshop on African languages in basic education reads: "Studies should be made to compare the progress of children in mother tongue medium classes with the

progress of children in English medium classes" (NIED, 1995: 5).[180] The
result of such research, which had been carefully planned and carried
out, might convince parents and principals more than comparable research having been carried out, for instance, in Nigeria.

Not only has the use of the Namibian languages as languages of instruction gone down since independence. So also has publishing in these
languages. It is a vicious circle; the fewer children who have a Namibian
language as language of instruction, the less profit publishers will make
publishing in these languages. And the less printed material there is in
the Namibian languages, the less parents and children will want to
choose that language as a language of instruction (Brock-Utne, 1995c).

PUBLISHING IN NAMIBIAN LANGUAGES AS BAD BUSINESS FOR NAMIBIA BASED PUBLISHERS

Meeting with publishers in Namibia in the fall of 1995, I was repeatedly
informed that they hoped I would be able to convince Norwegian donors
to support publishing in Namibian languages. Many of the publishers
had a real concern for these languages but they were now losing money
on most books published in the minor Namibian languages. Joseph
Auala, director of African Languages at Gamsberg Macmillian told me:
"We are publishing with closed eyes. We sell so few copies of some of
the books in Namibian languages we can't really publish. We have to see
if we can get some help from donors. So when are you going to open
those sweet lips of yours and tell us in what way you can assist us?"

---

[180]As it stands, however, this recommendation might work to the detriment of the
Namibian languages. As noted earlier, there is reason to believe that less qualified teachers often are given the classes with mother tongue instruction. Studies
set up to compare the progress of children in mother tongue medium classes with
the progress of children in English medium classes have to be well designed research, keeping constant all variables except the language of instruction. Such a
design may be difficult, but not impossible, to carry out. I was told that in Keetmanshoop yet another primary school—Minna Sachs Primary—had just applied
to switch the language of instruction from Khoekhoegowab to English. If one
could have half of the school switch and not the other half, some good research
could come out of this experiment. One would have to assign teachers of the
same standard to the Khoekhoegowab medium and the English medium class(es)
and see to it that both groups get equivalent teaching material. One would also
have to make sure that learners are comparable in socio-economic standing and
educational background of the parents.

According to *Namibian Books in Print* in September 1994 there were 904 Namibian books in print. Of these, 503 titles were in the Namibian languages—56% of the total (Reiner, Hillbrecht and Katjivivi, 1994). Of the 503 books that were published the following number were published in each Namibian language listed:

1. Oshindonga. 107
2. Oshikwanyama. 97
3. Otjiherero.. 65
4. Silozi. 62
5. Rukwangali. 54
6. Khoekhoegowab. 50
7. Thimbukushu 32
8. Rugciriku 30
9. Setswana.   6

No book was published by commercial publishers in the Bushman languages. Nevertheless, given the size of the population of Namibia, the record of 503 titles published in the local languages is not an inconsiderable achievement. In comparison, since independence in Mozambique only three books have been published in African languages (Coates, 1995).

Among the ten members of the Namibia Publishers Association,[181] several are small academic publishers of research reports. The publishing companies publishing in Namibian languages and partly for the school market are Gamsberg Macmillan; Out of Africa Publishers; Longman Namibia; New Namibia Books; and the religious publishing company, Eloch. At the end of 1995, a new publishing company was established, Africagraphix.

The first book published for the Namibian market was in a Namibian language, Nama. It was published in 1830, albeit in South Africa by the London Missionary Society. The first book recorded as being published in Namibia was a mission translation of Luther's catechism into Nama/Damara in 1855. In the early days, publishing in Namibia was

---

[181] The publishing business in Namibia seems still to be very white. Little seems to have been done to train black Namibians in publishing. Unless some affirmative action is taken, this situation does not seem likely to change soon. There are lots of bright black Namibians who could be trained in the publishing business. This goes also for those who write the textbooks.

done by the missions and was religious in nature. The longest-established publishing company in Namibia was established by Finnish missionaries in 1901, now ELCIN Press at Oniipa (Coates, 1995). A wider-scale publication of African-language titles began with the Department of Bantu Education. The *Inboorling-taalburo* of the Department of Bantu Education, rooted in the apartheid system of education, began publishing in the indigenous languages in 1968. Its publishing activities were of necessity strongly linked to the shift in the official education policy for blacks toward ethnic education, which was supposed to be carried out in the mother tongue. "The effect of this policy based on ethnic divisions, meant in publishing terms a significant contribution to an expansion of skills in local publishing" (Reiner et.al., 1994: 12–13).

In 1977 Gamsberg Macmillan was the first publishing company to start publishing schoolbooks in Namibian languages on a larger scale. That publishing company is still the largest schoolbook publishing company in Namibia. Gamsberg Macmillan developed through publishing in local languages. In the financial year ending 1992, 53% of Gamsberg Macmillan Publishers' turnover was from Namibian-language publishing. Two years later, however, this number dropped to 30% (Coates, 1995).[182] Gamsberg Macmillan now owns more than 50% of Out of Africa Publishers. Out of Africa Publishers is publishing the new first-grade books in math, science, and environmental studies. The print run for Oshindonga is stipulated at 26,000 copies; Oshikwanyama 20,000 (books in these two languages must cover up for the financial loss on the books in the other languages); Otjiherero, 6,000; Khoekhoegowab, 3,000; German, 500; and Setswana, 300. (The real price would here be U.S.$290 per book if the books were not subsidized.) A publishing company needs a lot of money to publish for the first grades in so many languages. Such publishing requires a big company, like Gamsberg Macmillan.

Longman Namibia is a sister company of Maskew Miller Longman in South Africa and part of the worldwide Longman group (UK/US). They publish regionally, have materials in Setswana on the market and they are investigating the market in Angola. They have no local ownership and most of their books come from South Africa. They have had no local editors but have recently embarked on the Pamwe creative writing competition in two different Namibian languages per year. The books

---

[182] Gamsberg Macmillan has 50% local ownership and 50% ownership from the worldwide Macmillan.

published so far look exciting and attractive. The first-prize winner for the Pamwe book in Oshindonga was an 83 year-old-woman. Unfortunately, the books have so far meant an economic loss to the publishing company. Longman Namibia has only received minute orders for them. The recently published Pamwe book was published in Otjiherero. Not much more than thirty copies of the book have been ordered. The books could have been used as supplementary material in schools, but the money from the Ministry seems to go to core material and not to supplementary reading, this in spite of the fact that it is a Ministerial policy that schools should have supplementary reading. Schools do not seem to order other books than the most necessary textbooks. Longman Namibia further conclude that people with some money to buy books would rather buy books in English.[183]

Though some books have been produced in Namibian languages for the secondary school, where the languages are taught as subjects, many more are in manuscript form and are not being published because of financial restrictions. Generally, teachers are more satisfied with the books for secondary school than for primary because more of them are original works. Both in Oshikwanyama and Oshindonga several textbooks exist. The Oshikwanyama learners should also get used to reading Oshindonga and vice versa. The situation is more difficult for other languages. An Otjiherero-speaking educator said at a meeting in Keetmanshoop:

> The textbook situation is a disaster. We don't have authors for Otjiherero. The people who could write the material *say* they are not able. We need a writer's workshop. To print books for the few learners who take Otjiherero in secondary school will be too expensive for commercial firms. We shall need to print some material at NIED. We do not have a culture of developing books. Most of the school libraries are full of books in Afrikaans. Some novels and poetry published by Gamsberg MacMillan in Khoekhoe are not in the library and not in the book-shop.

It is important to note, however, that the lack of texts in Namibian languages is not just a function of limited publishing of texts in general. Students taking English, German, or Afrikaans as language subjects have

---

[183] This, however, might not be quite true. One has to remember that there is a shortage of bookshops in the country. In many places books are not available. People are not used to reading books in their own languages that are not school textbooks. Many do not know that they exist.

a lot of supplementary reading material in all of these languages. New books are constantly being published. There are daily newspapers, and an abundance of magazines but hardly any newspapers or magazines are published in Namibian languages. There is a great need for a couple of monthly magazines in Namibian languages. One of the magazines should publish in Khoekhoegowab and Ju'hoan and another magazine in the Bantu languages.[184] The magazines could also be used as supplementary reading in school.

New Namibia Books is a locally owned company which started in 1991. It is an agent for Heinemann, East African Educational Publishing and Zimbabwe Publishing House. They have co-published five science books with Heinemann, two at the primary level and three at junior secondary. New Namibia Books has recently published ten booklets containing fairy-tales in Khoekhoegowab. The series is called *Tsi i ge ge hahi* (Once upon a time.) The fairy-tales have been compiled by Sigrid Schmidt and Veronica #Eiases with the support of the German Development Foundation, which has also supported the publishing. The book company has had the same experience as the other publishing companies —the local literature does not sell. They feel that although the local languages have been strengthened in the Constitution, they have not been so in reality. The Ministry has not even evaluated the Khoekhoegowab fairy-tale booklets for use in schools, so that they can get on the reading list as supplementary reading. I was informed that two to three years often pass between the time a book has been published and the Ministry approves it for use in school.

Since independence in Namibia there has been a widening of the publishing base, with new publishers entering the market and a stronger competition. This increased activity, however, has not resulted in an increase in the number of new titles published. The publishing manager of Gamsberg Macmillan Publishers, Nick Coates, claims:

> The heyday of publishing in the Namibian languages was just prior to and around the time of independence. The post-independence changes, and particularly the Language Policy, have made it more difficult for commercial publishers to publish in African languages . . . the apartheid

---

[184] The main newspaper in the Seychelles has articles both in Creole, French, and English every day. Such magazines with columns for politics, arts, health, and sports would both give people something to read and stimulate the culture of reading.

education policy encouraged the development of African languages and books were purchased. The new government, by making English the official language, has prioritised that language and a much higher percentage of government funds are now spent on English language books. (Coates, 1995: 2–3)

One would expect that a decolonization of the African mind, including the restoration of the African languages, would figure as the topmost priority of the universities in Africa. While a debate on this is, as we shall see in the last chapter, quite strong in post-apartheid South Africa (see Malherbe, ed., 1996) most universities in Sub-Saharan Africa are just struggling to survive. The Jomtien emphasis on basic education has made a difficult situation even harder for the universities in Sub-Saharan Africa. It is to their problems and potentials that we shall devote Part III.

A Life after Jomtien for the African Universities?

*In more recent years, with the decline in
"national planning," the triumph of the market,
the preponderance of foreign institutions in
policy-making (through so-called "policy
dialogues") any pretension to national
priorities providing guidelines to research has
simply vanished. Where national research
councils still exist the statement of priorities
is never more than a wishful declaration of
intent. One may note, parenthetically, the
irony in the fact that at the time when most
African governments insisted on their national
priorities there were few indigenous social
scientists and most of the experts were
expatriates who were not bound by national
priorities. Now that Africa has large numbers
of social scientists, African governments have
lost a significant degree of autonomy and in one
way or other are pursuing objectives imposed
by external financial institutions.*

(MKANDAWIRE, 1990: 28)

CHAPTER 7

Globalization of Learning—Whose Globe and What Learning?—the Role of the African Universities

As one goes around the Faculty of Medicine, one wonders whether, after a hundred years after Karl Peters landed here, a second partition of Africa is in progress or not. The Dental School seems to be run by the Finnish, the AIDS research program by the Swedes, community health programs by the Germans, with the British, Italian, Danish all having their own corners.

(HIRJI, 1990: 23)

In Part III the other two parts of the book come together. It asks the questions: What consequences does the Jomtien emphasis on basic education have for the universities in Africa? What is the role of the donors and the universities in the north? What are the possibilities of building a university curriculum based on African culture and using African languages? Starting with the first question, we shall in this chapter point to the problems and challenges facing the universities in Sub-Saharan Africa and also point to some creative solutions. The situation in South Africa is very different from the situation in other countries in Sub-Saharan Africa and will therefore not be dealt with in this chapter but treated separately in the next chapter. Here in Chapter 7 we ask: How is it possible to prevent the globalization of learning from meaning the integration of the African elites into the culture of the former colonial masters? How is it possible to develop an African counter-expertise without a strengthening of the African universities? Such strengthening would have as an aim the restoration of African languages and culture and stop the South's curriculum dependency on the North. Such strengthening would stop the flow from global producers to local consumers and would ensure a more multidirectional flow, such as flows going South–South or South–North.

WHAT ABOUT THE LANGUAGE ISSUE
AT THE UNIVERSITIES?

At this point in time, no university in Sub-Saharan Africa has an indigenous African language as the language of instruction. The languages of instruction at the universities in Sub-Saharan Africa are the European languages English, French, Portuguese, Dutch[185] (in South Africa), and Italian (when the university in Somalia was still functioning)[186]

Ali Mazrui (1994; 1996) argues that the choice of European languages as mediums of instruction in African universities has had profound cultural consequences for the societies served by those universities. He gives as an example professional Japanese scientists who can organize a conference and discuss professional matters entirely in Japanese. (He could for that matter also have mentioned Norwegian or Finnish scientists who do the same.) Mazrui states: "But a conference of African scientists, devoted to scientific matters, conducted primarily in an African language, is for the time being sociologically impossible" (Mazrui, 1994: 120–121).

As we shall see later, however, there is at least one research institute at an African university that is capable of conducting its conferences in an African language—and does so. But generally Mazrui is correct when he maintains that almost all black African intellectuals conduct their most sophisticated conversations in European languages. "It is because of this that intellectual and scientific dependency in Africa is inseparable from linguistic dependency" (Mazrui, 1994: 121). Mazrui quotes Jomo Kenyatta in the old colonial Kenya, who said: "When the white man came to Africa he had the Bible and we had the land. And now? We have the Bible and he has the land" (Mazrui, 1996: 5), Culture—including language—was offered in exchange for material goods. The West exported its ideas and languages and imported riches.

---

[185]Afrikaans, the language of the Boers and also the Colored of South Africa is, according to Dutch people I have talked with in South Africa, 95% Dutch.

[186]In Somalia the language of instruction in all the faculties except the Faculty of Education was Italian (even though the language of instruction in primary school was Somali and in secondary school English) because the University got development aid from Italy. The Faculty of Education was, however, sponsored by the Americans and therefore English was the language of instruction there (personal communication from Hassan Keynan from Somalia, who attended my "Education in Africa" seminar while in Norway and then was sent by UNESCO to try to build up a school system in his country, where there was no state and the people are fighting).

In its publication on higher education, the World Bank (1994) does not even mention the language question. For the further growth and development of a language, its use as language of instruction at higher levels is of fundamental importance. The west-African educational researcher Adama Ouane of Mali has accurately observed:

> Unless these languages (the indigenous African languages) can step beyond the door of primary schooling, and face the challenges of secondary and higher education, with increased number of subjects to deal with, their modernization will be achieved only half-way (Ouane, 1991: 10).

At the University of Dar es Salaam in Tanzania there is one department and one institute that use an African language as the language of instruction: the Department of Kiswahili and the Institute of Kiswahili Research. Referring to the history of the Department of Kiswahli, Zaline Makini Roy-Campbell (1992a, 1992b) counters the frequently heard argument that the African languages do not have a vocabulary that is developed enough to be languages of scholarship and instruction at higher levels in the educational system. She holds that this department gives a good practical example of the coinage of technical words which was undertaken in the process of changing from English to Kiswahili as the medium of instruction.

Prior to 1970 the courses in this department were taught in English. There were no Kiswahili terms for guttural sounds and phonemes, nor even for linguistics and vocabulary. However, once the decision was made to teach the courses in this Department in Kiswahili, words were developed in the process of teaching and later standardized. Some words were used side by side as synonyms. English terminologies were used until Kiswahili terms were developed. Some English terms became Kiswahilized and some terms were found in some of the other languages of Tanzania. The process of creating new words was done with the assistance of all teachers in the Department of Kiswahili and the Institute for Kiswahili Research.

ATTENTION TO LOCAL KNOWLEDGE

Even the Jomtien declaration mentions the need to base curricula in the South on local knowledge. In the preamble to the World Declaration on Education for All (WCEFA, 1990), it is recognized that "traditional knowledge and indigenous cultural heritage have a value and validity in their own right and a capacity to both define and promote development." In light of the "education for all" emphasis, professor Komba of the University of Dar es Salaam in an assessment of the Tanzanian "education for self-reliance" policy stresses the need to "analyze the possibilities to revive and use dying traditional learning systems in various tribes" (Komba, 1996: 6). To me the great question is: How is it at all possible to reconstruct the curriculum of African schools, to root it in African culture, without a great emphasis on indigenous research, preferably by African scholars who are clearly African-based in their outlook? Ali Mazrui (1978: 352) notes that "the full maturity of African education will come only when Africa develops a capacity to innovate independently." This independent innovation may incorporate elements from the West but must be based in African roots.

THE UNEVEN DISTRIBUTION OF RESOURCES FOR HIGHER EDUCATION

The International Development Research Centre (IDRC) suggests that differences between nations in their capacity to generate and utilize knowledge will create a new "global apartheid" (IDRC, 1994). And in the last decade there has been increasing inequality. The 1997 Human Development Report of the UNDP (United Nations Development Programme) notes the worsening gaps between the rich and the poor within and among countries:

> The share of the poorest 20 percent of the world's people in global income now stands at a miserable 1.1% down from 1.4% in 1991 and 2,3% in 1960. It continues to shrink. And the ratio of the income of the top 20% to that of the poorest 20 rose from 30 to 1 in 1960 to 61 to 1 in 1991 and a startling new high of 78 to 1 in 1994 (UNDP, 1997: 9).

As the UNDP report also indicates, the inequalities between the North and the South increased even more with respect to the development of scientific capacity and technological development than in terms of income distribution. In less than ten years, the North's advantage in the number of scientists and technicians expanded by 60%. Between 1980 and 1990, the gap in research and development spending widened by 170% (UNDP, 1994). The United States, the European Union, Japan, and the former Soviet Union share 88% of the world's resources for research (including some people born in the South who are part of the brain drain to the North.) The countries in Sub-Saharan Africa share less than 1% of the research and development-oriented scientists and engineers (many of whom are trained in the North) and about 0.2% of the global expenditures for such activities (Barré and Papon, 1993). This widening gap to the detriment of Africa occured in part because of an unequal flow of international assistance. For example, of all World Bank projects in support of science and technology in higher education and industry since 1970, no less than two-thirds were executed in the Asia/Pacific region. More than 75% of the value of all science and technology projects went to Asia, and somewhat less than 5 % went to the African region (Muskin, 1992).

In her paper on the power of knowledge Berit Olsson (1995) claims that the most glaring inequalities are demonstrated in the opportunities for higher education. In only fifteen years, the differences in university enrollment levels doubled in favor of the developed world (UNDP, 1992). While the most advanced countries have more than 5,000 students per 100,000 inhabitants, the least fortunate ones educate fewer than 25 per 100,000 (UNESCO, 1998). Table 7.1 presents selected data from the 1998 *World Education Report* from UNESCO concerning the enrollment in higher education in twelve African and six Western industrialized countries.

As shown in table 7.1, in most of the African countries named here only about 5% of those in the higher education age-group actually take one type of higher education. In the developed countries, half or more than half of the age-group are enrolled in higher education. It is these latter countries which through their commitment to the policies of the World Bank, are encouraging African countries to reduce their higher education enrollment even further.

THE ATTITUDE OF THE WORLD BANK TOWARD UNIVERSITY EDUCATION IN THE SOUTH

More than twenty years ago, the World Bank (1974) in its *Education Sector Working Paper* began the process of emphasizing the importance of primary and basic (including non-formal) education. At the same time the Bank urged that the proportion of education lending to this sector be increased (from 11% to 27%), thus reducing the proportion going to higher education (from 40% to 30%). Although non-formal and adult education soon dropped from Bank priorities, it did prove possible over the

Table 7.1 Gross Enrollment Ratios for Selected Countries, 1995

Countries	Number of Students per 100,000 Inhabitants	Gross Enrollment Ratio (%)
Botswana	403	4.1
Burkina Faso	96	1.1
Eritrea	102	1.1
Malawi	76	0.8
Mozambique	41	0.5
Namibia	738	8.1
Senegal	290	3.4
Swaziland	543	5.1
Uganda	142	1.5
Tanzania	43	0.5
Zambia	241	2.5
Zimbabwe	679	6.9
Canada	6,984	102.9
United States	5,395	81.1
Finland	4,033	66.9
France	3,617	49.6
Norway	4,009	45.5
United Kingdom	3,126	48.3

Source: UNESCO (1998: 148–151).

next twenty years to raise dramatically the proportion of lending for basic education and to reduce the proportion to higher education, as planned, to approximately 30% (King, 1995). *The Education Sector Policy Paper* at the beginning of the 1980s (World Bank, 1980) was remarkable in that there was no more than a page or two of discussion on higher education in some 100 pages of text.

At a meeting with African vice-chancellors in Harare in 1986, the World Bank argued that higher education in Africa was a luxury: that most African countries were better off closing universities at home and training graduates overseas. Recognizing that its call for a closure of universities was politically unsustainable, the Bank subsequently modified its agenda, calling for universities in Africa to be trimmed and restructured to produce only those skills which the "market" demands. Such was its agenda for university restructuring in, for instance, Nigeria, in the late 1980s (Mamdani, 1993). Isahaku Sadique (1995), through his analysis of the World Bank's involvement in the university sector in Nigeria, concludes that the World Bank sees university education for Africans as a luxury. He also shows how the Bank obliged the National University Commission (NUC) "to reallocate resources in order to shift emphasis from arts and humanities to science, engineering, and accountancy" (Sadique, 1995: 130). He further reports that the World Bank insisted on choosing the contractors who were to supply the needed materials (books, journals, laboratory consumables) and that these contractors were foreign companies.

Chapter 2 presented an analysis of the World Bank's 1988 paper on *Education Policies for Sub-Saharan Africa: Adjustment, Revitalization and Expansion (EPSSA)*. Even though African policy-makers at earlier meetings about World Bank policies for the educational sector had strongly opposed the suggestion of a stagnation in enrollments in higher education, this suggestion is, as noted in Chapter 2, advanced repeatedly in the *EPSSA* paper. It is suggested that students pay for their upkeep at the university. Cut-backs in funding to the universities are suggested in fields like the arts and humanities, exactly those fields which could most easily be focused on restoring the African heritage. The advice to cut back on higher education in Africa will increase the dependency of Africa on studies overseas, staffing their institutions of higher learning with expatriates and people who have been trained mainly overseas and given mostly Western, in any case, non-African concepts, ideas, outlooks, and research methodologies.

The brain-drain from Africa will continue and the need for expatriates increase. Sub-Saharan Africa lost 30% of its highly skilled manpower between 1960 and 1990, largely to the European Union countries. The United Nations Economic Commission for Africa estimates that since the 1960s more than 50% of the Africans who pursued tertiary studies in chemistry and physics in the United States never returned to Africa. On the other hand, more than 100,000 expatriates from the industrialized countries in the North are employed in Africa, and this costs U.S.$4 billion per year, accounting for nearly 35% of the continent's official development aid (Bekele, 1997).

The thinking of the World Bank was also quite instrumental in shaping the 1990 Jomtien conference "Education for All." In Chapter 1 we described some of the policies coming out of this conference and the fear of the countries in the South that the donor emphasis on basic education would mean a further starvation of higher education. At the Jomtien conference a whole series of countries were lobbying for more explicit safeguards for higher education, research, and access to high technology. The thrust of this concern was from Latin America, with other signatories coming from Africa and Asia, the Caribbean, and Europe. *NORRAG News* (1990: 6) claims that the pressure from the developing countries led to Article 8, point 2 in the World Declaration on Education for All:

> Societies should also insure a strong intellectual and scientific environment for basic education. This implies improving higher education and developing scientific research. Close contact with contemporary technological and scientific knowledge should be possible at every level of education. (WCEFA, 1990:8)

In an evaluation of the outcomes of the EFA conference from an African perspective, Aimé Damiba, the program specialist in education and planning in UNESCO's regional office in Dakar, Senegal concludes: "We must avoid the danger of limiting ourselves to basic education and neglecting high level manpower training and research. It is not possible to solve the problems of Education for All without a national pool of expertise and without an indigenous capacity for research" (Damiba, 1991: 11). Yet many officials of third world countries seem to interpret the outcomes of the Jomtien conference as a wish from the donor community to limit their renewed effort within the education sector to primary education and to tell developing countries to do the same. As we have already seen, their interpretation seems, unfortunately, to be correct.

There is considerable overlap between the *EPSSA* paper from 1988 and the 1994 World Bank paper *Higher Education: The Lessons of Experience*.[187] The proposed stagnation of higher education, which can be

[187] Of the 152 bibliographic references mentioned in the back of the 1994 World Bank booklet, only 32 (21%) are not World Bank publications or publications of Bank staff. This fact leads one to question whose experience is meant by the subtitle "The Lessons of Experience"? Fernando Reimers (1995) is struck by the fact that even UNESCO's 1993 policy paper *Strategies for Change and Development in Higher Education* is not mentioned as a publication from which to draw lessons of experience. Nor are any of the many important publications from the Eastern and Southern Africa University Research Project (ESAURP), written by African university people.

found in the *EPSSA* paper, is also a prominent feature of the higher education paper of 1994. The safeguards that people from the South thought they had managed to get into the Jomtien declaration do not seem to have had any effect on the World Bank's position. In the *EPSSA* study the focus on higher education was principally on the public university sector, whereas in 1994 one of the main themes was that there should be diversification of higher education with attention to the whole range of private sector and non-university institutions.

Lene Buchert (1995d) asserts that the expectation that the World Bank higher education paper would defend the higher education sector against other priorities, and argue its relevance among and support of other sub-sectors of education, is not fulfilled. If they should have been fulfilled, the arguments in the document would have centered on the importance of both traditional and modern goals of education. The paper would in that case have focused on higher education as a knowledge producer, a values and culture transmitter, and a capacity builder for industry and business. Instead, the lens through which higher education is seen in the Bank's document is primarily an economic one. The Bank wants to reduce government expenditures to higher education in Africa. Colclough (1995b), however, points to the need for increased support rather than reduction in the expenditures for higher education in many countries, particularly in Sub-Saharan Africa. In the World Bank's paper on higher education, recommended solutions are those which can simultaneously reduce costs and increase access specifically to those areas of education which support the utilitarian purposes of the university. The following are the main policy prescriptions around which the higher education paper (World Bank, 1994) is centered:

- **A Redefined Role for the State in Higher Education.** A predominant role is given to the market in relationship with the state. This ignores the fact that in most African contexts there is no local industrial dominance and no powerful private sector with which the state can share the responsibility for higher education. Moreover, as Keith Watson (1995) demonstrates in an article on redefining the role of government in higher education, in many of the key country cases (e.g., OECD countries and NICs) the state has maintained an interventionist role in the higher education sector.
- **Institutional Differentiation.** The World Bank gives a predominant role to the private sector in the relationship with higher education institutions.

- **Diversification of Funding.** This means cost-sharing measures, including user fees, university partnership with business—privatization and diversification of the higher education system. The assumption made by most advocates of user charges at the tertiary level is that net private returns would remain high enough, even after the imposition of fees for higher education, to make studies a rational personal investment. Yet, as argued by Colclough (1995a), most of the evidence upon which this assumption is based uses earnings data from the 1960s and 1970s, and does not accommodate the strong reductions in real earnings and earnings differentials between university graduates and other workers, which have been a characteristic of the 1980s in many developing countries and especially in Sub-Saharan Africa.
- **Policy Attention to Quality, Responsiveness, and Equity.** African countries have to prove themselves worthy of Bank support for higher education, and this worthiness is measured by results in terms of equity and quality at the primary and secondary levels. In his criticism of the 1994 World Bank paper on higher education, Kenneth King (1995) finds that the paper announces a new conditionality: *higher education only after adequate provision of primary and secondary education.* The World Bank paper ignores the importance of a well-functioning higher education system in efforts to achieve quality at other sub-sectoral levels.

THE EFFECTS ON HIGHER EDUCATION
OF A CONCENTRATION OF RESOURCES
ON BASIC EDUCATION

Knowing the attitude of the World Bank to higher education in Africa, there is reason to fear that the renewed emphasis on basic education will indeed lead to a further starvation of higher education and intellectual life in Africa. Studies after the 1990 Jomtien conference have shown that the focus of education aid among many multilateral and bilateral donor agencies is increasingly shifting to the basic education level. As noted in Chapter 1, Lene Buchert (1995c) shows that even agencies which had generally allocated by far the larger proportion of their bilateral education assistance to the higher education sub-sector, now have adopted policies in favor of the basic education level. This includes for example the Italian Development Cooperation, the Dutch development agency DGIS (Diretoraat-General Internationale Samenwerkung), the UK-based Overseas Development Administration (ODA) and the French Ministry of Development Cooperation.

The increase in resource allocation toward basic education is often clearly indicated by the donor agencies as being undertaken at the expense of higher education. For instance Wolfgang Kuper of the German development agency (GTZ) notes:

> Since the World Conference on Education for All in Jomtien, Thailand in 1990, the promotion of higher education institutions in developing countries by Ministries of Development Cooperation has no longer been popular—at least in Germany but also in some other industrialised countries. The promotion of basic education has been getting more emphasis—in our country initially at the expense of the promotion of higher education. (Kuper (1998: 23)

Donor policies have two direct consequences for the universities in Africa:

—An increase in user fees at the universities in Africa (and dropping of book allowances, food allowances, and free tuition) make the universities in Africa places of learning only for the well-to-do.

—African university people feel compelled to seek donor support for a department, a faculty, a research institute, building up links with more affluent universities in the West.

As for the first point, even World Bank figures are unequivocal in showing that the majority of students in Africa—an average of about 60%—come from the ranks of the peasantry, workers and small traders who are not likely to have the means to meet the increasing cost of university education. The natural outcome will be an increase in drop-out rates among students from poorer family backgrounds. In Kenya's Moi and Egerton universities, for example, with a combined population of about 6,000 students, over 2,000 students were deregistered in early May 1996 over non-payment of fees and tuition (Mazrui, 1997). These tuition "defaulters" are more likely to have come from lower than upper-class families. According to Alamin Mazrui: "The net effect of the World Bank's structural adjustment programmes in education, therefore, is increasingly to transform the African university into a "white collar" institution in terms of the parental background of its student population" (Mazrui, 1997: 40).

As for the second point, the support to the universities in Africa from the North could in theory come as a grant that the universities themselves could use as they wanted. This is, however, seldom the case. In a paper on North and South partnership models in the university sector, Endashaw Bekele (1997) of Addis Ababa University in Ethiopia asserts that the support his university gets from SAREC (Swedish Agency for Research Cooperation with Developing Countries) is superior to other donor support because they have been supplying a recurrent budget of foreign currency. This is much better support than the provision of equipment (which often breaks down and for which there is no budget to get spare parts) or long-term fellowships.

The so-called "experts" and university people from the North go to Africa to teach, to "transfer" knowledge. In reality those of us from Europe and North America may have more to learn from Africans than they have from us. The fact that we are "experts" in our own countries, for instance, in competitive sports of a Western kind, women's law in Norway, AIDS prevention in the North, or commercial forestry or fishery in the North Sea, does not make us experts on the use of the body in Africa, women's law in Africa, the spreading of AIDS in Africa, sexual norms among various African groups, African agro-forestry, or tropical multi-species fishery in shallow waters. Whenever there is a review of a department at an African university receiving donor support, one should ask questions like: How much has the support been given as a help to self-help, as a possibility for Africans to do research on their own culture, and how much has it been another "transfer of knowledge" project? How much do we from the North come to learn: language, culture, traditional law, and traditional medicine? How much do we listen and learn to appreciate the indigenous knowledge?

The support that universities in Africa normally get comes in the form of link arrangements between universities in the North and South. "Experts" from the North coming to teach and distribute the Western curricula are normally part of the link phenomenon. So are books written in the West, computers from the West, and scholarships for master's and Ph.D. students to go to the West to study the curricula offered there. Rarely are provisions made for students from the North to study in the South or for professors in the South to be visiting professors teaching in the North. No wonder then that many academics in the South become Westernized in outlook. Staf Callewaert, who has done extensive research in Namibia, Mozambique, and Guinea-Bissau, tries to explain why one seldom finds African researchers questioning Western schooling as such: "As a rule you cannot expect the educated African to use much energy to reconstruct and problematize the break, by which he or she became exactly what they are: educated in a modern Western sense of the word" (Callewaert, 1994: 108).

The newsletter of the Academic Staff Assembly at the University of Dar es Salaam further clarifies the dilemma surrounding university links with institutions outside the region:

> The situation at the University of Dar es Salaam is a microcosm of that in the nation as a whole. Here, in the midst of filthy toilets and classrooms with broken windows and furniture, thrives the LINK phenomenon. Virtually every department, under the threat of material and intellectual starvation, has been forced to establish links with one or more institutions, mostly from the West. We depend on the links for the training of our junior staff, for teaching material and equipment, and a host of other things. The link agreements are, almost without exception, as unequal as would be expected. This is despite some efforts to include clauses suggesting reciprocity . . . What is primarily at stake is that as we lose confidence in our own ability to sustain our education system we shall also have to abandon the pretence of determining our educational future (UDASA, 1990: 1).

In the same newsletter, Sheriff (1990: 2) writes about the way the once proud academic community of the University of Dar es Salaam "has been brought to its knees, begging from donors and the ubiquitous 'Links' merely to keep on breathing."

In 1990 the university teacher Karim F. Hirji came back to the Faculty of Medicine at the University of Dar es Salaam after eight years of studying and working abroad. The epigraph that opens this chapter is taken from a heartfelt article about his meeting with the LINK phenomenon. Hirji (1990: 23) further writes that he is definitely in favor of international exchange and that such exchange should be cultivated in any university: "However when such exchanges are solely conducted in the framework of a donor-recipient relation, what is there to guarantee that they are conducted on the basis of academic equality and mutual respect?"

To establish a North–South cooperation in the university sector which is truly symmetrical is an accomplishment that must be regarded as utopian, given the unequal distribution of resources in this world. The mere fact that one party is giving the money and is a "donor," while the other party receives the money and is a "recipient," is a disempowering and asymmetrical relationship. Below we shall examine a couple of examples of such cooperative links.[188]

THE FIELD OF LAW

In 1988 Norway took the initiative to start offering diploma courses in women's law in universities in eastern Africa. It is important to note that the courses were not started as a result of requests from East African institutions, but as an initiative from the Norwegian Development Agency (NORAD). At the time of the first review of the initiative, four courses had been conducted, with three taking place at the University of Oslo and the fourth at the University of Zimbabwe (UoZ). Participants came from Kenya, Lesotho, Mozambique, Swaziland, Tanzania, Uganda, Zambia, and Zimbabwe. An evaluation of these courses concluded:

> The Institute of Women's Law in Oslo seems to have over-played their role in terms of administrative and professional contribution to the implementation of the course. They seem to have disregarded, perhaps because of time constraints, the points of view of partners at the UoZ who, at times, felt that their role was minimized to being host for the Norwegian "directors." Clearly, also selection of candidates and the course content were taken out of the hands of the UoZ.
>   . . . Many participants question the relevance of the Norwegian approaches in various lectures. It appears that there were too many Norwegian lecturers with rather limited competence in the African women's living conditions and reality . . . In the future concerted efforts must be made to develop a course content taking the perspective of African women as a starting point. (Hyden, Kazembe, Lexow, and Wirak, 1991: VIII.)

The review mission quotes African researchers who maintain that there are difficulties regarding the application in an African context of feminist jurisprudence developed in Norway. They point to historical, cultural, social, and legal differences and the fact that in Africa the cultures and societies are deeply gender-rooted. They note that the position

---

[188]These are examples I happen to know. They involve Norwegian academics but there would be no problem finding other examples involving academics from other European or North American universities.

of an African woman is relational, in terms of her position in the extended family and kinship system, rather than individually based as in Europe. Furthermore, the dual system of customary and common law, which often coexist in many African countries, makes matters even more complex than in Norway.

The review mission cites the report of Mary Maboreke, the diploma course leader and lecturer at the Department of Private Law at the University of Zimbabwe. She states that, increasingly, both methodology lectures as well as those dealing with substantive topics tended to turn more and more toward customary law to try to identify aspects which could be used as bases for solutions which are both native/indigenous and appropriate to Africa as people felt that perhaps they should look "inward" for customary solutions for African problems rather than look "externally" for imported solutions in general law or other importations from Western countries. Maboreke illustrates this by looking at the way battered wives are sheltered in Western and African societies. In the African tradition, she claims, a woman who is beaten by her husband could always find sanctuary with one of the relatives either on her own or her husband's side, thus leaving the problem "a family matter," which is all important in African tradition. The Western form of "outside intervention" without first exhausting the process of family dispute resolution is foreign to African thinking.

Another African participant, Janet W. Kabeberi-Macharia, a lecturer of law at the University of Nairobi and a guest lecturer at the diploma course in 1990, states:

> So far the subjects/topics have been centred on a comparison between the Norwegian perspective and the African perspective. If we continue teaching women's law, using the above comparisons, there is a danger of regarding the Norwegian perspective as being the ultimate goal for "African" women's law. It is high time that this scope was expanded to include other perspectives from other countries. However, what is most important is the development of an African perspective on women's law, centred on the need of African women and their experiences. (quoted in Hyden, et al., 1991: 30)

One would think that the differences between a Norwegian perspective on women's law and an African one would make it interesting for Norwegian lawyers to come to Africa to learn about African law, to study the fascinating clashes between traditional law and codified law so well described, for instance, by Rwezaura (1985).[189] The danger that Norwegian (or other non-African) academics will be cultural imperialists is clearly there, if we come with the attitude that we are the teachers, the ones who know, and if we view our role as being in Africa to impart our knowledge, to enlighten and to inform, and not to learn. That attitude could certainly be found in the following example.

A DEPARTMENT OF PHYSICAL EDUCATION AT AN AFRICAN UNIVERSITY

Sendeu Titus Tenga, now completing his doctoral degree at the University of Sports and Physical Education in Oslo, Norway, in 1994 wrote a very interesting master's thesis on the Norwegian Sports for All project (SPA) in Dar es Salaam, Tanzania. This project was the fore-runner of the link arrangement between the University of Sports in Norway and the Faculty of Education at the University of Dar es Salaam. The project was run in Dar es Salaam from 1984 to 1990, by the Norwegian Federation of Sports (NIF) with support from the Norwegian Development Agency (NORAD).

In his thesis, Tenga (1994) mentions that the Sports for All project was initially an idea of the NIF which the Tanzanian side found undesirable but later accepted. He shows how the SPA project has been totally Norwegian-dominated and has not taken into account the indigenous culture or ways of doing things in Tanzania. For instance, the SPA people saw it as their aim to organize all soccer players into clubs. In Tanzania one just joins in when one sees someone kicking a ball. Young boys play soccer barefoot and with a home-made ball made out of newspapers and string—well suited for bare feet. The Norwegians organized the boys in clubs and supplied them with shoes and real footballs, sports equipment

---

[189]Baltazar Rwezaura (1985), who teaches law at the University of Dar es Salaam, has written a most fascinating study of the Kuria social system and traditional law in Tanzania. He writes about maritial disputes over property rights, regulation of bridewealth, disputes over the control of children, and judicial allocation of matrimonial assets. The *makamona* (woman-to-woman) marriages are explained through their economic and social significance and the legal problems they represent when met by codified law built on Christian principles. This is done by someone who has studied these systems through first-hand knowledge of them. It is sad to see that a book of such high importance for legal studies in Tanzania especially, but also in Africa generally, is published abroad and impossible to buy in Tanzania.

which made Tanzanians dependent and undermined their self-reliance strategy.

In his thesis Tenga discusses the health concept, how "sports for all" is a concept from the West to keep people fit; because of a sedentary lifestyle moving around in cars, sitting at work, or in front of the television, and a lot of eating, people in the West have problems with the heart and obesity. They need regular exercise and the sports equipment industry makes profits from this need. Tanzanians get exercise in their daily activities (a lot of walking, working in the fields, etc.). Their health problems are different; they include lack of nutritious food and clean water.

In another paper Tenga (1997) discusses how the traditional sports and games in Tanzania like wrestling, skipping-rope, gambling, and canoeing were integral to the traditional process associated with the general survival of the people. Exercise also took place during the traditional dances where everyone participated. There was a richness of indigenous games, initiation rites, and rituals. Modern sports, as they have been exclusively developed in the Western societies of Europe, were introduced to Africa during the colonial period. Tenga claims that:

> the introduction of modern sports was the most useful strategy used by the British colonial administration in moulding the people in order to serve the interests of the colonial masters. It introduced the people in the colonies to Western ways of life and value systems, and thus made it easier for colonial administrators to control and rule the people . . . During this period, traditional sport and games, just like the tribal languages, were completely prohibited in schools and missionary settings (Tenga, 1997: 3).

Post-colonial Africa was faced with the task of reconstructing society along lines that emphasize Africanization, restoration of pride, and cultural heritage, as well as unity among various ethnic groups. Tenga (1997) describes how Tanzania aspired to adopt the *ujamaa* ideology, whereby Africa should be developed on the basis of the traditional patterns of social life in African societies. Sports, both in its traditional (ngomas and dances) and modern forms, were included in the curriculum in order to promote the values of "cooperation" and "solidarity," the two principal values of *ujamaa* ideology.

The Sports for All project in Tanzania was dysfunctional because of its non-recognition of the socio-economic realities in Tanzanian society, its manipulative policy of free distribution of sports equipment and sport gear, and the non-incorporation of traditional sports and games into its programs.

> What needs to be emphasized here is the fact that rather than promoting mass sport, the project had been effectively promoting modern competitive sport, especially through its emphasis on "street club" formation. It should be noted that if the emphasis on "street club" formation had succeeded, it could have destroyed the whole flexible and accommodative culture of sport participation in Tanzania since that would have implied that an individual can only participate in sport through her/his registered club, a typical Norwegian model of sport participation (Tenga, 1997: 5).

Tenga (1997) tells how in his first week in Norway he was personally caught in this clash between the Tanzanian culture of anybody joining in when he or she sees someone playing soccer and the Norwegian culture of organized sports. On his way home to the student housing area he saw some people playing soccer on the ground beside a sport stadium. Very happy that he had finally found a place to play soccer, he decided to rush home to change and join them. But he was not allowed to play and instead was given the address of their club to apply for a membership!

Through the initiative of the Norwegian University of Sports and Physical Education (NUSPE), Norwegian sport aid has been responsible for the establishment of the Department of Physical Education, Sport, and Culture (PESC) at the Faculty of Education, University of Dar es Saalam (UDSM). Like the Sports for All project, the initial idea of this project also came from NUSPE. The staff of the Faculty of Education at the University of Dar es Saalam were initially not enthusiastic about the idea of a degree course in sport. As the head of Department of Educational Psychology, I was present in the faculty meeting when the initiative of the NUSPE was discussed. I remember well the initial lack of enthusiasm for that particular department. It was mentioned that a department of special education might be more needed. Tenga (1997) notes the fact that the degree course offered by the new PESC department puts more emphasis on the teaching of modern sports, and gives a very minimal regard to traditional African sports and games. He also notes the struggle in meetings and exchange of letters between NUSPE and UDSM for the inclusion of the word *culture* in the name of the new department. NUSPE wanted the department to be called Physical Education and Sports but the UDSM insisted on the inclusion of the word *culture* in order to give the department, and thus its degree, a broader perspective in line with sport in Tanzania. Including the word "culture" might also mean including traditional dances and traditional games. It took more than three months to resolve this dispute, after which the word *culture* was reluctantly accepted by NUSPE.[190]

INSTITUTION BUILDING—WHOSE INSTITUTIONS ARE BEING BUILT?

The Danish fishery biologist Henrik Gislason and I did a project review[191] of the diploma/Master of Philosophy courses in Fisheries Biology and Fisheries Management at the University of Bergen for candidates from developing countries. We were asked to assess the degree to which the course had led to institution building in the recipient countries. After visiting Tanzania, Zimbabwe, and Sri Lanka and looking at the facilities there and the cooperating institutes in Norway, we concluded:

> The degree to which the course has assisted in institution building in the recipient countries is difficult to assess. Very little of the total course budget has been spent outside Norway and it is far more obvious that the course has led to institution building in Norway than in the home countries of the participants (Brock-Utne and Gislason, 1993: 35).

Unfortunately, this observation holds true for very many projects within higher education in the third world which have made use of development assistance.

[190] I remember reading through the first newsletters appearing in 1990 from this "link," all published in Norway and sent back to Tanzania. Most of the articles were written by Norwegians who would use the term "Department of Physical Education and Sports." When Tanzanians wrote, they would always call the department the Department of Physical Education, Sports, and Culture.

[191] Donor-sponsored projects are from time to time reviewed by the donors. Project teams are chosen by the donor. They normally consist of people from the donor countries and some local experts, who are never as well paid as the expatriates and often do not have much say in how the report is written. Project reviews have become good business for development consultancy firms—and their full-time employees and contract workers—in the North.

GETTING INDIGENOUS KNOWLEDGE INTO THE FACULTIES OF FORESTRY AND AGRICULTURE AT AFRICAN UNIVERSITIES

In a project review of the Faculty of Forestry at the University of Agriculture, Morogoro, Tanzania, my colleagues and I learned that "women are the main managers of natural resources on land in Tanzania" (Brock-Utne et al., 1990: i). The review mission, therefore, expressed concern that very few women have graduated from the Faculty of Forestry and that there are no women at all among the academic staff. It also expressed concern about the curriculum at the Faculty which pays too little attention to farm and community forestry, including natural tree vegetation for domestic use. Too little emphasis is placed on agro-forestry and rural problems: "For women trees and forests are multifunctional, whereas men tend to concentrate on their commercial potential for timber and other goods" (p. 3). There are the so-called women trees, the multi-purpose trees used for food, fodder and fuel, and the men trees used for timber.

According to the Tanzanian biologists Adelaida Semesi and Felister Urassa (1991) many women have accumulated knowledge about some of the causes and effects of crop failures, and spoiled food, and have devised ways to overcome such problems. Some solutions work very well. Moreover, village women are great science teachers in the fields of agriculture, medicine, and food technology and they pass their knowledge on to their children, friends, and neighbors through practical training. A mother will show the children how to plant seeds, weed, select seed, and identify pests and she will even explain about the different soils suitable for the different crops. She will also talk about food processing and food preservation, for instance, through drying or smoking meat.[192]

---

[192] Since much of this knowledge is not documented, it is not easily developed or challenged. As a consequence the accumulated knowledge is seldom consulted to develop a better understanding of the environment. This can be illustrated by the Kongwa groundnut scheme, which failed because local people were not consulted to assess the suitability of the soils and reliability of the climate to cultivate groundnuts (Semesi and Urassa, 1991). Not *all* indigenous knowledge is sound, even though it can have survived for generations. At a session on 30 September 1997 within the "Education in Africa" seminar series, the Norwegian physicist Svein Sjøberg gave the example of the old indigenous advice handed down through generations that if your skin is freezing and has white stains (e.g., during a storm while cross-country skiing) you should rub the white stains with snow. He said that medical research had shown that such a thing is the worst thing you can possibly do. But much indigenous knowledge (e.g., within herbal medicine) is well worth listening to, to try out and learn from.

Lancy (1996) points to sensitive and open-minded research by ecological anthroplogists in recent years which has shown that the kind of subsistence practices followed by slash-and-burn horticulturalists, such as the Kpelle people in Liberia, far from being inefficient, are wonderfully adapted to the local ecology. He sees Western aid, whether in the area of agriculture or schooling, as something which destroys the original culture and sets the Kpelle society on to the *Kwii* way. *Kwii* in the Kpelle language is a general term that refers to Westerners and Liberians who dress and talk like Westerners, live in towns, participate in the cash economy, and so on. In order to avoid African societies going further on the *Kwii* way, African universities need to pursue research based on local experience in collaboration with the people of Africa.[193] What is most needed now is for African researchers to be able to develop academic fields from African roots.

Archie Mafeje (1992), writing on the indigenization of intellectual discourse in Africa, reminds African intellectuals of the guiding principle in Socratic thought: "Know thyself." Looking at African philosophical thought, he finds grounds for a new reconstruction and self-realization. He sees that unwritten accounts, transmitted in stories, legends, myths, and so on reflect in various ways African philosophical thought, and are sources of high significance and authenticity.

In an article on the teaching of philosophy in African universities, Kwasi Wiredu (1984) laments:

> An African may learn philosophy in a Western institution of higher learning abroad or at home and become extremely adroit in philosophical disputation; he may even be able to make original contributions in some branch of philosophy. The fact remains that he would be engaged in Western, not African philosophy. Surprisingly, many Africans accept this; they have even seemed to take it as a matter of course . . . The usual practice seems to reserve all references to African conceptions to classes on African philosophy. As far as the main branches of philosophy are concerned, African philosophical ideas might just as well be non-existent. This trend, I suggest, ought to be reversed (Wiredu, 1984: 31–32).

Wiredu makes himself a spokesperson for the strategy of "counterpenetration." This strategy is meant to impress upon the world that it has

---

[193] I have shown here that in the field of African languages, culture, and dances; physical education; philosophy; law, and environmental studies Africa has a lot to offer.

something to learn from Africa, that in the global culture which is evolving, the West does well to listen to Africa.[194] It is a strategy mentioned by Ali Mazrui (1978: 350), who raises the question whether African universities that have been so permeated by Western culture in turn can affect Western thoughts and values. He thinks this is possible and outlines his strategies of domestication, diversification and counterpenetration (Mazrui, 1978, 1992). The balance of cultural trade between the North and the South has to be restored. The strategy will not work, however, unless Africa builds on its own foundation and stops mimicking the West.[195]

I agree with Wiredu and Mazrui that African researchers need to develop academic fields from African roots. The West can help by showing interest in the endeavor, giving economic support, and no longer sending so-called "experts" who come to teach and not to learn, who have the audacity to impose Western culture on a defenseless continent that is lost and needs to return to a familiar point—its own roots—before rushing on.

BUT THERE ARE SUCCESS STORIES

In an interesting criticism of a Norwegian white paper on North/South policy, the Indian researcher Sanjit Bunker Roy (1993: 10), director of the Society for Work and Resources Centre in Tilonia, lists some priority areas for Norwegian South/North policy in sustainable development:

- Stop sending "experts" to the South and wasting resources. Instead the strategy should be to build local capacity. It should not be seen as an opportunity to provide jobs to Norwegians in the South. This is not "untied" aid.
- Put more time and energy into developing people to people projects and exchanges.
- Identify successes in approaches, methods, and implementation as a result of development aid that could be duplicated elsewhere in other countries in the South.

[194] There is much the West could learn from the black people of Africa about leading a good and harmonious life, taking care of each other and the beloved dead ones, and being one with nature and the spiritual world.
[195] Mahatma Gandhi gave the same advice to women, in whom he had much greater faith than in men when it came to creating peace in this world. This is what he said about a woman behaving like a man: "She can run the race but she will not rise to the heights she is capable of by mimicking men" (Gandhi, 1940; see Brock-Utne, 1985 and Brock-Utne, 1989 for a further discussion of women and peace).

- Promote low-cost, community-based innovations.
- Stop training engineers, doctors, and professionals in Norway. They become misfits in their own country.
- Top priority should be given to strengthening indigenous local institutions.

A program which to me seems to combine several of these priority areas is the ALLEX (African Language Lexicon) program, which is a joint project of the universities of Zimbabwe, Göthenburg, and Oslo designed to provide a range of monolingual dictionaries for the local languages in Zimbabwe, the chief of which are Shona and Ndebele. The project is a major step in upgrading some African languages to the benefit of the local people. The work is done by Zimbabweans who are native speakers of the languages in question. Financial aid is given through SIDA and NORAD (via the Norwegian University Fund (NUFU)—the organization for development aid through university cooperation). The Swedish and Norwegian lexicographers help with the computerization and share their experiences from working with Swedish and Norwegian dictionaries. They are taught about structures in African languages they did not know before and about meanings of different words rooted in a different cultural setting. The Zimbabweans engaged in this project claim that they really get a "help to self-help" in an area of the greatest importance for the masses of Africans.

A NORAD project which to me also seems to combine several of these priority areas in a successful way is a project that aims to build up the Department of Animal Science and Production at the University of Sokoine in Tanzania. Here NORAD has been successful in building local capacity. A master's of science course for this department was first built up at Ås College of Agriculture in Norway but with the clear intention from the start that after a few years the course would be transferred to the University of Sokoine. Here the number of students increased and the curriculum was partly indigenized. The staff morale and performance of this department is high. Hardly any of the staff members had left their position in the department when it was under review in 1992 (Brock-Utne, Chichaibelu, Kauzeni, and Wiktorsson, 1992).

The German Development Foundation (Deutsche Stiftung für Entwicklung, or DSE) has embarked on an interesting project to build educational research capacity in eastern and southern African. The project is enabling African educational researchers to meet, carry out small research projects, build networks, and exchange information. With a little seed money the project has enabled African educational researchers to come up with some original research from their own societies using qualitative methods (Mwiria, 1998; Brock-Utne, 1999).

THE LINK THAT IS REALLY MISSING

I ask the same question as Xabier Gorostiaga, rector of the University of Central America (UCA) in Managua, Nicaragua, asked when he analyzed the situation of Latin American universities:

> What, then, does it mean to train "successful" professionals in this sea of poverty? Does an institution that does not confront the injustice surrounding it, that does not question the crisis of a civilization that is ever less universalizable to the great majorities of the world, merit the name "university"? Would not such an institution be simply one more element that reproduces this unequal system? (Gorostiaga, 1993: 29)

What is really missing in most of the universities in the South is the link between academia and the ordinary people. Values and knowledge creation, particularly through independent and basic research, is critically important in order to develop the African continent as a creator of science and technology and not simply a consumer of imported versions. This knowledge creation has to be produced together with the local people. Examples of the missing link between local and university know-how can be found in most departments in all of the universities in Africa. University know-how has come about through studying texts which are relevant in the North but not in the South. Xabier Gorostiaga (1993) writes about professors of business administration in the South who cannot research businesses of twenty workers because such businesses do not use the sophisticated accounting systems that they studied in the texts and which are used by only a small minority of factories in the South. In countries where the immense majority of farms belong to small and medium-sized growers, some professors of agricultural administration are only comfortable with the business and state administration schemes that they know from the Harvard manuals.

The missing link is between the macro (national alternatives) and the micro (local experiences). There is a lack of what Gorostiaga calls "people-bridges" capable of creating communication links among different local experiences, of promoting experimentation among them, or of pushing viable national programs based on their successes. This gap between the macro and the micro subverts the efforts of people from the South to find an alternative national development model. Gorostiaga argues for a transformation of the universities of the South to include local knowledge. In a study on the African experience with higher education commissioned by the Association of African Universities, Ade Ajayi, Lameck Goma, and Ampah Johnson (1996) reach the same conclusion: African universities must serve the African masses and build on local knowledge:

> That the universities in Africa should seek to be more African than they are is no longer a matter of debate. The real challenge is to concretize this by doing things African with greater resolve and creativity. Regrettably, African universities have not taken up certain important African issues with the necessary determination, aggressiveness and continuity . . . How many African scholars have cared, for instance, to study and understand the successes of African market women?
>
> Or that in agriculture, some traditional methods seem to have been more successful than several of the environmentally unfriendly modern methods?
>
> Or the fact that traditional medicines are coming into vogue even in the industrialized countries? What remains of African traditional society is an extremely important source of material for the intellectual endeavour of African universities . . . The social sciences in African universities are presently not sufficiently detached from Western, especially American, jargon and influence. They have not really taken root in the African universities or been significantly inspired by the fundamental circumstances of African societies (Ajayi, Goma, and Johnson, 1996: 234–235).

"The Universality of Values" There is reason to beware of the tendency of the West to claim universality of values that are particular to Western history and culture.[196] To create intercultural awareness, we need to problematize the notion of the universality of values. Tandon (1995: 11) writes about the tendency of the West to claim a universality for their definition of human rights and, worse, applying them as conditionalities for aid. In doing so, "the West commits the classic error of

---

[196] For example, Yash Tandon (1995), former minister in Uganda now living in Zimbabwe, criticizes the way the concept of human rights has come to mean civil rights embedded in Western liberal and individual expression.

transposing its values on weaker populations who pretend to share those values for the sake of aid or development assistance."

It is not easy for us who live in the affluent West to start questioning our own values, our own behavior, and approach the culture of other people with an open mind and a willingness to learn from them. How much are men willing to listen to and learn from women? How much are we in the West willing to listen to the indigenous peoples of this world? As John Synott (1994: 75) observes: "Omission and silence are strategies of oppression as much as active oppression, as well the feminist movement has shown us."[197]

AFRICAN METHODS OF CONFLICT RESOLUTION

It is important that African peace educators do not derive their theories mostly from Western peace educators but search in their own heritage for an African way to deal with conflicts. The African Association for Literacy and Adult Education (AALAE), which is a Pan-African association, has outlined a three-year research project in peace education. Among the main objectives are the following:

- To research into the African concepts and terms of conflict, as well as into African methods, techniques and processes of conflict prevention, management and resolution.
- To establish and articulate a philosophy, principles and world outlook which underline African concepts of conflict, conflict prevention, management and resolution.
- To promote and generate public interest in African concepts of conflict, and methods, techniques and processes of conflict prevention, management and resolution as a resource for managing and solving contemporary conflicts. (AALAE, 1994: 19)

Thandika Mkandawire (1990: 26) sees the disintegration of the research infrastructure as the most strikingly visible feature of the crisis of

---

[197] In his article on the Australian Aboriginal constructions of humans, society, and nature, Synott (1994) explains the Tjukurppa—the holistic knowledge system of the Australian Aboriginal people. He shows how the indigenous people of the world, whose societies the West continues to oppress and destroy, are struggling to preserve and assert the very values and forms of social organization which peace educators are trying to promote.

social sciences in Africa. As a result of the "Book Hunger"[198] libraries are collapsing, means for travel to carry out field research hardly exist, and when they do exist, they are linked to some short-term consultancy work for government or an external agency.

In his article titled "The African Social Science Research Environment," Mkandawire claims that national priorities within research and education are vanishing all over Africa:

> In more recent years, with the decline in "national planning," the triumph of the market, the preponderance of foreign institutions in policy-making (through so-called "policy dialogues") any pretension to national priorities providing guidelines to research has simply vanished. Where national research councils still exist the statement of priorities is never more than a wishful declaration of intent. One may note, parenthetically, the irony in the fact that at the time when most African governments insisted on their national priorities there were few indigenous social scientists and most of the experts were expatriates who were not bound by national priorities. Now that Africa has large numbers of social scientists, African governments have lost a significant degree of autonomy and in one way or other are pursuing objectives imposed by external financial institutions (Mkandawire, 1990: 28).

Is there anything researchers in the North can do about the situation? What they should *not* do is to embark on so-called "collaborative research" where the research agenda is set in the North; the concepts, theories, and methods of analysis are Western methods; and Africa again serves the function of providing raw materials. We can come to learn, help to ask the questions, and let African voices speak. Carol Opok, a trainer of change agents in Uganda, asserted in a Norwegian TV interview aired in August 1995: "We Africans need to come back to ourselves as a people. It is only the African who knows best how he can describe and manipulate his circumstances, his environment. The real thing has to start from here. The questions must be asked here. You can help us ask the questions if you like, but the answers are here in Africa." She was

---

[198] "Book Hunger" means there is no money to buy new books and especially not to get hold of books relevant to Africa. There is a high mortality rate of journals. As noted in Chapter 4 books originating in developing countries, especially in Africa, are highly underrepresented in the world today.

addressing development workers from the North but she could have been addressing researchers from the North defining the questions to be researched and the answers to be given to African problems.

THE VOICE OF AFRICANS

African researchers know their environment better than any expatriate knows it and will be more likely to ask the right questions provided that they are allowed to ask them and not forced to work with questions of concern to Western donors and provided that they trust their own experiences and use those to form concepts instead of merely transferring concepts formed in the West and based on experiences in the northern hemisphere. Abu-Loghod (1991) states:

> Women, blacks, and people of most of the non-West have been historically constituted as others in the major political systems of difference on which the unequal world of modern capitalism has depended. . . . being studied by "white men". . . turns into being spoken for by them. It becomes a sign and instrument of their power. (Abu-Lughod, 1991: 142–143)

In the *Handbook of Qualitative Research* edited by Norman Denzin and Yvonna Lincoln (1994), John Stanfield discusses the work in the area of qualitative research that has been shaped by Eurocentric biases. He is himself an African-American sociologist with extensive research experiences in African-American and African institutions and communities. However, this does not make him an African. But like me, he wants to take up the challenge posed by Carol Opok and help to ask the questions. Maybe we shall be able to counteract some of the tendency of African researchers to rely mainly on Western sources and assist them in asking questions built on their own experiences and environment.

A concrete illustration of helping African researchers to ask questions occurred some years ago in my work at the University of Dar es Salaam, when a colleague of mine wanted to write a paper on the albino children in Tanzania. As a good researcher with a traditional training, she went to do a library search since there was no time and no money for a larger empirical study. The question she seemed to ask herself was: "What do the books in the library of the University of Dar es Salaam have to tell us about the albino children of Africa?" In the library she found American

differential psychology books which treated the phenomenon of albinoism. She found some useful information about genetic causes, but the
books did nothing to discuss living as an albino in the southern hemisphere. So she did not put anything about that into the paper. She had no
sources that covered such a phenomenon. She tried to make the paper
African through the sources she could find about the albino children in
Africa. These sources were written by Western anthropologists from their
viewpoint and described how albino children had been looked at as devils
in some tribes and killed right after birth or as creatures to be honored and
given prominence in other tribes. The Western bias was clear in the descriptions, but my colleague did not have the time to do research herself,
to interview elders in various tribes about their views on albino children
and find out about the treatment such children were and had been subjected to. So her paper became a mixture of these anthropological sources
from the West and the American textbooks on albinoism.

I knew that this colleague happened to have two albino sons herself.
She felt, however, that drawing on her own experiences with them was
not "scientific," that she would be accused of being subjective. She did
not dare to let her own experience speak through her own voice.[199]

I asked my colleague: "If you should tell me the three most important
problems your albino sons have encountered, what would they be?" She
thought for a while, mentally reformulating the research question she had
formally narrowed down to a library search into a more meaningful question: "What do my experiences tell me about raising albino children in
Africa?" After we had discussed the question a while, we could group the
main answers to the question into the following categories:

---

[199] The question of the legitimacy of personal experience as a source of scholarly
work is also faced by feminists and some other interpretivist researchers. For example, in an article titled "The Validity of Angels," the feminist scholar Patti
Lather (1995) relates that within the little work that does exist on narrative inquiry into the lives of persons with AIDS, women's voices are largely absent. In
an article dealing with the concept of voice, the American curriculum specialist
William Pinar (1995: 1) says: "There is a silence of women's experience and
voices, the splitting off of women's lived worlds from the public discourse of education." Janet Miller (1982: 5) asks: "How much does it take to break silence?"
It takes a lot. Maybe we as researchers from the northern hemisphere may help
legitimize the experiences of African researchers as the most valid knowledge
there is of African living and African education.

1. *White Skin in an Environment of Black People.* The fact that her sons were white, while all their friends were black, made them an object of teasing, often of bullying. One of the boys had had such a hard time at one school that they had to take him out of the school. Other children would say that their mother had been thinking of a white man when having sex with their father and cruel things like that.[200]

2. *The Amount of Sun in the Southern Hemisphere.* The fact that the sun shines all day the year around could make life a torture for these children. Waiting for the schoolbus could be especially painful. They sometimes had to wait for a long time and there was no shade where they waited.[201]

3. *The Poverty of the South.* The poverty of university staff in Tanzania made it almost impossible to get the things that would make life somewhat easier for the albino kids: sun-screen lotion with a strong factor, long-sleeved shirts, caps, and sun-glasses.

These three problems, however, had not been discussed in her paper because she did not find them described in any literature and did not think that a scientific and scholarly paper, which was going to count toward promotion, could build on her own personal experiences. I was trying to convince her that putting herself and her own experiences into the paper was not unscientific. On the contrary, her lived experiences through many years could be analyzed and were the most valid and reliable data she could find. Building on them would be describing African experience from an African viewpoint and would add to the knowledge base an indigenized perspective which was sorely needed.

In Chapter 4 I noted the need to do secondary research in African social science. There is, for instance, abundant information on African traditional education in works of European travellers and American and European anthropologists. But this information is often written from a biased view-point and needs a reanalysis based on oral literature from the elders in Africa. I noted also the study of riddling activity made by

[200] In Norway, for instance, albino children do not look very different from blond Norwegian children in the winter-time. They are not immediately branded as different-looking.

[201] The textbooks written in the North do not discuss this phenomenon. In the countries in the northern hemisphere it is cold most of the year, the sun is not up always, and it is easy to hide from it. When you are an albino, it is exceedingly more comfortable to grow up as a Norwegian than as a Masai.

one of my students, Ishengoma, and how he was able to argue against Western social anthropologists who looked at riddles as a form of entertainment and amusement for children. With his African background Ishengoma was able to ask the right questions when he collected his data, namely: What is the educational value of the riddling activity? What is learned through it? The way he has collected his data makes it easy for educational planners to answer the question; How can the riddling activity be used to build an education rooted in African daily experiences? The expatriates who look at riddling as an exotic type of folklore, comparing the activity to activities they found in the West and therefore branding it as amusement, were not able to ask the right questions and thus lowered the validity of their work.

A reanalysis from an African perspective also of the evaluation exercises performed by expatriate teams coming to Africa on brief missions would be fruitful. For example, the traditional quantitative input-output research design normally used in the larger World Bank studies assumes first that the adopted policy is actually implemented, and second that this process of implementation corresponds to the policy directive itself. A useful illustration of this is a major World Bank evaluation of the diversification of secondary schooling in Colombia and Tanzania (Psacharopolous and Loxley, 1985). For the Tanzania data, the statistical analysis was based upon comparisons of students from their designated curriculum choices. However, research of a more qualitative nature undertaken by Tanzanian researchers has shown that not only did the official choice often not correspond to the actual one (a fact that principals might not be prepared to disclose in their response to the questionnaires in the World Bank study), but also that the policy was not actually implemented in many secondary schools (Lema, 1972; Besha, 1973; Muganyizi, 1976; Mblinyi, 1976; Manase, 1978).

In regard to my colleague's writing on her experiences of living with albino children in Sub-Saharan Africa, we may say that such an autobiographical description has high ecological validity[202] since it is very likely that the three categories of problems experienced by my colleague would also be experienced by other black parents of albino children in Sub-Saharan Africa. In an autobiographical approach as in a case-study approach, anonymity is hard to uphold. Yet these approaches may be

---

[202] For a discussion of reliability and validity in qualitative research within education in Africa, see Brock-Utne (1996b).

those most needed in African educational research today, in a research that will restore the African dignity and not mimic the West.

RESEARCHING YOUR OWN SOCIETY THROUGH QUALITATIVE METHODS

Vigdis Stordahl (1994) has done anthropological research on the Sami population, the indigenous people of the north of Norway. She is herself a Sami and discusses the reaction of her own people to her presence as a researcher among them. She relates that most of the time the reaction from her Sami friends has been: "At last someone from our own people doing research on us and not only foreigners." She relates that she clearly is expected to bring forth a new understanding, which they will recognize and which is the *duohtavuohta* (the truth). But she also warns against culture blindness. Culture blindness is a phenomenon which has to do with the fact that you may become blind to what you experience every day. It is difficult to go from being a participant to an observer. And if you succeed in becoming an observer, it may also be difficult to "switch off" (Stordahl, 1994). She realizes that she is not an average "Sami." Her many years of study and her training as an anthropologist make her see things from a certain position. The truth Stordahl finds will be a "positioned truth."

This also holds true for African researchers who have spent many years of their life unlearning the presuppositions they brought from their home environment to school and becoming Westernized in outlook. As we shall see in the next chapter, those working in universities in South Africa also face the challenge of restoring the dignity of African culture and not mimicking the West, despite the fact that many of them have been socialized in ways that make them at least partially culturally blind.

CHAPTER 8

Africanization of the Universities of South Africa

> *It is obvious that transformation of universities in South Africa involves major academic, intellectual and philosophical arguments about who and whose knowledge to teach, learn and research. The transformation is about Africanism versus Europeanism on the African continent. . . . How on earth can the African majority acquire freedom, power and justice by remaining a shadow of another distant nation and culture?*
>
> (MAKGOBA, 1997: 173)

In the fascinating book *Mokoko—The Makgoba Affair* Professor William Makgoba (1997) describes his background and upbringing as well as the chain of events that forced him to resign as deputy vice chancellor of the University of Witwatersrand (in daily communication called Wits) in Pretoria. Makgoba also expresses his views on the universities in Africa in general and the universities in South Africa in particular. How much are these universities going to be copies of European universities and how much will they realize that they are situated in Africa on African soil? What does educational transformation mean in relation to the universities of South Africa?

Makgoba (1997: 174) realizes that the universities in Africa generally are still very much tied to the "colonial motherland in a rather *imitative and replicative fashion.*" Himself a medical doctor, he holds that most South African doctors today would find it easier to practice the medicine they were taught at medical schools in South African universities in the United Kingdom, than among the majority population of South Africa as the medical school curriculum in South Africa is based on and is a true replica of the British system of health care. The medical profession does not seem to realize that they are working in Africa and could have a lot to learn from the traditional healers of Africa:

We have not brought traditional healers into the system. If we western doctors were to interact more with traditional healers, we might learn a lot and we might be able to teach them too. The point is that without the participation of these people, we'll never be able to institute the primary health care system we need (Makgoba, 1997: 195).

The academic staff of the medical faculties in South Africa would have quite a bit to learn should they care to spend some time at the department of traditional medicine at the University of Dar es Salaam, for instance. Instead they are going overseas. Makgoba (1997: 198) argues that some shared values are fundamental features of African identity and culture:

> These, for example, include hospitality, friendliness, the consensus and common framework seeking principle, ubuntu,[203] and the emphasis on community rather than the individual. These features typically underpin the variations of African culture and identity everywhere. The existence of African identity is not in doubt. How African culture is maintained and articulated is another matter.[204]

SOUTH AFRICA IN AFRICA

While the average gross tertiary enrollment rate for Sub-Saharan Africa is 1.4%, for South Africa it is 19.8%. On average only 14 young people (10 men and 4 women) out of every 1,000 have the opportunity to attend a university or college in SSA. In contrast, in South Africa it is almost 200 (198), of whom 98 are women (Sutherland, 1997). But as we shall see in a moment these numbers gloss over large inequalities among the different racial groups in South Africa.

A count of the universities reported to be located in the 54 countries and island states that are considered most commonly to make up "Africa"

---

[203] *Ubuntu* is a Zulu word which is derived from the stem *-ntu* of the noun *umuntu* (person). It refers to a state of humaneness, goodness, virtue, quality, good character, honesty, uprightness, considerateness, mercy and understanding. These are, according to the researcher of Zulu traditions, Sibongile Ramelimetya Thandiwe Koloti (1999) the more important attributes of *ubuntu*.

[204] As mentioned in Chapter 4 Catherine Odora (1994) of Uganda is concerned about the way Western schooling destroys the communal character of African indigenous education. "The moment children go to school, they learn to talk about 'my chair, my homework, my position' and less and less about 'our,' 'we'."

suggests that there are about 160 universities in Africa. South Africa's 21 universities, comprising 12.8%, and Nigeria's 30 (18.2%) make up almost a third of the universities on the continent (Sutherland, 1997). If the pool of universities under consideration is limited to "anglophone Africa," almost two-thirds of the institutions under consideration are in either South Africa or Nigeria. In Africa, 8 countries have no university, 2 have a single institution, and 14 have fewer than 5 universities.

South Africa has not only one of the largest but also one of the oldest and most developed systems of higher education in Sub-Saharan Africa. Prior to 1943, South Africa and Egypt were the only two countries on the African continent that had functioning modern universities. Sutherland (1997: 2) mentions that while Egypt, Morocco, and Mali can lay claim to three of the most ancient seats of learning in the world, "it is in South Africa that the modern university has its longest roots." However, she does not discuss the fact that the South African universities have been very European in orientation. Prior to and during the colonial period, there were only a handful of university colleges in Sub-Saharan Africa, established by European colonial powers. The extraordinary spread of universities across the continent took place during a thirty-year period, between 1950 and 1980: over half of all universities (54%) on the continent were established during this period, and an additional 29% (primarily in Nigeria) were founded *after* 1980.

South Africa's dominance in higher education is very clearly seen both from the number of research articles published in internationally recognized journals and from the number of books in the university libraries. Sutherland (1997) has made an interesting compilation of the number of volumes in the ten major libraries on the African continent. Her data, extracted from *The World of Learning* (4th edition, 1996), are presented in Table 8.1.

As the table shows, seven of the ten universities on the African continent and seven of the eight universities in Sub-Saharan Africa, which have the highest number of volumes in their libraries, are in South Africa. Those readers who are familiar with South Africa will, however, note that *all* seven of these universities belong to the group called "historically white universities" (HWUs).

On an annual basis the *Science Citation Index* lists just over 600,000 journal articles from 3,300 major journals across 100 scientific disciplines. Table 8.2 (from Sutherland, 1997) is constructed on the basis of identifying the number of articles whose authors reside in one of the thirty-nine countries in Sub-Saharan Africa.

Table 8.1 Major Libraries in African Universities

Country	Institution	Volumes
South Africa	U. of South Africa	1,520,000
Egypt	Cairo University	1,162,700
South Africa	Witwaterstrand U.	1,015,604
Egypt	Alexandria U.	1,000,000
South Africa	U. of Pretoria	942,389
South Africa	U. of Cape Town	865,200
South Africa	U. of Stellenbosch	810,000
South Africa	U. of Natal	702,000
Nigeria	U. of Nigeria	700, 588
South Africa	Potchefstroom U.	635,000

Source: Sutherland (1997)

Table 8.2 Journal Articles Listed in *Science Citation Index* (1995)

Country/ Region	Articles	% of Total	% of SSA's Total
Grand total	607,409	100	-
Sub-Saharan Africa	5,857	0.96	100
South Africa	3,158	0.51	53.9
Nigeria	555	0.09	9.4
Kenya	479	0.07	8.2
Tanzania	154	0.02	2.6
Zimbabwe	152	0.02	2.6

Source: Sutherland (1997)

As the table shows, more than half of the research articles listed in the *Science Citation Index* and originating from Sub-Saharan Africa were written by authors working in South African institutions.[205] This

[205] It should be mentioned here that for many years prior to 1994 there was an academic boycott of South Africa which probably affected publication, as scholars from South Africa would not be given space in the journals in the West.

first of all tells something about the publishing opportunities for African academics, and the lack of refereed journals in Sub-Saharan Africa that appear regularly enough and have high enough stature to be listed in the *Science Citation Index*. Moreover, just as was the case for the library holdings, these statistics concerning South Africa gloss over, as we shall see in a moment, great inequalities between the historically white and the historically black institutions.[206]

A LEGACY OF INEQUALITY

In his book with the telling title, *A Legacy of Inequality*, Ian Bunting (1994a) describes the system of higher education in South Africa in the years immediately preceeding the April 1994 elections. His term "higher education" comprises the teachers' colleges, the technikons (technically oriented tertiary institutions), and the universities. My focus will be on the universities.

As noted earlier, there are currently twenty-one universities in South Africa. These comprise ten historically white, residential universities; the open university UNISA,[207] Durban-Westville, historically meant to cater

[206] In order to address these inequities the government has, through its new Education Act, decided to embark on an ambitious program of a reestablishment of a Culture of Learning and Teaching (COLT) (Moyo, 1997). Cecilia Moyo, when she was the Director of the South African Agency for Academic Development (SAAAD), described the new program: "Embedded in our thrust for reestablishing COLT, is a push for an egalitarian ideology for public education as well as principles and ideals of equity, redress and the quest for a democratic imperative in all our spheres of life in South Africa" (Moyo, 1997: 2). She goes on to tell how in South Africa education was used by previous apartheid era governments to perfect their discriminatory policies. "The stuggle to delegitimate these governments centered on education. It is therefore prinicipally and politically correct to galvanise the country's resources to reconstruct COLT" (p.9).

[207] The University of South Africa (UNISA) started in 1873 as the University of the Cape of Good Hope, purely an examining body for other institutions. In 1946 the University of South Africa was formed as a distance learning university. I was told in October 1995, when I gave a talk at that university located in Pretoria, that at that time it had 128,198 students. Of these students 40% were white, 4% colored, 46% black and 8% Asian; 54% of the students were female. In 1955 71% of the students at UNISA were white, 3% colored, 18% black, and 8% Asian. The average age of the students is 31. The academic staff told me proudly that UNISA had had open admission all through the apartheid period. I was later told by black colleagues both in South Africa and in Namibia that the teaching philosophy at UNISA had been characterized by fundamental pedagogics built on Christian national principles.

for the Indian population;[208] the University of Western Cape[209] historically meant to cater for the colored population; and eight universities created to serve Africans (i.e. black South Africans) primarily: the University
of Fort Hare, the University of the North, the University of North West
(previously named University of Bophuthatswana), the University of Zululand, the University of Transkei, the University of Venda, Medunsa University (a medical university in Johannesburg), and Vista University (an
open university with many campuses scattered all over the country).

HISTORICAL BACKGROUND

The Nationalist Party victory in 1948 launched the party's determination
to gain firm control over all educational institutions for blacks and implement its Christian National Education principles[210] formulated in 1939,
thus giving concrete meaning to the Afrikaner ideology of white su-
premacy. The Eiselen Commission in 1950 formulated more specific educational policies, namely, the Bantu Education Act of 1953, the Colored
Persons' Education Act of 1963, and the Indian Education Act of 1965.
Education was to be the principal instrument to achieve the aim of separate development. Mokubung Nkomo (1990: 293) quotes Verwoerd, then
Minister of Native Affairs, during the parliamentary debate on the Bantu
Education Bill in 1953: "Education must train and teach people in accor-
dance with their opportunities in life, according to the sphere in which
they live."

     The Afrikaans-speaking universities and university colleges specifi-
cally barred the admission of non-Europeans. Ajayi, Goma, and Johnson
(1996: 33) explain: "Without saying so, the English-speaking [universi-
ties] rarely admitted non-Europeans." Although white English-speaking
universities (Natal and Rhodes as well as the universities of Cape Town
and the Witwatersrand) claimed to practice open admissions, blacks were
required to obtain a permit from the Minister of Education for admission.
In some cases, blacks who were considered personae non grata[211] by the

---

[208]The proportion of Indian students at Durban-Westville fell from 87% in 1986
to 59% in 1990 (Bunting, 1994: 55).
[209]The proportion of colored students at Western Cape fell from 88% in 1986 to
68% in 1990 (Bunting, 1994: 55).
[210]These principles will be explained later in connection with the educational
methods named "fundamental pedagogics" (FP).
[211]Usually they attained this status because they had participated in some protests
against the government.

state were not admitted. Eisleen (1950) estimated that in 1948 there were only about 400 full-time African students in universities in South Africa. Most were registered at Fort Hare, or at the non-European section of the University of Natal. At the Witwatersrand and Cape Town "open" universities, there were less than 100 African students (Stolten, 1997). These figures indicate not only how few African students there were, but also the extent to which university education was already segregated. One of these few token black students at the University of Witwatersrand in those early days was Nelson Mandela. He tells about his experience:

> Despite the university's liberal values, I never felt entirely comfortable there. Always to be the only African, except for menial workers, to be regarded at best as a curiosity and at worst as an interloper, is not a congenial experience. . . . Although I was to discover a core of sympathetic Whites who became friends and colleagues, most of the Whites at Wits were not liberal or colour-blind (quoted in Makgoba, 1997: 185).

Makgoba finds that this statement, reflecting the experiences of Mandela in 1942 as a student, is as true today as it was then: "It encapsulates the experiences of many Blacks at Wits and in other so-called English-speaking universities such as UCT, Rhodes and Natal" (p. 185).

In the 1950s several contending models of university apartheid had circulated. Common to all of them was the contention that white and black students should study separately. Besides this there were three basic ideas voiced by those arguing for higher education of blacks:

1. A relatively non-interventionist version: black students should also have a right to attend universities; however, they should preferably be provided with segregated university education and students would make out of it what they could.
2. University colleges for blacks were needed to provide administrative and technical expertise required for development in the Bantustans (the separate homelands "allocated" to the majority population).
3. The university colleges were to provide a locus of political control—removing students from the stormy political influences of the cities and molding them to play a role in the broader strategy for political control based on the Bantustans.

In 1959 the apartheid government passed the Extension of the University Education Act and the Fort Hare Transfer Act. These two acts transformed tertiary education in South Africa.

The University of Fort Hare is the oldest and in many ways the most prestigious of the black universities. It was the one and only independent black university in South Africa before 1960. The university was erected by mission interests in 1916. It is the university not only of Nelson Mandela, Oliver Tambo[212] and Mongosuthu Buthelezi[213] but also of President Robert Mugabe of Zimbabwe; the former Botswana president, Sir Sertse Khama; and Prime Minister Ntsu Mokhehle of Lesotho.[214] By the 1950s Fort Hare had developed a political culture that was particularly galling to apartheid policy makers. In 1957, in a direct reference to Fort Hare, Minister of Native Affairs, Verwoerd,[215] warned that: "control of [black universities] by the government is needed as it is necessary to prevent undesirable ideological elements—such as has disturbed the non-white institutions not directly under the control of the government" (quoted in Balintulo, 1981: 149).

During the 1960s a systematic program was developed by the government to recast Fort Hare as an institution under the total control of the government, an institution which would, at best, develop a corps of African administrators for the two proposed "Xhosa" homelands (Beale, 1990). Academic staffing, curriculum development and student admission policies were radically changed to meet the perceived needs of the then new "homelands" policy. After 1960, government intervention at Fort Hare involved an intertwined political and educational strategy designed to clear the environment at Fort Hare which nurtured anti-

[212]In the beginning of 1999, Tambo, formerly the vice-president of South Africa, took over the presidency after Nelson Mandela.
[213]Buthelezi is the leader of the Inkata, the Freedom Party of the Zulus. Many of the Inkata members want Zululand to be an independent state.
[214]The University of Fort Hare in late 1995 had 5,599 registered students, among whom were 8 colored students but no white students. The university has the following seven faculties: theology (51 students), law (645 students), arts (2,651 students), science (661 students), education (596 students), economic science (672 students), and agriculture (323 students). About 95% of the students are undergraduate students. (The student numbers given in parentheses are numbers collected by me during my visit to the University of Fort Hare in October 1995.)
[215]In April 1958 Verwoerd became prime minister of South Africa and leader of the National Party. As prime minister he worked relentlessly to further the politics of apartheid he had begun as a Minister of Native Affairs.

apartheid political activity and to direct students instead toward a political future in the Bantustans.

In the 1950s pro-apartheid university officials had struggled to reconcile their need to maintain control over the direction of the university colleges with the principle of separate development, which required that control of the university colleges would eventually be transferred to the ethnic communities they served. In this context it had been explicitly articulated that where possible, African academics should be employed as teachers and administrators. But the general political climate together with the specific political dynamics at Fort Hare combined to make the need to control the institution a priority—even a higher priority than hiring African academics, let alone devolving authority to the administrators, faculty, and students.

Immediately after the passage of the Fort Hare Transfer Act in 1959, the Department of Bantu Education began to employ a range of tactics to purge the staff, including direct dismissals and the introduction of conditions which made remaining on the staff untenable. In late 1959 the department gave notice that eight senior staff members would be dismissed, including the rector and the registrar. The Minister of Bantu Education, W. A. Maree, said: "I disposed of their services because I will not permit a penny of any funds of which I have control to be paid to any persons who are known to be destroying the government's policy of apartheid" (*Rand Daily Mail,* 10 November 1959). In terms of the Transfer Act, the department also announced a set of stringent and repressive regulations. African members of staff were not allowed to engage in any political activity, not even in legal organizations. After considering the implications of this restriction, another ten members of the academic staff resigned. Among these was Professor Matthews, who was just a few months from retiring and who lost all of his retirement benefits by resigning a few months short of the deadline (Beale: 1990: 43).

At other South African university institutions staff members were employed by and answerable to the council of the respective university. At the African university colleges,[216] all academic members were officially employed by the Department of Bantu Education, and as a result, academic staff members were strictly controlled. Lecturers were reportedly in constant fear of dismissal. The academic staff was also monitored by the security police. The security police was involved in helping

---

[216]The university colleges for black students were in reality undergraduate colleges often controlled by a nearby white university.

to curtail contact with academics from other universities. In 1962 when some Fort Hare students were still completing courses being examined by Rhodes University, two Rhodes lecturers, who went to Fort Hare to give extra lessons, were escorted from the campus by the security police. The registrar, meeting them in a security police car, told them that no one had the right to visit the campus without his permission.[217]

Over the past two years I have had the opportunity of visiting five of these eight so-called historically black universities (HBUs). I also have had the privilege of participating, on behalf of SAAAD (South African Agency for Academic Development) and sponsored by DSE (Deutsche Stiftung für Entwicklung), as one of six facilitators in a series of research capacity-building workshops aimed at young academics in the HBUs. The aim of our research workshops was not solely to build research capacity among black academics but also to Africanize the research.[218] The pamphlet announcing the program for prospective participants describes the background of the program:

> The research generated by South African institutions does not reflect African experiences and realities and is dominated by Eurocentric research methods and epistemologies. In African culture there is an over-reliance on orality for the transmission of knowledge between generations. This knowledge must be captured and preserved through authorship.

All twenty-one of the participants in the series of research work-

---

[217] It should be mentioned that the University of Fort Hare gave early attention to African studies, particularly in the study of languages, literatures, and the traditional societies of the Xhosa, Sotho, Tswana, and Zulu, before African studies became politicized and distorted under the apartheid system (Ajayi et al.1996: 36).

[218] The series of workshops are follow-ups to similar workshops arranged in eastern and southern Africa where academics felt a need for more training in qualitative research methods since they had had little training in that type of research through their studies. The South Africans, especially under the leadership of the then director of SAAAD, Cecilia Moyo, saw the participation in this program for black academics as an opportunity to do valuable research of interest to the majority population and to start an Africanization of research in South Africa (see Brock-Utne, 1999).

shops were Africans coming from the HBUs. Three of the other five facilitators also came from HBUs, one worked at UNISA, and one came from Kenya. As facilitators we tried to help participants root their research in African experience, to learn to be producers of knowledge rather than mere reproducers. We tried to fulfill some of the hopes of Makgoba for knowledge production in the universities of South Africa. These hopes also correspond to the hopes voiced by Ali Mazrui (1978, 1980) for the African universities two decades ago.[219]

Having noted that several of my black South African colleagues, themselves working in the HBUs and dedicated to the black cause, prefer to send their own children to the historically white universities (HWUs), it is tempting to ask whether there is still a life after the death of apartheid for the HBUs. Will they remain a legacy of apartheid—undergraduate colleges for black students whose parents cannot afford to send them to the HWUs? Which will be the "real" universities? Will the HWUs continue to set the academic standards, insisting on their definition of "academic excellence" and "quality" in education also for the HBUs? Or are there tasks that the HBUs can do better? Can they become the producers of knowledge instead of reproducing what the HWUs are reproducing from the North? Can they become institutions reflecting African experiences and realities? Can they become academic centers with pride, centers that will draw researchers of all skin colors and from all over the world? Can they become the institutions from where a redefinition of curricular content for *all* South African universities can start?

According to Charles Dlamini (1995), during the apartheid period

---

[219] In the whole group I was the only non-African by skin color. This in itself was no unusual experience for me, in that in my years at the University of Dar es Salaam I was working among only black academics. (For a description of how my experiences in Tanzania might be of value for South Africans, see Brock-Utne, 1995.) There is, however, a great difference between being a white person in Tanzania and a white person in South Africa—even among academics.

Damian Ruth, a white South African teaching at the University of the North, in a lecture in my "Education in Africa" class in the fall of 1996, also told about the tension he felt being a white teacher of black South African students. In an article on teaching at a South African university he writes: "The white teacher/ black students relationship is keyed into the whole structure of repression and reaction. I am not just a teacher, and our interactions are infused with an intense, immediate and contestatory political dimension" (Ruth, 1996: 132).

the HBUs were regarded as outposts of the National Department of Education. They did not enjoy any autonomy or academic freedom.

DISTRIBUTION OF RESOURCES BETWEEN HBUS AND HWUS

A review of research funding patterns at tertiary institutions in South Africa shows that historically black universities are plagued by the legacy of apartheid. The formula for university funding in South Africa has favored historically white institutions, rewarding heavily the number of scientific articles published by staff and students in refereed journals.[220] In 1989, for instance, each article published in refereed journals received 10,000 rand (about U.S.$2,000). Table 8.3 indicates the number of articles published in 1993 by faculty at historically white institutions

Table 8.3 Comparison of Research Productivity in Universities in the Republic of South Africa (RSA), 1993[221]

	Research Articles Published	Master and Doctoral Graduates
HWIs	4,391	3,513
	83%	81%
HBIs	367	197
	7%	5%
Distance Learning	486	518
Universities	9%	12%
Total	5,244	4,228
	99%	98%

Source: NCHE, 1996:18.

[220]As noted in the beginning of the chapter, the number of published articles in professional journals is very high in South Africa compared to other countries in Sub-Saharan Africa.

[221]The table does not say, however, whether the articles have been published by white or black academic staff in the black institutions (there are hardly any black academic staff members in the white institutions). Nor does it say anything about the content of the articles, whose experiences they reflect, or the views of the gate-keepers who deem an article to be publishable or not.

(HWIs) and those by the academic staff in historically black institutions (HBIs).

The funding formula further subsidizes full-time students as well as passed credits (weighted by a factor of 1 for bachelor's and 4 for doctorate with distinction). As shown in Table 8.3, such a weighting formula privileges HWUs because they have been authorized to enroll a much larger group of graduate students. It is at these universities that graduate studies have been built up. Table 8.4 shows how the overall pattern of funding is biased against HBUs and how the government has favored the historically white universities.

The university Council and other authoritative bodies, according to the Deputy Minister of Education, in 1996 still reflected the pre-1994 political order: "They excluded stakeholders on the basis of race, gender and class background. As such these structures mirrored the undemocratic state" (Mkhatshwa, 1996b: 9). This undemocratic state was evidenced historically, in that about ten times more whites than Africans have completed degrees in science in South Africa, despite the fact that whites represent under 10% of the population. The undemocratic state is also

Table 8.4 Humanities Research Expenditure by University (thousands of rand)

Grouping	Government sector	University Funds	Bursary	Private and Foreign	Total
HWU	R4,439	R101,761	R8,783	R82	R115,065
Afrikaans	62%	43%	52%	9%	44%
HWU	2,348	79,056	7,872	745	90,121
English	34%	33%	47%	70%	34%
HBU	130	25,496	98	120	25,844
	2%	11%	1%	13%	10%
UNISA	104	30,070			30,174
	1%	13%	0	0	12%
Total	R7,111	R236,383			
	100%	100%			

Source: Bunting (1994b).

mirrored in the provisions made for black and white students to master science subjects.

As a legacy of apartheid, black university students are still going for "softer options" in their choice of subjects to study. There is now an over-supply of teachers of biblical studies, local languages, and Afrikaans and a very serious shortage of teachers of mathematics, sciences, English, and geography. The low number of African students in mathematics and science is especially alarming. At the University of the North, I was told that at the time the university was built, in 1959 the white administration had not wanted to invest in science and math teaching for black students as they considered these subjects as too difficult for the blacks to manage.[222] The apartheid government felt, however, that biblical studies would be of great value to the black students. The fact that the science subjects have been regarded as too difficult for Africans to cope with and not been offered at all at some of the HBUs may also explain the low pass rate of African students at the matriculation exams (commonly known as "ma-

Table 8.5 Matriculation Pass Rates for White and African Students in Physical Science, Biology, and Mathematics, 1990

Subject	White	African
Physical Science	95%	44%
Biology	88%	29%
Mathematics	91%	15%

Source: Fabiano and Naidoo (1997: 5).

[222] This is the same attitude that many school planners have nourished in relation to girls and mathematics. For instance, in Norwegian towns between 1938 and 1959, girls in the upper grades of primary school received fewer lessons per week in mathematics than boys and there were mathematical problems in the textbooks marked with an asterisk explaining: "The girls do not need to solve this problem" (Brock-Utne and Haukaa, 1980).

[223] Selection for tertiary education in South Africa is to a large extent based on achievement in the Senior Certificate examination. The examination is taken after 12 years of formal schooling in standard 10 and leads to the award of a school-leaving certificate with or without matriculation exemption. The candidates who achieve the matriculation exemption—in daily speech called "matric" —are eligible for undergraduate studies at university, subject to additional entrance requirements which the individual universities may set (Herman, 1995).

tric").[223] Many years of apartheid education have instilled in the African population a feeling that many subjects are too difficult for them to master, and the inferior pre-university and university education they generally received did not enhance African students' pass rates, as shown in Table 8.5.

The Centre for Educational Policy Development (CEPD) has made an attempt to identify the range of factors that account for the poor performance of African students. These include low per capita expenditures, high student-teacher ratios, teacher shortages, inadequate teacher quality, lack of print materials/textbooks and science equipment, language problems, inappropriate textbooks, irrelevant syllabi, and inappropriate teaching methods (Fabiano and Naidoo, 1997). The inappropriate teaching methods that have been used in black schools leading up to matric have been methods emphasizing facts and memory skills and examinations dominated by recall questions, methods associated with fundamental pedagogics.

THE LEGACY OF FUNDAMENTAL PEDAGOGICS

Catriona Macleod (1995) has analyzed data from interviews with seven remedial advisers employed in the old homeland departments of education. She has analyzed the conscious and unconscious discursive pedagogical and personal realities of the advisers. The analysis shows the strength fundamental pedagogics (FP), or Bantu education, retains in the black educational institutions. The methods embraced in this type of pedagogy were the ones the apartheid regime deemed fit to be used in institutions where the black majority population are taught.

Fundamental pedagogics (FP) presents itself as a science that sets out (a) to describe what is universally characteristic of education — which it defines as the process of the child being accompanied into adulthood by the adult or educator, and (b) to evaluate educational doctrines in the light of these "fundamental pedagogic essences." Those doctrines which do not match up to these "universal" standards were seen to have harmful effects on the child: "children educated in this manner will have their adulthood impaired" (Vries, 1986: 121). In order to create a science that is devoid of any "philosophy of life" whatsoever, the FP scientist employs a methodological technique known as "bracketing." This requires the person to set aside (bracket) any personal interpretations, beliefs, prejudices, or opinions in order to observe the educative event as it "really is."

Most black lecturers and administrators have been brought up in the tradition of FP, also called Bantu education or Christian national education (as Christianity is looked upon as a religion well suited to convey the principles of fundamental pedagogics). According to these principles, full compliance of the student is demanded, and authority is to be obeyed and feared. This type of education breeds an unquestioning attitude. Lecturers are expected to carry out instructions from heads of departments, who in turn get their instructions from the vice-rector and the rector. Critical thought is discouraged and the Bible is used to obtain subservience and compliance. Teaching strategies used are telling and informing learners who are expected to be passive and receptive. Thus, what Paulo Freire (1972) criticized as the banking concept of education has been emphasized in virtually all black South African schools, colleges, and even universities.

B. E. Gozo (1996: 79) of the University of Venda writes from his experiences at black universities and teachers' colleges when he describes the students as "normally passive in class, taking down whatever the teacher says without questioning its veracity or validity." Gozo tells that these conditions are so widespread and entrenched that a program for retraining teachers using distance learning has been started by a non-governmental organization very close to the government (South African Institute for Distance Education, 1994). The main thrust of the programme is to move away from FP and to start on a clean slate that has not been contaminated by fundamental pedagogics.[224]

Another product of the fundamental pedagogics tradition is reliance on particular textbooks which are prescribed by the authorities. Lecturers

---

[224]According to Gozo (1996), student politics has also been affected by the fundamental pedagogics tradition. Student organizations have been frustrated by the authoritarian structures in schools and colleges and, as a consequence, have tended to be extremist in their attempt to solve problems. Rather than negotiate, they demand; and if their demands are not met, they resort to measures such as forcing rectors and lecturers out of the campus or locking lecturers in or out of the campus. The fundamental pedagogics tradition, according to Gozo, has not prepared the students for negotiation; students are expected to be compliant, they have not been encouraged to question and argue. The result has thus been endless disruptions and stay-aways. It has to be remarked that the history of the struggle against apartheid also has to be taken into account when it comes to student protests. The struggle against apartheid was very pronounced at the black campuses, and methods which were used and developed at that time are easily mobilized anew when the conditions for students are tough.

follow the textbook chapter by chapter without reference to any other source. This breeds the approach that whatever is in that book is gospel truth and cannot be challenged. The approach also kills the culture of reading as students are not encouraged to look any further than the textbook. Damian Ruth (1996), who is a lecturer at the University of the North, tells the same story as Gozo (1996):

> Bantu education was designed to oppress. In its ethos, structure and content it promoted a dependent authoritarian mentality where avoidance of mistakes was a primary concern. It was, in other words, deeply antithetical to the notion of free enquiry and the exploration of difference. Furthermore, most of our students have been taught by educators who themselves were victims of the system (Ruth, 1996: 131).

Ruth goes on to tell how the high level of daily corporal punishment in South African schools, which is still going on despite its having been outlawed, has ingrained in students an association of education with fear, violence, and anxiety. At the same time, many are first-generation students, who carry a familial and community burden of opportunity and expectation.

Ruth (1996) tells how he tries to eschew standard textbooks and ask his students to be reflective. His students oppose his open-ended approach. When he suggested that his industrial psychology class should interview workers in the neighborhood and let that form the basis of their curriculum, his students were against such an approach. They wanted "The Text," the content of which is known, and against which they could be tested. And they wanted him to be "The Authority." He mentions that he has colleagues in other parts of the world who can also cite examples of the student who exclaims: "Just tell me what to say and I will say it," but explains: "But what is perhaps South African about the condition is the emotional and historical force of this distrust of free enquiry on the part of the students" (Ruth, 1996: 131). It will take a long time to do away with the mentality that fundamental pedagogics has created. What is the new government doing to try to address this issue?

THE TRANSFORMATION OF THE HIGHER EDUCATION SECTOR IN SOUTH AFRICA

A Framework for Transformation In February 1995 President Mandela appointed a National Commission on Higher Education (NCHE), which submitted its report, *A Framework for Transformation*, in August 1996. The NCHE document, although timely and useful, focused mainly on the structure of the system and did not critically and consistently interrogate current values, cultures, and process issues that are central in transforming the higher education system. It is not possible to change the higher education system by focusing mainly on structures. The resiliency of the system, traditional hierarchies, and residues from the past can only be successfully confronted by focusing on changing current discourses and practices in the higher education system. Cecilia Moyo (1996: 10), the former director of SAAAD (South African Agency for Academic Development), observes: "No structure can change the values and misplaced beliefs and cultures in some of our institutions that regard themselves as the Oxford(s) and Harvard(s) of Africa."

Green Paper on Higher Education Transformation The *Green Paper on Higher Education Transformation,* presented in December 1996 by the Minister of Education in South Africa, S.M.E. Bengu, uses the NCHE report as its primary resource. The public was invited to respond to the Green Paper by 15 March 1997. In the preface to the Green Paper Minister Bengu writes:

> The Green Paper signals the policy intentions of my Department in regard to the reconstruction and development of higher education in South Africa. I agree with NCHE's point of departure that while our higher education system has considerable capacity and internationally acknowledged areas of excellence, it is also fundamentally flawed by inequities, imbalances and distortions deriving from its apartheid history and present structure. (Bengu, 1996: preface)

A DANGEROUS MEMORY

A great challenge facing all education in South Africa is a rewriting of the curriculum in such a way that all South Africans become aware of the unfair and unequal treatment of the majority population of South Africa. Likewise distortions derived from the apartheid history of the country have to be addressed. Father Smangaliso Mkhatshwa (1996:2), the Deputy Minister of Education in South Africa, argues for the necessity of incorporating into the curriculum something he called "a dangerous memory," which he defined as recognizing "those manifestations of suffering that constitute a historical memory as well as immediate conditions of poverty, moral decay and human exploitation. The dangerous memory enables institutions to be the agents of change, to seek justice in all areas of civil society." The dangerous memory both deals with the historical memory of racism and suffering as well as gives a direction for the work for justice, not only between university students and teachers of different colors, but also between the intellectual population and the population at large.[225]

In the previous chapter we discussed the missing link in the university system in Africa. This is not the link between a university in the South and one in the North. The link that is really missing in most of the universities in the South is the link between the academy and the surrounding community. Values and knowledge creation, particularly through independent and basic research, are critically important in order to develop the African continent as a creator of science and technology and not simply a consumer of imported versions. This knowledge cre-

---

[225] It is necessary also for South African university students to pose the same question as Xabier Gorostiaga (1993), rector of the University of Central America (UCA), Managua, Nicaragua, whom we quoted in the preceding chapter. When analyzing the situation of Latin American universities Gorostiaga held that the universities had to confront the injustices surrounding them.

[226] Gorostiaga argues for a transformation of the universities of the South to include local knowledge. The HBUs will be in the best position to tap this local knowledge since the students and many of the lecturers speak the languages of the majority and have grown up in the culture of the majority population.

[227] I encounter this racial idea every single time I am in South Africa and can give many examples. For example, one day when I went into the bank at the airport in Johannesburg to change some money, there were three people (all black) in a line waiting to be served while the cashier (a black woman) was dealing with a customer (another black woman). When I came in, I took my place last in the line but the cashier immediately asked me: "What do you want?" and was prepared to serve me before the three who were waiting in line. I told her that I was going to change some money but would wait until it was my turn. The other three looked at me in surprise. That episode could not have taken place in Tanzania, where I certainly should have had to wait until it was my turn.

ation has to be produced together with the local people. Examples of the missing link between local know-how and university know-how can be found in most departments in all of the universities in Africa.[226]

For South Africans to do research on and learn from the culture of the majority population it is necessary to try to come to grips with the manner in which the racial idea that still haunts South Africans works, how it still governs everyday behavior.[227] In an article on race and identity, Crane Soudien (1996: 41) asserts: "But how race, or the racial idea, has worked in our society, as opposed to the United States or the United Kingdom, is something we as South Africans have never fully addressed." Soudien goes on to say that theorists, such as Dubrow (1994) and Manganyi (1991), are helping South Africans to understand the historical and psychological complexities of the racial idea, showing how successful the idea of race is in governing their everyday behavior. This racial idea shows itself in the nature of social relationships, leisure choices, political orientations, and a whole host of seemingly insignificant everyday situations. Soudien states:

> The polarizing logic of apartheid is deeply imprinted on our psyches and is evident even in our most anti-racist moments. Nowhere is this better illustrated than in the anti-racist movement's distinct inability to acknowledge and work with the cultural capital of those outside the mainstream, particularly their languages. (Soudien, 1996: 42)

Smangalisho Mkhatshwa (1996a), the Deputy Minister of Education in South Africa, asserts that teaching approaches in the transformed institutions of higher learning in South Africa should celebrate the diversity of cultures. Learning theories should recognize the positive attributes students bring into the learning situation. Assessment practices should be guided by the principles of constructive evaluation that build and don't destroy the confidence of the learner. In a keynote address the Deputy Minister of Education quoted the following passage from the paper *Framework for Transformation* by the National Commission on Higher Education:

> South Africa's higher education system has considerable capacity in research, teaching and physical and human resources. Yet the system is fundamentally flawed by inequities, imbalances and distortions deriving from its history and present structure. Higher education can play a

pivotal role in the political, economic and cultural reconstruction and development of South Africa. For it to do so, the strengths in the system must be maintained, but the weaknesses must be remedied. To preserve what is valuable and to address what is defective requires transformation (quoted in Mkhatshwa, 1996b: 6).

Mkhatshwa went on to talk about the significance of transforming the higher education sector in South Africa and the role of the Ministry of Education. "Transformation of the higher education sector is about reorientation," he said (p. 7).

THE "AFRICANIZATION" OF HIGHER EDUCATION IN SOUTH AFRICA

In an article in the *Sunday Independent,* Professor Sipho Seepe (1997), head of Mathematics and Science Education at the University of Venda, writes about the necessity of building the curriculum on African experiences, to "Africanize" higher education in South Africa. This Africanization, he claims, must start from the premise that most of the people in South Africa are Africans.[228] For this reason higher education should reflect the culture, experiences, and aspirations of this majority. Africanization, according to Seepe, resembles the concept of "Afrocentricity" (a term used by Asante, 1987, 1991a) in that it refers to a process of placing the African worldview at the center of the analysis. The concept of Afrocentricity, according to him, is preeminently about how one views data or information: "An Afrocentric perspective would challenge the notion that European classical music is the only classical music in the world."

Seepe does not see Africanization as a matter of having enough black faces in institutions. In fact, a white person may be Afrocentric in his or her teaching and research, while a black person might not. Africanization is about the grounds for knowledge, about epistemology, about objects of intellectual discourse. Seepe finds it disheartening to note how similar South African research agendas are to those of Britain and the United States. There is, for instance, little research on solar energy in South Africa, even though Africa has more exposure to the sun than most other continents. Given the fact that Europe has long winters, a lack of excitement over solar energy by Europeans might be understandable.

[228]Africans refers to blacks, the original inhabitants of Africa.

But the lack of attention to solar energy in South Africa can mostly be understood to result from the fact that the intellectual inspirations of South African academics are derived from Europe.

Seepe also writes about the necessity of teaching science and mathematics in African languages so that the majority population can get a better grasp of these subjects and see their connection to familiar things. He criticizes the existence of a "tight umbilical cord reflected in whites' preference to learn European languages rather than any of the other languages in South Africa" (Seepe, 1997). He further comments how the same people who argue against the use of African languages are the first to remind South Africans of the need to emulate the then emerging Asian economic tigers, none of which is developing on the basis of colonial languages: "What the Asian experience suggests is that sustained development must be structured on indigenous culture with selective inputs and adaptation from outside" (Seepe, 1997).

The vice principal at the University of Venda, Vincent Vera (1995), is also very concerned about the devaluing of African experiences. He finds that this devaluing is pronounced by the white gate-keepers to knowledge, who control the publishing companies, the editorial boards, and the refereeing system.

> Racism, the kingpin of the apartheid era, posed a further barrier for publication of research by African academics resulting in the proliferation of unpublished materials by these academics. The "maintenance of standards" by white publishers is a disguised apology for maintaining a monopoly of publications by these same white academics. (Vera, 1995: 1)

Vera takes the position that teacher education should include training in research as a way of equipping potential teachers with research skills. Joint research projects should be initiated "as a way of minimizing dependence on foreign experts whose research predilections are diametrically opposed to African interests" (p. 1).

At a colloquium on "Decolonizing the Mind" held at the University of South Africa (UNISA) in October 1995, the terms "Africanization" or "ways to Africanize" were in frequent use (e.g., see Koka, 1996, Vorster, 1995 and 1996). Africanization was explained as a necessary process to counter the domination of the Eurocentric consciousness and marginalization of the African consciousness which has existed in Africa. P. J. Vorster (1996: 157) sees Africanization as primarily an appeal to Africans to:

- Regard Africa as a basis from which to escalate and aspire
- Take pride in being African or of African descent
- Appreciate and cherish the African cultural heritage
- Assert African ideas, rights, interests, and ideals
- Anticipate a healthy self-concept as an African
- Develop an African rationality in an intercultural context

Vorster also sees Africanization as an appeal to Europeans and non-Africans to respect and accommodate Africans' endeavors to achieve the above objectives. The process of "Africanizing" the curriculum is a process that does not, according to Vorster, concern only blacks of African descent, but certainly also Europeans or whites of European descent in Africa. Eventually, however, such a process concerns all people associated with Africa. An Africanized curriculum should be taught also in the HWUs, though it can best be developed in the HBUs.

THE "MAINTENANCE OF ACADEMIC STANDARDS"

Seepe (1996) discusses an issue that he finds emerges with alarming regularity whenever the concept of Africanization is raised: the issue of African culture versus academic standards. The question of standards is often discussed as a way to create an impression that there exists a distinction between the ill-defined concept of internationally competitive standards and African standards. Often these internationally competitive standards do not mean truly international standards but Western, most frequently Anglo-American, standards. In order to make the academic standards truly international, the culture of the underprivileged people of this world has to be reflected in academia. In South Africa this means the culture, including the languages, of the majority population. There can be no quality in education without making this culture a central part of the curriculum.

From the end of 1996 and throughout the spring of 1997 an interesting debate took place in the education section of the *Sunday Independent* on the meaning of quality, excellence, internationalization, and "international standards," as well as the need for transformation of the university sector of South Africa. The debate also covered the issue of state intervention in higher education versus institutional autonomy. The debate started as an exchange between Mamphela Ramphele, vice-chancellor of the University of Cape Town, and Blade Nzimande, member of Parliament and chairman of the Education Portfolio Committee of the South African parliament. But others also joined the debate.

In an article, Ramphele (1996) claims that her vision of a transformed higher education system in South Africa is one that strives for excellence with equity. She sees policies that purport to pursue equity at the expense of excellence as destructive. She feels encouraged by the tone of what is in the report of the National Commission on Higher Education, which reflects, according to her, "a balanced approach to transformation." She sees the pursuit of scholarship as the most important distinguishing feature of the universities. Scholarship, she believes, should be measured in terms of the production of new knowledge through research, the dissemination thereof through teaching and publications, and the transmission of a culture of critical inquiry. She claims that one of the most successful projects of apartheid was the undermining of scholarship among institutions set aside for use by black people. She finds it important that active steps be taken to promote a culture of scholarship throughout the entire university system of South Africa. But little is done in this article to define what is meant by excellence or "a balanced approach to transformation."[229] She mentions that black students have a right "to be exposed to curricula that reflect the African reality as an important part of the culture of the global village" but why should only black students be exposed to curricula reflecting African reality?

Abrahams (1997) claims that since their inception, "liberal" English-medium universities in South Africa have looked to the United Kingdom for validation of what they do. He laments:

> What surprises and concerns me about the debate on internationalisation is the lack of confidence and huge inferiority complex we suffer in this country. . . . Contrary then to making our graduates cope with overseas realities, our slavish adherence to uncritical internationalisation has rendered graduates ineffective in articulating a world view shaped by their South African training. (Abrahams, 1997)

---

[229] Ramphele (1996) sees a change of the staff profile of the University of Cape Town as her topmost challenge. The staff is now largely male and white. But no mention is made of the fact that there are women who are "males in skirts" and blacks who are "coconuts" or "bounties" (black on the outside, white on the inside). There are also men who support the feminist cause and whites who support the black cause. As Cecil Abrahams (1997), the rector and vice-chancellor of the University of the Western Cape and chair of the Historically Black Universities Forum, explains: "true 'rainbowism' goes beyond skin colour."

In addition Abrahams (1997) warns against an uncritical use of the term "internationalization" fueled largely by the economic powers of Europe and North America. He holds that such use of the word will contribute nothing to the understanding and direction of internationalization in South Africa. He argues for an internationalization which "begins at home." He stresses that South Africa is "first and foremost an African country and internationalisation must begin on the African continent."

This same thought is voiced by Blade Nzimande (1997a) when he stresses the need for South African educationists to "create a national space and development agenda and forge strategic alliances with other Third World or Southern countries based on the developmental needs of this part of the world." Nzimande (1997b) sees the globalization process as the domination and advancement of the interests of transnational capital of rich Northern countries and the interests of third world elites. He sees globalization as a process of transforming the world into a single market dominated by the interests of multinational corporations. With its features of deregulation and privatization, globalization has been accompanied by a curtailment of the provision of basic social services and the cutting back of the state from service provision. The ideology of globalization, according to him, is neo-liberalism.[230] Neo-liberal discourse is based on a particular notion of competitiveness which radically redefines national territories as markets rather than socio-economic and political entities with their specific needs. He characterizes as extremely naive the educationists who assume that globalization is a value-free process that has as its core the information super-highway.

Blade Nzimande (1997a) detects a strong neo-liberal currency in South African higher education. This currency reflects itself through the argument that the best way to test whether South African institutions are up to standard is to judge the extent to which they fit internationally competitive standards. He argues against Ramphele, who he claims accepts uncritically a definition of international standards as Euro-American standards, which are certainly derived from other than the African context. He also accuses her of adopting an anti-state stance, not seeing that the cry for institutional autonomy can easily be abused by people who pursue anti-transformation agendas. Mkhatshwa (1996a), the Deputy Minister of Education in South Africa, seems to agree with Nzimande when he talked about the quality of education and the contested concept of "academic excellence": "Academic excellence in today's South Africa

---

[230] For further discussion of this topic see Beck (1997), Bradshaw and Wallace (1996), Brecher and Costello (1994), and Martin and Schumann (1996).

requires a fundamental change in how knowledge is constructed, disseminated and evaluated" (p. 1).

The challenge of all South Africans, the members of the so-called *rainbow nation*, is exactly to change the way knowledge has been constructed, to let the voices of the hitherto silenced within academic discourse speak. The universities that are closest to the majority population in South Africa are the HBUs. Creating favorable research conditions for the academics in these universities might be the best way not only to strengthen the HBUs, but also to build a South African culture for *all* South Africans, a culture built on African roots. This would really be a decolonization of the African mind.

CHAPTER 9

Yes, Whose Education for All Is It?

> *The impact of the Jomtien conference is that*
> *concepts such as "Education for All" and*
> *"Basic Education" are used in every report.*
> *Even the University library project in Namibia*
> *was initially referred to as a Basic education*
> *project for the very reason that the financial*
> *institution involved was only funding basic*
> *education.*
>
> (KANN, 1997: 9)

Ulla Kann's experience as an aid coordinator shows that recipients of aid are quick to learn donor psychology, the new "buzz" words. Now it is "education for all" or "basic education" that will open the purse strings of the donors. The title of Part I of this book, "Establishing Education Policies for Sub-Saharan Africa," pointed to the fact that there are outside influences establishing education policies *for* Sub-Saharan Africa. The three first chapters were concerned with these outside influences and how they determine education in Africa. In Chapter 1 we paid a visit to the "Education for All" conference in Jomtien in 1990, discussed what happened there, and what some of the countries in the South tried to achieve. We saw their concern that the Education for All drive would mean a starvation of higher education and that indigenous curriculum construction, non-formal and adult education would be down-played. These concerns form the basis for Part II dealing with the content of education and the possibility of rooting it in African culture, and Part III dealing with higher education in Africa.

In Part I we also looked at some of the most important documents the World Bank has written concerning education in Africa and which govern not only World Bank lending to the education sector but, as we saw in Chapter 3, even aid from the so-called "like-minded donors."

My critique of the 1988 World Bank document *Education Policies for Sub-Saharan Africa* (EPSSA) formed much of Chapter 2. As noted in that chapter, most of the donor policies on education in Africa can be found in the *EPSSA:* the emphasis on basic education, the wish to reduce higher education, and the World Bank definition of what quality in education means. The *EPSSA* is heavily biased regarding the sources that were consulted for information. Only studies which support the arguments made are referred to. Sometimes these studies are rather insignificant and exploratory and have severe limitations and methodological weaknesses. Other studies, sometimes of a much more thorough nature, and sometimes even commissioned by the World Bank itself, are not cited when they go against the arguments made in the 1988 document. The document is clearly biased in the direction of American sources, as evidenced by the bibliography at the back of the document. The absence of references to African researchers in African-based research institutes is remarkable.

In this book I have made a point of having African voices speak. I have used both direct interviews with African policy-makers in the education sector and African researchers, as well as done my utmost to get hold of writings by Africans. To be able to do that, one has to stay and work in Africa for some lengths of time because much of the literature is not readily accessible from the North. Through my years of working in the education sector in Africa, my participation in student-staff seminars as well as department, faculty, and senate meetings at the University of Dar es Salaam, I have been able to get an insider's perspective that not many people from the North get. Also through my many informal discussions with African educationists as well as parents and school-children, I have been able to learn about a perspective that often has been silenced. Janet Miller (1982: 5) asks: "How much does it take to break silence?" It takes a lot. Maybe we researchers from the North can help to legitimize the experiences of African researchers as the most valid knowledge there is of African living and African education. A Zimbabwean proverb runs like this: "Stories of the hunt will be stories of glory until the day when animals have their own historians." The history of what the donor interventions of the post-independence era did to education in Africa needs to be written. This book is my small contribution to that history.

I have noted that when I first wrote a critique of the *EPSSA* paper, it was on the basis of a seminar with my colleagues at the University of Dar es Salaam. The arguments I give are the ones they gave me. But several of my colleagues said they thought it was great that I wrote this critique. They would not have dared to have done so themselves, fearing that they would become black-listed and not get any consultancies from donors. They were dependent on consultancies for their living. Sometimes it is easier for an expatriate like me, committed to the African cause, to come up with the criticism the recipients of aid would like to give vent to.

This book has given to donor policies what some may consider a disproportionate space. This was done not only because these policies are important for determining the educational policies in the South, but also because I, as a person from the North who has also worked for several donor agencies, feel a responsibility for the policies we are forcing on the poorer countries of Africa. I am in a position where I can criticize the powerful donors and take the repercussions that may come. It is my hope that people in donor agencies also may start questioning the conditionalities tied to aid to the education sector.

For me as a Norwegian educator working in Tanzania at the time when the National Education Trust Fund (NETF) was put in place (an intervention I describe in Chapter 3), it is sad to note what Norway's uncritical adherence to a World Bank concept has led to. When my own writings about the NETF first came out, there was still time for Norway to get out of the marriage with the World Bank. But instead of acting on my criticism, the NORAD office in Dar reacted by letting me know that I would not be hired as a consultant to work for them in Tanzania! How much harder is it for people who are dependent on the donors for their living to criticize the powerful donors.

NORAD has recently acquired a new director, Tove Strand. The student organization SAIH (Students Academic International Help fund) arranged a debate between Strand and me on the educational policies of NORAD on Tuesday, 23 September 1997, in which she agreed with my harsh criticism of the educational policies of the World Bank. It will be exciting to see if her agreeing in that forum will mean a shift in the policies of NORAD in relation to interventions like the NETF.

Recipients of aid know that the combination of the buzz-words "education for all" and "targeting the girl child" will work particularly well with donors from the Nordic countries and UNICEF. I noted in Part I how in Swaziland a curriculum project involving continuous assessment and put in place by USAID, which stopped the funding in the middle of the project period was taken over by UNICEF and redefined to "target the girl child" to get hold of donor money given by Norway. In Part I, I also noted that all 329 UNESCO- or World Bank-funded sector studies on Africa conducted between 1990 and 1994 were undertaken by expatriate-led teams with only minimal representation or inclusion of local researchers who never served as senior consultants or document authors.

In the aftermath of the Jomtien conference, concepts such as "Education for All" and "Basic Education" are now used in almost every report. Cooksey (1996: 11), for example, argues that the formal commitment by the government in Tanzania to Universal Primary Education (UPE) "is the result of international agency pressure following the Jomtien Education for All conference." Brian Cooksey, with his many years of living and working within the education sector in Tanzania, is highly skeptical of preschool in Tanzania—something which now is presented as "a government priority" in a country where primary enrollment rates now are low and the starting age for primary school has risen to over nine years as opposed to the official seven. Lack of government funds means that only parents who are willing and able to pay for preschool will get any. He feels certain that "UNICEF's global concern with early childhood development is behind the misplaced emphasis on preschool education."

In Part I, I also discussed how the donor's emphasis on basic education can be found in the educational policies put in place after the Jomtien conference in one African country after the other. This is especially the case in the countries under structural adjustment programs. I noted how the market-driven policies of powerful Northern lenders and donors dictating a drastic reduction of the state's role in the social sector has led to an increasing drop-out rate in the poorer segments of the population. Jellema and Archer (1998: 3), describing the schizophrenic donor policies, state: "Though donors proclaimed their commitment to Education for All at the 1990's Jomtien Summit, their macro-economic policies toward the South result in Education for Some."

While Part I was concerned with the donor drive toward "Education for All," Parts II and III were devoted more to what happens (or does not happen) within educational institutions in Africa. What does "Education for All" mean? What type of education is it that donors want to expand and complain that children are dropping out of? One way to study this is to look at the wording of documents like the *World Declaration on Education for All* or the various policy documents as we did in Part I, though these documents do not say much about the content of education. Another way to study the concept is to look at the projects now supported under the label "Education for All."

In Part II, I mentioned that almost all of these projects deal with primary education of a Western type. I posed the questions: Whose education are we talking about and in whose language? Does "Education for All" mean "Schooling for Some?"—for the children of those parents who think that their children will find a place in the modern sector? What type of learning do the great masses of African children get through the many years of Western schooling where they have to sit passively for hours listening to the teacher speak a language she or he does not command well and the children do not understand? Maybe the declining enrollment rate in primary schools in Africa, that is of so much concern to the donors, has to do with the fact that poor parents do not see that the schools their children attend give them anything worthwhile. Instead the schools are preventing their children from learning and taking part in worthwhile activities in the village and around the farms. Maybe the high drop-out rate is a rational choice made by parents who find that the primary schools with their Western curricula and language of instruction, which the parents and the surrounding community do not speak, are alienating their children instead of furthering their education? Perhaps the drop-out rate stems from the parents' perception that the education their children get disempowers them instead of empowers them. If this is the case, then most of the donor money going into building new schools or producing new booklets in the former colonal languages is wasted. No wonder that parents are unwilling to pay for an education that is of little practical value for their children. Jellema and Archer (1998: 3) state: "Lacking the 'voice' to change the system, their reponse has instead been one of 'exit;' they have simply pulled their children out of school."

In Chapter 4 I showed how curriculum centers have been torn down in many African countries, and how curricula and assessment systems produced in the West are making their way into African schools. I noted the reluctance on the part of donors (especially the World Bank, USAID, and UNICEF) to make vocational activities a part of the curriculum of "Education for All." Yet the learning of vocational skills was the reason most frequently mentioned to me by pupils participating in non-formal primary education in Guinea. One of the outcomes of the evaluation of Mweshipandeka Secondary School in the north of Namibia was also that the vocational skills which were taught there were highly appreciated by the pupils (Brock-Utne, Appiah-Endresen, and Oliver, 1994).

If Africa is going to declare a war on poverty, which she must, then maybe some of the educational ideas which were useful during the war of liberation may prove useful again? In view of the growing employment problem in Africa, one solution for the local communities could be educational initiatives that are more attuned to their perceived needs and demands, initiatives with a rural focus involving the entire local community. As Anders Närman (1992: 150) argues: "It is high time to revisit some of the original African concepts of education, such as Education for Self-Reliance and Education with Production. We must take note of their inherent pedagogical value."

SCHOOLING VERSUS EDUCATION

Joseph Ki-Zerbo (1990) of Burkina Faso argues for the need to return to much of the content transmitted in the pre-colonial period. He claims that colonial domination introducing formal systems of classroom education has led to the breakup of the African educational system. For Ki-Zerbo "education" comprises both the socialization process, learning by doing and apprenticeship, learning through oral literature and rites, and the "formal system of classroom education" or schooling. However, the problem has been that "education," also among Africans, has come to mean "schooling," a system of Western formal education imported into Africa. "He has high education" to many Africans means that the person in question has gone through many years of formal schooling. This limited view of education was what professional African educators were taught by the colonialists. The faculties of education, even in Africa, are faculties of Western schooling. The ministries of education are ministries of schooling. African curriculum developers, often working in institutes of education or institutes of curriculum development, have looked more to how curricula in the same subjects were constructed in other countries, mostly overseas, than to the indigenous learning and knowledge systems of Africa.

The powerful money-lenders and donors to education in Africa have the power to define not only the type of schooling they see fit for African children but also the concept of "education" itself. This is witnessed by a statement made in the book and taken from an article by two World Bank education officers: "Logic dictates that if the poor cannot afford schooling, then by definition they are less educated" (Burnett and Patrinos, 1996: 275). This statement should be contrasted to a passage from Nyerere's *Education for Self-Reliance:*

> The fact that pre-colonial Africa did not have "schools"—except for short periods of initiation in some tribes—did not mean that the children were not educated. They learned by living and doing. In the homes and on the farms they were taught the skills of the society and the behaviour expected by its members . . . Education was thus "informal;" every adult was a teacher to a greater or lesser degree. But this lack of formality did not mean that there was no education, nor did it affect its importance to the society. Indeed, it may have made the education more directly relevant to the society in which the child was growing up (Nyerere, 1982: 236).

The statement of the World Bank writers equating schooling with education begs the question: Whose logic are they talking about? Whose education? Built on whose frame of reference?

In Part II I mentioned that the basic African consciousness of life is fundamentally different from the European or Arabic, however much Christianity or Islam may have proselytized in Africa. I argued for opening up curriculum content to African culture as expressed through language, sciences, arts, crafts, and religious beliefs. This involves reconceptualization of content from an African perspective. In the African tradition knowledge is experientially and socially based rather than propositionally derived. As Avenstrup (1997a: 4) points out:

> There could hardly be a greater contrast than between Decartes' con-
> text-less mentalist individualism in Cogito, ergo sum (I think, there-
> fore I am) and the African contextually pregnant, social constructivist
> relationalism of umuntu umuntu babantu (I am because you are).

I mentioned in Chapter 4 that also Catherine Odora (1994: 84) of Uganda stresses the communal character of African life. She is concerned about the way Western schooling destroys the communal character of African indigenous education. Odora (1994: 84) criticized:

> The moment children go to school, they learn to talk about "my chair,
> my homework, my position," and less and less about "our," "we." The
> risks of alienation get more profound the higher one climbs up the lad-
> der in search for the elusive certificate.

It is the European encyclopedic tradition (from Decartes via Diderot) that has underpinned curriculum development in Africa from colonial times. Before colonialism, education was an indispensable component of societies. The education given at that time was functional to the requirements of each given social unit. As Melber (1997: 66) argues:

> This communication of knowledge, in contrast to what is understood
> by formal education and training in a European—and in the meantime
> a universal—context, did not primarily serve the distribution of posi-
> tions of power. The transmission of knowledge was a necessity of life,
> and for this very reason not selective.

Melber wants people once again to decide on their own system of knowledge transmission and its content, in local units, corresponding to their

particular conditions of life and their specific social and cultural structures: "What I wish for is a universal redefinition of education by the people it claims to be for" (p. 69).

EDUCATION FOR ALL—IN WHOSE LANGUAGE?

Chapters 5 and 6 were both devoted to the extremely important question of language of instruction in African schools. I agree with Kwesi Kwaa Prah (1993: 9), who argues: "African languages may be today possibly the most crucial link in the planning, propagation and development of culture, science and technology based on known and historical foundations rooted in the practices of people." It is these languages that represent the socio-cultural patterns of African people. The overwhelming masses of Africans have little or poor grounding in European languages. Almost all social intercourse is conducted in African languages, yet these languages are not deemed fit to be used as languages of instruction. Prah argues that throughout Sub-Saharan Africa the use of European languages of the former colonial masters arrested the processes of education, literacy, mass communication and development.

The scant attention paid to the problem of in whose language "Education for All" is going to be delivered illustrates my point that EFA is not about education, but about Western schooling, which means alienation from the indigenous culture. In Chapter 5 I showed how some African states have struggled to revive the African languages as the languages of instruction. I discussed the political battle around the language of instruction, the alliance between parts of the African elites (called in Kiswahili: *wazungo waeusi*—the black Europeans; in South Africa: "coconuts" or "bounties"—black on the outside, white on the inside) and parts of the donor community (especially that part with a colonial past in Africa). Some African states have, however, formed alliances with donors in favor of the use of African languages as languages of instruction. Among these donors we find the Swiss and the Germans, while the Nordic donors do not seem to pay much attention to this question even though, and here I agree with Obanya (1980: 8), "the main learning problem of the African child is linguistic."

Ouane (1995) makes a point of the fact that linguists, educational planners, and politicians seldom discuss language planning. Camps have been built up of people who think alike on the language issue in Africa and preach to the converted, seldom getting out of their ivory towers. Obanya (1995b) deplores that the most important educational decisions like the choice of language of instruction are taken by politicians with scant knowledge of linguistics and learning problems. He argues for increased attention to linguistic and educational matters and decreased attention to political and economic matters when it comes to choosing the language of instruction.

The choice of language of instruction is, however, an extremely sensitive political question that some donors say they want to stay away from. *Not* considering the question, however, is *also* highly political, as it mostly implies a strengthening of the European languages and the small elites in the African countries who master these languages. It means a further integration of these elites into the elites of the North and a further alienation of the same elites from the masses of Africans. At times in this book I have treated the betrayal of parts of the African elites, including some African researchers, towards their people. Staf Callewaert (1994: 108), who has done extensive research in Namibia, Mozambique, and Guinea-Bissau, tries to explain why one seldom finds African researchers questioning Western schooling as such: "As a rule you cannot expect the educated African to use much energy to reconstruct and problematize the break, by which he or she became exactly what they are: educated in a modern Western sense of the word." There is certainly a need for Africa to reclaim the concept of education.

Donors who are concerned about democracy in Sub-Saharan Africa should, however, give a thought to the fact that in many African countries communication between the government and the people is in a language the people do not understand. The further development of African languages for instructional purposes and the printing of textbooks and newspapers[231] in the local languages may be expensive. But when this argument is used, the costs to democratization and development of Africa in using languages people do no understand should be considered.

I strongly believe that "Education for All" can only be reached in our time through the strengthening of the indigenous languages of Africa, the languages most people speak.[232] I totally agree with the

----

[231]For a guide to establishing a rural press in Sub-Saharan Africa and for creating post-literacy reading material in local languages, see Ouane (1989).

[232]Yet, as mentioned, many donors (among them also NGOs) to the education sector in Africa do not seem interested in supporting these languages. An evaluation of Norwegian support to the building up of a secondary school in the north of Namibia, found that the only department that had not received any computers or any donor aid was the Home Language department. (Brock-Utne, et. al., 1994). However, after the evaluation report pointed to this injustice and their great need for a computer, they got one.

socio-linguists Skutnabb-Kangas and Phillipson (1996: 184) when they argue:

> Just as some development agencies aim to incorporate a gender dimension or a human rights dimension (e.g., in Scandinavia), the language dimension should also be made explicit. This would imply, for instance, that any poverty-oriented projects would necessitate support to local languages. It could well mean that in aid to education there should be a major shift to teacher training, curriculum work and materials production in local languages rather than European languages.

Chapter 5 dealt generally with the language issue in African education, giving examples not only of countries where the colonial languages are moving in again after a period of strengthening the African languages, but also of countries that have recently embarked on a language policy meant to strengthen the African languages. Chapter 6 examined more specifically the language policies of two countries in which I have studied these policies in some detail: (1) The chapter focuses on Tanzania, a nation that after independence decided to have an African language as the language of instruction, at least in primary school, and (2) Namibia, a nation that *could* have adopted a language policy at independence that would have strengthened the African languages but did not do so.

In Tanzania, Kiswahili is the medium of instruction in primary schools, in adult education, and in teacher's colleges. It is also the language used in Parliament, in government offices, in the radio and television. It is estimated that only 5% of the population have some knowledge of English. In their book on the language crisis in Tanzania, Zaline M. Roy-Campbell and Martha A. S. Qorro (1997) argue convincingly for the need to switch from English to Kiswahili as the medium of instruction in secondary schools as well as in the universities in Tanzania. They hold that the English language should no longer be allowed to act as a barrier to the attainment of knowledge.

I showed in Chapter 6 how the decision from the beginning of the 80s to switch to Kiswahili in secondary and tertiary education was reversed in the mid-1980s, under the pressure of structural adjustment, the return of USAID to Tanzania, and the introduction of the large English Language Support Project of the British Council.

George Urch (1991) tells how from 1985 to 1988 the United States Information Agency ran a three-year programme at the Dar es Salaam College of Education, a key institution for preparing secondary school teachers in Tanzania with the aim of strengthening secondary and teacher education in the areas of science, math, and English. To implement the program, a grant was awarded to the University of Massachusetts' Center for International Education. A whole group of teachers from Tanzania were enrolled in specially designed master's degree programs at the University of Massachusetts while personnel from the United States were in residence at the Dar es Salaam College. This type of collaboration is rather typical of the asymmetrical link arrangements between institutions of higher learning in the South and the North described in Part III.

A recent consequence of the introduction of a multi-party system in Tanzania was that the subject *siasa* (civics or "political education"—a subject much connected to the ideology of the CCM party), which was taught in Kiswahili in the secondary school of Tanzania, has had to give way to "social studies" taught in English. Later in Chapter 6 I described how Namibia, also through the influence of the United States and the British Council, after independence in 1990, has concentrated hard on making English the official language and the language of instruction in Namibia. This effort has been to the detriment of the Namibian languages.

In a discussion in the fall of 1995 Dr. Diaz, director of culture in Namibia, said to me:

> Namibia has the skin of a leopard. The skin of a leopard is so beautiful. It has this diversity of colors. If you look at the skin of a leopard through a microscope, you can find that also the black spots have some white in them, the white spots some black. The lion is strong, but the African kings—Zulu kings, Swasi kings, Setswana kings all wanted to adorn themselves with the skin of a leopard. We must keep this diversity, the multitude of colors, traditions, languages we have.

Toward the end of Chapter 7 I dealt with the concerns raised by Dr. Diaz. How much will Namibia be able to retain its skin of a leopard, its cultural diversity and multitude of languages?

Also Adama Ouane (1995: 5) describing the language situation in Africa, exclaims: Vivre la diversite (long live diversity). A country with many languages is a culturally rich country. People seem to be more concerned with endangered species than endangered languages. When a language dies, culture dies with it and the whole of humankind loses.

In the discusion of Namibia in Chapter 6, I also explained that the multitude of languages in Africa is not so great as some seem to think.

Many of the languages are more like dialects of each other put into writing by missionaries who just got to know one of the dialects.

RECLAIMING THE CONCEPT OF "EMPOWERMENT"

Several times in this book I have mentioned that just as there is a need to reclaim the concept of "education," there is also a need to reclaim the concept of "empowerment." The term "empowerment" was coined by the women's movement in the mid 1970s and has been an important concept within feminist discourse.[233] The concept has also found its way into donor documents like the 1989 World Bank report, *Sub-Saharan Africa: From Crisis to Sustainable Growth*, and the *World Declaration on Education for All* (1990).

Ben Turok (1992), who is the director of the Institute for African Alternatives, criticizes the co-optation of this concept by the Bank and claims that it has nothing to do with the popular participation of people normally associated with this concept. He claims that the reason the World Bank now stresses "empowerment" seems to be

> a desire to open space for individual entrepreneurs, who are to be empowered over the state sector in the economy. . . . People's empowerment is here not directed at greater self-reliance and sustainable development, but at further entry to world markets. . . . The proposals are all in the context of the firm disciplines of structural adjustment which are centrally and externally imposed and have nothing to do with people's empowerment (Turok, 1992: 51).

There is good reason to reclaim the concept of "empowerment", give it back its original meaning of power to the people, of self-reliance and self-determination. Lene Buchert, in her analysis of the current foreign aid policies on education in developing countries of DANIDA, SIDA, and DGIS whom she calls "likeminded frontrunners when it comes to aid to the education sector in the South," concludes: "With respect to education, aid must be given in favour of empowerment and self-

---

[233]See Stromquist (1993) for a discussion of the concept of empowerment. A whole seminar on this concept and what it means in women's education in the wake of Jomtien was held at the UNESCO Institute of Education in Hamburg, Germany, in January 1993. See also Brock-Utne (1989a: 25–27) for a further discussion of the concept of power in feminist thought.

help . . . Sadly, however, this goal is not immediately apparent in the current assistance patterns even of the 'likeminded' frontrunners" (Buchert, 1993: 13).

Is it at all possible that aid could be given in favour of empowerment and self-help? Is not the expression "educational aid for empowerment" a contradiction in terms? In a way it is. The mere fact that the one party is giving the money and is a "donor" while the other party receives the money and is a "recipient" sets up a disempowering and asymmetrical relationship. The Norwegians have come to Tanzania to teach, to "transfer" knowledge. In reality we may have more to learn from Africans than they have from us.

The empowerment approach to teaching sees cultures not only as social forms passed on from one generation to another, but as continually constructed and reconstructed in response to social and political conditions.[234] La Belle and Ward (1994) in their book on multicultural education note that there are groups in the United States which advocate a multiculturalism which promotes and empowers groups that have not previously had access to decisions about what is appropriate knowledge and how it should be transmitted. Afrocentrism and the related Afrocentric education are examples of such knowledge.

Afrocentrism supports infusing more about Africa, Africans and African-Americans and their experiences into curricula in the United States, curricula which are dominated by European knowledge and exclude information about Africa and the role African peoples have played in both African and American history. There is certainly a need to infuse more about Africa into the curricula in Europe too. Nordkvelle (1998) argues that almost 100% of the authors put on the required reading list within the field of education in the affluent countries of the West come from those Western countries. These same authors are, however, also on the required reading lists of the faculties of education in Africa. Saha (1991: 253) claims that 95% of the scientific literature read in third world countries is imported from the industrialized countries.

Afrocentrists argue that racism among history and classics scholars has distorted history, de-emphasizing, for example, Egypt's important

---

[234]Teaching students to analyze childhood poverty makes them aware of the fact that issues of ethnicity, race, gender, and poverty are intertwined. According to the U.S. Department of Education (1991), just over 14% of white children in the U.S. lived in poverty in 1988, whereas nearly 44% of African American children lived in poverty. For Hispanics, the figure was close to 38%.

role in the development of civilization, its influence over the Greeks, and its status as an African society and in the diffusion of African culture across the world (Asante, 1991a; Bernal, 1987; Diop, 1991). Much of the Afrocentrists' efforts in the United States have been to infuse material into the curriculum in history and the humanities. Some school districts have also tried to add Afrocentric perspectives into the teaching of science and mathematics. These efforts have, on occasion, led to controversy in districts where those who do not accept the Afrocentrist viewpoint have challenged specific readings. La Belle and Ward (1994) claim that the often complex and technical arguments about historical accuracy, with which those of the more Euro-centric view meet the Afrocentrists, demonstrate the desire for groups to shape and control the knowledge that is passed on to their children.

La Belle and Ward (1994: 34) describe Afrocentric research and teaching in the United States as a field of study that is meant to strengthen the self-concept and identity of African Americans: "Afrocentrism offers African American scholars alternatives to Eurocentric frames of reference." Afrocentrism goes much further than this, however. It has to do with a wish to correct and rewrite history and have African view-points and culture permeate the main-stream curriculum.

In Part III I wrote about the role of the universities in Sub-Saharan Africa to restore indigenous knowledge and make it part of the "Education for All" drive. In Chapter 7 I cited Kwasi Wiredu (1984) who claims that the problem is that the research on African philosophy is now ghettoized into classes on "African philosophy" but ought to be taught in regular philosophy classes.

In an assessment of the Tanzanian "education for self-reliance" policy in light of the "education for all" emphasis, Donatus Komba of the University of Dar es Salaam stresses the need to "analyze the possibilities to revive and use dying traditional learning systems in various tribes" (Komba, 1996: 6). In Chapter 7 I posed the question: How is it at all possible to reconstruct the curriculum of African schools, to root it in African culture, without a great emphasis on indigenous research at African universities and research institutes, preferably by African scholars who are clearly African-based in their outlook?

I mentioned in Chapter 7 the joint meeting of the United Nations Economic Council of Africa and the vice chancellors of the universities in Sub-Saharan Africa in Harare in the beginning of 1987. At that meeting the World Bank document on educational policies was heavily criticized because it was seen to perpetuate Africa's dependency by discouraging the training of their own high-level work force. It has been maintained that Africa needs "experts" from the industrialized countries because Africa has not developed the necessary expertise. The meeting in Harare stressed that if African institutions of higher learning do not undertake this training, the dependence on expatriates will grow.

As shown throughout this book, the World Bank continues to argue for a reduction of the activities of the African universities. There is also a clear donor shift of aid from higher to basic education which will make African intellectual life even more dependent on the West. This policy is a recipe for ensuring that "Education for All" becomes "Schooling for Some"—schooling in Western knowledge.

In Chapter 8 I explored the particular situation of the universities in South Africa that have the West within their midst. Will the most prestigious of these universities continue to model themselves after the West, become the Harvards and Oxfords of South Africa, or will they realize that they are located in Africa and help restore the African heritage and learn from some of the good work which has been going on under harsh financial restraints at some of the universities in Africa (like in the faculty of traditional medicine at the University of Dar es Salaam)? Will the historically black universities advance from their position of undergraduate colleges highly influenced by the historically white universities to research centers for African culture of interest for both blacks and whites outside and inside of Africa? It is only when this transformation occurs that South Africa will be able to create an "Education for All" that is really for all of its citizens.

What is the nature of the present struggle within the education sector in Africa? A possible answer is that the struggle attempts to consolidate gains made at independence, including opening up educational opportunities for the majority populations of Africa, introducing African languages as languages of instruction, constructing indigenous curricula, and liberating Africa from intellectual recolonization. This recolonization has occurred through the imposition of educational policies designed elsewhere; the forced adoption of Euro-American curricula, tests, and textbooks; and the erosion of the African languages as languages for intellectual pursuit.

Yash Tandon (1996) claims that in the short to medium run, Africa is on the road to "recolonization" by the West. Africa's political gains are under threat. In this book I argued that this recolonization is strongly felt within the education sector of most African countries. Africa's intellectual gains made during both the pre- and early post-colonial periods are under threat.

I agree with Noel McGinn when he accurately observes: "Education for All requires culturally relevant curricula and instruction in local languages" (McGinn 1994: 295). But I find it important to add that the construction of culturally relevant curricula and the strengthening of the use of local languages require that emphasis be put on the building up of institutions of higher learning in Africa where independent, or at least not foreign colonized, minds are fostered. It also requires the existence and further development of independent curriculum centers as well as a strengthening of teacher training.

IS THERE ANY CHANCE OF IMPROVING THE SITUATION?

Some of the best advice to recipient countries of aid that I have come across can be found in a document written by Jacques Hallak (1995) titled *Negotiation with Aid Agencies: A Dwarf against a Giant.* Hallak provides a checklist of sixteen suggestions for negotiations with aid agencies, divided into four categories: (1) Prior to negotiation, (2) What to negotiate? (3) How?, and (4) When? He reminds recipient countries that the costs of mistakes to donors (misallocations of aid resources) are normally small, if not negligible whereas the costs to governments could prove to be catastrophic no matter how small the share of aid in the education budget. As Hallak (1995: 8) argues:

> A donor-driven agreement leading to a national policy development coming up with the kind of answers the donors were looking for, may, at best, prove politically impossible to implement, and, at worst, put countries in blind alleys, imported from donors' own perceptions of what is rational for a society with a completely different political culture. Given the time factor in implementing changes in education systems and their impact over at least one generation of youth and adults, the consequences of wrong donor-induced policy reforms cannot be overlooked.

Keeping this in mind, Hallak suggests that negotiation should not start without the recipient country having made prior inquiry about the aid agencies' concern. Gathering information on their agenda, culture, modalities of operation, and perspectives is a crucial first step to be considered by any government in trying not only to balance the existing asymmetry in information between lenders and borrowers, but also, he claims, to build national capacity for communication with donors. Hallak warns against the adoption of complex programs within the education sector, as they may easily hinder national capacity building and generate donor-driven bureaucracies with limited scope for effective implementation and donor co-ordination. He claims that the donor move from project investment to credit agreement to support change in policy environment frequently hides major challenges needing to be addressed by local governments. He sees the challenge for borrowers in resisting the strong pressures from some aid agencies to negotiate an *overall policy framework* on the grounds that the only purpose of the credit agreement is to support changes in the policy environment. Hallak's advice to recipient governments on how to resist such potential pressures from donors and lenders is as follows:

1. Use the donors' own rhetoric on *capacity building* and *'sustainability.'*
2. Disclose information generally not available to donors on problematic consequences of adoption of donors' agendas.
3. Publicize the failure of many attempts by donors to use aid funds to persuade governments to introduce policy changes. (Hallak, 1995: 11)

Ulla Kann, who has worked as aid coordinator in Namibia for many years and whose experiences were referred to in Chapter 3, tells how little power is often left to the recipient government in aid negotiations. She offers the following advice from her twenty-five years of experience working for governments in Africa:

> **Don't forget the word NO.** It is admittedly difficult during negotiations to decline an aid offer. It is more difficult for a very poor country than for a less poor country. Whatever is the case it is the recipient country that will have to live with the decision made. A NO indicates that the recipient country is serious and may open up for a better discussion. Remember, it is the business of donor agencies to disburse aid. (Kann, 1997: 7, emphasis added)

One country that has lived up to this advice is Mauritius, which elaborated a master plan in 1991, eight years after the then minister had, upon taking office, decided not to accept the structural adjustment measures the donors wanted the country to adopt. Catherine Odora Hoppers (1998) tells that Mauritius took its time in preparing its master plan, and that despite the appointment of a coordinator who originated in the Ministry of Finance rather than education, and the presence of donor agencies, the main agenda remained clearly a Mauritian one. She quotes the following passage from a document of the Association for the Development of Education in Africa (ADEA, 1996:12 quoted in Odora Hoppers, 1998: 165).

> [S]ubsequent events suggest that (Mauritius's) refusal to apply adjustment measures to the education system harmed neither the education system not the macroeconomic climate. On the contrary, . . . by maintaining the reliability of the education system and its capacity to deliver uninterrupted services to the population,—instead of focusing on the elimination of inefficiences with potentially disruptive consequences—the Mauritian policy contributed to the enabling environment that preceded the country's strong economic growth.

Hallak (1995) relates in more detail how the government of Mauritius organized a "donors meeting" at UNESCO Headquarters. Some aid agencies expressed interest in supporting some components of the master plan; others requested additional studies. The World Bank opted to respect its own approach (commissioned sectoral work, program preparation, and appraisal). UNDP welcomed the initiative of Mauritius and gave its support. The process culminated in the signing of different agreements inspired by the master plan. In April 1995, once more at the initiative of the government, a mid-term review was organized with observers from other African governments and with representatives from aid agencies. Hallak (1995) notes that the main guiding principle of the review was the master plan, not *donor-driven programs*.

Ulla Kann finds that in the late 1990s an increasing awareness has developed among donor agencies and banks regarding the importance of leaving some space for the recipient countries to take the lead. It is high time. There is reason to believe that donors have done more harm than good to the education sector in Africa.

Julius Nyerere, the first president of an independent Tanzania, did much to change the content of education in his country. His wish was to have an education built on Tanzanian roots. As mentioned several times in this book, his educational philosophy outlined in "Education for Self-

Reliance" had a wide impact also in other African countries. But most of the self-reliance activities are gone, education with production is gone, curriculum centers are disappearing, foreign publishers are back in Africa, and in many African countries the colonial languages have been strengthened over the last fifteen years. There is reason to claim that over the last fifteen years under the donor pressures of structural adjustment an intellectual recolonization of Africa has taken place.

Some may ask if Africa was ever intellectually decolonized. No, probably not. But attempts were made at independence in one country after the other of building education in Africa on African roots. I claim that these attempts have been stifled over the past ten to fifteen years.

Some educators in the West see that we Westerners have a lot to learn from other continents. We need to change our Euro-centric curriculum to incorporate non-Western understanding, not only to do justice to oppressed groups but also because this change will make for a fruitful cross-fertilization of ideas. In our time of up-heavals and migration, it is important that as many people as possible, and especially educationists, develop a cross-cultural perspective. We in the West have so much to learn from Africa if she is allowed to develop from her own roots. Researching indigenous knowledge, within mathematics for instance, may lead to penetrating knowledge which also may change conceptions in the West. In the words of a mathematician from the West: "research on mathematics in non-western societies is changing our understanding of this fundamental human activity and helping educators develop more effective teaching strategies as well" (Struik, 1995: 36). There can be no global village without the knowledge we find in the villages of Africa.

References

AALAE (African Association for Literacy and Adult Education), November 1990. *Education for All: Issues and Guidelines for a Popular Alternative.* Adopted by the Second General Assembly of the African Association for Literacy and Adult Education (AALAE), Mauritius.

AALAE, December 1994. *The Third Three-Year Programme 1995–97.* Nairobi: Author

AASAP (African Alternatives to Structural Adjustment Programmes), 1989. A Framework for Transformation and Recovery. United Nations Economic Commission for Africa. *E/ECA/CM.15/6/REV.2.* Fifteenth Meeting of the Conference of Ministers Responsible for Economic Planning and Development. Addis Ababa, Ethiopia, 6–10 April 1989. Ch. 5.

Abrahams, Cecil, 1997. Higher Education Must Accommodate SA Reality. South Africans Have "Slavishly" Adhered to Internationalisation, Making Our Graduates Ineffective in Articulating a World View. *Sunday Independent.* April 1997.

Abu-Loghod, Lila, 1991. Writing against Culture. In Fox (ed.), *Recapturing Anthropology.* School of American Research Press.

ADEA (Association for the Development of Education in Africa), 1996. *Formulating Education Policy: Lessons and Experiences from Sub-Saharan Africa.* Paris: International Institute of Educational Planning.

Ajayi, Ade J. F., December 1963. The Development of Secondary Grammar
School Education in Nigeria. *Journal of the Historical Society of Nigeria.* pp. 517–535.

Ajayi, Ade J. F., Lameck K. H. Goma, and G. Ampah Johnson, 1996. *The African Experience with Higher Education.* Accra: The Association of African Universities. London: James Currey.

291

Akinnaso, F. Niyi, 1993. Policy and Experiment in Mother Tongue Literacy in Nigeria. *International Review of Education* 39(4): 255–285.

Akinnaso, F. Niyi, 1994. Linguistic Unification and Language Rights. *Applied Linguistics* 15(2): 139–168.

Alexander, Neville, 1989. *Language Policy and National Unity in South Africa/ Azania.* Cape Town: Buchu Books.

Altbach, Philip (ed.), 1992. *Publishing and Development in the Third World.* London/New York: Hans Zell Publishers.

Angula, Nahas, 1993. Language Policy Evaluation and Implementation: Choices and Limitations. In MEC (Ministry of Education and Culture), *Namibia National Conference on the Implementation of the Language Policy for Schools.* Ongwediva Training Centre, 22–26 June 1992. Windhoek: Longman Namibia. pp. 16–24.

Asante, Molefi Kete, 1987. *The Afrocentric Idea.* Philadelphia: Temple University Press.

Asante, Molefi Kete, 1991a. *Afrocentricity.* Trenton, NJ: Africa World Press.

Asante, Molefi Kete, 1991b. Multiculturalism: An Exchange. *The American Scholar.* pp. 267–272.

Avenstrup, Roger, 1995. Whose Education for All? *Plenary paper*, 1995 NASEDEC (Nordic Assciation for the Study of Education in Developing Countries) Conference "The Role of Aid in the Development of Education for All," 15–17 June, Oslo, Norway.

Avenstrup, Roger, 1997a. Introduction to the Proceeedings of the Sub-Regional Curriculum Conference: Shaping Africa's Future through Innovative Curricula. In Roger Avenstrup (ed.), *Shaping Africa's Future through Innovative Curricula.* Windhoek: Gamsberg Macmillan. pp. 1–6.

Avenstrup, Roger (ed.), 1997b. *Shaping Africa's Future through Innovative Curricula.* Windhoek: Gamsberg Macmillan.

Bäcklund, Stellan, and Anders Närman, 1993. Non-Governmental Organisations: Which Way? *Development Today* 12: 11.

Bakar, Abdourahim Said, 1988. Small Island Systems: A Case Study of the Comoro Islands. *Comparative Education.* Vol. 24. No. 2. pp. 181–191.

Baker, C., 1988. *Key Issues in Bilingualism and Bilingual Education.* Clevedon: Multilingual Matters.

Balintulo, M, 1981. The Black Universities in South Africa. In J. Rex (ed.), *Apartheid and Social Research.* Paris: UNESCO Press.

Bamgbose, Ayo, 1984. Enseignement en langue maternelle et reussite scolaire au Nigeria. *Perspective 14(1): 89–96.*

Banya, Kingsley, 1993. Illiteracy, Colonial Legacy, and Education: The Case of Modern Sierra Leone. *Comparative Education* 29(2): 159–171.

Barré, Remi, and Pierre Papon, 1993. Science and Technology Systems: Global Overview. In *World Science Report*. pp.139–150. Paris: UNESCO.

Beale, Em, 1990. The Task of Fort Hare in Terms of the Transkei and Ciskei: Educational Policy at Fort Hare in the 1960s. *Perspectives in Education 12(1): 41–54.*

Beck, Ulrich, 1997. *Was ist Globalisierung?* Frankfurt am Main: Suhrkamp.

Becker, Gary, 1962. Human Capital: A Theoretical and Empirical Analysis. *Journal of Political Economy Supplement* 70(5): 9–45.

Befring, Edvard, I. Hasle, and A. M. Hauge,1991. Tospråklig undervisning i internasjonalt perspektiv (Bilingual Teaching in an International Perspective). *Rapport* fra undersøkelse av tilgjengelig internasjonal forskning om tospråklig undervisning (Report from an Examination of Available International Research on Bilingual Teaching). Universitetet i Oslo: Institutt for Spesialpedagogikk.

Bekele, Endashaw, 1997. The North and South Partnership Models, and Views for Partnership in the Future. *Paper* submitted to the Norwegian Council of Universities Committee for Development Research and Education (NUFU) on a conference titled "Partnership Models, Experiences, and Trends So Far and Views for Partnership in the Future." University of Tromsø, Norway, 3–4 June 1997.

Bengu, S.M.W., 1996. Preface. *Green Paper on Higher Education Transformation*. Pretoria: Ministry of Education

Bennell, Paul, 1996. Using and Abusing Rates of Return. *International Journal of Educational Development.* 16(3): 235–248.

Berman, Edward (ed.), 1975. *African Reaction to Missionary Education.* New York/London: Teacher's College Press.

Bernal, M., 1987. *Black Athena: The Afroasiatic Roots of Classical Civilization.* New Brunswick, NJ: Rutgers University.Press.

Besha, M. R., 1973. Education for Self-Reliance and Rural Development *(mimeo).* Dar es Salaam: Institute of Education.

Beshir, M. O., 1974. *Education in Africa: Two Essays.* Khartoum: Khartoum University Press.

BEST (Basic Education Statistics for Tanzania), 1994. Dar es Salaam: Ministry of Education.

Bgoya, Walter, 1990. Economics of Publishing in Africa. *Paper* read at the 1990 Oslo Book Fair.

Bgoya, Walter, 1992. The Challenge of Publishing in Tanzania. In Philip Altbach (ed.), *Publishing and Development in the Third World.* London/New York: Hans Zell Publishers. pp. 169–190.

Bhaiji, A. F., 1976. The Medium of Instruction in our Secondary Schools. A Study Report. In *Papers in Education and Development.* No. 3. pp. 111–125. University of Dar es Salaam: Department of Education.

Blundell, R., C. Heady, and R. Medhora, 1994. Cote d'Ivoire. In S. Hurton, R. Kanbur and D. Mazumdar (eds.). *Labour Markets in an Era of Adjustments.* Vol. 2. Case studies. pp. 259–315. Washington DC: World Bank, Economic Development Institute.

Boois, J., L.Skrywer, and Levi Namaseb, 1995. The Findings of the Research Done from 20–27 April 1995 and 10–21 August 1995 on the Situation of Khoekhoegowab in Grades 1–3. *Paper* presented at the National Workshop on African Languages in Basic Education held at NIED in Okahandja, 18–22 September 1995.

Bradshaw, York, and Michael Wallace, 1996. *Global Inequalities.* Thousand Oaks: Pine Forge Press.

Brecher, Jeremy, and Tim Costello, 1994. *Global Village—Economic Reconstruction from the Bottom Up—or Global Pillage?* Boston: South End Press.

Brenzinger, Matthias, Bernd Heine, and Gabriele Sommer, 1991. Language Death in Africa. In Robert H. Robins, and Eugenius M. Uhlenbeck (eds.), *Endangered Languages.* Oxford/New York: Berg. pp. 19–45.

British Council, 1983. *British Council Annual Report.* London: Author.

Brock-Utne, Birgit, 1985. *Educating for Peace.* New York/Oxford: Pergamon Press.

Brock-Utne, Birgit, 1989a. Women and Third World Countries: What Do They Have in Common? *Women's Studies International Forum* 12(5): 495–503.

Brock-Utne, Birgit, 1989b. *Feminist Perspectives on Peace and Peace Education.* New York/Oxford: Pergamon Press.

Brock-Utne, Birgit, 1991. Women and Education in Tanzania. Report from a new African research group and a seminar. *Women's Studies International Forum* 14(1/2): iii-v of *Feminist Forum.*

Brock-Utne, Birgit, 1992. The Feminist Experiences and Social Change in Europe and Africa. In Elilse Boulding (ed.), *New Agendas for Peace Research: Conflict and Security Reexamined.* Boulder: Lynne Rienner Publishers. pp. 33–43.

Brock-Utne, Birgit, 1993a. Education in Africa. *Rapport* No. 3. Oslo: Institute for Educational Research.

Brock-Utne, Birgit, 1993b. Language of Instruction in African Schools: A Sociocultural Perspective. *Nordisk Pedagogik.* No. 4. pp. 225–247.

Brock-Utne, Birgit, 1994a. The Distinction between Education about Peace and Development and Value-Centered Education Intended to Promote Them. In

Douglas Ray (ed.), *Studies in Comparative Education: Education for Human Rights—An International Perspective.* Paris: UNESCO, International Bureau of Education. pp. 55–83.

Brock-Utne, Birgit, 1994b. Reflections of a Cultural Commuter. In Jill Bystydzienski, and Estelle Resnik (eds.), *Women in Cross-Cultural Transitions.* Bloomington: Phi Delta Kappa Educational Foundation. pp. 121–132.

Brock-Utne, Birgit (ed.), 1994c. Indigenous Forms of Learning in Africa. *Rapport* No. 7. Oslo: Institute for Educational Research.

Brock-Utne, Birgit, 1995a. Educating All for Positive Peace: Education for Positive Peace or Oppression? *International Journal of Educational Development 15(3):* 321–331.

Brock-Utne, Birgit, 1995b. Cultural conditionality and aid to education in East Africa. *International Review of Education* 15(3): 177–197.

Brock-Utne, Birgit, 1995c. The Teaching of Namibian Languages in the Formal Education System of Namibia. *A consultancy report* requested by the Ministry of Basic Education and Culture in Namibia through the National Institute for Educational Development (NIED) and with the support of the Namibia Association of Norway (NAMAS).

Brock-Utne, Birgit, 1995d. What Could South Africa Learn from the Failures of Other Countries in Sub-Saharan Africa? *Paper* presented at the colloquium on "Decolonizing the Mind" held at the University of South Africa, Department of Philosophy 12–13 October.

Brock-Utne, Birgit (ed.), 1995e. States or Markets? Neo-Liberalism in the Educational Policies of Sub-Saharan Africa. *Rapport.* No. 1. Oslo: Institute for Educational Research.

Brock-Utne, Birgit, 1996. Globalisation of Learning: The Role of the Universities in the South: with a Special Look at Sub-Saharan Africa. *International Journal of Educational Development* 16(4): 335–346.

Brock-Utne, Birgit, 1996b. Reliability and Validity in Qualitative Research within Education in Africa. *International Review of Education.* 42(6): 605–621. ISNN 0020–8566.

Brock-Utne, Birgit, June 1996c. Who Has the Power to Define Basic Education? *NORRAG NEWS* No. 19. pp. 17–18.

Brock-Utne, Birgit, August 1996d. Some Thoughts on the Capacity Building Aspects of the DSE Training Programme for Young African Researchers. *QUARESH:* Newsletter of Qualitative Educational Researchers in Eastern and Southern Africa. Issue 3. p. 2.

Brock-Utne, Birgit, 1996e. Brief Field Notes from a Brief Field Visit to Guinea, 22–25 November 1996. *Memo* to the Royal Norwegian Ministry of Foreign Affairs. Multilateral division. Delivered 1. December.

Brock-Utne, Birgit, 1996f. What Could South Africa Learn From the Failures of Other Countries in Sub-Saharan Africa? In J. Malherbe, (ed.), *Decolonizing the Mind*. Proceedings of the second colloquium on African Philosophy held at the University of South Arica, Pretoria, October 1995. pp. 13–31.

Brock-Utne, Birgit and Janne Lexow, 1996: *Rapport* fra møter i Yaounde, Kamerun og Johannesburg, Sør-Afrika om UNICEF- programmet om "girls and education in Africa" samt fra EFAs mid-decade konferanser for henholdsvis Vest- og Øst-Afrika. Februar 1996. (*Report* from meetings in Yaounde, Kameroun and Johannesburg, South-Africa about the UNICEF-program on "girls and education in Africa" as well as the EFA mid-decade conferences for West and East-Africa February 1996).

Brock-Utne, Birgit, 1997a. Internationalisierung des Bildungswesens-eine kritische Perspektive. In Christoph Kodron, Botho von Kopp, Uwe Lauterbach, Ulrich Schäfer, und Gerlind Schmidt (Hrsg): *Vergleichende Erziehungswissenschaft: Herausforderung-Vermittlung-Praxis*. Festschrift für Wolfgang Mitter zum 70. Geburtstag. Köln/Weimar/Wien: Böhlau Verlag.

Brock-Utne, Birgit, 1997b. Brief Field Notes from a Brief Field Visit to Uganda, 25–27. August 1997. *Memo* to the Royal Norwegian Ministry of Foreign Affairs. Delivered 8. September.

Brock-Utne, Birgit, 1997c. Brief Field Notes from a Brief Field Visit to Botswana, 1–4. September 1997. *Memo* to the Royal Norwegian Ministry of Foreign Affairs. Delivered 8. September.

Brock-Utne, Birgit, 1997d. Language of Instruction in Namibian Schools. *International Review of Education* 43(2/3): 241–260.

Brock-Utne, Birgit (ed.), 1997e. Decolonizing the African Mind? *Report* No. 8. Oslo: Institute for Educational Research.

Brock-Utne, Birgit and Janne Lexow, 1997. Report from a short field trip to Swaziland 2–4 February 1997. *Memo* to the Royal Norwegian Ministry of Foreign Affairs. Delivered 10.February.

Brock-Utne, Birgit, 1998a. Multicultural Education and Development Education: Similarities and Challenges to Peace Education. *Nordisk Pedagogik* 18(1): 1–15.

Brock-Utne, Birgit, 1998b. The Nordic Dimension in Education. Does It Exist? Where Are the Nordic Countries Heading? *Invited keynote* given at the 18th CESE (Comparative Education Society conference in Europe) conference held in Groningen, Holland, 5–10 July.

Brock-Utne, Birgit, 1998c. Norsk utdanning i et globaliserings-perspektiv (Norwegian Education in an Era of Globalization). *Invited keynote* given at the 7th National Conference on Educational Research, hosted by the Norwegian Research Council held at Lillehammer, Norway, 17–19 November.

Brock-Utne, Birgit, 1998d. Brief field-notes from a brief field visit to Niger 22–26 April 1998. *Memo* to the Royal Norwegian Ministry of Foreign Affairs. Delivered 4.May 1998.

Brock-Utne, Birgit, 1999a. African Universities and the African Heritage. *International Review of Education*. vol. 45. No. 1. pp. 87–104.

Brock-Utne, Birgit, 1999b. *Building Educational Research Capacity among Black Academics in South Africa: A Focus on Qualitative Research Methods*. Bonn: Deutsche Stiftung fur Entwicklung.

Brock-Utne, Birgit, and Runa Haukaa, 1980. *Kunnskap uten Makt. Kvinner som lærere og eleve* (Knowledge without Power. Women as Teachers and Pupils) Oslo/Bergen/Tromsø: Universitetsforlaget. Reprinted 1981 and 1984. German edition in 1986. *Wissen ohne Macht. Frauen als Lehrerinnen und Schülerinnen*. Giessen: Focus Verlag.

Brock-Utne, Birgit, E. Mnzava, Adelaida Semesi, Lars Strand, and Arnulf Ødegaard, 1990. *Project Review* of the Faculty of Forestry at the University of Agriculture, Morogoro, Tanzania. Oslo: The Norwegian Forestry Society.

Brock-Utne, Birgit, and Naomi Katunzi (eds.), April 1991. Women and Education in Tanzania. Twelve papers from a seminar. Arranged by WED 17–20 September 1990 at IDM, Mzumbe, in cooperation with the Women's Group, IDM. *WED-REPORT.* No. 3. Dar es Salaam.

Brock-Utne, Birgit, Beyene Chichaibelu, Athanas Stephen Kauzeni, and Hans Wiktorsson, 1992. *Project Review of the Department of Animal Science and Production (TAN 69)*, Sokoine University of Agriculture, Morogoro, Tanzania. Dar es Salaam, NORAD.

Brock-Utne, Birgit, and Henrik Gislason, November 1993. Review of the Diploma/M.Phil. Course in Fishery Biology and Fishery Management, University of Bergen. *Project review.* NORAD: Education Division.

Brock-Utne, Birgit, and Tove Nagel (eds.), 1996. The Role of Aid in the Development of Education for All. *Report.* No. 8. Oslo: Institute for Educational Research.

Brock-Utne, Birgit, and Marianna Miettinen, 1998. Making a Field of Study: The First Years of the "Education in Africa" Seminar at the University of Oslo. *Report* No. 5. Oslo: Institute for Educational Research.

Brock-Utne, Birgit, and Gunnar Garbo (eds.), 1999. Globalization—on Whose Terms? *Report* no. 5. 1999. Oslo: Institute for Educational Research.

Buchert, Lene, 1993. Current Foreign Aid Patterns and Policies on Education in Developing Countries: The Case of DANIDA, SIDA, and DGIS. *Paper* presented at the Oxford conference on the Changing Role of the State in Educational Development, 24–28 September.

Buchert, Lene, 1995a. Current Foreign Aid Patterns and Policies on Education in Developing Countries among Some Like-Minded Nations: Some Key Issues. *Scandinavian Journal of Educational Research* 39(1): 61–74.

Buchert, Lene, 1995b. *Recent Trends in Education Aid: Toward a Classification of Policies.* Paris: International Institute for Educational Planning.

Buchert, Lene, 1995c. The Concept of Education for All: What Has Happened after Jomtien? *International Review of Education* 41(6): 537–549.

Buchert, Lene, 1995d. Introduction. In Lene Buchert, and Kenneth King (eds.), Learning from Experience: Policy and Practice in Aid to Higher Education. *CESO Paperback* No. 24. The Hague: CESO. pp. 9–17.

Buchert, Lene, 1997a. *Education Policy Formulation in Tanzania: Coordination between the Government and International Aid Agencies.* Paris: International Institute for Educational Planning.

Buchert, Lene, 1997b. Coordination of Aid to Education at the Country Level: Some Experiences and Lessons from Tanzania in the 1990s. *Paper* presented at the Oxford International Conference on Education and Development, "Education and Geopolitical Change," 11–15 September.

Buchert, Lene, and Kenneth King (eds.), 1995. Learning from Experience: Policy and Practice in Aid to Higher Education. *CESO Paperback* No. 24. The Hague: CESO.

Bunting, Ian, 1994a. *A Legacy of Inequality: Higher Education in South Africa.* Cape Town: UCT Press.

Bunting, Ian, 1994b. Research Expenditure in the Humanities in South African Universities. *Paper* presented to the Launching Conference of the Social Science Research and Development Forum (SORSDEF), University of Fort Hare, January.

Burnett, Nicholas, and Harry A. Patrinos, 1996. Response to Critiques of Priorities and Strategies for Education. *International Journal of Educational Development* (16)3: 273–276.

Callewaert, Staf, 1994. Are African Pupils Different? Paul Riesman's Contribution to Ethno-pedagogics. In Karsten Schnack (ed.), Export of Curriculum and Educational Ideas. Didaktiske studier. *Studies in Educational Theory and Curriculum.* Vol. 14. Copenhagen: Royal Danish School of Eductional Studies. pp. 99–129.

Carnoy, Martin, 1995. *Encyclopedia of Economics of Education,* 2nd. ed. Oxford: Pergamon Press.

Chambers, Robert, 1997. *Whose Reality Counts? Putting the First Last.* London: Intermediate Technology Publications.

Chiduo, 1988. Third World Countries to Produce Own Learning Material. *Daily News,* 2 March, p. 1.

Chimundu, Herbert, 1997. Language Standardization without Policy or Planning: Zimbabwe as a Case Study. In Unni Røyneland, *Language Contact and Language Conflict*. Volda: The Ivar Aasen Institute/Volda College.

Chung, Fay, 1985. *Socialism, Education, and Development: A Challenge to Zimbabwe*. Harare: Zimbabwe Publishing House.

Clayton, Thomas, 1998. Explanations for the Use of Languages of Wider Communication in Education in Developing Countries. *International Journal of Educational Development* 18(2): 145–157.

Coates, Nick, 1995. Publishing in Namibian Languages. *Paper* presented at the National Workshop on African Languages in Basic Education held at NIED in Okahandja, 18–22 September.

Colclough, Christopher, 1991. Structuralism versus Neo-Liberalism: An Introduction. In C. Colclough and J. Manor (eds.), *States or Markets? Neo-Liberalism and the Development Policy Debate*. Oxford: Clarendon Press.

Colclough, Christopher (with Kurt Lewin),1993. *Educating All the Children. Strategies for Primary Schooling in the South*. Oxford: Clarendon Press.

Colclough, Christopher, 1995a. Raising the Private Costs of Public Schooling: The User-Fees Debate. In Birgit Brock-Utne (ed.), *States or Markets? Neo-Liberal Solutions in the Educational Policies of Sub-Saharan Africa*. Proceedings from a seminar. *Rapport No. 3*. Oslo: Institute for Educational Research. pp. 39–79.

Colclough, Christopher, 1995b. Diversifying the Funding of Tertiary Institutions: Is the Bank's Agenda the Right One? In Lene Buchert and Kenneth King (eds.), Learning from Experience: Policy and Practice in Aid to Higher Education. *CESO Paperback* No. 24. The Hague: CESO. pp. 145–157.

Colclough, Christopher, 1997. Aid to Basic Education in Africa: Opportunities and Constraints. *Evaluation Report No. 1.97*. Oslo: Ministry of Foreign Affairs.

Coleman, James, 1988. Social Capital in the Creation of Human Capital. *American Journal of Sociology*. pp. 95–120.

Commonwealth Secretariat and SWAPO, 1983. English Language Programme for Namibians. *Seminar Report*. Lusaka, 19–27 October 1983.

Coombs, P., 1985. *World Crisis in Education: View from the Eighties*. New York: Oxford University Press.

Conrad, Joan, 1994. A Discussion of the Concept of Quality in Relation to Educational Planning, Taking Nepal as an Example. *Paper* presented at the NASEDEC conference on Quality of Education in the Context of Culture in Developing Countries, Tampere, Finland, 13–15 January.

Cooksey, Brian, November 1996. The Pitfalls of Piecemeal Social Engineering: Funding Agency Support to Primary Education in Tanzania. *Paper*. Dar es Salaam: TADREG (Tanzania Development Research Group).

Cornia, Giovanni Andrea, 1989. Wirtschaftlicher Niedergang und menschliches Wohlergehen in der ersten Hälfte der 80er Jahren. In Giovanni Andrea Cornia, Richard Jolly, and Frances Stewart (eds.), *Anpassung mit menschlichem Gesicht. Wege aus der Schuldenkrise: Eine Studie für UNICEF.* pp. 29–93. Bielefeld: Luther-Verlag.

Cornia, Giovanni Andrea, Richard Jolly, and Frances Stewart, 1987. *Adjustment with a Human Face: A Study for UNESCO.* Oxford: Oxford University Press.

Crawford, James, 1989. *Bilingual Education: History, Politics, Theory, and Practice.* Trenton, NJ: Crane Publishing.

Criper, C. and W. Dodd, 1984. *Report on the Teaching of English Language and Its Use as a Medium of Education in Tanzania.* Dar es Salaam: British Council.

Daily News. Tuesday 3 March, 1992. PM sheds light on primary schools. p.3

Damiba, Aimé, 1991. The World Conference on Education for All and Africa's Expectations. *UNESCO AFRICA,* March 1991, pp. 8–11.

Darnell, Frank, and Anton Hoem, 1996. *Taken to the Extremes: Education in the Far North.* Oslo: Universitetsforlaget.

Davids, Laurentius, 1997. Centralisation and Identity: Sub-Regional Language Cooperation. In Roger Avenstrup (ed.), *Shaping Africa's Future through Innovative Curricula.* Windhoek: Gamsberg Macmillan. pp. 101–108.

Davidson, Basil, 1992. *The Black Man's Burden.* London: James Currey.

Denzin, Norman K, and Yvonna S. Lincoln (ed.) 1994. *Handbook of Qualitative Research.* Beverly Hills, CA: Sage Publications

Diouf, Mamadou and Mahammod Mamdani (eds). 1994. *Academic Freedom in Africa.* Dakar: CODESRIA Book Series.

Diop, Cheik Anta, 1974. *The African Origin of Civilization: Myth and Reality.* Brooklyn: Lawrence Hill Books.

Diop, Cheik Anta, 1991. *Civilizaton or Barbarism?* Brooklyn: Lawrence Hill Books/Chicago Review Press.

Dlamini, Charles R. M., 1995. The Transformation of South African Universities. *South African Journal of Higher Education* 9(1): 39–46.

Dubow, S., 1994. Ethnic Euphemisms and Racial Echoes. *Journal of Southern African Studies* 20(3): 355–370.

ED-82/MINEDAF/REF.5. 1992 The Use of African Languages as Languages of Education. The 1982 Harare Meeting of Ministers of Education in Africa. pp. 111–131.

Editorial, 1990. After the World Conference on Education for All, What Next? *Jomtien Journal.* 10 March 1990.

Editorial, 1994. Mayday! Mayday! *Journal of Education for Teaching* 20(2): 139–141.

Edwards, 1994. The Universities Council for the Education of Teachers: Defending an Interest or Fighting a Cause? *Journal of Education for Teaching* 20(2): 143–153.

Elderkin, E.D., 1995. Ju'hoan Orthography. *Paper* presented at the National Workshop on African Languages in Basic Education held at NIED in Okahandja, 18–22 September.

Elderkin, E.D., 1998. Silozi and Namibia. In: Karsten Legere, 1998 (ed.). *Cross-Border Languages. Reports and Studies. Regional Workshop on Cross-Border Languages.* NIED. 23–27 September 1996. Windhoek: Gamsberg Macmillan Publishers. pp.205–226.

Elugbe, Ben, 1995. The Use of African Languages in Basic Education in Nigeria with Particular Reference to Lower Primary and Functional Literacy. *Paper* presented at the National Workshop on African Languages in Basic Education held at NIED in Okahandja, 18–22 September.

EMIS, (Education Management Information System). 1994. *EMIS Statistical Yearbook.*

ERNESA. (Education Research Network of Southern and Eastern Africa), May 1987. In *NORRAG NEWS,* pp. 32–34.

ESAURP, (Eastern and Southern Africa University Research Project)1987: *University Capacity in Eastern and Southern African Countries.* London: James Currey.

Eshiwani, George S. 1993. *Education in Kenya since Independence.* Nairobi: East African Educational Publishers.

Fabiano, Emmanuel, and Prem Naidoo, 1997. Science and Technology Education Reform in Africa: An Examination of Some Contextual Factors and Reform Initiatives. *Paper* presented at a seminar at the Institute for Teacher Training and School Development at the University of Oslo, 7 May.

Fafunwa, Babs A., 1982. African Education in Perspective. In Babs A. Fafunwa, and J. U. Aisiku (eds.), *Education in Africa: A Comparative Survey.* London: Allen & Unwin. pp. 9–28.

Fafunwa, Babs A., 1990. Using National Languages in Education: A Challenge to African Educators. In UNESCO-UNICEF, *African Thoughts on the Prospects of Education for All.* Selections from papers commissioned for the Regional Consultation on Education for All, Dakar, 27–30 November. pp. 97–110.

Fafunwa, Babs A., and J. U. Aisiku (eds.), 1982. *Education in Africa: A Comparative Survey.* London: Allen & Unwin.

FAWE (Forum for African Women Educationalists), 1995. *School Dropout and Adolescent Pregnancy.* Nairobi: FAWE.

Finnegan, R., 1970. *Oral Literature in Africa.* Oxford: Clarendon Press.

Freire, Paulo, 1972. *Pedagogy of the Oppressed.* Harmondsworth: Penguin Books.
Freire, Paulo, 1985. *The Politics of Education: Culture, Power, and Liberation.* Massachusetts: Bergin & Garvey Publishers.
Fyle, Clifford, 1993. Educational Research and Teaching Methodologies in the African States. In Peter Muyanda-Mutebi, and Martin Yiga Matovu (eds), *Educational Research for Development in Africa.* Dakar: UNESCO-BREDA/ASESP. pp. 23–33.
Gaarder (now Brock-Utne), Birgit, 1972. Spesielle psykologiske virkninger av to-språklighet (Certain psychological effects of bilingualism). *Nordisk Psykologi* 24(4): 321–330.
Galabawa, Justin, 1990. Implementing Educational Policies in Tanzania. *World Bank Discussion Papers.* Africa Technical Department Series. No. 86. Washington DC: World Bank.
Galabawa, Justin C. J., and N. R. Alphonse, February 1993. The National Education Trust Fund: Implementation, Initial Takeoff, Constraints, and Sustainability. *A Consultancy Report* prepared for NORAD, Dar es Salaam.
Gandhi, Mahatma, 1940. What Is Woman's Role? *Harijan* 24. February.
Garbo, Gunnar, 1993. *Makt og bistand* (Power and Aid). Oslo: Spartacus Forlag.
Garbo, Gunnar, 1995. *Kampen om FN* (The Battle over the UN). Oslo: Universitetsforlaget.
George, Susan, 1989. *A Fate Worse than Debt: A Radical New Analysis of the Third World Debt Crisis.* Harmondsworth: Penguin Books.
George, Susan, 1994. *Faith and Credit.* Harmondsworth: Penguin Books.
Ginsburg, Mark (ed.), 1991. *Understanding Educational Reform in Global Context: Economy, Ideology, and the State.* New York and London: Garland Publishing. pp. 201–229.
Gorostiaga, Xabier, 1993. New Times, New Role for Universities of the South. *Envio: The Monthly Magazine of Analysis on Central America* 12(144): pp. 29–40.
Government of Tanzania, Ministry of Education and Culture and Prime Minister's Office, March 1996. *Primary Education. Master Plan: A Framework and Strategic Action Plan.* Draft 2. Ministry of Education and Culture. March.
Goverment of Uganda, 1992. *Government White Paper. Education for National Integration and Development.* Kampala: Government of Uganda.
Gozo, B. E., 1996. Teacher Education Reform in South Africa: The Need and Strategies. In P. T. M. Marope, and S. G. Weeks (eds.), *Education and National Development in Southern Africa.* Published by Comparative Education Interest Group (CEIG), Botswana Educational Research Association (BERA) for Southern African Comparative and History of Education Society (SACHES). pp. 77–85.

Graham-Brown, Sarah, 1991. *Education in the Developing World. Conflict and Crisis.* London: Longman.

Graphium Consult AB (formerly Esselte Print Consult AB). November 1991 – January 1992. *Proposed Future Schoolbook Provision System in Tanzania. Longterm Structure and Transition Period 1991.* Stockholm: Author.

Grimes, Barbara (ed.), 1992. *Ethnologue: Languages of the World. 12th.* Dallas: Summer Institute of Linguistics.

Grov, Hege, 1999. COPE (Complementary Opportunity for Primary Education) and Non Formal Education: Strategies Toward Education for All. A Focus on Relevance and Learning. *Thesis* for the Cand. Polit. degree in Education. Spring term. Oslo: Institute for Educational Research.

Habte, Akilu, 1997. The Future of International Aid to Education. *Paper* presented at the Oxford International Conference on Education and Development, "Education and Geopolitical Change" 11–15 September.

Haggerty, Olly Coopers & Lybrand International, 1991. *Developing a Privatization Program for Tanzania: A Proposal.* Presented on Friday 6. Dec. 1991.

Hallak, Jacques, 1991. *Education for All: High Expectations or False Hopes?* London: IEUL.

Hallak, Jacques, 1995. Negotiation with Aid Agencies: A Dwarf against a Giant. *IIEP contributions.* No. 19. Paris: UNESCO: IIEP.

Harlech-Jones, Brian, 1995. Attitudes of Teachers Towards English and Other Namibian Languages: Revisiting a Survey. *Paper* presented at the National Workshop on African Languages in Basic Education held at NIED in Okahandja, 18–22 September.

Harlech-Jones, Brian, February 1998. Viva English! Or Is It Time to Review Language Policy in Education? *Reform Forum.* pp. 9–15.

Hawes, Hugh, and Trevor Coombe (eds.), 1986. *Education Priorities and Aid Responses in Sub-Saharan Africa.* London: University of London, Institute of Education. HMSO Publications.

Henriksen, Spæt, 1993. Tanker om handlekompetence i kulturmødet med Letland (Thoughts about "Action Competence" in the Cultural Meeting with Lithuania). In B. B. Jensen, and Karsten Schnack (eds.), Handlekompetance som didaktisk begreb ("Action Competence" as a Didactical Concept). Copenhagen: Danmarks Lærerhøjskole: *Didaktiske studier.* Bind 2. pp. 70–75.

Herman, Harold, 1995. School-Leaving Examinations, Selection and Equity in Higher Education in South Africa. *Comparative Education* 31(2): 261–274.

Heward, Christine, 1997. The Women of Husseinabad and the Men in Washington: The Rhetoric and Reality of "Educating the Girl Child." *Paper* presented at the Oxford International Conference on Education and Development. "Education and Geopolitical Change," 11–15 September.

Heyneman, Stephen, 1995. Economics of Education: Disappointments and Potential. *Prospects* 4(25): 559–583.

Hinchliffe, K. 1989. Economic Austerity, Structural Adjustment and Education: The Case of Nigeria. *IDS Bulletin* 20(1): 5–10.

Hirji, Karim, 1990. Academic Pursuit under the Link. *UDASA Newsletter/Forum.* No. 10. pp.11–26. Issued by University of Dar es Salaam Academic Staff Assembly.

Hongoke, Christine, 1991. Consequences of Educational Planning on the Future Career of Girls in Tanzania. In Birgit Brock-Utne, and Naomi Katunzi (eds), Women and Education in Tanzania. Twelve papers from a seminar. *WED Report* No. 3. pp. 64–78.

Hoppers, Wim, 1989. The Response from the Grass-Roots: Self Reliance in Zambian Education. *IDS Bulletin* 20(1): 17–23.

Hyden, Håkan, Joyce Kazembe, Janne Lexow, and Anders Wirak, 1991. *Review of Diploma Course in Women's Law.* Commissioned by NORAD/Oslo. Oslo: DECO (Development Consulting).

IDRC (International Development Research Center), 1994. Development Ain't What It Used to Be: The Critical Role of Knowledge in Development. *Brief to the special joint committee reviewing Canadian foreign policy.* Ottawa: Author.

ILEA, 1990. *Language and Power: Afro-Caribbean Language and Literacy Project.* London: Harcourt Brace Jovanovich.

Indire, F. F., 1972. Towards a New Curriculum for Schools. *The Kenya Teacher.* 14(December): pp.14–26.

Ishengoma, J. M. R., 1988. Riddles as an Agent of Socialization and Social Learning among the Haya Children. *Term Paper* for Ed. 605: Social Psychology. University of Dar es Salaam: Faculty of Education.

Ishumi, Abel 1985. Educational Research in Tanzania—some issues. In: Abel Ishumi, Donatus. Komba , Y.M. Bwatwa, , Herme Mosha , Naomi Katunzi, S.T. Mahenge (eds.) 1985: Educational Research in Tanzania. *Papers in Education and Development,* Number 10, University of Dar es Salaam: Department of Education. February 1985. pp.2–23.

Ishumi, A. G,. D. Komba, Y. M. Bwatwa, H. J. Mosha, N. B. Katunzi, and S. T. Mahenge (eds.), February 1985. Educational Research in Tanzania. *Papers in Education and Development.* No. 10, University of Dar es Salaam, Department of Education.

Ishumi, A. G. M., J.Pendaeli, Y. D. M. Bwatwa, H. J. Mosha, D. Komba, K. M. Osaki, N. B. Katunzi (eds.), 1986: *The Educational Process: Papers in Education and Development.* No. 11. University of Dar es Salaam; Department of Education.

Jansen, Jonathan, 1989. Curriculum Reconstruction in Post-Colonial Africa: A Review of the Literature. *International Journal of Educational Development* 9(3): 219–231.

Jansen, Jonathan, 1993. Curriculum Reform in Zimbabwe: Reflections for the South African Transition. In Nick Taylor (ed.), *Inventing Knowledge: Contents in Curriculum Construction.* Cape Town: Maskew Miller Longman. pp. 58–69.

Jayarajah, C., and W. Branson, 1995. *Structural and Sectoral Adjustment: World Bank Experience, 1980–92.* Washington, DC: World Bank.

Jellema, Anne, and Archer David, 1998. Who's in power? Who's in prison? An education campaign for the Millennium. *ACTIONAID* 10(October): 3–4.

Jones, Phillip W., 1992. *World Bank Financing of Education: Lending, Learning and Development.* London: Routledge.

Jones, Phillip W.,1997. The World Bank and the Literacy question: Orthodoxy, Heresy, and Ideology. *International Review of Education* 43(4): 367–375.

Jones, Thomas Jesse, 1924. *Education in East Africa: A Study of East, Central, and South Africa by the Second African Education Commission under the Auspices of the Phelps-Stokes Fund.* London: Edinburgh House Press.

Kalid, Abdullah, 1977. *The Liberation of Swahili: From European Appropriation.* Nairobi: East African Literature Bureau.

Kalugula, Charles, 1991. The Policy Implications of Sex Role Stereotypes in Textbooks for Girls in Tanzania. In Birgit Brock-Utne, and Naomi Katunzi (eds.), Women and Education in Tanzania. *WED Report* No. 3. pp. 152–175.

Kamusi Sanifu Ya Biolojia, Fizika na Kemia, 1990. Taasisi Ya Uchunguzi wa Kiswahili Chuo DSM, TUKI/UNESCO/SIDA.

Kann, Ulla, 1997. Aid Coordination. A Personal Retrospective from Botswana and Namibia. *Paper* presented at the Oxford International Conference on Education and Development, "Education and Geopolitical Change," 11–15 September.

Kashoki, Mubanga E., M. E. Katengo, and M. Mundia, 1998. Cross-border Language Perspectives: Experiences and Lessons from Zambia—Focus on Silozi. In: Karsten Legere, 1998 (ed.). *Cross-Border Languages. Reports and Studies. Regional Workshop on Cross-Border Languages.* NIED. 23–27 September 1996. Windhoek: Gamsberg Macmillan Publishers. pp.168–205.

Kaye, Stafford, and Bradley Nystrom, 1971. Education and Colonialism in Africa. *Comparative Education Review* 25(2): 240–59.

King, Kenneth, 1986. Problems and Prospects of Aid to Education in Sub-Saharan Africa. In Hugh Hawes, and Trevor Coombe (eds.), *Education*

Priorities and Aid Responses in Sub-Saharan Africa. London: University of London, Institute of Education. HMSO Publications. pp. 113–134.

King, Kenneth, 1991. *Aid and Education in the Developing World: The Role of the Donor Agencies in Educational Analysis.* Harlow: Longman.

King, Kenneth, 1992. External Agenda of Aid in Educational Reform. *International Journal of Educational Development* 12(4): 257–263.

King, Kenneth, 1995. World Bank Traditions of Support to Higher Education and Capacity Building: Reflections on "Higher Education: The Lessons of Experience."In, Lene Buchert, and Kenneth King (eds.), Learning from Experience: Policy and Practice in Aid to Higher Education. *CESO Paperback* No. 24. The Hague: CESO. pp. 19–41.

King, Kenneth, 1997. Aid to South African Education and Training in the Context of the New Aids Paradigm: A Case of the Reluctant Recipient? *Paper* presented at the Oxford International Conference on Education and Development, "Education and Geopolitical Change," 11–15 September.

King, Kenneth, and David Court, 1986. The Interaction of Quantity and Quality in Tanzanian Primary Schools. In A. G. M. Ishumi et al. (eds.), The Educational Process. *Papers in Education and Development.* No. 11, University of Dar es Salaam, Department of Education. pp. 23–42.

Ki-Zerbo, Joseph, 1990. *Educate or Perish: Africa's Impass and Prospects.* Dakar, Senegal: BREDA with WCARO (UNESCO-UNICEF, Western-Africa).

Knapert, 1969. The Discovery of a Lost Manuscript from the Eighteenth Century. *African Language Studies* 10: 1–30.

Koka, D. K., 1996. The Impact of Euorocentric Systems of Education on the African Mind: Decolonizing the Mind. In Jeanette Malherbe (ed.), *Decolonizing the Mind. Proceedings of the Colloquium held at UNISA,* October 1995. Pretoria: Research Unit for African Philosophy at UNISA. pp. 49–57.

Koloti, Sibongile Ramelimetya Thandiwe, 1999. Language and Culture in South Africa—Policy and Practice. *Paper* presented at the NASEDEC (Nordic Association for the Study of Education in Developing Countries)conference in Vasa, Finland 5–9 May 1999.

Komba, Donatus, 1996. Education for Self-Reliance Revisited in Light of the World Declaration on Education for All. *Papers in Education and Development.* No. 17. pp. 1–7.

Kumar, Krishna, 1991. *Political Agenda of Education: A Study of Colonialist Ideas.* New Delhi: Sage Publications.

Kuper, Wolfgang, 1998. The End of Development Cooperation in the Universities? *NORRAG NEWS* 23(October): 23–25.

La Belle, Thomas J., and Christopher R. Ward, 1994. *Multiculturalism and Education: Diversity and Its Impact on Schools and Society.* Albany: State University of New York Press.

Laitin, D., 1977. *Politics, Language, and Thought: The Somali Experience.* Chicago: University of Chicago Press.

Lancy, David, 1996. *Playing on the Mother-Ground. Cultural Routines for Children's Development.* New York/London: Guilford Press

Lather, Patti, 1995. The Validity of Angels: Interpretive and Textual Strategies in Researching the Lives of Women with HIV/AIDS. *Qualitative Inquiry* 1(1): 41–68.

Lauglo, Jon, 1992. Vocational Training and the Bankers' Faith in the Private Sector. Essay review of: Vocational and Technical Education and Training: A World Bank Policy Paper. *Comparative Education Review* 36(2): 227–36.

Lauglo, Jon, 1996. Banking on Education and the Uses of Research: A Critique of World Bank Priorities and Strategies for Education. *International Journal of Educational Development* 16(3): 221–235.

Lawuo, Z. E., 1978. The Beginnings and Development of Western Education in Tanganika. The German Period. In Abel G. M. Ishumi, and G. R. Mmari (eds.), *The Educational Process. Theory and Practice, with a Focus on Tanzania and Other Countries.* Department of Education, University of Dar es Salaam. pp. 47–65.

Legere, Karsten, 1995. Languages in Namibian Education: Achievements and Problems. *Paper* presented at the National Workshop on African Languages in Basic Education held at NIED in Okahandja, 18–22 September.

Legere, Karsten, 1998 (ed.).*Cross-Border Languages. Reports and Studies. Regional Workshop on Cross-Border Languages.* NIED. 23–27 September 1996.Windhoek: Gamsberg Macmillan Publishers.

Legere, Karsten, 1998. Oshikwanyama in Namibia. In: Karsten Legere, 1998 (ed.). *Cross-Border Languages. Reports and Studies. Regional Workshop on Cross-Border Languages.* NIED. 23–27 September 1996. Windhoek: Gamsberg Macmillan Publishers. pp.40–75.

Lema, A. A. 1972. *Education for Self-Reliance:. A Brief Survey of Self-Reliance: Activities in Some Tanzanian Schools and Colleges.* Dar es Salaam: Institute of Education.

Lillis, K. M., 1985. Processes of Secondary Curriculum Innovation in Kenya. *Comparative Education Review* 29(1): 80–96.

Little, Angela, 1992. Education and Development: Macro-relationships and Micro-cultures. *Silver Jubilee Paper 4.* Sussex: Institute of Development Studies.

Little, Angela, 1994. The Jomtien Conference and the Implementation of Primary Education Projects. In Angela Little, Wim Hoppers, and Roy Gardner (eds.), *Beyond Jomtien. Implementing Primary Education for All.* London: Macmillan. pp. 1–20.

Little, Angela, Wim Hoppers, and Roy Gardner (eds.), 1994. *Beyond Jomtien: Implementing Primary Education for All.* London: Macmillan.

Lockheed, Marlaine E., and Adriaan M. Verspoor and Associates, 1990. *Improving Primary Education in Developing Countries: A Review of Policy Option.* Oxford/New York: Oxford University Press (published for the World Bank).

Loxley, John, 1987. The IMF, the World Bank, and Sub-Saharan Africa: Policies and Politics. In Kjell Havnevik (ed.), *The IMF and the World Bank in Africa,* Uppsala: Scandinavian Institute of African Studies. pp. 47–65.

Lugoe, W. L., 1989. Growing Up as a Boy in the Jita Subnation in Mara Region. *Term paper* in social psychology. University of Dar es Salaam. Spring 1989.

Lund, Bernt, November 1995. Educationally Marginalised Children. *A desk study* submitted by Bernt H. Lund. Okahandja/Elverum.

Lwaitama, A. F., and J. M. Rugemalira, 1988. The English Language Support Project. *Seminar Paper* presented to the Department of Education and the Department of Foreign Languages and Linguistics, University of Dar es Salaam. 29.September.

Lynch, John, 1994. The Working Group on School Examinations Completes Its Program. *DAE Newsletter* 6(1).

Macleod, Catriona, 1995. Transforming Pedagogy in South Africa: The Insertion of the Teacher as Subject. *Perspectives in Education* 16(1): 63–82.

Mafeje, Archie, 1992. African Philosophical Projections and Prospects for the Indigenisation of Political and Intellectual Discourse. *Seminar Paper Series* No. 7. Harare: Sapes Books.

Makgoba, William, 1997. *MOKOKO: THE MAKGOBA AFFAIR. A Reflection on Transformation.* Lea Glen: Vivlia Publishers & Booksellers.

Malekela, George, 1983. Access to Secondary Education in Sub-Saharan Africa: The Tanzanian Experiment. *Ph.D. Thesis,* University of Chicago.

Malekela, George, 1984. Secondary School Girls in Tanzania: What Do We Know about Them? *Paper* presented to the staff-student seminar, October 18. University of Dar es Salaam, Department of Education.

Malherbe, Jeanette (ed.), 1996. *Decolonizing the Mind.* Proceedings of the second colloquium on African Philosophy held at the University of South Africa, Pretoria, October 1995.

Maliyamkono, T. Luta (ed.), 1980. *Policy Development in Overseas Training.* Dar es Salaam: Eastern African Universities Research Project and Black Star Agencies.

Maliyamkono, T. L., 1987. *Comments on the World Bank Document on "Financing Education in Developing Countries," a World Bank Publication.* Stenciled. University of Dar es Salaam.

Maliyamkono, T. Luta, A. G. M. Ishumi, and Wells, S. J., 1982. *Higher Education and Development in Eastern Africa.* London/Ibadan/Nairobi: Heinemann.

Mamdani, Mahmood, 1993. University Crisis and Reform: A Reflection on the African Experience. *Review of African Political Economy* No. 58. pp. 7–19.

Manase, T. J. 1978. Ideological State Apparatus Reproduces Existing Productive Relations: The Case of Mdanda Educational Institutions. In Abel Ishumi, and Geoffrey Mmari (eds), *The Educational Process.* University of Dar es Salaam, Department of Education.

Manganyi, N. C., 1991. Treachery and Innocence. *Psychology and Racial Difference in South Africa.* Johannesburg: Ravan Press.

Martin, Hans-Peter, and Harald Schumann, 1996. *Die Globalisierungsfalle. Der Angriff auf Demokratie und Wohlstand.* Reinbek bei Hamburg: Rowohlt.

Mazrui, Alamin, 1997. The World Bank, the Language Question, and the Future of African Education. *Race & Class. A Journal for Black and Third World Liberation* 38(3): 35–49.

Mazrui, Ali, 1978. *Political Values and the Educated Class in Africa.* Berkeley: University of California Press.

Mazrui, Ali, 1980. *The African Condition.* Cambridge University Press.

Mazrui, Ali, 1994. The Impact of Global Changes on Academic Freedom in Africa: A Preliminary Assessment. In Mamadou Diouf and Mahmood Mamdani (eds.), *Academic Freedom in Africa.* Dakar: CODESRIA Book Series. pp. 118–141.

Mazrui, Ali, 1996. Perspective: The Muse of Modernity and the Quest for Development. In Philip Altbach and S. M. Hassan (eds.). *The Muse of Modernity; Essays on Culture as Development in Africa.* Trenton, New Jersey: Rica World Press.: 1–18.

Mbala, R. M., F. M. Maayumbelo, and R. W. Matongo, 1995. Research on the Role and Attitudes Towards Silozi in Basic Education. *Paper* presented at the National Workshop on African Languages in Basic Education held at NIED in Okahandja, 18–22 September.

MBEC (Ministry of Basic Education and Culture), 1995. *Curriculum Guide for Formal Basic Education.*

Mblinyi, Majorie, 1976. The Study of Education and the "Community." In Kenneth King (ed.), *Education and Community in Africa.* University of Edinburgh: Centre of African Studies.

Mbunda, Alois, 1997. Curriculum under Pressure: Tanzania's Experiences. In Roger Avenstrup (ed.), *Shaping Africa's Future through Innovative Curricula.* Windhoek: Gamsberg Macmillan. pp. 178–184.

McFadden, Patricia, 1987. Adjustment and Its Impact on Industry and on Women. Paper presented at a CODESRIA (Council for the Development of Economic and Social Research in Africa) conference in Dakar, 27–29 October 1987.31 pp.

McGinn, Noel, 1994. The Impact of Supranational Organizations on Public Education. *International Journal of Educational Development* (14)3: 289–299.

McGinn, Noel F., 1997. Toward an Alternative Strategy for International Assistance to Education. *Prospects*. 27(2): 231–246.

McGrath, Simon, 1997. "The Famished Road": The Search for Sustainable Education and Development. *Paper* presented at the Oxford Conference, Education and Geopolitical Change, New College, Oxford, 11–15 September.

MEC (Ministry of Education and Culture), 1993a. *Namibia National Conference on the Implementation of the Language Policy for Schools*. Ongwediva Training Centre, 22–26 June 1992. Windhoek: Longman Namibia.

MEC, 1993b. *Toward Education for All: A Development Brief for Education, Culture, and Training*.

MEC, 1993c. *The Language Policy for Schools 1992–1996 and Beyond*.

MEC/NIED (Ministry of Education and Culture/National Institute of Educational Development in Namibia), February 1994. Monitoring Secondary Reform: The Junior Secondary Certificate Examination, 1993. *Mimeo.*

Mehrotra, Santosh, 1998. Education for All: Policy Lessons from High-Achieving Countries. *International Review of Education*. Vol. 44. No.5/6. pp.461–484.

Melber, Henning, 1997. Centralisation/Decentralisation in the Context of Educational Globalisation. In Roger Avenstrup (ed.), *Shaping Africa's Future through Innovative Curricula*. Windhoek: Gamsberg Macmillan. pp. 63–69.

Mendelsohn, John, Patti Swarts, and Roger Avenstrup, 1995. Marginalisation in Education: The Case of Bushman-Speaking People. *EMIS Bulletin*. No. 3. June.

Miller, Janet, 1982. The Sound of Silence Breaking: Feminist Pedagogy and Theory. *Journal of Curriculum Theory* 4 (1): 5–11.

Ministry of Education. 1996. *Green Paper on Higher Education Transformation*. Pretoria:

Mkandawire, Thandika, 1990. The African Social Science Research Environment. *UDASA Newsletter*. No. 10. February. The University of Dar es Salaam. pp.26–33. Also published in *CODESRIA Bulletin*, 1988. No. 4. pp. 1–4.

Mkhatshwa, Smangaliso, 1996a. The Significance of Implementing the Transformation Charter in the Teaching and Learning Context. *A short address* delivered at the unveiling of the Transformation Charter at the Vaal Triangle Technikon, 17 September.

Mkhatshwa, Smangaliso, 1996b. The Significance of Transforming the Higher Education Sector and the Role of the Ministry of Education. *A keynote address* delivered at the Summit on the Transformation of Potchefstroom University for Christian Higher Education, 21 September.

Mlama, P., and M. Matteru, 1978. *Haja ya Kutumia Kiswahili Kufundishia Katika Elimu ya Juu.* (The Need to Use Kiswahili as a Medium of Instruction in Higher Education). Dar es Salaam: Bajita.

Mordaunt, Owen G, 1990. Swaziland's Language Policy for Schools. *Educational Studies.* Vol.16. No.2. pp.122–136.

Mosha, Herme Joseph, 1988. A Reassessment of the Indicators of Primary Education Quality in Developing Countries: Emerging Evidence from Tanzania. *International Review of Education* 34(1): 17–45.

Moumouni, Abdou, 1968. *Education in Africa.* London: Andre Deutsch.

Moyo, Cecilia, 1996. Rationale for an Audit of the Higher Education Sector. Prepared for the Deputy Minister of Education. Johannesburg. June 20.

Moyo, Cecilia, 1997. Issues in the Construction of the Culture of Learning and Teaching in South Africa. *Paper* presented at the Oxford International Conference on Education and Development, "Education and Geopolitical Change," 11–15 September.

Mudenda, Gilbert, 1987. Adjustment, De-Industrialization and the Urban Crisis: The Case of Zambia. *Paper* presented at a CODESRIA conference, Dakar, 27–29 October.

Muganyizi, L., 1976. Implementation and Usefulness of Self-Reliance in Schools: Findings of Research Carried Out in Bukoba District. *Papers in Education and Development.* 2. pp. 97–121.

Mukyanuzi, F. B., April 1978. Implications of Colonial Examination System in Secondary Schools in Tanzania. In Majorie Mbiliny, Martha Mvungi, S. T. Mahenge, A. Ishumi, M. P. Besha, I. M. Omari, and G. V. Mmari (eds.), *Papers in Education and Development.* No. 6. University of Dar es Salaam, Department of Education. pp. 76–106.

Mulenga, Derek, 1995. *Impact of Structural Adjustment Programs (SAPs) on Policy Formation in Adult/Basic/Nonformal Education in Africa and Asia.* Hamburg: UNESCO Institute of Education.

Mumford, W.B.,1936. *Africans Learn to be French.* London: Evans Bros. Ltd.

Muskin, J., 1992. World Bank Lending for Science and Technology: General Operational Review. *PHREE*/92/51R. Washington, DC: World Bank.

Mutorwa, John, 1995. *Statement* delivered at the National Workshop on African Languages in Basic Education held at NIED in Okahandja, 18 September.

Muyanda-Mutebi, Peter, and Martin Yiga Matovu (eds.), 1993. *Educational Research for Development in Africa.* Dakar: UNESCO-BREDA/ASESP.

Mwiria, Kilemi, July 1998. *Building Educational Research Capacity in Malawi, Zambia, and Zimbabwe: The DSE Experience.* Nairobi: Kimkam Development Consultants.

Nababan, P. W. J., 1982. Indonesia: The Language Situation. In Richard Noss (ed.), Language Teaching Issues in Multilingual Environments in South-East Asia. *Anthology Series* 10. SEAMEO Regional Language Centre. RELCP 154–82. pp. 1–45.

Nagel, Tove, 1993. Quality Between Tradition and Modernity: Patterns of Communication and Cognition in Teacher Training in Zimbabwe. *Dr. Polit. thesis.* Oslo: Institute for Educational Research.

Namuddu, Katherine, 1991, Educational Research Priorities in Sub-Saharan Africa. In Gary Miron, and Karen Sorensen (eds.), *Strengthening Educational Research in Developing Countries.* Paris: UNESCO and IIE. pp. 39–73.

NCHE, 1996: National Commission on Higher Education: Discussion Document: A Framework for Transformation. Pretoria.

Närman, Anders, 1991. Local Initiative in Planning for Development: The Kenyan Harambee Movement. In Gun Mickels, Kirsti Floor, and Anita Toro (eds.), *The Third World, the Fourth World: Dimensions of Development in the Peripheries. Occasional Paper.* No. 26. Helsinki: Finnish Association For Development Geography. pp.109–114.

Närman, Anders, 1992. Basic Education and Relevant Schooling in Africa: the Need to Bridge the Gap. In Lene Buchert (ed.), *Education and Training in the Third World.* The Local Dimension. *CESO Paperback* No. 18. The Hague: CESO. pp. 143–153.

Ngulube, Naboth, 1989. *Some Aspects of Growing Up in Zambia.* Lusaka: Nalinga Consultancy.

NETF (National Education Trust Fund), 1994. *Amounts of Funds Disbursed to Schools as of 24 June 1994.* Dar es Salaam: Author.

NIED, 1995. *Summary of conference proceedings and recommendations* from the National Workshop on African Languages in Basic Education held at NIED in Okahandja, 18–22 September.

Nkomo, Mokubung, 1990. Post-Apartheid Education: Preliminary Reflections. In Mokubung Nkomo, (ed), *Pedagogy of Domination.* Trenton, NJ: Africa World Press. pp. 291–325.

Nnana, Marie-Claire, 1995. Livres scolaire: Vers une guerre nord-sud? *Afrique Education.* September.

NORAD (Norwegian Development Agency), October 1986. *ZAM 021, the Maintenance Programme.* Report from the joint Zambian/Norwegian review mission. Oslo: Author.

NORAD/AFR-1989. *Agreed Minutes* from Policy Consultations on Development Cooperation between Tanzania and Norway following the meeting held in Dar es Salaam 10–12 April 1989. (Storløkken/ Aarbakke 21.04.1989)

NORAD, September 1990. *Strategies* for Development Cooperation. Oslo: Author.

NORAD, September 1992. *Strategier* for bilateral bistand-del II (Strategies for Bilateral Aid. Part II). Oslo: Author.

Nordkvelle, Yngve, 1998, Globalisering og postkolonialistisk teori: mulige konsekvenser for pedagogikk som vitenskapsfag, studiefag og fagdidaktikk (Globalization and Post-Colonial Theory: Possible Consequences for Education as a Scientific Discipline, Field of Study and Pedagogy). *Paper* presented at the conference "Pedagogikk: normalvitenskap eller lappeteppe?" (Education: A Normal Scientific Field or a Quilt?) Lillehammer Regional College. 17–19. November.

NORRAG (Northern Research Review Advisory Group) NEWS, June 1990. Published at the University of Edinburgh.

Ntondo, Zavoni, 1998: The Sociolinguistic Situation of Oshikwanyama in Angola. In: Karsten Legere, 1998 (ed.). *Cross-Border Languages. Reports and Studies. Regional Workshop on Cross-Border Languages.* NIED. 23–27 September 1996. Windhoek: Gamsberg Macmillan Publishers. pp.75–82.

Nyerere, Julius, 1967. *The Arusha Declaration and TANU's Policy on Socialism and Self-Reliance.* Dar es Salaam: Publicity Section. TANU.

Nyerere, Julius, 1968. (issued in March 1967). Education for Self-Reliance, In *Ujamaa, Essays on Socialism.* Dar es Salaam: Oxford University Press. pp. 44–76.

Nyerere, Julius, 1982. Education in Tanzania, (extracts taken from Education for Self-Reliance) In Babs A. Fafunwa, and J. U. Aisiku (eds.), *Education in Africa. A Comparative Survey.* London: Allen & Unwin. pp. 235–254.

Nyquist, Annette, 1999. Challenges Facing the Instructor in the COPE (Complementary Opportunity for Primary Education) Centres: A Focus on the Paraprofessional Teacher in Non-Formal Education Programmes. *Thesis* for the Cand.Polit. degree in Education. Spring term. University of Oslo: Institute for Educational Research.

Nzimande, Blade, 1997a. Neo-Liberal Ideologues Are Hijacking the Transformation of Education. Higher Education Transformation Must Not Be Distracted from the Goals of the Anti-Apartheid Struggle by a Globalisation Process Driven by Neo-Liberal Ideologies. *Sunday Independent.* 23. February.

Nzimande, Blade, 1997b. Ramphele Is Using a Smokescreen to Conceal What Amounts to Intellectual Blackmail of Me. Academic's Criticism of the Chairman of Parliament's Education Portfolio Committee Has "Hidden Motive". *Sunday Independent.* 23. March.

Obanya, Pai, 1980. Research on Alternative Teaching in Africa. In E. A. Yoloye, and Flechsig, Karl Heinz (eds.), *Educational Research for Development.* Bonn: Deutsche Stiftung für Internationale Entwicklung. pp. 67–112.

Obanya, Pai, 1995a. Case Studies of Curriculum Innovations in Western Africa. *International Review of Education* 41(5): 315–336.

Obanya, Pai, 1995b. Un aperçu sur la place des langues dans les programmes d'alphabetisation et d'education de base en Afrique. In Adama Ouane (ed.), *Vers une culture multilingue de l'education.* Hamburg: Institut de l'UNESCO pour l'Education. pp. 195–211.

Ocitti, J. P. 1973. *African Indigenous Education: As Practised by the Acholi of Uganda.* Nairobi: East African Literature Bureau.

Ocitti, J. P. 1990. Indigenous Education for Today: The Necessity of the Useless. *Adult Education and Development.* No. 35. pp. 347–357. German Adult Education Association.

Ocitti, J. P. 1991: An Introduction to Indigenous Education in Sub-Saharan Africa. A Select Annotated Bibliography. *Bibliography No .9.* The Hague: Centre for the Study of Education in Developing Countries.

ODA (Overseas Development Administration), 1995. *Aid to Education in 1993 and Beyond.* London: Author.

Odora, Catherine, 1992. Decentralisation and the Re-Validation of the Indigenous Learning Systems.In Lene Buchert (ed.), *Education and Training in the Third World: The Local Dimension. CESO Paperback.* No. 18. The Hague: CESO. pp. 77–90.

Odora, Catherine, 1993. Educating African Girls in a Context of Patriarchy and Transformation: A Theoretical and Conceptual Analysis. Stockholm University: *Master's Degree Study* from the Institute of International Education. No. 7.

Odora, Catherine, 1994. Indigenous Forms of Learning in Africa with Special Reference to the Acholi of Uganda. In Birgit Brock-Utne (ed.): Indigenous Education in Africa. *Rapport* No. 7. Oslo: Institute for Educational Research.

Odora Hoppers, Catherine 1998. Structural Violence as a Constraint to African Policy Formation in the 1990s: Repositioning Education in International Relations. *Doctoral thesis.* University of Stockholm, Institute for International Education.

OECD (Organization for Economic Cooperation and Development), 1996. *OECD Development Cooperation 1996.*

OECD 1997: *Education at a glance. OECD Indicators 1997.* Paris:OECD. Centre for Educational Research and Innovation.

Ohly, R., 1987. *Primary Technical Dictionary: English-Kiswahili.* Institute of Production Innovation. University of Dar es Salaam and Deutsche Gesellschaft für technische Zusammenarbeit.

Okkelmo, Kjersti Franciszka. Some gender related challenges in primary education in Swaziland. *Thesis* for the cand.polit. degree in education. Spring term. University of Oslo: Institute for Educational Research. Published as Report No.2.1999 from the Institute for Educational Research, University of Oslo.

Olsson, Berit, 1995. The Power of Knowledge: A Comparison of Two International Policy Papers on Higher Education. In Lene Buchert, and Kenneth King (eds.), *Learning from Experience: Policy and Practice in Aid to Higher Education. CESO Paperback* No. 24. The Hague: CESO. pp. 235–247.

Onimode, Bade, 1992. *A Future for Africa. Beyond the Politics of Adjustment.* London: Earthscan Publications.

Ouane, Adama, 1989. *Handbook on Learning Strategies for Post-Literacy and Continuing Education.* Hamburg: UNESCO Institute for Education.

Ouane, Adama, 1991. Language Standardization in Mali. In Utta von Gleich, and Wolff Ekkehard (eds.), *Standardization of National Languages.* Symposium on Language Standardization, 2–3 February. *UIE-Reports.* No. 5. Hamburg: UNESCO Institute of Education. (joint publication with the Research Centre for Multilingualism and Language Contact, University of Hamburg). pp. 1–11.

Ouane, Adama, 1995. Introduction: Regard de l'interieur de la prison linguistique. In Adama Ouane, (ed.), *Vers une culture multilingue de l'education.* Hamburg: Institut de l'UNESCO pour l'Education. pp. 3–21.

Ovando, Carlos, 1990. Politics and Pedagogy: The Case of Bilingual Education. *Harvard Educational Review* 60(3): 341–57.

Payer, Cheryl,1987. The IMF and India. In Kjell Havnevik (ed.), The IMF and the World Bank in Africa: Conditionality, Impact and Alternatives. *Seminar Proceedings* No. 18. pp. 65–85. Uppsala: Scandinavian Institute of African Studies.

Phillipson, Robert, 1992. *Linguistic Imperialism.* Oxford: Oxford University Press.

Phillipson, Robert, Tove Skutnabb-Kangas, and Hugh Africa, 1985. Namibian Educational Planning: English for Liberation or Neo-Colonialism? In K. Mateene, J. Kalema, and B.Chomba (eds.), *Linguistic Liberation and Unity of Africa.* Kampala: OAU Bureau of Languages. *OAU/BIL Publication 6.* pp. 42–59.

Pinar, William, 1995. *Regimes of Reason and Male Narrative Voice.* (mimeo)

Polome, E., 1979. Tanzania Language Policy and Swahili. *Word.* No. 30.

Prah, Kwesi Kwaa, 1993. *Mother Tongue for Scientific and Technological Development in Africa.* Bonn: German Foundation for International Development.

Psacharopoulos, G., and Loxley, W. 1985. *Diversified Secondary Education and Development: Evidence from Colombia and Tanzania.* Baltimore: Johns Hopkins University Press.

Ramphele, Mamphela, 1996. Universities Must Encourage Dancers to Take the Floor Even if They Have to Step on Toes. *Sunday Independent.* 20 October.

Ranaweera, A. Mahinda, 1976. Sri Lanka: Science Teaching in the National Languages. *Prospects* 6(3): 416–423.

Rand Daily Mail, 10 November 1959 (interview with Minister of Bantu Education, W. A. Maree).

Reh, Mechthild, and Bernd Heine, 1982: *Sprachpolitik und Sprachplanung in Afrika.* Hamburg: Buske.

Reimers, Fernando, 1995. Higher Education: The Lessons of Experience. Book Review. *Comparative Education Review* 39(2): 245–247.

Reimers, Fernando, and Luis Tiburcio, 1993. *Education: Adjustment and Reconstruction: Options for Change.* Paris: UNESCO Publishing.

Reiner, Peter, Werner Hillbrecht, and Jane Katjivivi, 1994. *Books in Namibia: Past Trends and Future Prospects.* Association of Namibian Publishers.

Rodney, Walter, 1972. *How Europe Underdeveloped Africa.* Dar es Salaam: Tanzania Publishing House.

Roy, Sanjit Bunker, May 1993. The Right to Basic Needs and Making Choices. Norwegian Aid Policies Prevent People's Organisations from Taking Roots. In *Split Vision: Southern Reflections on the Norwegian White Paper on North-South Policy.* Oslo: Forum for Environment and Development. pp.7–18.

Roy-Campbell, Zaline Makini, 1992a. The Politics of Education in Tanzania: From Colonialism to Liberalization. In Horace Campbell, and Howard Stein (eds.), *Tanzania and the IMF: The Dynamics of Liberalization.* Westview Press. pp. 147–169.

Roy-Campbell, Zaline Makini, 1992b. Power or Pedagogy: Choosing the Medium of Instruction in Tanzania. *Ph.d. thesis.* University of Wisconsin-Madison.

Roy-Campbell, Zaline Makini, 1998. Language as the Repository of Knowledge and Culture: Deconstructing Myths about African Languages. *Paper* presented to the CIES annual meeting held in Buffalo, New York, March 18–22.

Roy-Campbell, Zaline Makini, and Martha Qorro, 1987. *A Survey of the Reading Competence in English of Secondary School Students in Tanzania.* University of Dar es Salaam, Department of Foreign Languages and Linguistics.

Roy-Campbell, Zaline Makini, and Martha A. S. Qorro, 1997. *Language Crisis in Tanzania. The Myth of English versus Education.* Dar es Salaam: Mkuki na Nyota Publishers.

Rubagumya, Casmir, (ed.), 1990. *Language in Education in Africa: A Tanzanian Perspective.* Clevedon. Philadelphia: Multilingual Matters.

Rubagumya, Casmir, 1991. Language Promotion for Educational Purposes: The Example of Tanzania. *International Review of Education* 37(1): 67–87.

Rugemalira, J. M., C. M. Rubagumya, M. K. Kapinga, A. F. Lwaitama, and J. G. Tetlow, 1990. Reflections on Recent Developments in Language Policy in Tanzania. In C. M. Rubagumya (ed.), *Language in Education in Africa: A Tanzanian Perspective.* Clevedon. Philadelphia: Multilingual Matters. pp. 25–36.

Ruth, Damian, 1996. Teaching at a South African University. *Teaching in Higher Education* 1(1): 129–133.

Rwezaura, Baltazar, 1985. *Traditional Family Law and Change in Tanzania.* Baden-Baden: Nomos Verlag.

Sadique, Isahaku, 1995. The Image of the World Bank within Nigerian Universities. In Birgit Brock-Utne (ed.), *States or Markets? Neo-Liberal Solutions in the Educational Policies of Sub-Saharan Africa.* Proceedings from a seminar. *Rapport No. 3.* Oslo: Institute for Educational Research. pp. 108–135.

Saha, Lawrence, 1991. Universities and National Development: Issues and Problems in Developing Countries. *Prospects.* 21(2): 248–257.

Samoff, Joel, 1993. The Reconstruction of Schooling in Africa. *Comparative Education Review* 37(2): 181–222.

Samoff, Joel, 1996. Which Priorities and Strategies for Education? *International Journal of Educational Development* 16: 249–71.

Samoff, Joel, and Suleman Sumra, 1992. *From Lighting a Torch on Kilimanjaro to Living in a Shanty Town: Education and Financial Crisis in Tanzania.* Paris: UNESCO.

Sanou, Fernand, 1990. Who's Afraid of National Languages as Instructional Media and Why? In UNESCO-UNICEF, *African Thoughts on the Prospects of Education for All.* Dakar: Breda. pp. 75–97.

Scanlon, David, 1964. *Traditions of African Education.* New York: Columbia University Teachers' College.

Schmied, J., 1989. English in East and Central Africa. *Bayreuth African Studies Series,* No. 15.

Schuller, Tom, and John Field, 1998. Social Capital, Human Capital, and the Learning Society. *International Journal of Lifelong Education* 17(4): 226–236.

Schultz, Theodor, 1961. Investment in Human Capital. *American Economic Review* 5(1): 1–17.

Seepe, Sipho, 1997. Africa Must Be Measured in Its Own Right, Not as a Fringe of Europe. *Sunday Independent.* January 5.

Semesi, Adelaida, and Dr.Urassa, April 1991. Educating Female Scientists in Tanzania. In Birgit Brock-Utne, and Naomi Katunzi (eds.), *Women and Education in Tanzania.* Twelve papers from a seminar. *WED-Report 3.* Dar es Salaam. pp. 124–135.

Sheriff, A. 1990. Incentive Schemes, Scopo, and the Need for a Living Wage. *UDASA Newsletter/Forum.* No. 10 (February): 2–10. Issued by University of Dar es Salaam Academic Staff Assembly.

Sikwibele, Anne, 1996. Foreign Aid and Globalisation of Educational Policy in Post Colonial Africa. *Southern African Review of Education* 2(October): 19–31.

Skutnabb-Kangas, Tove, 1984. *Bilingualism or Not: The Education of Minorities.* Clevedon, Avon: Multilingual Matters.

Skutnabb-Kangas, Tove, 1988. Multilingualism and the Education of Minority Children. In Tove Skutnabb-Kangas, and Jim Cummins (eds.), *Minority Education. From Shame to Struggle.* Clevedon: Multilingual Matters. pp. 9–44.

Skutnabb-Kangas, Tove, 1990. *Language, Literacy, and Minorities.* London: Minority Rights Group.

Skutnabb-Kangas, Tove (ed.), 1995. *Multilingualism for All.* Lisse: Swets & Zeitlinger.

Skutnabb-Kangas, Tove, and Jim Cummins (eds.), 1988. *Minority Education. From Shame to Struggle.* Clevedon: Multilingual Matters.

Skutnabb-Kangas, Tove, and Robert Phillipson, 1996. The Possible Role of Donors in a Language Policy for All. In Birgit Brock-Utne, and Tove Nagel (eds.), *The Role of Aid in the Development of Education for All. Report.* No. 8. Oslo: Institute for Educational Research. pp. 161–202.

Soudien, Crain, 1996. Issues of Race and Identity. *Academic Development.* Vol.2. No.1. pp. 37–47.

South Center, 1996. *For a Strong and Democratic UN: A South Perspective on UN Reform.* Geneva: Author.

Stevenson, G., 1991. *Adjustment Lending and the Education Sector: The Bank's Experience.* Washingon DC: World Bank.

Stewart, Frances, 1996. Globalisation and Education. *International Journal of Educational Development* 16(4): 327–333.

Stolten, H. E., 1997. Academic Apartheid and Progressive Response. Historical Images of Social and Ethnic Implications of the Introduction of University Apartheid, 1950–1960. *Paper* presented at the "Africa Days" at the Nordic Africa Institute in Uppsala, 19–21 September.

Stordahl, Vigdis, 1994. *Same i den moderne verden:. Endring og kontinuitet i et samisk lokalsamfunn* (Sami in the Modern World: Change and Continuity in a Sami Community). Karasjok.

St. meld nr. 74, 1984–85. Om Norges samarbeid med utviklingslandene i 1984 (On Norway's Cooperation with the Developing Countries in 1984). Government White Paper.

Stromquist, Nelly, 1993. The Practical and Theoretical Bases for Empowerment. *Paper* presented at the International Seminar on Women's Education and Empowerment organized by the UNESCO Institute for Education, Hamburg, January.

Struik, J. Dirk, 1995. Everybody Counts: Towards a Broader History of Mathematics. *Technology Review.* Aug./Sept. pp. 36–44.

Sumra, Suleman, and Naomi Katunzi, 1991 The Struggle for Education: School Fees and Girls Education in Tanzania. *WED Report.* No. 5. Dar es Salaam: Women, Education, Development (WED), University of Dar es Salaam.

Sumra, Suleman, September 1994. An Analysis of National and Regional Enrollment Trends in Primary Education in Tanzania. *Report* submitted to UNICEF, Dar es Salaam.

Sumra, Suleman, 1996. Education Policies in Tanzania Since Independence. In Birgit Brock-Utne, and Tove Nagel (eds.), *The Role of Aid in the Development of Education for All. Report.* No. 8. Oslo: Institute for Educational Research. pp. 202–226.

Sutherland, Carla, 1997. University Transformation in South Africa: Lessons from the Rest of the Continent. *Paper* presented at the Oxford International Conference on Education and Development. "Education and Geopolitical Change," 11–15 September.

Swain, M. 1981. Bilingual Education for Majority and Minority Language Children. *Studia Linguistica* 35: pp. 15–30.

Swain, M., and S. Lapkin, 1982. *Evaluating Bilingual Education. A Canadian Case Study.* Clevedon, Aven: Multilingual Matters.

SWAPO, (South West Africa People's Organization) 1982. *Preliminary Perspectives into an Emergent Educational system for Namibia.* Luanda: Department of Education and Culture. SWAPO of Namibia.

SWAPO, 1989. *Swapo Election Manifesto: Towards an Independent and Democratic Namibia.* SWAPO's Policy Positions.

Symiris, S., 1988. *Sector Review: The Financing of Education in Tanzania-Overview.* Paris: UNESCO.

Synott, December John, 1994. Australian Aboriginal Constructions of Humans, Society and Nature in Relation to Peace Education. In Åke Bjerstedt (ed.), *Education for Peace: A Conference Report from Malta. Peace Education*

Reports. No. 13. Malmö: Department of Educational and Psychological Research. pp. 71–83.

Taasisi Ya Uchunguzi wa Kiswahili, 1990. *Kamusi Sanifu Ya Biolojia, Fizika na Kemia.* (Dictionary of biology, physics and chemistry) Dar es Salaam: Chuo DSM/TUKI/ UNESCO/ SIDA.

Tadadjeu, Maurice, 1989. *Voie africaine: Esquisse du communautarisme africain.* Cameroon: Club OUA.

Tadadjeu, Maurice, 1997. The Challenge of Language and Education in African Development. *Plenary talk* 12. September and *paper* presented at the Oxford International Conference on Education and Development, "Education and Geopolitical Change," 11–15 September.

Takala, Tuomas, 1995. Textbook Provisions under the Conditions of Economic Liberalization: Cases of Zambia, Mozambique, and Namibia. In Birgit Brock-Utne (ed.), *States or Markets? Neo-Liberalism in the Educational Policies of Sub-Saharan Africa. Rapport* No. 1. Oslo: Institute for Educational Research. pp. 162–182.

Takala, Tuomas, 1998. Making Educational Policy under Influence of External Assistance and National Politics: A Comparative Analysis of the Education Sector Policy Documents of Ethiopia, Mozambique, Namibia, and Zambia. *International Journal of Educational Development* 18(4): 319–335.

Tandon, Yash, 1995. Norwegian South Policy for a Changing World. *Development Today* 5(5): 10–11.

Tandon, Yash, 1996. Continuing Struggle of the African People in the Era of Globalization. *Paper* presented at the Anti-Imperialist World Peasant Summit, Manila, Philippines, November.

TANU (Tanzania National Union), 1971: *TANU Guidelines.* Dar es Salaam.

Tenga, Sendeu Titus, 1994. The Norwegian Sports for All Project in Dar es Salaam, Tanzania 1984–90. An evaluation of the training programmes. *Master's thesis.* Oslo: Norwegian University of Sport and Physical Education. Spring term.

Tenga, Sendeu Titus, 1997. How Can the Sociology of Sports Use Globalization Theory to Analyze Sports in Africa? *Paper* written for an exam as part of the degree of dr. scient. Oslo: Norwegian University of Sport and Physical Education. Spring term.

Tetlow, Julian G., 1988. The English Language Support Project. *Seminar Paper* presented to the Department of Education and the Department of Foreign Languages and Linguistics, University of Dar es Salaam. 29. September.

Theal, G. M., 1910. *History and Ethnography of Africa, South of the Zambezi before 1795.* London: Allen and Unwin.

Thiong'o, Ngugi wa, 1986. *Decolonising the Mind: The Politics of Language in African Literature.* Nairobi/Portsmouth: Heinemann.

Tilak, Jandhyala, 1992. Education and Structural Adjustment. *Prospects* 22(4): 415–422.

Tomasevski, Katarina, 1997. *Between Sanctions and Elections: Aid Donors and Their Human Rights Performance.* London: Pinter.

Tungesvik, Ragnhild, 1998a. To Make Every Child a Successful Learner: Continuous Assessment as a Contribution to Quality Improvement in Primary Education in Swaziland. *Thesis* for the cand.polit. degree in education. Spring term. University of Oslo: Institute for Educational Research. Published as *Report* No.3.1999 from the Institute for Educational Research, University of Oslo.

Tungesvik, Ragnhild, 1998b. English as the Language of Instruction in African Schools: Some Perspectives on Learning Processes and Power Structures. *Term paper* for the cand. polit. degree in education. Spring term. University of Oslo: Institute for Educational Research.

Turok, Ben, 1992. What Does the World Bank Mean by Empowering Ordinary People? In Mary Turok (ed.), *The African Response: Adjust or Transformation.* London: Institute for African Alternatives. pp. 46–58.

Uchendu,V. (ed.), 1979. *Education and Politics in Tropical Africa.* New York: Conch.

UDASA (University of Dar es Salaam Academic Staff Assembly), February 1990. The Squeeze of Education. *UDASA Newsletter/Forum.* No. 10. February 1990. Issued by University of Dar es Salaam Academic Staff Assembly. 45 pp.

UNDP (United Nations Development Program), 1992. *Human Development Report.* New York: Author.

UNDP, 1994. *Human Development Report.* New York: Author.

UNDP, 1997. *Human Development Report.* Oxford: Oxford University Press.

UNECA (United Nations Economic Commission for Africa), 1989. *African Alternative Framework to Structural Adjustment Programs for Socioeconomic Recovery and Transformation.* Addis Ababa: Author.

UNESCO (United Nations Educational, Scientific, and Cultural Organization), 1970. *The Use of Vernacular Languages in Education.* Paris: Author.

UNESCO, 1985. *African Community Languages and Their Use in Literacy and Education.* Dakar: BREDA.

UNESCO–UNICEF, 1990. *African Thoughts on the Prospects of Education for All. Selections from papers commissioned for the Regional Consultation on Education for All,* Dakar 27–30 November,1989. Dakar: Breda and Abidjan: WCARO

UNESCO, 1993. *Education for All: Status and Trends.* Paris: Author.

UNESCO, 1996. *Statistical Document: Education for All, Achieving the Goal.* Mid-Decade Meeting on the International Consultative Forum on Education for All, Amman.

UNESCO, 1997. *Statistical Yearbook 1996.* Lanham: UNESCO Publishing & Bernan Press.

UNESCO, 1998. *World Education Report 1998.* Paris: UNESCO Publishing.

UNESCO/UNECA, 1961. *Outline of a Plan for African Educational Development.* Paris.

UNIN (United Nations Institute for Namibia), 1981. *Toward a Language Policy for Namibia: English as the Official Language—Perspectives and Strategies.* Lusaka: Author.

Urch, George, 1991. Shifts in Socioeconomic and Educational Policy in Tanzania: External and Internal Forces. In Mark Ginsburg (ed.), *Understanding Educational Reform in Global Context: Economy, Ideology, and the State.* New York & London: Garland Publishing. pp. 201–229.

URT (United Republic of Tanzania),1972. *Economic Survey, 1970–71.*

URT (United Republic of Tanzania),1988. *Hali ya Uchumi wa Taifa katika miaka 1983–88* (the state of the Economy of the country in the years 1983–88)

URT (United Republic of Tanzania), 1993. *The Tanzania Education System for the 21st Century: Report of the Task Force, 1993.* Dar es Salaam: United Republic of Tanzania, Ministry of Education and Culture and Ministry of Science, Technology, and Higher Education. (Printed by the Print Service, a division of University of Leeds Media Services)

URT (United Republic of Tanzania), 1995. *Education and Training Policy.* Ministry of Education and Culture.

U.S. Department of Education, 1991. *The Condition of Education 1991. Vol. 1. Elementary and Secondary Education.* Washington, DC: Author.

Vera, Vincent N., 1995. Multifaceted Joint Research: A Strategy for Fostering a Culture of Research in HBUs. *Paper* presented at the Faculty of Education Symposium titled "Re-thinking the Culture of Teaching, Learning and Administration at Historically Black Institutions of Higher Learning in South Africa." The University of the North 7. October.

Vera, Vincent N., 1996. The Politics of Transforming Higher Education in South Africa. *Paper* presented at the National Conference of Black Political Scientists (NCOBPS), Savannah State College, Georgia, 6–10 March.

Verspoor, Adriaan, 1993. More Than Business-as-Usual: Reflections on the New Modalities of Education Aid. *International Journal of Educational Development* 13: 103–112.

Vorster, P. J., 1995. Africanisation: An Explanation and Some Educational Implications. *South African Journal of Education* 15(1): 6–12.

Vorster, P. J., 1996. Decolonizing the Mind through Africanisation. In Jeanette Malherbe (ed.), *Decolonizing the Mind. Proceedings of the Colloquium held at UNISA,* October 1995. Pretoria: Research Unit for African Philosophy at UNISA. pp. 154–162.

Vossen, Rainer, 1990. *Patterns of Language Knowledge and Language Use in Ngamiland, Botswana.* Bayreuth African Studies Series. No. 13. Bayreuth: Bayreuth University.

Vries, C. de, 1986. *Orientation in Fundamental Education Theory.* Stellenbosch: University Publisher & Booksellers.

Wardaugh, R. 1987. *Languages in Competition.* New York: Basil Blackwell.

Watson, Keith, 1994. Caught between Scylla and Charybdis: Linguistic and Educational Dilemmas Facing Policymakers in Pluralist States. *International Journal of Educational Development* 14(3): 321–337.

Watson, Keith, 1995. Redefining the Role of Government in Higher Education: How Realistic Is the World Bank's Prescription. In Lene Buchert, and Kenneth King (eds.), *Learning from Experience: Policy and Practice in Aid to Higher Education.* CESO Paperback No. 24. The Hague: CESO. pp. 125–145.

Watson, Keith, 1996. Banking on Key Reforms for Educational Development: A Critique of the World Bank Review. *Mediterranean Journal of Educational Studies* 1(1): 43–61.

Watson, Keith, 1997. Languages, Power and Geopolitical Changes. *Paper* presented at the Oxford International Conference on Education and Development. "Education and Geopolitical Change," 11–15 September.

WCEFA (World Conference on Education for All), April 1990. *World Declaration on Education for All.* New York: Author.

WCEFA, (World Conference on Education for All) 1990: *World Declaration on Education for All: Our Framework for Action to Meet Basic Learning Needs,* Jomtien, 5–9 March 1990.

Westley, David, 1992. Language and Education in Africa: A Select Bibliography, 1980–1990. *Comparative Education Review* 36(3):355–368.

White, Bob W.,1996: Talk about School; Education and the Colonial Project in French and British Africa (1860–1960). *Comparative Education.* Vol. 32. No. 1. pp. 9–25.

Whiteley, W., 1969. *Swahili: The Rise of a National Language.* London: Methuen.

Wickmann, Kenth, 1993. Swedish Support to Schoolbook Provision in Tanzania. *Promemoria* 29.12.1993. Stockholm: SIDA, Undervisningsbyrån.

Wiredu, Kwasi, 1984. *Philosophical Research and Training in Africa: Some Suggestions.* Paris: UNESCO.

Wold, Astri Heen, 1989. Tospråklighet. Språklige, intellektuelle og skolemessige konsekvenser (Bilingualism: Linguistic, Intellectual, and Educational Consequences). *Tidsskrift for Samfunnsforskning* 1(30): 3–26.

Wold, Astri Heen, 1992. Holdbare og ikke holdbare argumenter i debatten om morsmålsundervisning for barn fra språklige minoriteter (Valid and Not Valid Arguments about Teaching in the Vernacular for Children from Language Minority Groups). *Norsk Pedagogisk Tidsskrift.* 76(5): 240–249.

Wolff, Ekkehard H., 1991. Standardization and Varities of written Hausa (West Africa). In Utta von Gleich, and Wolff Ekkehard (eds.), Standardization of National Languages. Symposium on Language Standardization, 2–3 February. *UIE Reports.* No. 5. Hamburg: UNESCO Institute of Education (joint publication with the Research Centre for Multilingualism and Language Contact, University of Hamburg). pp. 21–33.

World Bank 1974: *Education Sector Working Paper.* Washington D.C.: Author.

World Bank, 1978. Teacher Training and Student Achievement in less Developed Countries. *Staff Working Paper* No. 310. Washington, DC: Author.

World Bank, 1980. *Education Sector Policy Paper* (3rd ed.). Washington, DC: Author.

World Bank, 1981. *Accelerated Development in Sub-Saharan Africa: An Agenda for Action.* Washington, DC: Author.

World Bank, 1984. *Toward Sustained Development in Sub-Saharan Africa: A Joint Program of Action.* Washington, DC: Author.

World Bank, 1986. *Financing Education in Developing Countries: An Exploration of Policy Options.* Washington, DC: Author.

World Bank, 1988a. *Education Policies for Sub-Saharan Africa: Adjustment, Revitalization, and Expansion.* Report No. 6934. Washington, DC: Author.

World Bank, 1988b. *Financing Adjustment with Growth in Sub-Saharan Africa 1986–1990.* Washington, DC: Author.

World Bank, 1989. *Sub-Saharan Africa: From Crisis to Sustainable Growth.* Washington, DC: Author.

World Bank, 1990a. *Primary Education: A World Bank Policy Paper.* Washington, DC: Author.

World Bank, April 1990b. Staff Appraisal report: *The United Republic of Tanzania-Education Planning and Rehabilitation Project.* Document of the World Bank. United Republic of Tanzania, Population and Human Resources Division, Southern Africa Department of the World Bank. Report No. 7998–TA.

World Bank, 1991a. *Vocational and Technical Education and Training:* A World Bank Policy Paper. Education and Employment Division, Population and Human Resources Department. Washington, DC: Author.

World Bank, 1991b. *The African Capacity-Building Initiative (ACBI): Toward Improved Policy Analysis and Development Management.* Washington, DC.

World Bank, 1994. *Higher Education. The Lessons of Experience.* Washington, DC: Author.

World Bank, 1995a: *Priorities and Strategies for Education:* A Review. Washington, DC: Author.

World Bank, 1995b. *Tanzania Social Sector Review.* Washington, DC: Author.

World Bank/ODA (Overseas Development Agency), 1988: *Book Sector Study.* Washington, DC: Author.

WDEFA, 1990: *World Declaration on Education for All: Our Framework for Action to Meet Basic Learning Needs,* Jomtien, 5–9 March 1990. New York: Author.

Yoloye, E. Ayotunde, 1986. The Relevance of Educational Content to National Needs in Africa. *International Review of Education* 42: 149–172.

Index

327